SCHOOL FINANCE AND AND EDUCATION POLICY

Second Edition

SCHOOL FINANCE AND EDUCATION POLICY

Enhancing Educational Efficiency, Equality, and Choice

JAMES W. GUTHRIE
University of California, Berkeley

WALTER I. GARMS
University of Rochester

LAWRENCE C. PIERCE
Oregon State System of Higher Education

PRENTICE HALL, Englewood Cliffs, New Jersey 07632

LIBRARY OF CONGRESS
Library of Congress Cataloging-in-Publication Data

Guthrie, James W.
   School finance and education policy : enhancing educational
efficiency, equality, and choice / James W. Guthrie, Walter
I. Garms, Lawrence C. Pierce. -- 2nd ed.
     p.   cm.
   Includes index.
   Rev. ed. of: School finance / Walter I. Garms, c1978.
   ISBN 0-13-793324-X :
   1. Education--United States--Finance. 2. Education and state-
-United States. 3. School management and organization--United
States. I. Garms, Walter I. School finance. II. Garms, Walter
I. III. Pierce, Lawrence C. IV. Title.
LB2825.G88 1988
371.1'1'0973--dc19   87-34303
                                   CIP

Editorial/production supervision
   and interior design: Rob DeGeorge
Cover design: George Cornell
Manufacturing buyer: Peter Havens

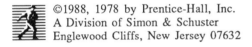 ©1988, 1978 by Prentice-Hall, Inc.
A Division of Simon & Schuster
Englewood Cliffs, New Jersey 07632

Previously published under the title *School Finance: The Economics and Politics of Public Education*

Printed in the United States of America

10 9 8 7 6 5 4 3 2

ISBN 0-13-793324-X

PRENTICE-HALL INTERNATIONAL (UK) LIMITED, *London*
PRENTICE-HALL OF AUSTRALIA PTY. LIMITED, *Sydney*
PRENTICE-HALL CANADA INC., *Toronto*
PRENTICE-HALL HISPANOAMERICANA, S.A., *Mexico*
PRENTICE-HALL OF INDIA PRIVATE LIMITED, *New Delhi*
PRENTICE-HALL OF JAPAN, INC., *Tokyo*
SIMON & SCHUSTER ASIA PTE. LTD., *Singapore*
EDITORA PRENTICE-HALL DO BRASIL, LTDA., *Rio de Janeiro*

for

H. Thomas James
Charles S. Benson
James A. Kelly

This book is dedicated to these three individuals. They are persons from whom we have all learned much, both professionally and personally. Also, each of them has contributed in a remarkably productive manner to the shaping of school finance as a field of scholarly study and professional standing. We are pleased to be associated with them. Contrary to conventional practice in such matters, all three are very much alive. We thought we would express our gratitude to them in this manner while they are still young enough to appreciate it.

CONTENTS

PART FOUR: EDUCATIONAL REFORM

PREFACE

The original edition of this text, *School Finance: The Economics and Politics of Public Education* (1978), emphasized primarily the education reform movement then taking place. This period of policy reshaping was heavily oriented toward achieving intrastate financial equality for local school districts. A second theme in that volume was the coming era of fiscal limits. We could easily predict that sliding school enrollments would continue, at least temporarily, and it appeared that fiscal resources would decrease at least commensurately, and perhaps faster. The only evidence we had regarding the economy was the rapidly growing inflation rate under the Carter administration. We could not predict the damaging 1979 oil shortage that the Organization of Petroleum Exporting Countries (OPEC) would provoke or the deep recession that would accompany the initial two years of the Reagan administration. We had correctly projected the direction of events, but had not properly assessed their intensity. Many schools and professional educators had to tighten their fiscal belts far more than we had anticipated.

DECLINING PRODUCTIVITY

Our 1978 theme seemed to be timely and modestly accurate. Nevertheless, it is now clear that we missed one of the most significant developments occurring in the United States—plummeting economic productivity. The signals were everywhere present and had been evolving for more than a decade. Increasing importation of technologically sophisticated, inexpensive, foreign-made consumer items, growing inability to sell United States products overseas, shoddy quality control on domestically manufactured goods, salary and wage increases unjustified in terms of productivity gains, and reduced investment in research and development were symptomatic of America's underlying economic malaise. In Chapter 1 of this book we provide the details. Suffice it to say here that national measures of economic productivity leveled off significantly throughout the 1970s and actually became negative during the early 1980s.

The declining ability to produce goods and services efficiently triggered all manner of other economic ills, such as an inability to compete effectively in international trade, a loss of domestic jobs, a reduced standard of living, and the transfer to subsequent generations of a legacy of mounting national debt. Critics and analysts blamed such diverse conditions as the fundamental flaws of capitalism, the infiltration of a socialist ideology into the popular ethos, the prodigal spending of the military-industrial conspiracy, an appalling failure of civic leadership, an enveloping late-twentieth-century narcissism, erosion of the American Dream, and a loss of national vision. As one might imagine, schools came in for a share of the blame also.

Although many may disagree on the root cause, there is little escaping the day-to-day manifestations of the problem. It is not simply that the United States is no longer the preeminent world leader in technological prowess, scientific advances, entrepreneurial vision, commercial development, and investment acumen. In addition, United States economic conditions are tied to developments in other nations far more intensely now than probably at any other point in its history since the era of colonial exploration. Millions of existing and potential jobs have escaped overseas. The economy experiences periods of stagnation and uncertainty; components of the business cycle appear far less predictable than before. In short, we are no longer in complete control of our nation's economic destiny.

If only national pride were at stake, concern need not run too deeply. A resounding Olympic victory or having regained the America's Cup might solve the problem. The United States is by no means teetering on the brink of hopelessness or national chaos. There continue to be numerous signs of American vitality. The nation's history, even if shorter than that of many of its European and Asian competitors, is replete with inspiring successes. The American national character contains a large element of creativity and persistence that may well rise to the challenge. Nevertheless, there is also evidence of national anxiety regarding the economy and America's future in the highly competitive world of international trade. This uncertainty manifests itself in a number of ways, one of which is a widespread public desire for more effective and more productive schools.

EDUCATION REFORM AND THE ISSUE-AGENDA CYCLE

Anthony Downs, the economist, has written persuasively on the public issue-agenda cycle. He postulates that policy issues progress through stages that range from widespread citizen ignorance, to an attention-riveting circumstance or set of events, to intense alarm and frantic search for solutions, to growing disillusion, and through eventual transition to the next issue. The fact that the mass media now "market" news and the public has come to regard current events as prime-time entertainment, only facilitates the flow of citizen attention through Downs's cyclic stages. Newspaper and television journalists are almost always in search of the next newly breaking exciting story in order to retain their share of viewers or readers. Media market competition virtually promotes the invention of news and the provoking of public crises, out of which policy issues frequently flow.

Measures of United States student achievement began a two-decade decline in the 1960s. Throughout the 1970s, many public and private expectations regarding school performance, such as graduation requirements and college admission standards, were permitted to slide. Beginning in the latter 1970s and continuing until the mid 1980s, financial resources for United States schools were badly diluted. These distressing education conditions were developing against a national backdrop of increasing economic instability and intensifying foreign trade competition. The publication in 1983 of *A Nation at Risk,* a report by the National Commission on Educational Excellence, chaired by David P. Gardner, focused public attention upon the necessity for school reform.

Throughout the mid 1980s, state after state initiated policies aimed at rendering schools more rigorous academically. It is still too early to judge the success of these efforts. Questions regarding significant student performance increases remain to be answered. Equally unknown is the degree to which public interest will remain focused on education. Is Downs correct in predicting that the attention of citizens and their government representatives will soon recycle onto the next media-manufactured "crisis," however insignificant in contrast with education?

We do not know the answer to this question. As advocates for education, we hope that public attention will forever be riveted to schooling issues. But this is unrealistic. Reforms have come in waves previously, and are likely to do so in the future. There is one dimension of which we are relatively sure, however. The problems of productivity underlying the present economic distress will not succumb to simple solution. In order to sustain its position as a world leader and to continue to provide hope and comfort to its citizens, the United States must revitalize its productive capacity. This will necessitate pulling many policy levers, and we are by no means sure of all of them or of the sequence in which they should be engaged.

One condition does appear evident. In almost any plan to restore national productive capacity, education must be a vital element. Consequently, at least if rationally directed, the current school reform effort should be sustained for some years to come. The education decline that has characterized much of the last quarter century is the result of complicated forces with enormous inertia. To brake this decline and refocus the energies of America's three-million professional educators is not an overnight assignment. It is an awesome challenge requiring vision, leadership, practical ideas, fiscal resources, human talent, and individual commitment. The major theme of this book is education and productivity. The analyses and ideas in this volume are intended to assist in restoring American schools to a vital and more highly respected position.

By advocating continued attention to school reform, particularly productivity and educational efficiency, we by no means intend to overlook the values of equality and liberty. The *equality* agenda, to which we devoted substantial attention in the 1978 volume, has not been fully accomplished. Again, had we been asked in 1978 to predict the next focus of the reform pendulum, we probably would have said *liberty* rather than efficiency. We still contend that the American system of education could benefit from a greater measure of liberty. It is not necessary to forego either equality or efficiency to attain greater choice. To be sure, compromise among all three values is a continuing necessity, but it can be achieved. Consequently, in Part IV we describe reforms that could simultaneously advance equality of educational opportunity, promote productivity, and enhance consumer choice.

THE PLAN OF THE BOOK

This book is primarily about school finance. However, schooling is such a significant component of American society and occupies such a large amount of society's resources that the financing of schools is heavily linked to politics and government. Thus, this book is also about government and the linkage among politics, government policy, and school finance. How schools utilize their financial resources influences their success in educating students and shapes public opinion about schools and school policy. Thus, this book also focuses on the deployment of financial resources within schools and how they might be utilized more effectively. In this way, it is also a book about school effectiveness.

This volume is divided into four major sections. Part I concentrates on the three major influences on policy. Chapter 1 describes "technical" conditions of demography and economics that shape government policy. Chapter 2 explains the three major preferred value dimensions that underlie public policy: equality, efficiency, and liberty. Chapter 3 explains the role of government in mediating technical and value conditions and in shaping the delivery of educational services.

The chapters in Part II describe the economic and political dynamics of school finance. They cover the functions of all three levels of government—local, state, and federal—in generating and distributing resources for schools. They also explain the interaction between the political and economic systems in decision-making on the financing of schools.

Part III is devoted to procedures for managing schools effectively. Planning, budgeting, evaluation, resource management, technology, economic incentive systems, human motivation, and organizational change are all covered in this section. The four chapters in this section are based on the most recent research results regarding effective schools and efficient resource allocation.

Part IV describes comprehensive reform plans that could provide a needed new balance among the policy objectives of equality, efficiency, and liberty.

We have retained selected components of our prior volume that we believe are still relevant. All of the material has been rewritten and brought up to date. Moreover, eight of the chapters in the present edition are altogether new.

ACKNOWLEDGMENTS

We were again assisted by many people, both in the compilation of ideas and in the production of the book itself. We wish to acknowledge our appreciation to:

Jacob E. Adams, Jr., Gregg Bender, Charles S. Benson, Guy Benveniste, Helen Cagampang, Geraldine J. Clifford, Paul Disario, Terry Emmett, John W. Evans, Linda Forsyth, William H. Gerritz, Bernard R. Gifford, W. Norton Grubb, Ardis Hartry, Eric Hartwig, Gerald C. Hayward, Guilbert Hentschke, Linda C. Humphrey, Michael W. Kirst, Julie Koppich, Michael La Morte, Donna Kay LeCzel, Suzan Liao, Judith Warren Little, Jim Moser, Kristin Palmquist, Allan Odden, Marge Plecki, Rodney J. Reed, Pamela M. Robbins, Judy Snow, David Stern, René Verdin, Darren H. Wong, and Derek Woo.

We also wish to acknowledge the assistance of Mr. Richard K. Pratt of the State of California Legislative Analyst's Office, for contributing to Chapter 9, and of Sarah Guthrie Holtzapple, who did the index. We wish particularly to thank Norma Needham who undertook the repeated computer entry of text and revisions. Her patience was truly remarkable, as was her attention to detail. If mistakes remain, it is because we entered something in the Macintosh without letting her know.

Readers who are long of tooth may notice that the sequence of authors has been rotated in this book compared with the prior volume. Not much should be made of this. We are all equal contributors or equally culpable, depending upon the issue.

James W. Guthrie   Walter I. Garms   Lawrence C. Pierce
Berkeley, California   Rochester, New York   Eugene, Oregon

SCHOOL FINANCE
AND
EDUCATION POLICY

chapter one

SHAPING AMERICAN EDUCATION

The purpose of this book is to explain and analyze (1) the way the United States finances public schools, (2) the relationship between school finance and educational policy, and (3) the link between school finance and educational practice. To do justice to these diverse commitments, we must describe the structural and dynamic features of education in the United States and the various social forces that give form and substance to those conditions. This chapter explains the broad boundaries of a policy paradigm, summarizes demographic and economic trends that have recently influenced American education and are likely to shape its future, and weighs four central dimensions of the American educational system: (1) enrollments, (2) personnel, (3) governmental arrangements, and (4) financial costs.

A PRELIMINARY POLICY PARADIGM

A *policy* is a uniform decision rule that guides action. Social policy, which includes educational policy, encompasses those decision rules that apply to members of a society or its important subgroups. All societies have policies on common dimensions such as health, marriage, commerce, political participation, and criminal justice. All of these policies prescribe how members of the society will act or be treated by others. If a policy is governmentally enacted and codified, it is typi-

1

cally known as a *statute* or *law*. Informal, uncodified policies exist in every society, and may be every bit as prescriptive as statutes. Anyone doubting this should attempt to cut into a queue in England and experience the consequences.

Social policies are strongly influenced by three fundamental considerations which are respectively technical, cultural, and political: (1) demographic and economic dynamics, (2) preferences among three values—equality, efficiency, and liberty—and (3) political arrangements. The flow of influence among these three conditions is substantial and multidirectional. For example, demographic or economic circumstances can trigger political system changes, and vice versa. Thus, this paradigm provides no mechanical model for precisely predicting which policies will emerge from which conditions at which time.[1] Public policy is continually influenced by variables outside this paradigm, such as human determination, acts of God, and elements of caprice. Simply knowing pertinent "facts" will not necessarily permit policy predictions. For example, it would have been difficult to predict from their past performance that President Lyndon B. Johnson would be an ardent advocate of civil rights, President Jimmy Carter a proponent of governmental deregulation, or President Ronald Reagan the administrator of a vastly unbalanced federal budget.

The complex social world of human interactions constitutes a vast primordial policy ooze out of which technical, cultural, and political conditions periodically coalesce to create policy predispositions. An individual or an idea may, however, spark actual policy change. Components of the policy paradigm, while not lending themselves to precise prediction, nevertheless alert one to the broader patterns of policy emergence and influence.[2]

Figure 1.1 illustrates these three predispositions. Chapter Two concentrates on the cultural dimension of policy influence—values. Chapter Three describes the political dimension—government. The remainder of this chapter is oriented toward the technical influences on policy—economics and demographics.

DEMOGRAPHIC AND ECONOMIC DYNAMICS

Throughout the world, educational policy, and its eventual expression in schooling, is driven by two variable conditions, *demography* and *economics*. These conditions are themselves related, though the nature of the relationship at any point in time depends upon many additional conditions, such as a society's level of technical development and its climate. For example, in a technologically undeveloped society, an explosion in the birthrate may trigger famine, poverty, and great human hardship. Conversely, in a technologically sophisticated, commercially oriented society,

---

[1] Insight into the emergence of public policy issues is provided by Anthony Downs in "Up and Down with Ecology: The 'Issue Attention Cycle,'" *Public Interest*, no. 29 (1972), 39-50.

[2] The authors acknowledge the contribution of Frederick Wirt in conceptualizing these matters.

FIGURE 1.1 Preliminary Policy Paradigm

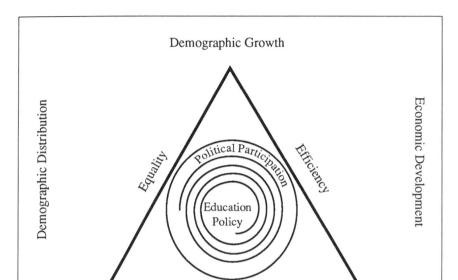

a dramatic upsurge in births may spur economic expansion and an increase in living standards.

Two economic dimensions exert important influences upon policy: level of overall economic *development* and rate of economic *growth*. Obviously, a technologically sophisticated industrialized or information-oriented economy will have different policy concerns and predispositions than an agricultural or preindustrial society. Similarly, low productivity and the absence of economic growth may create conflict between elites and the poor and, depending upon a society's political dynamics, may focus policy discussions obsessively on issues of economic redistribution.

Demography also has a two-dimensional influence. A society's policy predispositions are influenced not only by overall *population size*, but also by the *geographic, ethnic,* and *age distribution* of the population. A society in which the median age is relatively low might invest a disproportionate share of its social resources in children and youth. Conversely, when the median age rises, as is currently the case in the United States, senior citizens may begin to attract a disproportionate share of social resources. Also, a geographically compact and racially heterogeneous society may have different domestic policy concerns than a sparsely settled or racially homogeneous people.

Demographic Developments

The Census Bureau estimated the United States population to be 240 million in 1987. The medium-range projection is for an increase to 268 million by the year 2000. These figures rank the United States behind only China, India, and the Soviet Union in terms of overall population. Nevertheless, major domestic policy consequences of demography in the United States do not flow as much from sheer population size or recent rates of growth as from trends in geographic, racial and ethnic, and age distribution.

GEOGRAPHIC LOCATION

The most significant geographic trend is the population growth of the so-called *sunbelt* states in the South and West. Table 1.1 displays the rate of population change between 1970 and 1980 in the five fastest-growing and slowest-growing states. This shift is occasioned by the increasing number of retired citizens seeking warmer climates, displaced frostbelt workers seeking jobs in technologically more advanced industrial and informational fields located in the sunbelt, and recent patterns of Latin-American immigration, about which more is said in a subsequent section.

These population changes have been accompanied by significant alterations in economic and political patterns. The most obvious is the shift to sunbelt states of greater political influence. For example, because of its population growth, California has replaced New York as the state with the largest delegation in the U.S. Congress. The sunbelt has taken on added economic significance as well. Some changes are obvious. New job openings have reduced unemployment in the South and West below that in many midwestern industrial states. Other economic changes are more subtle. For example, sunbelt states derive the economic advantage of retiree spending from pension income earned earlier in the North and Midwest. Also, something of a "brain drain" has occurred. Sunbelt areas benefit from education investments made earlier in the school lives of recent immigrants from the North and Midwest.

Education policy has also been affected by these population dynamics. State contributions to school revenues in northern industrial and agricultural states were sustained during the decade 1970–80 because declining enrollments made it easier to spend more money on a shrinking pupil base. Conversely, sunbelt states have had to increase school spending overall, particularly on items such as school construction and intense recruiting to fill teacher shortages.

Initially, sunbelt states had difficulty adjusting to the new growth patterns. Note in Table 1.1 that their per-pupil expenditures did not keep pace with spending increases in the frostbelt states from 1970 to 1980. However, in the more dynamic economy of 1980–85, the sunbelt states began to spend more money per pupil. That is, they generated new revenues to cover both pupil population growth and added demand for education services. These sunbelt states were among the leaders in the educational excellence movement of the 1980s.

TABLE 1.1 Change in Population and Per-Pupil Expenditures for the Five Fastest- and Slowest-Growing States, 1970-80

| | 1970 | | | 1980 | | | | CHANGE IN SPENDING | |
	POPULATION IN THOUSANDS	STUDENT ENROLLMENT IN THOUSANDS	PER-PUPIL EXPENDITURES	POPULATION IN THOUSANDS	STUDENT ENROLLMENT IN THOUSANDS	PER-PUPIL EXPENDITURES	CHANGE IN POPULATION	TO 1980	TO 1985
Fastest-Growing States									
California	20,023	4,598	$922	23,771	4,119	$2,791	18.5%	303%	357%
Texas	11,224	2,755	581	14,320	2,873	2,283	27.1	393	566
Florida	6,851	1,408	710	9,784	1,508	2,452	43.5	345	480
Arizona	1,795	418	766	2,731	509	2,565	53.1	335	357
Georgia	4,604	1,113	600	5,482	1,079	1,945	19.1	324	449
Slowest-Growing States									
New York	18,259	3,514	$1,237	17,575	2,958	$4,228	−3.7%	324%	422%
Rhode Island	951	180	904	949	152	3,326	−0.3	368	453
Massachusetts	5,697	1,147	753	5,743	1,047	3,326	0.8	442	513
N. Dakota	619	148	621	652	117	2,537	5.7	409	523
S. Dakota	667	167	657	690	133	2,255	3.7	343	428

Sources: U.S. Bureau of the Census, *Current Population Reports*, ser. p. 25, no. 944; U.S. Dept. of Health, Education and Welfare, Office of Education, *Statistics of Public Schools* (1970); National Education Association, *Estimates of School Statistics*; National Center for Educational Statistics, *Digest of Education Statistics*.

RACIAL AND ETHNIC COMPOSITION

Following the colonial period of national development, the United States experienced five major population migrations. The first was the 18th- and 19th-century "manifest destiny" expansion into western lands. The second was the massive immigration from Europe during the nineteenth century. The third was the shift of rural blacks from the South to the cities beginning in the late 1930s and escalating greatly during World War II and immediately after. The fourth was the flow of middle-class families from cities to the urban periphery during and shortly after the black migration. The most significant recent movement is the large wave of immigration from Latin America and secondarily from Asia.

Each of these migrations has affected education policy and practice. Massive nineteenth-century migrations from southern and eastern Europe intensified the assimilation functions of public schools. Many immigrants could not speak English and were not familiar with American forms of government. Also, many of these new citizens were Catholic and found public schools of that day far from religiously neutral. Reacting to the Protestant orientation of public schools, and probably desiring institutions over which they could have more influence, the new immigrants greatly expanded and participated in the nation's Catholic school system.[3]

The twentieth-century migrations of blacks to cities and middle-class families to suburbs also precipitated educational policy changes.[4] The segregated school systems of the agricultural South did little to provide new city dwellers with the educational skills necessary to succeed in an industrial and commercial environment. The migration of middle-class families to the suburbs deprived city schools of an informed citizen constituency and an experienced cadre of lay leaders. The 1965 enactment of the Elementary and Secondary Education Act (ESEA) was in large measure a response to these conditions.[5]

The 1980s immigration has also challenged school systems. Assimilation of new immigrants continues to be a necessary function. As in the nineteenth century, today's immigrants frequently do not speak English as their first language. Several big-city school districts have had to cope in the 1970s and 1980s with students arriving from dozens of nations and speaking different languages. Also, secondary school dropout rates are disproportionately high among first- and second-generation Hispanic students.[6] Conditions such as these have prompted legislative and judicial decisions regarding bilingual education and dropout prevention.[7]

---

[3]Nathan Glazer and Daniel P. Moynihan, *Beyond the Melting Pot* (Cambridge, Mass: MIT Press, 1970).

[4]Nicholas Lehman, "The Origins of the Underclass," *Atlantic*, 257 (June 1986), 31-43.

[5]This legislation is described in greater detail in Chapter 7. The ESEA was combined in 1981 with several other statutes to form the Education Consolidation and Improvement Act (ECIA).

[6]Kevin F. McCarthy and R. Burciaga Valdez, *Current and Future Effects of Mexican Immigration in California* (Santa Monica, Calif.: Rand Corporation, 1985).

[7]For example, *Lau v. Nichols*, 414 U.S. 563 (1974).

AGE DISTRIBUTION

The age distribution of the American population is undergoing dramatic changes that have major policy implications. The population is aging rapidly. In 1950, the median age was 30.2. By the year 2000, it is projected to be 36.3. This evolving condition is a consequence of vastly reduced birthrates and medical advances that have significantly extended longevity for both women and men. In 1986, 12 percent of the United States population was 65 or older. By 2000, the proportion of citizens over 65 is estimated to reach 20 percent—higher than that in any other large nation in the world.

The aging of the American population will continue to have important policy implications, education included. The larger number of older people may entail changes in the composition of government services. The elderly may well be more interested in a different mix of economic, energy, transportation, income, and criminal justice policies than would a younger society. The distribution of government spending and public debt might be significantly altered.[8]

Education is no exception to the possible policy changes. Older individuals may not be as directly concerned about schooling. Moreover, public school students and their parents now constitute a smaller percentage of the electorate. This may have important implications for school-related politics. For example, states or localities with particularly large concentrations of retirees may not be able to generate conventional levels of political support for public schooling. Alternatively, senior citizens may want a larger portion of the school budget devoted to adult education. Their numbers among local voters may enable them to express this preference forcefully through the electoral process.

Economic Developments[9]

Despite a gross national product (GNP) second to none (almost $4 trillion in 1987), United States' hegemony over the world's economy had greatly diminished by the mid 1980s. In November 1986, Japan's per-capita GNP matched that of the U.S. By 1987, average workers' compensation in West Germany, Sweden and several other European nations exceeded the United States.[10] This change is illustrated practically by the remarkable spectrum of foreign-produced consumer goods widely purchased throughout the nation, intense foreign investment in fundamental finan-

---

[8]Phillip Longman, "Justice Between Generations," *Atlantic*, 255 (June 1985), 73-81.

[9]An excellent analysis on this topic is provided in Richard M. Cyert and David C. Mowery, (eds.), *Technology and Employment: Innovation and Growth in the U.S. Economy* (Washington, D.C.: National Academy Press, 1987).

[10]See Kenneth H. Bacon, "Shrinking Wage Gap Helping U.S. Firms," *The Wall Street Journal*, March 23, 1987, p. 1.

cial and manufacturing activities,[11] and the diluted standard of living experienced by many Americans. [12]

If the United States' declining economic supremacy were simply a function of growing international interdependency, it might be of less concern to policy makers and the informed public. However, such is not the case. Worrisome economic conditions are not a function simply of intense commercial competition between aggressive trading equals. Rather, two decades of declining or stagnant productivity, unmatched federal government deficits, mounting international trade imbalances, unprecedented reversals in foreign indebtedness, growing personal debt, and roller-coaster ups and downs in currency value, unemployment, and interest rates have had their own unsettling effects. These uncertain economic conditions were summarized, at least symbolically, by the dramatic stock market drop of Monday, October 19, 1987, when the market lost more than 20% of its value. In short, much of the nation's economic distress is a consequence of its past policies and cannot be attributed simply to expansionism by aggressive international competitors.

A few features of the United States' economic malaise are amenable to short- and medium-range corrections through manipulations of government *monetary* and *fiscal* policy.[13] For example, by altering the discount rate—the cost to commercial banks of borrowed money—the United States Federal Reserve Board can exercise short-run influence over interest rates on items such as consumer loans. There exist, however, several secular trends that cannot be altered so easily and that portend longer-run economic distress for the United States. We will discuss three of these— economic productivity, debt, and international competition. There is substantial interaction among the three, but we treat each independently.

PRODUCTIVITY

This index is crucial to a nation's well-being. It is an economist's measure of a nation's ability to produce goods and services. Productivity can be measured for an entire nation in aggregate terms, for example, of total national income or total hours at work. It can also be measured on a unit basis, such as national income per capita, output per hour at work, or output per employee. If productivity is high, a nation's standard of living can increase. If productivity is low or falling, the standard of living cannot increase or will decline. A nation's policies can encourage or discourage long-term economic growth. Thus, it is easy to envision the connection between a nation's economy and its political environment.

The quarter century following World War II was a robust period. Between 1948 and 1973, U.S. productivity increased by every measure. As can be seen in

[11]In 1986, of the world's ten largest banks in terms of total financial assets, only one was based in the United States; four were Japanese. Also, the Japanese education system was being frequently compared with that of the United States. See Nobuo K. Shimahara, "Japanese Education Reforms in the 1980's," *Issues in Education*, 4, no. 2 (Fall 1986), p. 1.

[12]By 1987, average weekly earnings for Americans had receded in purchasing power to the 1963 level.

[13]*Monetary* policy is concerned with the government-influenced availability of money in its various forms, such as currency and credit. *Fiscal* policy deals with government spending and borrowing intended to influence economic growth.

Table 1.2, for example, national income increased 3.7 percent, national income per employed person increased 2.16 percent, and national income per capita increased 2.21 percent. Over the following seven years, productivity grew much less rapidly. National income increased by only 2.61 percent, national income per employed person by only 0.36 percent, and national income per capita by only 1.59 percent. The next three years were particularly dismal. Aggregate national income and national income per employed person decreased 0.54 percent; national income per capita declined 1.55 percent.

Year-to-year variations in productivity are too great to permit easy generalization. Thus determination of valid trends is best done through extrapolation over an extended period. Since 1983, United States economic productivity, though again increasing, still has not matched post-World War II levels or equaled that of current competitor nations such as Japan, Taiwan, and South Korea. Table 1.3 examines productivity from another standpoint—a comparison of the manufacturing and service sectors. It is evident that productivity in the manufacturing sector has been improving. It is in the service sector that productivity lags badly.

If productivity per worker, particularly per service worker, or productivity per capita cannot be increased, then the United States will face many difficult choices. For example, the nation will not be able to pay off its rising national and international debt without either reducing private standards of living or cutting back significantly on public services. In short, the nation must increase its productivity or forego some items and services that many members of the public have felt to be important to this point.[14]

TABLE 1.2   Output and Productivity in Terms of Annual Percentage Growth Rates, 1948–82

ITEM	1948-73	1973-79	1979-82
National Income	3.70	2.61	−0.54
National income per person employed	2.16	0.36	−0.54
Total hours at work	0.97	1.62	−0.83
National income per hour at work	2.70	0.98	0.28
National income per capita	2.21	1.59	−1.55
Personal consumption expenditures per capita	2.15	2.17	0.47
Implicit price deflator for GNP	2.80	7.52	8.18

Source: Edward F. Denison, *Trends in American Economic Growth, 1929-1982* (Washington, D.C.: Brookings Institution, 1983), p. 4, Table 1.1.

[14]One economist contends that the United States has already exhausted all available "tricks" in maintaining its citizens' standard of living. By tricks he is referring to the trend of both marriage partners being employed, delaying having children, having fewer children so as to maintain high levels of disposable income, and assuming more of consumer debt. Frank Levy, "We Are Running Out of Tricks to Keep Our Prosperity High," *Washington Post*, December 14, 1986, pp. H1, H4.

TABLE 1.3   Nonfarm Productivity
           Average Annual Percentage Increases

PERIOD	MANUFACTURING	NON-MANUFACTURING	TOTAL
1948 4Q to 1973 4Q	2.7	2.1	2.3
1973 4Q to 1981 3Q	1.5	0.1	0.6
1981 3Q to 1986 3Q	3.8	0.1	1.1

Source: Paul W. McCracken, "The Rust Belt's Coming Revival", *The Wall Street Journal,* March 30, 1987, p. 9.

Productivity is a function of several conditions, such as capital investment, managerial effectiveness, and education. A calculation of the factors spurring productivity growth from 1929 to 1982 suggests that education is exceeded in significance only by advances in knowledge—themselves products in large measure of research in higher education institutions. *Education accounted for 26 percent of productivity growth in this period.*[15] The sagging U.S. productivity is likewise a function of many conditions, among them poor management in America's industrial sector and poor government leadership. Recovery of past productivity rates probably will depend heavily on an effective system of schooling. This explains, at least partially, the enthusiasm for education reform that captured the American policy agenda during the mid 1980s.

DEBT

By 1987, the United States' federal government debt exceeded $2 trillion.[16] This is an amount so large as to lose meaning for most individuals. It can be understood only in relative terms. During the nation's first one-hundred years, cumulative national debt was only $1 billion. Total federal debt reached $1 trillion by 1950 and remained relatively constant for the next quarter century. Then it began to escalate precipitously. By 1987, the federal debt was growing six times faster than the GNP and had equaled half the GNP. The national debt had reached the point where interest payments alone amounted to $20 million an hour, twenty-four hours a day, 365 days a year. Total debt—government, business, and consumer—was higher than at any point since 1920 and was twice the value of GNP.[17]

Moreover, United States borrowing was not simply domestic. Between 1984 and 1985, the United States experienced a dramatic lending reversal. In 1982, the

[15] Edward F. Denison, *Trends in American Economic Growth, 1929-1982* (Washington, D.C.: Brookings Institution, 1983), p. xvi.

[16] On this topic of debt, see Carolyn Webber and Aaron Wildavsky, *A History of Taxation and Expenditure in the Western World* (New York: Simon & Schuster, 1986).

[17] Between 1960 and 1966, the average federal deficit equaled 0.6 percent of the GNP. By 1980-86 the federal deficit was averaging 4.5 percent of the GNP, according to figures published by the Federal Office of Management and Budget.

United States was the world's leading foreign investor, with more than $147 billion in net overseas assets; it ended 1985 as the world's largest net debtor, owing other nations over $100 billion.[18] By contrast, as late as 1980, Japan's net overseas holdings were only $12 billion. This figure had increased tenfold by 1986. In the United States, political rhetoric regarding the need for national deficit reduction was intense. Reality was less impressive.

The distressing debt situation affects education in several ways. The most obvious is that if money is needed to pay national debt interest and reduce principal, then the share of the public sector's fiscal pie available to fund schools is reduced, or at least subjected to even more intense competition. If money becomes scarcer, interest rates increase and taxes must be elevated to generate the added public funds necessary to service the debt. Voters subjected to a greater federal revenue burden are reluctant to have state and local taxes increased to pay for schools. If the federal government counteracts the short money supply situation by creating more money, increased inflation is possible, and that can prove to be the cruelest tax of all, particularly for low- and fixed-income individuals. The least painful solution to a burdensome debt situation is increased national productivity. Education can help.

INTERNATIONAL COMPETITION

By the middle of 1987 the United States had an annual international trade deficit approaching $200 billion. Lower oil prices and a vastly devalued dollar throughout 1986 and 1987 did not correct the imbalance. Low productivity continued to price United States goods out of many markets. This was true even of agricultural products, previously an export mainstay. Not only was manufacturing a problem, but so were services. The United States was surprised to learn that by 1987 the value of its imported *services* exceeded that of its exported services.

Availability of lower-priced foreign goods and services has the advantage of dampening inflation. However, there is a trade-off in jobs. The flow of manufacturing to other nations results in a loss of many millions of jobs. United States unemployment exceeded 10 percent in the early 1980s. By the mid 1980s it had settled in the 5-7 percent range. It would have worsened if not for demographic dynamics. The number of youths entering the labor market had been declining since 1985. Had the number of high school graduates stayed at 1970s levels, unemployment would probably have been higher. The precipitous 1987 drop in the value of the U.S. dollar against selected Asian and Western European currencies stimulated U.S. exports, but still did not balance the trade deficit.

The international trade situation has consequences for education and education policy. During the 1970s and 1980s the U.S. economy created millions of new jobs. Many, though not most, of these jobs were part-time, low-paid service positions requiring low skills. The relative absence of high-paying jobs for low-skilled youth may act as a partial deterrent to high school graduation. Students not seeing the prospect of eventual rewarding employment may become discouraged and drop

---

[18]Figures cited in Lester Brown et al., *State of the World 1986* (New York: W. W. Norton & Co., Inc., 1986), p. 4.

out. However, not all outcomes are negative. The public's view that Japan and other nations are able to sustain high productivity because of their rigorous schooling prompted the United States in the early 1980s to allocate more resources and greater attention to education.

The question is, will the United States do enough soon enough? Writing in the October, 1987, *Atlantic*, Peter G. Peterson said

> More important, it is hard to imagine any long-term economic renaissance—especially one built on "working smarter"—without a determined investment in the most precious of our assets: the skills, intellect, work habits, health, and character of our children. Yet this is precisely where we may be courting our most catastrophic failure. In the words of one analyst cited by the 1983 National Commission on Excellence in Education, "For the first time in the history of our country, the educational skills of one generation will not surpass, will not equal, will not even approach, those of their parents." Recent trends indicate that each year the typical American child is increasingly likely to be born in poverty and to grow up in a broken family. And a study by the Committee for Economic Development points out that without major educational change, by the year 2000 we will have turned out close to 20 million young people with no productive place in our society. The CED study continues, "Solutions to the problems of the educationally disadvantaged must include a fundamental restructuring of the school system. But they must also reach beyond the traditional boundaries of schooling to improve the environment of the child. An early and sustained intervention in the lives of disadvantaged children both in school and out is our only hope for breaking the cycle of disaffection and despair." Our children represent the furthest living reach of posterity, the only compelling reason that we have to be serious about investing in the future. And we are failing them.

As suggested repeatedly, productivity is at the heart of American economic problems and is simultaneously the key to many solutions. Education can be a major stimulus to productivity, and subsequent sections of this book explain how. First, however, it is necessary to understand the magnitude and complexity of the United States education system. Only in this way can one come to appreciate the difficulties involved in reforming America's schools and thus placing them in a better position not only to assist the nation's economy but also to fulfill the aspirations of individual citizens.

EDUCATION IN THE UNITED STATES

Demand for Schooling: Enrollments

United States enrollment in kindergarten through twelfth grade peaked at 51 million in 1971. Enrollments had grown dramatically following World War II. Indeed, at the peak of the "baby boom," one out of every four Americans was enrolled in school. More than half the adult electorate had children in public schools.

Annual birthrates began to decline in the mid 1960s, a trend that persisted until a mid-1970s low point. First-grade enrollment generally lags births by approximately five years. Thus, the overall pupil population in public and private schools declined to a 1981 low point of approximately 45 million. This shrinkage marked a period of unprecedented contraction for many United States school districts, particularly in the Northeast and Midwest. School closings and teacher layoffs provoked controversy and distress for many communities and individuals.

Since the early 1980s, enrollments have been increasing nationwide. This is a consequence both of more live births and of increased immigration. By 1987, total K–12 enrollment stood at 47 million students. Even though enrollment is growing, it still represents only one out of every five persons in the total population. Also, only about 40 percent of the current electorate are parents of schoolchildren. Schools have recovered from their 1970s low point in enrollment but they have not recaptured their previous potential political influence. Throughout the 1980s, elementary enrollments have expanded the most. Secondary schools continued to shrink and were not projected to begin to grow until the mid to late 1990s. Figure 1.2 displays the historic and projected path of total pupil enrollments.

NONPUBLIC SCHOOLS

On the basis of percentages, public schools in the United States have a virtual monopoly on education. Private school enrollments approximate only 10 percent of the total school-age population. However, this percentage represents a large number—almost 5 million pupils. Moreover, there is substantial geographic variation

FIGURE 1.2   Enrollment in Regular Day Schools, 1960-1992

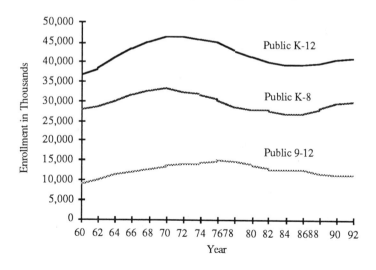

Source: U.S. National Center for Educational Statistics, *Projections of Education Statistics* (biennial), *Digest of Educational Statistics* (annual).

in private school attendance patterns.[19] In New York and Massachusetts, up to 25 percent of children attend nonpublic schools. In Montana, almost 99 percent attend public schools. The overwhelming proportion of nonpublic schools are affiliated with the Catholic church. However, the fastest-growing segment comprises so-called Christian schools.[20]

GEOGRAPHIC VARIATION

Although K-12 enrollments have been increasing since the early 1980s, they have not been doing so at an even pace. The vast migration to sunbelt states has meant a corresponding increase in school enrollment. Enrollments have remained stable, or have continued to decline, in a few northern and midwestern areas. Conversely, sunbelt states such as Florida, Georgia, Arizona, and California are having difficulty constructing schools fast enough and finding enough qualified teachers to meet burgeoning demands.

Nor do migrants from other nations distribute themselves evenly. In 1986, 25 percent of all new immigrants to the United States settled either in the Los Angeles or San Francisco regions. School systems in these two areas found themselves faced with enormous problems simply in finding teachers who spoke the eighty different languages of the new students. South Florida, New Mexico, Texas, New York, and Illinois also experienced intense enrollment spurts because of migrations from other nations.

FUTURE TRENDS [21]

Current enrollment growth may not be long-lived. The mid-1970s upturn in the birthrate was a consequence of an increase not in the fertility rate but in the number of women entering their prime childbearing years.[22] Even though each woman is having fewer children than before in the United States, the expanded

[19]There has been historic variation as well. In 1955, private institutions accommodated 7 percent of the total United States school population. By 1967, this figure had climbed to 14 percent. By 1975, it had returned to 7 percent. The increase was accounted for almost completely by southern white parents attempting to avoid court-ordered racial desegregation. Ironically, a quarter century after the United States Supreme Court's *Brown v. Board of Education* desegregation decision, many southern schools were better integrated than those in the north. See Raymond Wolters, *The Burden of Brown: Thirty Years of School Desegregation* (Knoxville: University of Tennessee Press, 1984). Also, on the general topic of private schools see Daniel J. Sullivan, *Comparing Efficiency between Public and Private Schools* (Stanford, Calif.: Stanford University School of Education, Institute for Research on Education Finance and Governance, 1983).

[20]For more about such schools see Alan Peshkin, *God's Choice: The Total World of a Fundamentalist Christian School* (Chicago: University of Chicago Press, 1986).

[21]This discussion draws on the Center for Educational Statistics, *Pre-School Enrollment: Trends and Implications* (Washington D.C.: Office of Educational Research and Improvement, U.S. Department of Education, 1986).

[22]Technically, *birthrate* refers to the number of live births per 1,000 women, aged 15-44, per each 1,000 population. *Fertility rate* refers to the number of children on average born to each female during her lifetime.

number of post-World War II females has created a baby boom "echo." This echo begins to reverberate through the schools some five years later.

What will occur after baby boom mothers have passed their peak childbearing period? What will happen to enrollments? Immigration aside, the likely answer is that enrollments will stabilize or decline slightly. The number of live births peaked again in 1987 at approximately 3.7 million. Present polls of prospective mothers typically reveal a preference for small families. Women in the United States must average 2.1 children to stabilize the population. Surveys suggest, though, that women currently prefer smaller families—an average of 1.7 children each. Unless immigration accelerates, enrollments will reach a plateau or begin a mild decline in the twenty-first century.

CHALLENGES

There exists a picture more poignant than statistics alone can capture. Harold L. Hodgkinson, a former high-level official in the federal Department of Education, compiled a startling portrait of the United States school population. In 1986, he wrote,

> There is a tendency to think of the typical American family in terms of an old Norman Rockwell magazine cover, the working husband, the housewife, and two schoolchildren. Today, the description fits only 7 percent of American households.
> Consider the implications of these realities about today's children:
> • 14 percent are illegitimate.
> • 40 percent will be living with a single parent by their 18th birthday.
> • 30 percent are (so-called) latchkey children.
> • 20 percent live in poverty.
> • 15 percent speak another language.
> • 15 percent have physical or mental handicaps.
> • 10 percent have poorly educated parents.[23]

There have always existed poor, handicapped, and deprived children. In the past, however, advocates for them were few in number and policy makers only paid cyclical attention to their plight. This neglect may be about to change on at least two fronts. First, even though the above-listed percentages somehow never encompass all American children, the absolute numbers in any particular category are huge. Secondly, many of the above-depicted students are not simply from economically deprived households. These distressing conditions increasingly encompass middle-class children as well. Such conditions may serve to provoke greater public and policy concern. Regardless, educators will be additionally challenged to identify appropriate resources to assist such students.[24]

[23] Harold L. Hodgkinson, *All One System* (Washington, DC: Institute for Educational Leadership, 1985), p. 3.

[24] In this vein see also Andrew Hahn and Jacqueline Danzberger, *Dropouts in America* (Washington D.C.: Institute for Educational Leadership, 1987).

Suppliers of School Services: Personnel

Education in the United States is big business. Schools employ approximately 4 million individuals. There are more school employees than uniformed military personnel, more K-12 teachers than physicians and attorneys combined. The number of preprimary through twelfth-grade teachers, both in public and private schools, was an estimated 2.5 million in 1988. The overwhelming proportion (87 percent) of these teachers are in public schools. The remainder, some 337,000 individuals, are employed in a wide variety of religiously affiliated and nondenominational private institutions. Catholic schools employ the largest number, approximately 150,000.

The number of teachers has been growing steadily. During the previously mentioned enrollment decline of the 1970s, states such as Ohio, Michigan, and New York experienced attrition and layoffs. During the same period, teacher hires increased 3 percent nationwide. Education makes intensive use of labor, and there appears little prospect in the near future of substituting capital for labor. Therefore the current number of employed teachers is predicted to increase by almost 10 percent by 1993.

Schools also employ a substantial number of other professionals (an estimated 500,000) such as administrators, counselors, psychologists, librarians, and nurses. Approximately 1 million additional employees serve as custodians, clerks, bus drivers, cafeteria workers, and so on. These latter are typically known as *classified* employees. Their employment is more like civil service employment and typically does not require state licensure.

Table 1.4 summarizes various statistics for the current teacher work force. Here we can see that the teaching profession is composed overwhelmingly of women.[25] Women teachers outnumber men two to one. Secondary school staffs are almost balanced with regard to gender. However, elementary teachers are almost 80 percent women. This has been the historic pattern among American teachers. Teaching in the United States is a feminine occupation.

The teacher work force has been aging. In 1986, half the public school teachers in the United States were forty years of age or older. Twenty percent were fifty or older in 1983. Seventeen percent have taught for twenty years or longer. These statistics have important implications for future employment demand, a topic subsequently covered in detail. America's teachers are white. Less than 12 percent are nonwhite. These racial proportions have changed little in the last two decades. More than 99 percent of teachers hold a Bachelor of Arts or higher degree. More than 50 percent hold a master's degree or have had at least six years of college. In contrast, in the early 1960s almost 15 percent of America's teachers had not even graduated from college. Less than a quarter had any graduate preparation. Thus, if education level is associated with work-force improvement, there have been significant gains for teachers over the last quarter century.

---

[25] And it has been for over 200 years. See Myra H. Strober and Audri Gordon Lanford, *The Percentage of Women in Public School Teaching: Cross Sectional Analysis, 1850-1880*, Institute for Research on Educational Finance and Governance, Program Report No. 84-B11 (Stanford, Calif., 1984).

Another dramatic change over the last quarter century has been the unionization and politicization of teachers. The National Education Association (NEA) is the largest teacher union, with almost 1.5 million members. The American Federation of Teachers (AFT), affiliated with the national labor organization the AFL-CIO, has more than 600,000 teachers. The AFT's membership tends to be concentrated in large city school districts. The NEA membership is more representative of suburban and rural districts. Both unions contribute money and member time to state, federal, and sometimes local political campaigns.

PROJECTING THE FUTURE

Expanding enrollments and increasing teacher attrition are creating an intensely renewed demand for educators. According to prediction, the United States will need 140,000 to 175,000 additional public school teachers every year from 1988 to 1993. Private schools will employ an additional 22,000 to 36,000 teachers annually over the same period.[26] Because private schools are not required by law to hire credentialed personnel, the precise nature of the labor market competition between them and public schools is not known. Nevertheless, it stands to reason that there is some market overlap for new instructors. Adding these two sets of figures may not yield an absolutely accurate picture of the competitive bidding for licensed teachers. Nevertheless, the sum of the two suggests the magnitude of the market demand for teachers.

The coming demand for new teachers will amount annually to approximately 20 percent of all United States college graduates.[27] This is an impressive figure; if it is accurate for each year from 1988 to 1993, and perhaps thereafter, one out of every five U.S. college graduates will be needed to staff the nation's schools. This situation can be mitigated to the degree to which the "reserve pool" of already credentialed but nonteaching teachers can be induced to work or to work again in schools. Subject areas such as mathematics, science, foreign language, and special education are predicted to be in particularly short supply.[28] Also, secondary enrollments will begin to increase after 1990, possibly triggering intensified demands in other subjects. This will precipitate a race for talent. Can the schools compete? Despite the millions of employed teachers, there seldom has been an absolute shortage of teachers in the nation's history. Generally, legislative bodies resolve the problem by lowering entry qualifications. Thus, the problem becomes one of *quality*, not quantity.[29]

[26]National Center for Educational Statistics, *Conditions of Education, 1985*, U.S. Department of Education (Washington, D.C., 1985), p. 144.

[27]Ibid., p. 124.

[28]Ibid., p. 146, Table 3.2.

[29]The projected shortage is denied in a controversial report by Emily Feistritzer, *Teacher Crisis: Myth or Reality?* (Washington, D.C.: National Commission on Educational Information, 1986). Also, by 1987 enrollments in teacher training programs were beginning to increase. See Blake Rodman, "AACTE Debates Accreditation: Releases New Enrollment Data," *Education Week*, 4, no. 22 (February 25, 1987), p. 1.

TABLE 1.4   Selected Characteristics of Public School Teachers: United
States, Spring 1961 to Spring 1986

	1961	1966	1971	1976	1981	1986
Median age (years):						
All teachers	41	36	35	33	37	40
Men	34	33	33	33	38	41
Women	46	40	37	33	36	39
Age Distribution (%):						
Under age 30	NA	33.9	37.1	37.1	18.7	11.0
Age 30-39	NA	22.8	22.8	28.3	38.8	37.7
Age 40-49	NA	17.5	17.8	19.1	23.1	30.1
Age 50 and over	NA	25.8	22.3	5.5	19.4	21.2
Gender (%):						
Elementary						
Men	12.2	10.2	16	12.8	17.7	13.8
Women	87.8	89.8	84	87.2	82.3	86.2
Secondary						
Men	56.8	54.2	54.5	52.2	46.9	50.4
Women	43.2	45.7	45.4	47.8	53.1	49.6
Ethnicity (%):						
Black	NA	NA	8.1	8.0	7.8	6.9
White	NA	NA	88.3	90.8	91.6	89.6
Other	NA	NA	3.6	1.2	0.7	3.4
Teaching Experience (%):						
1-2 years	14.3	18.4	16.8	11.3	5.3	4.6
3-4 years	13.2	14.4	15.6	16	8.2	4.8
5-14 years	34.5	35.9	39.6	46.2	49.2	40.0
15-19 years	10.4	9.8	9.7	12.5	15.4	23.1
20 or more years	27.6	21.4	18.3	14.1	21.9	17.5
Median years experience	11.0	8.0	8.0	8.0	12.0	15.0
Highest degree held (%):						
Less than bachelor's	14.6	7	2.9	0.9	0.4	0.3
Bachelor's	61.9	69.6	69.6	61.6	50.1	48.3
Master's or 6 years	23.1	23.2	27.1	37.1	49.3	50.7
Doctorate	0.4	0.1	0.4	0.4	0.3	0.7

Source: National Education Association, *Status of the American Public School Teacher*
(Washington, D.C., 1985-86, 1987).

Note: Data are based on sample surveys of public school teachers; because of rounding,
percentages may not add to 100.

Governmental Arrangements

In the United States it is government that acts overwhelmingly as a broker between those demanding school services and those willing to supply instruction. This governmental role is analyzed in detail in Chapter Three. Our purpose here is to describe the governmental structures involved.

The most significant structural characteristic of the governance of American education is its decentralized nature. The United States is one of the few major nations in the world that does not have a nationally operated system of schools.[30] History accounts greatly for the decentralized American arrangement. The framers of the U.S. Constitution distrusted the central authority of the British Crown.[31] They desired to distribute power widely in hopes of diluting the discretion of government generally, and the national government particularly. One of their inventions was the separation of power into three branches of government–*executive, legislative,* and *judicial.* Another invention was the dispersal of decision discretion over three levels of government–*national, state,* and *local.*

During the colonial period, education developed as a state and local function. The majority of participants in the Constitutional Convention of 1787 did not believe this practice ought to be altered. Consequently, the document they drafted contains no explicit mention of *education* or *schooling.* The Tenth Amendment, subsequently drafted, expresses the *social contract theory* of government and makes explicit the framers' intent regarding power:

> The powers not delegated to the United States by the Constitution, nor prohibited by it to the states, are reserved to the states respectively, or to the people.

The omission of schooling and education, when viewed in tandem with the Tenth Amendment, explains the absence of a central role for the national government in providing instruction. Also, each of the fifty states has an education provision in its constitution. Consequently, the *plenary* role of states in education is triply reinforced, and for many practical purposes the United States has fifty systems of education.[32]

During the colonial and early federal periods, the primitiveness of transportation and communication constrained the state government role in the provision of schooling. States relied on local school districts to deliver educational services, and state statutes facilitated the wide discretion of local authorities.[33] This set of arrangements promoted the perception and reality of *local control.* While never hav-

---

[30] Others include Canada, Australia, and West Germany.

[31] Christopher Collier and James Lincoln Collier, *Decision in Philadelphia* (New York: Ballentine, 1986).

[32] The District of Columbia and the various Trust Territories, each of which also has a separate system of schooling, makes the picture even more complex.

[33] The history of United States school governance is described by James W. Guthrie, Diana K. Thomason, and Patricia A. Craig in "The Erosion of Lay Control," National Committee for Citizens in Education, *Public Testimony on Public Schools* (Berkeley, Calif.: McCutchan, 1975), chap. 5.

ing strong standing as a legal concept, local control nevertheless played a major ideological and practical role in early American school governance. Even today, the majority of day-to-day decisions regarding school operation are made by locally selected policy makers and professional educators.

At the peak of local control there were approximately 128,000 individual school districts in the United States. Since this high point in the 1920s, state-issued incentives and mandates have reduced the number of districts ninefold. By the mid 1980s, the number of local school districts had been reduced to slightly more than 15,000.[34] Even this number is deceptive, because a fifth of these districts are concentrated in five states alone—California, Texas, New York, Illinois, and Nebraska. Southern states have historically aligned school districts with counties. As a consequence, there are many fewer districts in the south than in other regions of the nation.

The movement to consolidate school districts occurred during great population increases. Consequently, school districts, on average, have come to contain more pupils and adult residents. Near the beginning of the twentieth century, each school board member represented fewer than 200 citizens. Today, the comparable figure is approximately 3,000 citizens. There are still small rural districts, some with one school or a one-room school. However, what used to be local control of education is increasingly a rhetorical myth. Local school districts are larger, more bureaucratized, more subject to influence by professional educators, and more dominated by state government than at any time in American history. Be that as it may, educational governance is still less centralized in the United States than in almost any other nation in the world. It simply is not as decentralized as before and local control is probably nowhere as strong as many laypersons continue to believe it is.

Finances

The financial magnitude of schooling is seldom well understood.[35] An undertaking directly serving 20 percent of the population, operating throughout every state and most localities, and employing 4 million persons could reasonably be expected to involve a great deal of money, and it does. In 1988, the United States was expected to spend approximately $200 billion on elementary and secondary education. Postsecondary schooling would bring the total to more than $300 billion. This is approximately 7 percent of the GNP, the total value of all goods and services produced annually in the United States. The nation spends more only on defense, health and welfare, and annual interest payments on the national debt.

The amount of money spent per pupil is also impressive. Expenditures per pupil for 1988 were estimated at more than $4,000. The comparable figure in 1940 was $100. Even when compensating for the diluted value of today's dollar, the nation has increased school spending per pupil by more than 500 percent over the last

---

[34]The number of schools has been vastly reduced also and continues to shrink. For example, there were 84,000 schools in 1983–approximately 6,000 fewer than in 1971. *Conditions of Education, 1985*, p. 28.

[35]State statistics in this section are based on National Education Association, *Rankings of the States, 1986*, (Washington, D.C., NEA, 1986).

half century. For proponents of education, this may be insufficient. Nevertheless, it is an impressive accomplishment.[36]

New York State currently spends more than $5000 per pupil, Arkansas only half as much.[37] Sources of spending also differ greatly among states, and national averages are deceptive. Throughout the entire United States, locally generated school revenues constitute approximately 45 percent of the total, state funds make up approximately 49 percent, and federal funds provide the remainder. There is wide variation, however. At one extreme is Hawaii, where the overwhelming proportion of school costs, typically 90 percent, is borne directly by the state; the remainder results from federal funding. At the other extreme is New Hampshire, where the figures are almost reversed: local government contributes almost 90 percent of school revenues through the property tax, the state 8 percent, and federal revenues the remainder.

However broad the variation among states, the diversity of patterns within many states is wider yet. Some wealthy local school districts spend fifteen or twenty times as much per pupil as other districts.[38] These expenditure disparities have provoked repeated efforts at school finance reform. The 1970s constituted one of the most intense such reform periods, with proponents of greater equality seeking change through imaginative use of the courts. This book contains numerous references to and explanations for the governmental arrangements that permit such inequities. The next chapter begins this process by reviewing the legal findings resulting from judicial challenges to historic patterns of school financing.

SUMMARY

The purpose of this book is to explain the relationship between the financing of schools and educational policy. This chapter therefore began with a discussion of policy and the kaleidoscopic web of technical conditions and social forces that continually interact to shape policy. The significance of demography and economics is stressed. Specifically, the evolving composition of the overall population, together with several decades of declining productivity, has placed the United States in a vulnerable economic situation. Education is viewed by the public and policy makers as one potential solution to this problem. However, the magnitude and complexity of the decentralized system of schooling in the United States make it difficult to quickly reform educational policy and practice. Alterations in the education system must evolve from a complicated set of exchanges among proponents of three major value streams—equality, efficiency, and liberty. These interactions are the focus of the next chapter.

[36]For added evidence on rate of spending increases see Allan R. Odden, "The Economics of Financing Educational Excellence" (paper delivered at the American Educational Research Association Conference, Washington D.C., 1987).

[37]Alaska typically spends half again as much as New York, but its cost of living is on another scale.

[38]For evidence, see Joel S. Berke, ed., *Answers to Inequity* (Berkeley, Calif.: McCutchan, 1974).

chapter two

PUBLIC VALUES AND SCHOOL POLICY

The potential influence of economic and demographic changes on policy is mediated by culture, political arrangements, and values. Americans through their culture hold three strongly preferred values that significantly influence public policy: *equality*, *efficiency*, and *liberty*. Government actions regarding national defense, housing, taxation, antitrust regulation, racial desegregation, and hundreds of other policy dimensions, including education, are molded by one or more of these three values.[1]

Equality, liberty, and efficiency are viewed by an overwhelming electoral majority as conditions that government should maximize. They are not ends in themselves but criteria against which policy processes and products are judged. These three values are considered good, just, and right. Belief in them has historical roots that are deeply embedded in America's heritage. This belief permeates the ideologies promulgated by political parties, religions, schools, and other social institutions.

---

[1] An explanation for the manner in which individuals' political preferences are influenced by their culture is offered by Aaron Wildavsky in *Choosing Preferences by Constructing Institutions: A Cultural Theory of Preference Formation*, Survey Research Center Working Paper Series, (Berkeley, Calif.: 1987). The topic is also addressed by Thomas Sowell, *A Conflict of Visions* (New York: Morrow, 1987).

Despite widespread popular devotion to these values as abstract goals, their simultaneous fulfillment is well nigh impossible. At their roots, the three desired conditions are inconsistent and antithetical. Exclusive pursuit of one violates or eliminates the others.

For example, imagine that government, in an effort to increase equality, nationalized the construction industry and mandated standardized production of housing. Presumably all citizens above a specified age would be guaranteed a government-produced home. Only one or a limited number of building types, perhaps with minor variations, would be manufactured. Consequently, all eligible housing consumers would be provided with identical products and would, by definition, have equal housing. Added technical efficiency might be achieved, at least in the short run, through high-volume manufacturing of uniform products.[2] Unit cost of houses might be reduced.

However attractive the goals of equality and efficiency, in this instance liberty would be sacrificed. A limited variety of housing would severely restrict or totally prevent choice. In the absence of choice, there is no liberty. Moreover, in time, lack of competition might discourage the search for new production techniques and thus impair economic efficiency. Reasonable people might disagree about whether the absence of slums would be worth the presumed loss of freedom and efficiency. Policy makers constantly must face trade-offs such as these, most of which are far more subtle and many of which are more controversial than this hypothetical example.

Pursuit of equality exclusively will restrict or eliminate liberty and efficiency. Conversely, complete attention to either liberty or efficiency will diminish other values. Efforts to rearrange society so as to maximize one of the three values are constrained by forces for preserving the status quo. This dynamic equilibrium among the three values constantly shifts, with the balance at any particular point being fixed as a consequence of a complicated series of political and economic compromises.

Education is one of the prime instruments through which society attempts to promote all three values. Educators and officials involved in educational policy making are well advised to be informed about and alert to the interactions among these values. The purpose of this chapter is to describe the practical and policy consequences for public schools of these interactions and to illustrate the trade-offs policy makers face in attempting to maximize liberty, equality, and efficiency.

Before proceeding, we should recall the demographic and fiscal conditions of education in the United States described in the preceding chapter. It is only against this statistical backdrop that we can comprehend the remarkable magnitude of the United States system of schooling and appreciate the complexity of the value preference trade-offs about to be described.

[2] A distinction is made in Chapter 14 between *technical* and *allocative* efficiency.

DEMOCRATIC GOVERNMENT AND A MARKET ECONOMY

Nowhere is the tension among equality, efficiency, and liberty better mirrored than in the practical conflicts between democracy and a market-oriented, profit-motivated economy.[3] American political ideology champions equality and freedom. In reacting to the social rigidity and inherited privilege that dominated seventeenth- and eighteenth-century Europe, Thomas Jefferson proclaimed in the Declaration of Independence that "All men are created equal. . . ."[4] Subsequently, a constitution was adopted containing an elaborate system of governmental checks and balances to discourage overaccumulation of political power and thus to preserve individual liberty. Private ownership of property was seen as an important additional protection against political tyranny.

In the formative years of the United States, the relative absence of inherited social position, the freedom of individuals to own the means of production, and the freedom to choose one's occupation encouraged pursuit of private profit. Profit seeking was justified partly on the grounds that it contributed to economic efficiency. The ability to reap returns from their own efforts and benefits from new ideas and methods motivated entrepreneurs to pioneer increasingly better products, often at lower prices. Both consumers and producers were held to benefit from such increased efficiency. The prospect of benefiting from profit inspires manufacturers to expand the range of their products. The resulting proliferation of choice reinforces the possibility of liberty. However, social approval of profit promotes economic disparity. If political power accrues with compilation of capital, a private-property, profit-motivated economy may contradict the democratic idea of political equality. The absence of political equality jeopardizes liberty. Again, the three values are inextricably linked.[5]

Much of the government reform in the United States over the last two hundred years has been directed at adjusting tensions between social equality and economic efficiency. Antitrust legislation, personal and corporate income taxes, social security, unemployment insurance, medicare, food and housing subsidies, and inheritance taxes are all intended to protect against poverty or the accumulation of great wealth.

Where these reforms have touched the economy, they may have contributed to inefficiency. Perhaps the economy would grow more rapidly if capital were permitted to pyramid perpetually rather than being dispersed through transfer payments for welfare purposes. Perhaps there would be greater productivity if the work force did not benefit from a minimum standard of living provided by minimum wages, social security, unemployment insurance, medicare benefits, and food and housing

---

[3]This is the topic of an extraordinarily thoughtful volume by Arthur M. Okun, *Equality and Efficiency: The Big Tradeoff* (Washington, D.C.: Brookings Institution, 1975).

[4]See Carl Becker, *The Declaration of Independence: A Study in the History of Political Ideas* (New York: Knopf, 1942).

[5]A philosophical analysis of the interaction between equality and liberty is contained in John Rawls, *A Theory of Justice* (Cambridge, Mass.: Harvard University Press, 1971), particularly Chaps. 2 and 4; and Kenneth J. Arrow, "Some Ordinalist-Utilitarian Notes on Rawls' Theory of Justice," *Journal of Philosophy,* 70 (May 10, 1973), 245–63.

subsidies. Perhaps agricultural production would be more efficient and less costly if farmers were not advantaged by a complicated parity system of food-price supports.[6] However, against the potential loss of economic inefficiency one must weigh the value of social equality and the increased political stability that it fosters.[7] The reforms just mentioned may represent a trade-off between short-term economic inefficiency and long-term political stability. The absence of stability can contribute mightily toward the economic failure of a government. Of course, political stability in itself is no guarantee of personal liberty. Many repressive governments have been "stable." However the lack of stable government may lead to loss of liberty if the weak or unprotected are overcome by the powerful.

EDUCATION AS A POLICY VARIABLE IN THE PURSUIT OF EQUALITY, EFFICIENCY, AND LIBERTY

The eighteenth-century leaders of the new American republic viewed education as a means to enable citizens to participate as equals in affairs of government,[8] and thus essential to ensure liberty.[9] It was not until the nineteenth century that education began to assume significance in economic terms. The increasing demands of industrial technology necessitated an educated work force; henceforth schooling was taken as an important contributor to economic efficiency. By the twentieth century, intensified technological development and economic interdependence had made formal schooling a prerequisite both for society's survival and for an individual's economic and social success. Consequently, education assumed new importance as a means of maximizing equality. Beginning with the 1954 United States Supreme Court decision in *Brown v. Board of Education*[10] and continuing with the increase in the federal education programs of the 1960s and the school finance reform efforts of the 1970s, a major portion of mid-twentieth-century education policy has been directed at achieving greater equality. Consequently, our discussion of values and school policy begins with equality.

[6]According to the Census Bureau, in 1976 the total dollar cost of all levels of U.S. government required that an average employed person work two hours and thirty-nine minutes of each eight-hour day, or almost four months of each year, to pay taxes. By 1984, the average total tax burden had shrunk to 21 percent of income. This meant that an individual worked one hour and forty-one minutes of each eight-hour day, or three months out of each year, to pay taxes.

[7]The economic basis for political revolution has been the subject of substantial research. For example, there are those who speculate that instability is intensified if, after a period of progress toward equality, there is a slide toward greater inequality. This contention emphasizes that it is not the absolute level of disparity that provokes revolution but rather the level of expectation about equality.

[8]See Frederick Rudolph, ed., *Essays on Education in the New Republic* (Cambridge, Mass.: Harvard University Press, 1969).

[9]For more on this topic see Chapter 1 in John W. Gardner, *Excellence: Can We Be Equal and Excellent Too?* (New York: Harper & Row, Pub., 1961).

[10]For perspective on *Brown* see Raymond Wolters, *The Burden of Brown: Thirty Years of School Desegregation* (Knoxville: University of Tennessee Press, 1984).

Education and Equality

For educational policy purposes, equality has almost always been translated as "equality of educational opportunity." Few have seriously argued that education should be absolutely equal for each individual. Such an objective would make unsupportable the assumptions regarding genetically endowed abilities, standardized instruction, and similarities of environmental effects upon human tastes. Consequently, most policy debates center in interpretations of "equal educational opportunity." Over time, this concept has evolved through several major stages.[11]

EQUAL ACCESS TO EDUCATION

Equal access assumes that provision of at least a minimum level of school resources will ensure equality of educational opportunity. This approach, operating far longer and in many more states than any other, initially implied that schools, of whatever quality, be made available to all students. In the nineteenth century, the fact that schooling was provided at all was taken to constitute equal educational opportunity.

The definition evolved to mean more than simple access. The quality of available services also was taken into account: every child should be provided with at least the same minimally adequate school services. Typically this was translated into a policy whereby states guaranteed a minimal education expenditure level. Local school districts were then expected to transform these dollars into *minimally adequate programs.*

Equal access to a minimally acceptable level of school service is reflected in the language of most state school finance statutes—for example, "foundation program" or "basic aid." If localities choose to add their own resources to the state-guaranteed minimum, they are free to do so. One outcome of local discretion, explained more fully in Chapters 4 and 5, is the present variation in per-pupil expenditure among school districts in most states.

The probability is high that wide expenditure differences, at least at the extremes, represent actual disparities in the quality and kind of school services available to students. All other things being equal, it is hard to imagine that students from poorly funded school districts with large classes, inadequately prepared teachers, and limited course offerings have the same opportunity to learn as their more fortunate counterparts in districts spending two or three times the state average. What historically was an adequate minimum, available equally to all students throughout a state, has been transformed over time into a low level of service exceeded substantially by districts with greater wealth to tap, greater willingness to tax themselves, or both. Some states—for example, New Hampshire and Connecticut—did not attempt until the 1970s even to guarantee such a minimum.

[11]The historical development of the concept of equal educational opportunity is described by James S. Coleman in "The Concept of Equality of Educational Opportunity," *Harvard Education Review,* Winter 1968, pp. 7-22. A detailed discussion of varying definitions of this concept is provided by John D. Danner in an M.A. thesis entitled "Equality of Educational Opportunity: The Search for the Meaning of the Motto" (University of California, Berkeley, 1974). See also Arthur Wise, *Rich Schools: Poor Schools* (Chicago: University of Chicago Press, 1970).

Whatever the reason for inequalities in educational expenditures and services, they have triggered a series of lawsuits questioning the legality, under both state and federal constitutions, of the school finance arrangements in over forty states. These legal maneuvers influenced school finance reform throughout the late 1960s and 1970s and have had a residual effect in the 1980s. A chronology of the "equal protection" cases and a summary of their legal logic and practical consequences are presented in Chapter 8.

EQUAL EDUCATIONAL TREATMENT

This definition of equal educational opportunity is based on the premise that learners have widely varying characteristics and abilities, from which it logically follows that available school services should be tailored to each student's specific circumstances. Minimally adequate school services, by this definition, are insufficient because what is appropriate for some students does not put less fortunate children at the "starting line" in the race for life's rewards. The *equal educational treatment* definition assumes that under ideal conditions, each student's school-related strengths and weaknesses would be assessed. Subsequently, additional services would be supplied those who, for whatever reason, were judged to be deficient in some learning abilities. This definition is reflected in efforts to provide special educational services to students who are physically or mentally handicapped. The drive for so-called compensatory education, initiated in the mid 1960s with enactment of the federal Elementary and Secondary Education Act (ESEA), also reflects this definition of equality of educational opportunity. Under the Education Consolidation and Improvement Act (ECIA), the 1981 successor to the ESEA, states and school districts are eligible for federal funds in proportion to the number of students they enroll from low-income households. Added funding is justified on grounds that such students are likely to be environmentally disadvantaged in their ability to benefit from schooling. Federal funds are intended to provide compensatory school services.[12] This attempt to balance any potential learning deficit theoretically results in equal treatment of all pupils but clearly demands unequal resources. This program is described in detail in Chapter 7.

EQUALITY OF EDUCATIONAL OUTCOME

Beginning in the early 1970s, a number of social theorists and policy analysts began to construct a new definition of equal educational opportunity. Their position stemmed from the observation that academic achievement had become crucial for personal success. Consequently, they proposed that the appropriate measure of equality be equal student learning, at least in terms of minimum or basic skills. Presumably, the objective would be fulfilled if, upon graduating from secondary school, for example, every student were able to perform at least at an eighth-grade level in reading, mathematics, and composition. Schools would be held responsible

[12]This program is described in detail in Chapter 7.

for achieving such equal minimal outcomes regardless of the resource level necessary.[13]

On occasion, this *equal outcome* definition is extended to include the schools' responsibility for providing an "equal life chance." By this definition, school services and resources should be deployed so as to assure every normal child, upon graduation from secondary school, an equal opportunity to compete with any other student. Achievement of this goal could be measured by the degree to which race, socioeconomic status, ethnic origin, and similar social measures no longer predicted adult income or occupation. However, even if one assumed that pedagogical techniques could be so refined and applied as to make such an objective attainable, the resource level necessary to implement it would undoubtedly be large.

Education and Efficiency

American culture's attachment to the concept of efficiency is borne out not only in age-old adages such as "a penny saved is a penny earned" and "a stitch in time saves nine," but also by a number of practical applications. Appeals to frugality are widespread in advertising, and exhortations to become more productive are commonplace in work settings. Efficiency as an ideal stems from components of the Protestant work ethic and is continually reinforced by the profit motive.

In simple terms, economic efficiency is increased by a gain in units of output per unit of input. This can occur either by holding output constant and decreasing input or by deriving greater production from the same level of input. Nonspecialists frequently label the first condition *greater effectiveness* and the second as *added productivity*. From the viewpoint of economic analysis, the two are similar.

Efficiency is often achieved by implementing new production techniques, such as those effected by new tools. The steel plow, internal combustion engine, electronic computer, and "miracle grains" are dramatic examples. However, gains in efficiency are not dependent solely upon creation of new material items. New techniques may simply involve workers' adopting new patterns of action or interaction. For example, through experience, better training, or both, a wood-carver or bricklayer may be able to accomplish more during a workday. Similarly, manufacture of many material items has become more efficient not only because of new equipment made available during the industrial and electronic revolutions but also because of new manufacturing techniques. The concept of interchangeable parts permitted assembly lines and promoted greater output per worker. By specializing in a narrow portion of the production process, each worker could perform functions more rapidly, with greater precision, or both. By the 1980s, limitations to this production approach were becoming more evident, and manufacturers were seeking a middle ground between assembly-line specialization and worker identification with

---

[13]The equal outcome definition is suggested and explained by authors such as Charles S. Benson, *The Cheerful Prospect: A Statement on the Future of Public Education* (Boston: Houghton Mifflin, 1965); Henry S. Dyer, "The Measurement of Educational Opportunity," in *On Equality of Educational Opportunity,* ed. Frederick Mosteller and Daniel P. Moynihan (New York: Random House, Vintage Books, 1972), pp. 513–21; and James W. Guthrie et al., *Schools and Inequality* (Cambridge, Mass.: MIT Press, 1971).

overall production outcomes.[14] Nevertheless, the general rule still holds: greater specialization leads to more efficient production.

Schools are no exception to the American desire for efficiency. There have been repeated efforts to increase educational efficiency. For example, during the first half of the nineteenth century, an elaborate British system of tutors and monitors, the so-called Lancastrian System,[15] was used in an effort to boost school output. Under this method, a single headmaster instructed older and presumably the most able students, who then reinforced their learning by transmitting it to younger students. Elaborately tiered seating corresponding to this hierarchical pattern was introduced to facilitate supervision by a master and instructional efforts by the student "monitors." Similarly, near the turn of the twentieth century, American schools were greatly influenced by the scientific management movement then popular in the manufacturing sector. This was the era of "cheaper by the dozen," time-and-motion studies, and efficiency experts.[16] The hope was that schooling could be reduced to a series of scientific principles amenable to implementation by professional school administrators. Implementation of such managerial principles was expected both to enhance learning and to reduce costs.

Heated competition for public sector resources accompanying government-sponsored social programs in the 1960s triggered another cycle of concern for efficiency. This time *accountability* became the fashionable label under which to seek added school productivity. Two decades later, economic uncertainty and intense international trade competition stimulated further efforts on behalf of school productivity.[17] Following the publication in 1983 of *A Nation At Risk*,[18] a federal commission's report on education, hundreds of high-level task forces, blue-ribbon panels, study groups, and legislative committees began prescribing reforms intended to make America's schools more efficient. The banner this time was *excellence*.

Schools have remained remarkably resistant to these repeated attempts to increase efficiency. Between 1940 and 1986, per-pupil school expenditures for U.S. public schools increased 500 percent, even when inflation is discounted. School costs have outstripped growth in the GNP.[19] Yet it is not immediately evident that

[14]See Tom Peters and Nancy Austin, *A Passion for Excellence* (New York: Warner Books, 1986).

[15]For more on this and other techniques of instruction introduced at the time to enhance school efficiency, see David B. Tyack, *The One Best System* (Cambridge Mass.: Harvard University Press, 1974).

[16]See Raymond Callahan, *The Cult of Efficiency* (Chicago: University of Chicago Press, 1962).

[17]See James W. Guthrie, "The Educational Policy Consequences of Economic Instability: The Emerging Political Economy of American Education," *Educational Evaluation and Policy Analysis*, 7, no. 4 (Winter 1985), 319–32.

[18]National Commission on Educational Excellence, *A Nation at Risk* (Washington, D.C.: Government Printing Office, 1983).

[19]According to the U.S. Department of Health, Education, and Welfare's National Center for Educational Statistics, total expenditures for education as a percentage of GNP increased from 2 percent in 1943 to a high point of 8 percent in 1975. By 1987, they had declined to approximately 6 percent.

FIGURE 2.1   Average SAT Scores, Differences From Lowest Year

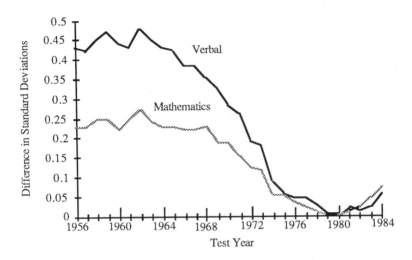

Sources: Hunter M. Breland, *The SAT Score Decline: A Summary of Related Research* (New York: College Board, 1976), Table 1; and College Entrance Examination Board, *National College-Bound Seniors, 1985* (New York: College Board, 1985).

such increases have been accompanied by elevations in productivity. Students do not complete schooling any more quickly, and measures of academic achievement are, at best, mixed. In fact, if one were to judge by the rather narrow criterion of student scores on various achievement tests administered between 1960 and 1985, as shown in Figure 2.1, school performance has actually declined in the last quarter century.[20] United States school performance has also been slipping relative to that of other nations.[21]

IMPEDIMENTS TO SCHOOL EFFICIENCY

Conflicting expectations and weak incentives. A host of conditions inhibit attempts to make public schools more efficient. First, increased productivity requires agreement about the expected product. What is it that the American public school system is to produce? There are no easy answers to this question. The fact that school districts have become larger, more bureaucratized, and possessed of less decision-making discretion inhibits efforts to decide on common goals. The virtual

[20]Although many tests show similar patterns of student achievement, testing experts have been unable to agree conclusively on the causes of test-score declines. The most comprehensive explanation is that put forward by the College Entrance Examination Board, Willard Wirtz, chairman, *Advisory Panel on the Scholastic Aptitude Test Score Decline* (New York, 1977).

[21]See International Association for the Evaluation of Educational Achievement, *The Underachieving Curriculum: Assessing U.S. School Mathematics from an International Perspective* (Champagne, Ill.: Stipes Publishing Co., 1987); and Arthur N. Applebee, Judith A. Langer, and Ina V. S. Mullis, *Learning to Be Literate in America* (Princeton, N.J.: Educational Testing Service, 1987).

monopoly of public schools on the education market impedes expression of consumer choice, which might otherwise reveal public preferences for school outputs. School purposes are determined through the political process by elected officials. This contributes to complexity (see cartoon). Another complication is the widespread concern for equality previously discussed. Attempts to maximize equality frequently conflict with efforts to increase economic efficiency.

Also, educational techniques and materials of production are extraordinarily primitive compared with standard manufacturing processes. Despite the growing sophistication of research on instruction,[22] fundamental pedagogical processes have changed little since the time of Socrates. Moreover, the schools' relative absence of rewards for better instructional techniques and technology renders dramatic breakthroughs unlikely. There may well be a "better mousetrap" for schools, but it is improbable that the inventor will much benefit economically from its creation. There are few stimuli in public schooling equivalent to the profit motive in the private sector. The standard reward for successful educators is to be "promoted" so as not to be near students. This obviously does not motivate teachers to seek practical instructional breakthroughs. In fact, it has probably dampened school productivity by inducing many able instructors to leave classroom teaching.

Value conflicts. Attempts to achieve equality frequently decrease school efficiency. For example, whether it be court-mandated or voluntary, racial integration usually entails added transportation costs. If contact with students of other races promotes mutual understanding and social cohesion, then the expenditure may be

Source: Danziger, in *The Christian Science Monitor,* ©1987 TCSPS.

[22]See Jere E. Brophy and Thomas L. Good, "Teaching Behavior and Student Achievement," in *Handbook of Research on Teaching*; ed. Merlin C. Wittrock (New York: Macmillan, 1986), pp. 328–75.

cost-effective. Without such outcomes, funds spent for busing are simply added school costs.[23]

There are less ambiguous examples of the conflict between equality and efficiency. For instance, in the late 1960s an effort was made to increase school productivity by utilizing *performance contracting*.[24] Private entrepreneurs were encouraged to contract with local school districts to provide specified instructional services—most often in reading. Contractors were to be paid in proportion to pupils' measured gains in reading achievement. For many reasons the experiments were eventually halted; prominent among the causes was the revelation that a few contractors had concentrated on the students who demonstrated the greatest propensity for large-scale improvement and neglected the others. For contractors this was economically efficient—as long as the output was measured in terms of *average class gains*. However, concern for equal treatment of all students contributed strongly to the demise of performance contracting as a federal government–sponsored experiment.

A second value conflict pits economic efficiency against a concern for liberty. Compulsory attendance statutes and the strong monopolistic quality of public schools limit individual liberty. This situation is mitigated not only by the availability of private schooling but also by a modest range of options within public school systems. Particularly in secondary schools, students are usually not confined to a single program of study; they can choose among elective courses. Frequently, the range of electives is broad, including music, language, science, drama, art, business, and other courses. Provision of electives is consistent with the value of liberty. However, school officials, in attempting to respond to the public's desire for services, can offer only as wide a choice as budgets permit. The delicate balance between range of offerings and tax rates is decided by elected officials, usually school board members. Clearly it would be less costly to provide only a modicum of electives. One could delete expensive options such as vocational training or advanced foreign language classes with their typically small enrollments. Under such restricted arrangements, unit costs of schooling would be reduced. However, this trade-off might prove sufficiently unattractive and unresponsive to parents' and students' needs to arouse public ire. In such circumstances, efficiency gives way, at least in part, to liberty.

[23]The effectiveness of racial integration as a strategy for improving the performance of minority-group students has been the subject of argument among social science researchers. Early interpretations of Coleman Report findings suggested that integrated schooling enhanced the school performance of black students. See, for example, James S. Coleman et al., *Equality of Educational Opportunity* (Washington, D.C.: U.S. Government Printing Office, 1966), pp. 330–33. This general conclusion was subsequently challenged by the research of David Armor, who asserted that integration was associated with no positive outcomes for minority children; David J. Armor, "The Evidence on Busing," *Public Interest*, no. 28 (Summer 1972), 90–126. Armor's position has itself been subject to serious criticism. See Thomas F. Pettigrew et al., "Busing: A Review of the Evidence," *Public Interest*, no. 30 (Winter 1973), 88–114. Contemporary debate on the topic is provided by David L. Kirp in *Just Schools: The Ideal of Racial Equality in American Education*, (Berkeley: University of California Press, 1982).

[24]This experiment is described in Edward M. Gramlich and Patricia P. Koshel, *Educational Performance Contracting: An Evaluation of an Experiment* (Washington, D.C.: Brookings Institution, 1975).

Private sector spillovers. Conventional wisdom holds that gains in economic efficiency are shared by labor and investors. If an invention enables labor to produce twice as much in the same amount of time, newfound gains are transmitted to workers in the form of higher wages or more leisure time, and to owners in the form of added profits. Most productivity gains occur in the private sector. Public sector endeavors, particularly education, are highly labor-intensive. They have not yet been similarly susceptible to added efficiency through new technology. Nevertheless, because the public sector competes with the private sector for labor, it must match salaries and working conditions if it is to attract employees. Thus, public sector labor costs frequently increase even in the absence of gains in economic efficiency. This renders the unit costs of "producing" education even higher—that is to say, it makes schools more inefficient.[25] However, if schools could not compete with the private sector for talent, they could become even less attractive to their clients and thus might be even more inefficient. In obtaining the services of talented individuals, public schools are probably already at a competitive disadvantage when compared with the total hiring market. This topic is addressed in detail in Chapter 11.

MEASURING EFFICIENCY

In the face of conflicting expectations for school output, competing values, weak incentive systems, and private-sector spillover effects, how can public schools attempt to become more efficient? For reasons described in subsequent chapters, efforts to apply purely economic methods of efficiency to public schools are often naïve and limiting. However, efficiency need not be defined solely in mechanical economic terms. It is possible to expand the definition to signify maximum consumer satisfaction at minimum costs. By this definition efficiency can result from an ingenious blend of politics and economics.

Public schools can be restructured to offer a wider range of choice to direct consumers—households of parents and children. Dissatisfaction because of disagreement over educational goals is lessened by permitting households to select among schools. Provided a choice, clients will presumably select schools stressing objectives they believe important. By requiring a minimum standard curriculum at each school, the state could ensure an adequate amount of education is provided, reduce the likelihood of undesirable levels of inequality in school output, and encourage social cohesion. Meanwhile, individual schools could be encouraged to be responsive and efficient. They would stand to lose clients if they did not meet parent and student expectations. Presumably the more efficient a school in deploying available income, the broader the range or the higher the quality of services it could offer. By constantly attempting to outperform other schools in its sector, a school would not only retain but possibly increase its enrollments.

Such a plan for maximizing consumer preference might evolve through several different avenues. It could take the form of a voucher plan wherein families are

[25]The classic explanation of the relationship between private and public sector efficiency is that of William Baumol, "Macroeconomics of Unbalanced Growth: The Anatomy of Urban Crisis," *American Economic Review,* June 1967, p. 57.

provided with a warrant in the amount spent per pupil within their public school district.[26] The warrant would be redeemable at a school of their choice, private or public. Restricting parent choices to schools within the public system would be a less drastic change and thus might be politically more feasible.[27] The trade-off would be less competition. A still milder reform would be merely to encourage greater consumer participation by establishing parent advisory councils at each school and giving them decision-making power over program offerings and personnel.[28] These and other strategies are analyzed in detail in subsequent chapters. The purpose in listing them here is to indicate that even though there are no perfect paths to efficiency in public schools, it may be possible to construct better approaches.

Education and Liberty

The third value deeply affecting the direction of American educational policy is liberty.[29] This value provided a major ideological justification for the revolution that gave birth to the United States. After the war with England, James Madison wrote:

> In Europe, charters of liberty have been granted by power. America has set the example, and France has followed it, of charters of power granted by liberty.[30]

For Americans, liberty has meant the freedom to choose, to be able to select from among different courses of action. The desire for choice fueled the historical American affection for a market economy. Competition among producers, among other benefits, is held to expand the range of items from which consumers can choose. In the public sector, responsive governmental institutions are taken to be a crucial link in the preservation of choice and liberty.

In the view of those who designed the American social contract, governmental authority was vested in the citizenry, who then delegated the power to govern to selected representatives. A measure of representatives' effectiveness was their responsiveness to the will of those they governed. Remarkably enough, lack of responsiveness is still viewed today as eroding the power of the citizenry and thus constitutes grounds for removal from office.

---

[26]Many varieties of voucher plans have been proposed. The acknowledged twentieth-century forerunner is described by Milton Friedman in *Capitalism and Freedom* (Chicago: University of Chicago Press, 1967). The explanation and set of proposals described by John E. Coons and Stephen D. Sugarman in *Education by Choice: The Case for Family Control* (Berkeley: University of California Press, 1978) is particularly complete. (See Chapter 14).

[27]Many of these plans have been proposed as well. A good description of this movement during the 1960s and 1970s is provided by Mario Fantini, "Alternative Educational Experiences: The Demand for Change," in National Committee for Citizens in Education, *Public Testimony on Public Schools* (Berkeley, Calif.: McCutchan, 1975), pp. 160–82.

[28]This is the primary recommendation of the National Committee for Citizens in Education in *Public Testimony on Public Schools*.

[29]See F. A. Hayek, *The Constitution of Liberty* (Chicago: University of Chicago Press, 1960).

[30]Quoted by Bernard Bailyn, *The Ideological Origins of the American Revolution* (Cambridge, Mass.: Harvard University Press, 1967), p. 55.

A second means for preserving liberty was to disperse governmental authority widely. This accounts for the balancing of powers among three branches and over various levels of government. Efforts to inhibit accumulation of power also account for the deliberate constitutional fragmentation of decision-making authority: specific powers are accorded the federal government, some are left to the states, and some reserved to the people themselves. Historically, power to make educational decisions evolved in the same fashion. Centralized authority was viewed as perilous because it might exert widespread control and uniformity. Formation of thousands of small local school districts, portending both inefficiency and inequality, was intended as an antidote to accumulation of power. Proximity to constituents, coupled with the electoral process, was taken as a means to enhance governmental responsiveness and to preserve liberty.

GOVERNMENTAL CYCLES AND THE DILUTION OF RESPONSIVENESS

America has evidenced the liberty-efficiency dichotomy in proposals from three groups of citizens: (1) advocates of responsiveness, (2) those favoring greater centralization of authority —a stronger executive—and (3) those espousing expert professional management. Early American government, as just emphasized, stressed the first value—representativeness. In large measure this was a colonial reaction to the strong authority of the English Crown, focus of intense revolutionary hatred. Whatever its advantages for expression of the popular will and preservation of liberty, strong representative government is cumbersome, time-consuming, demands compromise, and can obscure responsibility. To avoid such liabilities and gain greater decisiveness and accountability, Americans have tended periodically to favor a strong executive and greater centralization of government decision-making authority.[31]

On other occasions, public opinion has opposed both representativeness and executive authority. The former is accused of being prone to an excess of partisan politics and the latter overly open to persuasion by selfish interests. In such periods, the argument has been made for the advantages of nonpartisan, disinterested governmental officials who perform government tasks free from personal bias and narrow interest. The model here is the expert, the professional or technician, who presumably is apolitical and therefore does what is "right." Such arguments formed the basis of the progressive era reforms at the turn of the twentieth century and led to development of merit systems and the civil service arrangements now existing at all levels of government.

Actual mechanisms of government, whether at the federal, state, or local level, reflect constant adjustments among *representativeness, executive authority,* and *professional management.* School governance is no exception to the cyclical emphasis placed in turn upon these three views of the governing process. Representativeness peaked early in the twentieth century, to be superseded by centralized authority and professional management . Since these shifts in the pattern of gover-

---

[31]The cyclical nature of governmental forms is described by Herbert Kaufman in *Politics and Policies in State and Local Government* (Englewood Cliffs, N.J.: Prentice-Hall, 1963), chap. 2.

nance have strongly colored public education and promise to be equally influential during the last decade of the twentieth century, it is appropriate to review briefly the historical events that provoke such pendulum swings.

SCHOOL DISTRICT CONSOLIDATION

As mentioned in Chapter 1, by 1932 the number of local school districts in the United States had reached its high point, approximately 128,000. By 1988 this number had been reduced to approximately 15,500.[32] This drastic reduction in the number of units of a specialized form of local government constitutes one of the most dramatic of all changes in America's internal political patterns. There were several motives for consolidating thousands of small rural school districts, many of them with only one school, frequently a one-room school at that. It was argued that small school districts were inefficient. Specifically, it was asserted that they could not provide a sufficient array of services, impeded the ability of teachers to specialize, and generally inhibited attainment of economies of scale in matters such as purchasing and maintenance. Enticed by the carrot of financial inducements and driven by the stick of legislative penalties, local districts combined into larger units.

PROFESSIONAL MANAGEMENT

Reduction in the number of school districts, and increases in population, resulted in the creation of school district organizations too large to be managed by school boards themselves. Originally, local board members were directly responsible for matters such as hiring teachers, purchasing supplies, setting school curricula, establishing school regulations, and listening personally to citizens' complaints. In short, for school matters they performed the three functions of government—*rule making, rule implementation,* and *rule adjudication.*[33] Formation of large districts brought such practices to a close. It became clear that school districts would require full-time managers. Consequently, beginning in New York in the 1870s, elected school boards began to employ professional school superintendents and turn over to them day-to-day operations.[34] This trend spread across the nation. In the process, representativeness was further diluted.

The professional school administrator movement was bolstered in the early twentieth century by the growth throughout the United States of *scientific management.* Beginning in the private sector, the philosophy and methods of efficiency experts—time-and-motion analysis—spread to the public sector.[35] The argument

---

[32]*A Century of U.S. School Statistics* (Washington, D.C.: U.S. Department of Health, Education and Welfare, 1974); and *The Conditions of Education: 1986* (Washington, D.C.: U.S. Department of Education, 1986).

[33]For further elaboration of this means of viewing government functions see David Easton, "An Approach to the Analysis of Political Systems," *World Politics,* no. 9 (1957), 383–400, and *A Framework for Political Analysis* (Englewood Cliffs, N.J.: Prentice-Hall, Inc., 1965).

[34]Theodore L. Reller, *Development of the City Superintendency of Schools* (Boston: Privately printed, 1935).

[35]See Callahan, op. cit; and Tyack, op. cit.

was made that government, school government included, could be made more efficient and less prone to excesses and corruption of the political process if managed by experts. School operation would be entrusted to those skilled in education, those capable of making scientific judgments regarding school management. Schools of education began preparing "scientifically trained" administrators imbued with a philosophy that while school boards might make policy, there was a strict line between policy and practice and only an administrator was responsible for the latter.

The scientific management movement was abetted by an uncovering of widespread political scandal, particularly in large cities, during the early 1900s.[36] This provided an added boost to those who argued that representativeness led only to an excess of politics, pettiness, and corruption. Thus, it was believed, by reducing the number of school board members, centralizing authority in fewer persons, and ceding management reins to trained professionals, people could run schools more efficiently. But by the 1960s, as we will see shortly, there was a strong reaction to this decline in representativeness.[37]

COLLECTIVE BARGAINING

In the 1950s, teachers began to organize unions to engage in collective bargaining with school boards. This development was initiated in large cities and spread to almost every school district in the United States. Increases in organizational size, bureaucratization, and the number of administrative levels probably accounted, in large measure, for teachers' feelings of inefficacy and alienation and prompted them to unionize. Though teachers' representatives frequently come to the bargaining table with genuine concerns for student welfare and respect for the public interest, their primary allegiance is to teachers. They cannot legitimately claim to represent the larger public. Nevertheless, duly elected public representatives—the school board members—must share decision-making authority with them. The outcome is to further centralize school policy making and to erode the ability of the public to participate in the process.

ESCALATING STATE POWER

Though state government has always held ultimate legal responsibility for school decision making, historically state governments have delegated policy discretion to local units of government. Since World War II, however, state-level participation has increased because of the politicization of school decisions and intensified efforts to achieve greater equality of educational opportunity and more efficient use of school resources.[38] This increased state participation has removed much of decision-making discretion from local education authorities. For example, areas

[36]See Joseph M. Cronin, *The Control of Urban Schools* (New York: Free Press, 1973).

[37]See Judith Gruber, *Controlling Bureaucracies: Dilemmas in Democratic Governance* (Berkeley: University of California Press, 1986).

[38]See James W. Guthrie and Paula H. Skene, "The Escalation of Pedagogical Politics," *Phi Delta Kappan,* No. 54 (February 1973), 386–89; and Les Pacheco, "The Politicization of Education at the State Level: A Case Study of California, 1947–72" (Ed.D. dissertation, University of California, Berkeley, 1975).

such as school curriculum, teacher salaries and working conditions, graduation requirements, and school architecture increasingly have been incorporated into state specifications. More decisions regarding schools are now determined by fewer persons. Choice is restricted, the ability of local officials to respond to constituent preferences is constrained, and, at least in a legal sense, local autonomy and liberty—and perhaps efficiency—have been diminished.

REACTION

By the latter half of the 1960s, a reaction to the diminished status of representativeness had begun. Requests for change stemmed initially from ethnic enclaves in large cities, who perceived themselves as relatively impotent in affecting the operation of their children's schools. They demanded what was then labeled *community control*.[39] For example, several community control experiments were undertaken in the New York City schools. The state legislature ultimately recognized this growing political momentum by fractionating New York City into thirty-two elementary school districts. Since each of the thirty-two averaged 30,000 students, approximately the size of the entire school district in cities such as Syracuse, the system could not realistically be characterized as under "community control." Nevertheless, each of New York City's local districts was authorized to elect a nine-member local board of education. Thus, New York City's elected school policy makers grew from 9 to 297.[40]

Reaction to dilution of representativeness also reached Congress. Federal education acts were amended in the early 1970s to mandate parent participation in decisions about federal program funds.[41] Also, by the mid 1970s several state legislatures were requiring formation of parent advisory councils at school sites,[42] and numerous local school districts were voluntarily implementing plans for wider involvement of citizens in decision making.

Reforms intended to increase public participation in educational planning were justified on grounds that schools had become dominated by professional experts and, as a consequence, were insensitive to public preferences. Those opposed to reform were quick to threaten recurrences of corruption and other political horrors and to cite the inevitable inefficiency accompanying widespread participation. By the mid 1980s, it appeared that opponents' fears had been realized, at least partially . Corruption had not escalated, other than perhaps in a few large city districts, but inefficiency had manifested itself in falling pupil performance. The previously described lament offered in *A Nation at Risk* testified to the sorry depths to which United States school standards had sunk. The result was an intense wave of state-directed reform, much of which bypassed local decision makers. The stage was set for an-

---

[39]See Henry M. Levin, *Community Control of Schools* (Washington, D.C.: Brookings Institution, 1970).

[40]See Melvin Zimmet, *Decentralization and School Effectiveness* (New York: Teachers College Press, 1973).

[41]The previously mentioned ECIA diluted this requirement.

[42]For example, by 1975 both California and Florida had enacted statutes to this end.

other round of change. The only question was whether proponents of equality or proponents of liberty would capture the next reform agenda .

Other chapters throughout this volume explain policies to inject a larger element of balance and stability into school decision making. It should be clear, however, that the pendulum of change is constantly in motion and that the present generation's zealously sought reforms can be transformed into tomorrow's insufferable social ills. Continued adjustments among alternative forms of government and the competing values of equality, efficiency, and liberty will undoubtedly persist. One should suffer no delusion that particular reform recommendations will prove appropriate indefinitely.

EQUALITY, EFFICIENCY, LIBERTY: RESOLVING THE TENSION

As mentioned previously, it is impossible to pursue one of the three major values without placing the other two at risk. Thus, governmental bodies are engaged in an almost constant readjustment. A new public sector program, a new economic policy, a new technological invention, or any of a number of other changes can trigger an imbalance in the relationships among the three values and provoke political action to establish a new equilibrium. Moreover, government action to maximize one of the three values in one sphere may provoke disequilibrium in another sphere, For example, attempts to achieve greater equality for the poor by public provision of low-cost housing can impair the property-tax revenue base of a local school district and thus hinder it from providing equal educational opportunity.

All three branches and all levels of government are engaged in this balancing process. However, the judicial branch offers particularly dramatic examples of the continual search for stability. More than either executive officers or legislators, judges must publicly explain their decisions. Their actions—judicial opinions—are visible and available for examination. Court decisions also offer particularly apt illustrations of the trade-offs among equality, efficiency, and liberty, because—as noted by Alexis de Tocqueville in the middle of the nineteenth century—there is a tendency in the United States for questions of deep political significance eventually to be settled by the judicial branch.[43] Consequently, a discussion of court decisions on schools and equality can illustrate how these tensions are resolved.

Equal Protection and School Policy

In 1868, the Fourteenth Amendment to the U.S. Constitution was ratified. Known at the time as the Reconstruction Amendment, it prescribed conditions for the South's renewed participation in the Union. The second sentence of the amendment's first section states: "No state shall...deny to any person within its jurisdiction the equal protection of the laws." This *equal protection clause* has served as the federal constitutional basis for judicial redefinition of equality of educational

---

[43] Alexis de Tocqueville, *Democracy in America* (New York: Mentor, 1965; originally published in 1835).

opportunity.[44] Court cases have also rested on state constitutional provisions, both equal protection clauses and education sections.[45] In the remainder of this section we review an important school finance court case in order to illustrate the legal logic of efforts to achieve reform through the judicial process.

State Equal Protection: *Serrano v. Priest*

In 1967 John Serrano, a father in a Los Angeles area school district, complained to the principal of his son's school about the quality of services available. The principal informed the parent that the school district simply could not afford more or better instruction and counseled the father to move to a wealthier district nearby. The senior Serrano viewed this advice, no matter how well intentioned, as worthless; he was not able to move. Instead, he joined with others and brought suit against selected state executive branch officials.[46]

Complicated judicial procedures extended the case until December of 1976, when the state's supreme court issued a comprehensive ruling.[47] The court declared California's school finance arrangements to be in violation of the state constitution's "equal protection" provision and specified a deadline by which the legislature was to arrive at a judicially acceptable reform plan.

Attorneys for Serrano argued that education is a "fundamental interest," availability of which cannot be conditioned on wealth. They reasoned that individuals must be educated in order to pursue rights explicitly guaranteed by government in matters such as voting, free speech, and religion. Consequently, in the absence of a compelling justification, the state could not discriminate in the quality of school services made available to students.

Throughout the court proceedings, plaintiffs' counsel cited information and statistics to demonstrate that children residing in property-poor school districts tended to have less money spent upon their education, even though residents of such districts frequently were willing to tax themselves at higher rates than wealthy districts.

To dramatize the disparities permitted, perhaps even encouraged, by the existing California school-finance system, the plaintiffs argued that in 1968–69 the Beverly Hills school district, with property wealth totaling more than $50,000 per

[44]For details see Michael W. La Morte, "The Fourteenth Amendment: Its Significance for Public School Educators," *Educational Administration Quarterly*, 10, no. 3 (1978), 1–19.

[45]A summary analysis of equal protection suits is provided by Michael W. La Morte and Jeffrey D. Williams in "Court Decisions and School Finance Reform," *Educational Administration Quarterly*, 21, no. 2 (Spring 1985), 59–89.

[46]Reasonably, the defendant should have been the state legislature. However, one needs the legislature's consent to sue it. Therefore, plaintiffs named state officials as defendants. Priest in this instance was Ivy Baker Priest, then California state treasurer.

[47]The initial California Supreme Court decision was upon a demurrer. The court held that if the facts were as alleged by plaintiffs, the state's equal protection provision was being violated. The court remanded the case to the court of original jurisdiction for a trial on the facts. The initial California Supreme Court decision was *Serrano v. Priest*, 96 Cal. Rptr. 601, 437, P.2d 1241 (1971), known as *Serrano I*. The subsequent decision favored plaintiffs.

pupil, spent $1232 per pupil at a tax rate of only $2.38. Conversely, nearby Baldwin Park, with property valued at $3706 per pupil, spent only $577 even though it taxed itself at $5.48, a rate more than twice that of Beverly Hills. State aid offset differences somewhat: Beverly Hills received only $125 per pupil from the state whereas Baldwin Park received $307. Nevertheless, there remained an expenditure discrepancy between the two in excess of $450 per pupil. Keep in mind that these figures were for the mid 1960s; school superintendents and other experts attested that a dollar difference of this magnitude translated to significant disparities in the quality and quantity of school services.

No argument was made that the state can never discriminate in the delivery of services. For example, there are certainly compelling reasons for treating adults differently from juveniles, criminals differently from noncriminals, drivers differently from pedestrians, and so on. However, the plaintiffs in *Serrano* contended that it was unfair to discriminate simply because of an "accident" of location—residence in a property-poor school district. Residence in such a school district was argued to be a *suspect classification*, one in which discriminatory treatment was unjustified.

Having heard the legal arguments, California's high court decided initially in favor of the plaintiff. The court commented:

> Affluent districts can have their cake and eat it too; they can provide a high quality education for their children while paying lower taxes. Poor districts, by contrast, have no cake at all.[48]

The court subsequently ruled that differences in school spending exceeding $100 per pupil could not be wealth-related and allowed the legislature five years in which to comply.[49] In 1983, plaintiffs appealed on grounds that the state had not yet reformed sufficiently. The trial and appeal courts agreed that the original $100 per pupil spending difference should be interpreted in light of high subsequent rates of inflation. But, when the inflation index was applied, the courts decided that the state had complied and specified that no further action to reform California's school-finance arrangements was required.[50]

During the twenty years in which *Serrano* wound its way through California courts, a number of other equal protection school-finance suits were argued.[51] A review of several of these cases (see Chapter 8), some of which were decided in favor of plaintiffs, some not, aids in understanding the translation of public values into public policy.

[48]*Serrano v. Priest*, 96 Cal. Rptr. at 611–12; quoted in Betsy Levin, "Recent Developments in the Law of Equal Educational Opportunity," *Journal of Law and Education*, 4, no. 3 (July 1975), 429.

[49]The story of *Serrano*'s implementation is contained in Richard F. Elmore and Milbrey Wallin McLaughlin, *Reform and Retrenchment: The Politics of California School Finance Reform* (Cambridge, Mass.: Ballinger, 1982).

[50]In 1987, the California Supreme Court was again asked to review the *Serrano* decision. It decided that the state had complied effectively with prior judgments.

[51]In fact, between 1971 and 1973, fifty-two court actions were cited in thirty-one states. Elmore and McLaughlin, op. cit., p. 430.

SUMMARY

This chapter describes tensions among equality, efficiency, and liberty, three values central both to American public policy in general and to American educational policy in particular.

The value of equality, when applied to educational policy making, usually revolves around the concept of equality of educational opportunity. In the United States, educational equality first meant equal access to education: every child was to be provided with at least the same, minimally adequate school services. Equality later came to mean equal educational treatment. That is, educationally handicapped students should receive special remedial treatment that will place them in a position equal to that of other students. Most recently, educational equality has come to mean equality of educational outcome—the notion that schools ought to produce students all of whom have the same minimum or basic skills.

Although U.S. schools constantly strive for greater efficiency, the cost of education has skyrocketed while student achievement appears to have decreased. Impediments to educational efficiency are to be found in the conflicting expectations about what education ought to do, the lack of an incentive system for promoting efficiency, and the rising costs necessitated by competition with the private sector, even though education labor costs seldom benefit from private-sector productivity gains. Moreover, educational efficiency conflicts at times with educational equality and liberty.

The value of liberty, when applied to education, often refers to the freedom to choose, and is ensured by governmental responsiveness. Responsiveness, at first strengthened in the United States by the large number of local school districts, was later eroded by school district consolidation, professional management in the interests of efficiency, labor-management collective bargaining, and the increased influence of state governments acting in the interest of equality.

The chapter concludes with a discussion of equal protection and a major court case, *Serrano v. Priest*. This case illustrates the practical trade-offs among the values of equality, efficiency, and liberty.

chapter three

THE ROLE OF GOVERNMENT IN FINANCING EDUCATION

Thomas Jefferson wrote that no nation could remain both ignorant and free. In order to protect freedom as well as to provide a trained work force, the United States gradually developed an elaborate system of free public schools. From modest beginnings, free public education has now become an integral part of American life.

Broad political and economic support for public education has not immunized schools against criticism, however. Political conservatives have argued that public provision of schooling is an unnecessary extension of government responsibility.[1] Criticism of public schools in the 1970s eroded political support and contributed to a citizens' revolt against local property-tax support of public education.[2] During the same period, many school programs were attacked by conservatives as being costly luxuries and by liberals and radicals as being infringements on the rights of students and parents.[3]

During the 1980s, public schools came under close scrutiny by numerous national and state commissions.[4] Claims of a "rising tide of mediocrity" led to sug-

[1]Milton Friedman, *Capitalism and Freedom* (Chicago: University of Chicago Press, 1962).

[2]Charles Silberman, *Crisis in the Classroom* (New York: Random House, 1970).

[3]Jonathan Kozol, *Death at an Early Age* (Boston: Houghton Mifflin, 1967).

[4]See, for example, National Commission for Educational Excellence, *A Nation at Risk* (Washington, D.C.: Government Printing Office, 1983).

gestions for improving elementary and secondary schools, including extending the length of the school day and the school year. Schools in the United States were frequently compared with those in Japan and the assessment was not always favorable.[5] This wave of public criticism forced a reexamination of assumptions about public education. Where does public responsibility for education begin and end? Who benefits from public education? How much education is enough?

This chapter explores these and other questions regarding the role of government in education. It is organized around four main topics: public and private benefits from education, ways of measuring the economic returns of education, economic factors affecting education supply and demand, and political factors influencing the price and quantity of public education.

PUBLIC RESPONSIBILITY IN EDUCATION

Educating young people is a major responsibility of adult society. At birth children depend on parents for many necessities: food, shelter, protection, and affection, among others. This dependence continues for many years, until children have adequate experience and education to function independently in society.

Education, of course, is not free. It requires an expenditure of time and resources—which could be used to produce other things valued by society. The dollar costs of formal schooling (which is only part of the total educational experience of children) amount to billions, making schooling one of the nation's most important economic and social activities.

While most everyone recognizes the significance of education, there is some debate about whether its provision is a public or private responsibility. On one hand, the family, which continues to be the basic social unit, is recognized as having the greatest concern and responsibility for educating the young.[6] No other social unit is better able to care for a child's well-being or to listen to a child's concerns, or is sufficiently small to respond consistently to each child's interests.

On the other hand, the predominance of the family in education has been gradually diminished by government assumption of new areas of educational responsibility. Originally, schools provided the minimum basic education needed by an individual to function in society. Schooling has expanded, however, to include vocational education, special education for physically and economically disadvantaged students, and many higher educational experiences. Even moral education, long regarded as a function of the family and church, is being recommended for public school curricula.[7] These accretions have been justified on the grounds of their public benefits, or of the failure of the family and private institutions to pro-

---

[5]See, for example, Thomas P. Rohlen, *Japan's High Schools* (Berkeley: University of California Press, 1983); and U.S. Department of Education, *Japanese Education Today* Washington, D.C.: (Government Printing Office,1987).

[6]Mary Jo Bane, *Here to Stay* (New York: Basic Books, 1976).

[7]See statements by Education Secretary William J. Bennett—for example, those in *Education Week*, 6, no. 32 (May 6, 1987), 1.

vide these educational experiences. However, when does public responsibility end? Because of a high divorce rate, will young people be required to earn a family-responsibility certificate in school before they are allowed to marry? Certainly a precedent exists, in that driver education is required in many school districts. Will disillusionment with public officials lead someone to suggest that aspiring politicians enroll in political science courses before running for office? Even more perplexing is the problem of public schools doing a poor job of providing services that may better be provided privately.[8] Private failure is a ready excuse for public activity. Is public failure an equal justification for returning responsibility to individuals?

Tensions between private and public responsibility in education can be clarified by examining private and public benefits of education. Private benefits are those that accrue to a child or a child's family. Public benefits are those received by individuals outside the family of the child being educated. Public financing and provision of education are usually rationalized, at least from an economist's point of view, in terms of supplementing private education to ensure that societal benefits are forthcoming.

Private Benefits of Education

There is clearly an element of pure consumption in many of the benefits of education. Although not all children are fond of attending school, doing so has obvious advantages, including learning about new things, meeting friends, engaging in sports, and, in some cases, having a good meal. The consumption component of education probably increases the longer an individual attends school, becoming most intense in the many how-to-do-it adult courses offered by community colleges and some school districts.

Most of the literature on the private benefits of education emphasizes future economic returns of educational investment. A high school education is now necessary to ensure good prospects in the job market. Currently, advanced training in business, computer science, electrical engineering, or medicine promises the likelihood of higher-than-average future earnings. Many studies have compared expected lifetime earnings of individuals completing different amounts of schooling. Those with four or more years of college are likely on average to earn more than those with only a high school degree. The latter, in turn, can expect to earn more than those with only an elementary school experience.[9] During the 1970s the economic value of a college education seemed to decline partly because of a large bulge of college graduates.[10]

---

[8]James S. Coleman and Thomas Hoffer, *Private High Schools* (New York: Basic Books, 1987).

[9]See, for example, U.S. Bureau of the Census, Consumer Income: Money Income of Households, Families and Persons in the United States: 1983. *Current Population Reports,* ser. P-60, no. 146 (Washington, D.C.: Government Printing Office, 1985).

[10]Richard A. Freeman, *The Declining Economic Value of Higher Education and the American Social System,* An Occasional Paper of the Aspen Institute for Humanistic Studies (New York, 1976).

During the 1980s a new debate emerged about the value of education. Some believe that high technology will relegate an increasing proportion of the work force to low-skill jobs.[11] Others believe that more advanced training will be needed to prepare workers to stay abreast of changing technology and the many service jobs the new information and technology will create.[12] Regardless of the outcome of this debate, most economic analyses suggest that education, particularly primary and secondary education, is a good investment.

Studies of the economic returns of education concentrate on monetary returns and thus often ignore educational values difficult to measure in dollars. Most people change jobs several times during their working years. A well-educated person can adapt more easily to new job situations and has a wider set of opportunities; he or she can thus *hedge* against future unemployment. Education also provides access to educational and professional possibilities. For example, one value of a high school education is the opportunity to attend college or be selected for on-the-job training in business or government. Other nonmonetary returns to education include more informed consumer behavior and improved ability to manage one's financial affairs.

Finally, men and women who pursue education and then choose to become homemakers often cannot identify a precise economic return to their education. That same education is likely, however, to improve their families' cultural and social opportunities and enhance their children's educational prospects. The economic value of education for those who do not enter the labor force, in other words, is not necessarily lost. Educated parents tend to motivate their children to obtain an education and to excel in school. The education of one generation is passed on to the next and thus plays an important part in perpetuating an educated citizenry.[13]

Public Benefits of Education

In addition to conferring benefits on students and their families, education benefits others. These benefits are frequently labeled *external benefits*, or *externalities*. Educational services that result in considerable public, or external, benefits are viewed by policy makers quite differently from services that confer only private benefits. Individuals can, of course, be expected to continue purchasing a service until the costs of an additional unit of that service exceed the additional benefits received. Since private benefits of education accrue solely to the individuals served, the amounts of service resulting from individual decisions should theoretically produce an optimal level of service. When, on the other hand, public benefits that

[11]Henry M. Levin and Russell W. Rumberger, *The Educational Implications of High Technology,* Institute for Research on Educational Finance and Governance (Stanford, Calif.: School of Education, Stanford University) February 1983.

[12]Bill Honig, *Last Chance for Our Children: How You Can Help Save Our Schools* (Reading, Mass: Addison-Wesley, 1985).

[13]An extended discussion of the relationship of public education to private advantage is provided in Henry M. Levin, "Education as a Public and Private Good," *Journal of Policy Analysis and Management,* 6, no. 4 (1987), pp. 628-41.

normally would not be considered in purely private decisions are involved, government intervention is justified.

The public, as opposed to a student and his or her family, benefits from a student's education in at least two ways. First, one person's education may improve his or her co-workers' productivity. Second, education may improve the social environment of a community, making it a better place for everyone to live.

External economic benefits of education are closely related to the increasing interdependence of modern industrial society. Most work processes today, whether in the private sector or in government, require coordination, cooperation, and interaction among many people. Consequently, each worker's training and skills spill over to other workers. Just as the presence of good students in a classroom appears to enhance their classmates' performance, so advanced training of a worker or supervisor is reflected in the added productivity of his or her colleagues.[14] The transfer of benefits to other workers can be simple. A better-educated person may set an example for others. Education may make a person more aware of recent technology, or more flexible in applying new technology or ideas to work situations. To the extent that a manager's training, for example, improves subordinates' performance, both owners and other employees benefit directly from the manager's education. In addition, workers with higher educational attainment are likely to have improved communication skills and more highly developed mental discipline.[15]

Another important external economic benefit of education is the long-term cost savings to a community that result from education. For example, there is a strong relationship between low levels of education and crime. One study indicates that approximately 40 percent of those in the nation's jails are illiterate.[16] Another concludes that 34 percent of offenders between twelve and seventeen are illiterate, compared to only 4.8 percent of all adolescents between these ages.[17] By providing education for all its citizens, a community may reduce the costs of dealing with crime and delinquency. Furthermore, education reduces the probability of unemployment, thereby lowering welfare costs and, conversely, increasing total taxable income. The effects may be even greater than the simple increase in a community's economic resources, however, since higher-income families may also consume fewer public services.

Perhaps the most common external benefit attributed to education is its contribution to economic growth. The idea here is simple, although its implications

---

[14]Theodore W. Schultz, "Education and Economic Growth," in *Yearbook of the Committee on Social Forces Influencing American Education,* Nelson B. Henry, ed. (Chicago: National Society for the Study of Education, 1961), pp. 74–75.

[15]J. R. Davis and J. F. Morrall, *Evaluating Education Investment* (Lexington, Mass: Heath, Lexington Books, 1974).

[16]J. Ronnie Davis, "The Social and Economic Externalities of Education," in *Economic Factors Affecting the Financing of Education,* ed. Roe L. Johns et al. (Gainesville, Fla.: National Educational Finance Project, 1970), p. 66.

[17]B. Hodges and D. Mahrer, "Competency Based Education: Implications for Education in Juvenile Corrections Settings," *Journal of Correctional Education,* 32, no. 3 (1981), 14–16.

for public policy are complicated. According to the argument, because education contributes to an economy's productivity (the amount of goods and services produced by a unit of labor), investment in education, or in *human capital,* should be considered on the same basis as physical investments in a nation's economy. If, for example, investment in education leads to greater economic productivity than investment in roads, then educational investment should be increased until the marginal productivity of investing in education is equal to that of investing in roads. Furthermore, if private educational investment in a society is insufficient to produce desired levels of educational investment, then government should intervene to close the gap between the two. According to this schema, economic growth— that is, the opportunity for higher per-capita future income—is enhanced by investing in education to reduce the social costs of potential unemployment.

Education contributes to economic growth in a number of ways. Most important, perhaps, is the direct improvement in productivity associated with upgrading of labor skills. Workers who can read, write, and perform everyday mathematical calculations, or who possess more specialized work skills, all produce more efficiently than the uneducated. Education allows employees to enter the work force at a higher level, to adjust to changes in the requirements of the position, and to progress to more complicated tasks more rapidly. In addition, better-educated workers produce an improved product, provide services more skillfully, and produce more goods and services over a specified period.[18]

It is important to identify a particular type of externality called *spillover effects.* Spillovers are benefits persons carry from a community in which they receive an education. For example, the state of Illinois may incur costs of $200,000 to educate a medical student who establishes a practice in Ohio. Illinois citizens pay the costs but receive no benefits because the doctor is providing services in Ohio. If Illinois-trained doctors consistently moved to Ohio, Illinois legislators would become increasingly reluctant to support medical schools. However, the fact that medical education benefits spill over into another state is irrelevant to the education investment decisions of the family whose child is studying to become a physician.

In addition to improving a community's economic well-being, education produces important noneconomic benefits. Democratic government requires a citizenry with a common fund of values and an understanding of and commitment to democratic rules. Inculcating an understanding of history, geography, and the nation's and community's cultural heritage is an often overlooked task of education. Learning how and why the Revolution, the Civil War, and the social reforms of the 1930s and 1960s occurred contributes to a common perspective on current political problems. Knowledge of other languages, athletic skills, and interpersonal proficiency enhance children's communication and interaction in community settings. Finally, and perhaps most important, education conveys from generation to generation the rules by which social and political discourse is conducted. In a democracy, a large proportion of actions are voluntary. Individuals are not required to participate in community affairs, vote, work, or do many other things essential to society's func-

[18]H. R. Bowen, *Investment in Learning* (San Francisco: Jossey-Bass, 1977).

tioning. Education aids in perpetuating norms and values that guide citizens' behavior in a free society.

Education also helps maintain social cohesion by reducing social inequalities. A famous nineteenth-century educator, Caleb Mills, believed that public schools could ameliorate class conflict. In the colorful language of the time he argued that public schools

> contribute more than any other one agency, to mould and assimilate the various discordant materials to be incorporated into the body politic and render them homogeneous in character and sympathy. How often have we all seen in those nurseries of knowledge, aristocratic pride humbled, plebeian roughness refined, rustic conceit corrected, haughty insolence rebuked and repressed, gentle modesty emboldened, unobtrusive worth encouraged, and the many asperities of character give place to lovelier traits, all contributing to swell the aggregate of human happiness, domestic peace and civil freedom.[19]

Furthermore, to the extent that people still believe the amount and kind of education play a significant role in determining income distribution, availability of free public education may dampen demands for more rapid or radical redistribution of wealth and privilege. The ability of each new generation to rise above its social and economic beginnings, in other words, encourages tolerance of remaining social and economic inequalities.

Public Benefits and Government Intervention in Education

From an economist's point of view, government's role in education is justified in terms of education's public or external benefits. If educational benefits were limited to those receiving education and to their immediate families, then there would be no good economic reason for government to become involved.[20] Individuals would purchase an optimal amount of schooling in the private market. Those who could not afford to pay the full cost of schooling could theoretically borrow what they needed, since the rate of return would be sufficient to justify private loans.[21]

As we have indicated, however, education contributes not only to the well-being of a student and his or her family but to the well-being of others in society as well. External benefits are therefore important for two reasons. First, from an equity point of view, if costs of private or public services are to be borne by those who benefit from them, then those who receive external benefits should contribute to the

---

[19]Charles W. Moores, ed., *Caleb Mills and the Indiana School System*, Indiana Historical Society Publications, 3, no. 6 (Bloomington, Ind., 1905), p. 585.

[20]There are undoubtedly exceptions to this general statement. For example, citizens may vote against property tax increases for schools even though they still stand to benefit as parents. Their reasoning is probably that state or federal funds will become available to supplement or replace local property tax support for schools.

[21]Under current capital market conditions lenders may be reluctant to make loans for education without a physical asset as collateral. A free society is unlikely to permit lenders to bind (or indenture) students to future service. Such imperfections in capital markets could be dealt with, however, without government financing or provision of education per se. For example, federal loan guarantees or income deductions might solve the problem.

financing of education. Second, an optimal level of educational expenditure will result only if external benefits are included in the determination of educational spending. If they are omitted, too little education will be consumed from an economic-efficiency perspective. Educational spending must be more than that resulting from equating only private benefits and costs.

The quest for a socially equitable way of distributing education costs is discussed in detail in Chapters 6 and 8. The remainder of this section examines alternative ways government can intervene to ensure efficient levels of educational services are provided. When external benefits are desirable (as one assumes they are for any progressive society), government can intervene in a least three ways to provide a more efficient level of educational services.[22] The simplest is for government, while not actually providing schooling, to require that citizens obtain a minimum amount of education. Government can also subsidize education to reduce private costs and thereby increase the amounts of it demanded. A third possibility is for government to provide the service itself.

GOVERNMENT REGULATION

Suppose education were provided privately. Some families would purchase technical training. Others would send their children to religious schools. Some might opt for apprenticeships in business after a few years of basic education. Still others would invest not only in basic education but also in higher education and professional training. Each family would obtain as much education as it felt it wanted and could afford.[23] From a social point of view, too little education might be purchased. However, a community could agree upon a minimum of eight or ten years of basic education as yielding a minimum level of citizenship. Less than that amount might leave students ill prepared to find employment or participate in community affairs. This situation would place an economic burden upon others and increase social tensions in the community. In the presence of such externalities, government could require each student to receive a minimum number of years of basic education. It could then require that basic skills in reading, writing, arithmetic, and citizenship training be included in the basic education programs. As Milton Friedman writes:

> What kind of governmental action is justified by this particular neighborhood effect? The most obvious is to require that each child receive a minimum amount of schooling of a specified kind. Such a requirement could be imposed upon the parents without further government action, just as owners of build-

[22]Friedman, *Capitalism and Freedom.*

[23]Many argue that such a system would deprive working people of an adequate education. E. G. West points out, however, that before public support of education in England, working-class parents were paying directly for their children's education and that literacy among working-class children was high. E. G. West, *Education and the State* (London: Institute of Economic Affairs, 1965), chaps. 10–11.

ings, and frequently of automobiles, are required to adhere to specified standards to protect the safety of others.[24]

Compulsory attendance laws, curriculum requirements, and minimum requirements for the length of the school day and school year are regulatory mechanisms used by government to ensure adequate provision of education services.

Friedman suggests further that costs of the required minimum level of education be borne by parents, and that government subsidy be available only to low-income families. The argument for having parents finance their children's education is based on efficiency and does not consider whether it is equitable for those receiving external benefits to avoid contributing. Friedman maintains that private financing would eliminate the administrative costs of public collection and distribution of taxes. It would minimize the tendency of government budgets to grow as personal income and tax receipts increase even though the need for government programs may have remained the same or even declined. Private financing of basic education would also place the cost of having children directly on parents, and thus promote a more rational determination of family size.

GOVERNMENT SUBSIDY

This second method of ensuring an adequate supply of basic education is based on the premise that individuals and families will purchase more of something at a lower price than at a higher price. The utility of subsidies in promoting an efficient level and type of educational performance depends upon the sources of the subsidy and the methods by which it is distributed. A head tax on school-age children redistributed to households according to number of children would have little or no effect on the purchase of educational services. (The administrative costs of collecting and distributing the tax would leave families with less for education than they had before the tax.) A general property or sales tax, on the other hand, would reallocate education costs among all households. In fact, the larger the public subsidies, the more money those families with children would have for purchasing additional education.

The actual effect of subsidies in reducing a family's educational costs, and thereby determining the level and kind of education purchased, depends also on the kind of subsidy. Suppose a community decided that all students should have ten years of basic education, including citizenship and moral instruction. A subsidy distributed to families in the form of equal dollar amounts per school-age child would not be an efficient way of accomplishing a community's objective. Families would tend to use public funds to purchase vocational and professional training, which have high private benefits. To achieve the desired public benefits, the community would have to restrict the subsidy's use to particular programs and perhaps to particular schools. If the community, in addition to desiring minimum citizenship training, also wanted to reduce income inequalities, it might decide to provide larger subsidies for children from low-income families. Other things being equal,

[24]Friedman, *Capitalism and Freedom*, p. 96.

more highly subsidized families would purchase relatively more education and improve their children's chances of earning higher lifetime earnings.

GOVERNMENT PROVISION

Public provision of education is a third means of ensuring that individuals take account of education's external benefits. This is the method currently used in the United States, along with certain requirements imposed on all children, even those attending private schools. But if a socially desirable level of educational services that makes provision for public as well as private benefits can be ensured through minimum standards along with subsidies, why is it necessary to create a $200 billion public educational industry? One answer is that public schools are necessary to maintain a common core of values and thus to promote social cohesion and political stability. Some allege that a system of private schools, even if supported with public funds and required to adhere to minimum standards, would not provide a sufficiently uniform educational experience. Instead, private schools would emphasize individualistic values and transform education into a divisive rather than a unifying force.

This argument, while possibly persuasive, seems inconsistent with many facts about public and private education in the United States. In the first place, public schools are noteworthy for their differences as well as their likenesses. Even though the physical features of schools and the organization of the school day appear similar, there is great variety in educational climate and pupil performance expectations. The tensions and hostility permeating many urban high schools are less frequently found in middle- and high-income suburban high schools. Even within a large urban high school, the educational experiences of children taking general education courses tend to be different from those enrolled in college preparatory programs or vocational education programs.[25] It is not at all clear, in other words, that public school children are acquiring a common core of values, or that the values they are acquiring always enhance social cohesion. In fact, state constitutional provisions requiring a general and uniform educational program may produce conflict in large urban communities with diverse ethnic and social populations. Confronted with demands for greater emphasis on bilingual education, vocational education, compensatory education, basic education, and a myriad other educational services, school boards reach compromises that frequently satisfy virtually no one.[26]

Similarly, it is not clear that a system of private education would be as divisive as some believe. The conventional case against private schools is that they intensify class differences and emphasize sectarian rather than patriotic values. Under the current U.S. educational system, private schools may foster class differences because they often are available only to those who can afford both public school taxes and private school tuition. If parents were not penalized by having to pay

[25]Jeannie Oakes, "Keeping Track, Part 1: The Policy and Practice of Curriculum Inequality," *Phi Delta Kappan*, 68, no. 1 (September 1986), 12–17.

[26]See Mancur Olson, *The Logic of Collective Action* (Cambridge, Mass.: Harvard University Press, 1965).

twice to send their children to private schools, however, and particularly if public financial support of both public and private schools were weighted in favor of low-income families, then wealth would be a less important determinant of private school enrollment. Children preferring educational programs organized around the arts, for instance, would be brought together regardless of income or social background.

The second claim—that private schools do not instill values supporting democratic government—is not validated by survey results. Greeley and Rossi, for example, found that Catholics in parochial schools were slightly less rigid and intolerant and more socially conscious than Catholics attending public schools.[27]

Another argument for government provision of education is that other alternatives (regulation and subsidy) do not provide adequate incentives to overcome what economists call the *free-rider problem*. Assume, for example, that education is financed through voluntary contributions. Under such a system there would be inadequate provision for education's external benefits, because enjoyment of external benefits by one person usually does not diminish similar enjoyment by others. If, for instance, an additional two years of public schooling increases the expected rate of economic growth, reduces juvenile delinquency, or in any number of other ways creates a more enjoyable community, those benefits are shared by everyone. Nevertheless, any single individual in the community might be reluctant to pay voluntarily for added amenities. In other words, people may refuse to express their true educational philosophy if it means they will have to pay for something they might otherwise obtain free. One solution is a system in which people reveal their educational preferences through democratic processes and then spread the costs of those decisions to everyone in the community.[28]

SUMMARY

Under what conditions, therefore, is government intervention in education desirable? Clearly, to the extent that education produces public or external benefits for families other than that of the student, government should intervene both (1) to ensure that those who receive external benefits share the costs of their provision, and (2) to ensure that external benefits are considered in a community's decisions about the supply of education. Minimum standards, subsidies, or public provision can be used.

As a general rule, the greater the public or external benefits of a particular type of education, the stronger the case for government financing and provision of education. A good case can be made, therefore, for government support of a minimum basic education required for citizenship. The case for government support of vocational education and higher education is weaker, but not entirely absent. There may be, for instance, substantial public benefits from vocational training for handicapped children and for many students who have difficulty in traditional classrooms,

---

[27] Andrew M. Greeley and Peter H. Rossi, *The Education of Catholic Americans* (Chicago: Aldine, 1966), pp. 136–37.

[28] For a more detailed discussion of this problem, see Davis, "The Social and Economic Externalities of Education," pp. 76–80.

because such preparation may make these individuals more employable and reduce the costs of various social programs. Similarly, although many higher education benefits are private, activities such as university research projects increase economic productivity and economic growth. Where both private and public benefits are substantial, government can prorate support according to the desired blend of external and private benefits. For example, medical students agreeing to study family medicine and practice in rural communities lacking medical services could receive more public support for their medical school costs than those whose specialty already suffers from an oversupply of qualified physicians.

MEASURING THE BENEFITS OF EDUCATION

Conceptually, policy makers justify public support of education in terms of the benefits it provides. Before deciding how much to spend on public schools, however, decision makers need an idea of the extent of the benefits. This raises some crucial questions: How can education benefits be measured? Are conceptual justifications for public education confirmed by actual social benefits?

Policy makers also need to know who is likely to benefit from public support of schools. Spending for education, as for every other public program, has redistributional consequences. In the case of education, there is clearly a redistribution of resources from taxpaying adults to school-age children. Public education also results in a transfer of resources from families without school-age children to those with school-age children, because almost every family pays the taxes used to support the schools. Some people also argue that public education benefits businesses at the expense of working people, because education reduces on-the-job training costs. While it is obvious that education produces social benefits and that more of those benefits accrue to some people than to others, it is not so easy to assess those benefits.

Several reasons for the difficulty of measuring educational benefits have already been mentioned. Many of the external benefits of education are nonexclusive: their enjoyment by one person does not reduce their enjoyment by others. In such cases, therefore, one cannot say that a group carrying the cost burden benefits more than any other group. Then, of course, many of the benefits of education are long-term and can only be hypothesized. In addition, governments have not been helpful in identifying the beneficiaries of education, partly because insufficient research has been conducted on the distributional consequences of education.

Private Returns

Despite difficulties in identifying and obtaining information on the beneficiaries of education, there is a body of economic theory and analysis that casts light on this issue. According to *human capital theory*, young people acquire a stock of human capital in much the same way as businesses acquire a stock of physical capital.[29] Acquisition of education has many of the attributes of an investment. Just as an investment requires a commitment of time and resources, acquisition of education requires a substantial commitment of a student's time as well as the time and resources of his or her parents. The returns or benefits of education accrue to both students and their parents, and are subject to uncertainties, as with any investment borne privately. Education capital may become obsolete as technological changes result in requirements for different skills and knowledge.[30] Human capital theory helps explain the allocation of educational resources and the effects of education on economic growth, distribution of income in society, and social mobility of groups in succeeding generations.

Economists measure the benefits of human capital investment in several ways. One approach is to analyze increases in lifetime earnings associated with additional years of education. Typically data are collected on incomes of individuals of different ages who have completed varying levels of education. Summing the average incomes of different age groups with, for example, a high school education provides an estimate of the total lifetime earnings of someone graduating from high school. Because future income is less valuable than current dollars, an estimate of it is usually discounted by some assumed rate of interest to obtain present values, which can then be compared with present values of the income of, for instance, college graduates.[31] Not all differences in discounted lifetime earnings should be attributed to education alone. Credit is also due to intelligence and parents' education and income, both of which are highly correlated with the length of time a child remains in school as well as with future income. The specific effect of formal education on lifetime earnings is undoubtedly smaller, therefore, than most returns-to-education studies suggest.

An example of this approach to measuring the private benefits of education is presented in Table 3.1. In the study on which this table is based, it was found that lifetime earnings increase with years of education, but the extent of the increase depends on the assumed discount rate. The higher an assumed discount rate, the less the lifetime value of additional years of education.

A second approach for estimating education value is to compare rates of return on investments in varying amounts of education. The methodology of computing an *internal rate of return* is much like that used to compute the present value of education. The internal rate of return is simply the discount rate, which, when applied to increases in a lifelong stream of expected income from each level of education, equals education costs. The higher the expected increments of income and the lower the costs of education, the higher the rate of return. Differing amounts of education can then be compared in terms of their merits as investments.

[29]Theodore W. Schultz, "The Human Capital Approach to Education," in *Economic Factors,* ed. Roe Johns et al., pp. 47–54.

[30]Theodore W. Schultz, *Investing in People: The Economics of Population Quality* (Berkeley: University of California Press, 1981).

[31]W. Lee Hansen, "Total and Private Rates for Return to Investment in Schooling," *Journal of Political Economy,* 71 (April 1963), 128–140; and Charles S. Benson, *The Economics of Public Education* (Boston: Houghton Mifflin, 1978), pp. 77–85.

TABLE 3.1 Value of Lifetime Income Associated with Education

CATEGORY	TOTAL INCOME	PRESENT VALUE AT 5 PERCENT	10 PERCENT
White males			
1–3 years high school	$427,633	$132,262	$60,488
4 years high school	478,280	147,951	66,940
1–3 years college	534,013	153,187	63,151
4 or more years college	699,771	184,831	68,902
White females			
1–3 years high school	94,693	28,872	13,377
4 years high school	125,428	35,072	14,780
1–3 years college	147,986	40,580	16,729
4 or more years college	276,640	70,769	27,043
Nonwhite males			
1–3 years high school	268,268	86,543	40,636
4 years high school	309,765	99,817	46,323
1–3 years college	355,265	106,002	44,850
4 or more years college	423,395	116,268	44,622
Nonwhite females			
1–3 years high school	111,041	35,027	16,539
4 years high school	139,863	40,277	17,213
1–3 years college	176,101	49,494	20,515
4 or more years college	361,002	94,639	36,357

Notes: The assumption is made that real incomes in 1967 dollars at any given age will increase at 1.62 percent per year as a result of expansion of the economy.

Amounts shown are present values at age 16 of incomes from age 16 to 65, before taxes. Basic data are from U.S. Bureau of the Census, *Current Population Reports,* Series P-60, No. 60, "Income in 1967 of Persons in the United States" (Washington: U.S. Government Printing Office, 1969). Incomes during periods individuals are students are from Robert G. Spiegelman, *A Benefit/Cost Model to Evaluate Educational Programs* (Menlo Park, Calif: Stanford Research Institute, 1968).

Median incomes were used, to help correct for the upward bias caused by using income rather than earnings data. Data, given by the Bureau of the Census at 10-year age intervals, were positioned at the midpoint of the interval and values for other years were determined by linear interpolation. A mortality correction is included.

Figures shown are for incomes *associated* with education. They include the effect of noneducational causal factors correlated with education.

Source: Walter I. Garms, "A Benefit-Cost Analysis of the Upward Bound Program," *Journal of Human Resources,* 6, no. 2 (Spring, 1971), 213.

In 1970, Theodore Schultz, who pioneered much of the research on the human capital approach to education, compared return rates of various kinds of education to rates of return in the U.S. private economy, which range from 10 to 15 percent.[32] He concluded that returns for investment in elementary and secondary education are high. His estimate for elementary school was 35 percent. Other studies specify the

[32]Schultz, "The Human Capital Approach to Education."

rate of return of elementary schooling at over 100 percent.[33] Schultz estimated the rate of return for high school education at approximately 25 percent.

In a more recent study, Schultz noted that rates of return for education continue to exceed rates of return for physical capital.[34] This is a result in large part of the growth in real compensation paid workers. The share of income accruing to property has declined since 1900 from 45 to 20 percent. The share accruing to labor has increased from 55 to 80 percent. One consequence of the increasing importance of human capital in the production of goods and services is a decrease in the distributional inequality of personal income over this period.[35]

Schultz and Richard Freeman contend that the rate of return for college education is lower than that for elementary and secondary education. Their estimates for the former are 15 percent and only 7 percent, respectively.[36] Also, instead of increasing, as returns to primary and secondary education have done since World War II, returns from college education may be falling.[37] An interesting finding in Freeman's research is that the general conclusion about lower rates of return for college education does not apply to black students or to women. In both of these groups, returns of college education are increasing.[38]

Schultz concludes from his review of human capital studies that there is a serious underinvestment in elementary education, particularly in the rural areas of the South, the Southwest, and Appalachia as well as in our largest cities. Associated with inadequate resources is neglect of the quality of elementary and secondary education throughout the nation. The rate of return for high school education has been rising but is only slightly above the domestic rate of return for physical capital. In other words, improvements in the quality of high school education are suggested, but the economic case for greater investment there is less compelling than that for elementary schooling.

There is greater controversy about increased investment in higher education. Freeman argues that the nation may be suffering from an overinvestment in higher education. He attributes the poor U.S. economic performance, falling productivity, and high inflation of the late 1970s to a particularly large supply of college graduates.[39] Schultz, for example, believes United States economic problems are due more to an undereducated population than to an overeducated one, and blames the declining quality of education.[40]

[33]W. Lee Hanson, "Total and Private Rates for Return to Investment in Schooling," *Journal of Political Economy*, 71 (April 1963), 128–40; and Giora Hanoch, "An Economic Analysis of Earnings and Schooling," *Journal of Human Resources*, 2, no. 3 (Madison: University of Wisconsin Press, 1967), 310–29.

[34]Schultz, "The Human Capital Approach to Education."

[35]Schultz, *Investing in People.*

[36]Schultz, "The Human Capital Approach to Education"; and Freeman, *The Declining Economic Value of Higher Education.*

[37]See Richard B. Freeman, *The Overeducated American* (New York: Academic Press, 1976).

[38]Richard B. Freeman, *Black Elite: The New Market for Highly Educated Black Americans* (New York: McGraw-Hill, 1976).

[39]Ibid.

[40]Schultz, "Education in an Unstable Economy."

Certainly, given the scarce resources for education, an economic argument can be made for reallocating money from higher education to elementary education. Schultz suggests that higher education financing be rearranged so that those receiving the benefits of higher education pay a higher proportion of its costs.[41] Samuelson assumes an even more strident position. In an early 1987 article he asserted

> ...our chief error has been overspending on what's euphemistically called "higher education." ...Higher education spending is now about two-fifths of all of education spending. ...The result has been to weaken the entire education system.[42]

On the other hand, many states are increasing investments in higher education to promote economic development. The quality of higher education institutions is near the top of the list of factors as considered important by executives seeking locations for new businesses. Political leaders, economists, and educators are increasingly coming to the view that the U.S. economic problems (its lack of competitiveness) are due more to the undereducated population than to an overeducated one.

Public Returns

Public or social returns to education are much more difficult to measure than private returns. Assuming that public benefits are available at all, there is no economically feasible way of determining how much value each person acquires. If a course in moral education, for example, reduces a community's crime rate, how much does each individual community member benefit? A few studies, however, suggest the extent of the contribution of education to important public policy objectives.

During the 1980s education received much attention because of its importance to economic performance. According to the National Commission on Excellence in Education and the 1986 report of the National Governors' Association, *A Time for Results*, high quality education is essential to the competitiveness of the American economy.[43] The relationship of education to economic growth has been the focus of a number of comparative studies. Edward Denison attempted to determine the contribution of education to the rates of growth in national income of nine Western countries. Table 3.2 reveals several interesting facets of the determinants of economic growth that emerged in his study. The most striking observation, displayed in column 8, is the high percentage of growth unexplained by any input listed in the table. Another observation is the wide variation in education effects among the countries. The calculated contribution of education in the United States is considerably higher than that of European nations, except for Belgium and the United Kingdom. This difference may be attributable to the important role played by capi-

---

[41]Schultz, "The Human Capital Approach to Education," p. 53.

[42]Quoted in *The Wall Street Journal* February 6, 1987, p. 18.

[43]National Commission on Excellence in Education, *A Nation at Risk*, p. 6; National Governors' Association, *Time for Results: The Governor's 1991 Report on Education* (Washington, D.C., 1986), p. 2.

TABLE 3.2. Sources of Economic Growth in Nine Western Nations: 1950–62

AREA	CONTRIBUTIONS OF FACTOR INPUTS					INCREASED OUTPUT PER UNIT OF INPUT (6)	PROPORTION OF TOTAL GROWTH EXPLAINED BY	
	TOTAL GROWTH (1)*	PHYSICAL CAPITAL (2)	EMPLOYMENT (3)	EDUCATION (4)	OTHER LABOR ADJUSTMENTS (5)**		EDUCATION (7)	OUTPUT PER UNIT OF INPUT (8)
United States	3.36	0.83	0.90	0.49	-0.27	1.41	15	42
Italy	5.95	0.70	0.42	0.40	0.14	4.29	7	72
Northwestern Europe:								
Total	4.70	0.86	0.71	0.23	-0.11	3.01	5	64
Belgium	3.03	0.41	0.40	0.43	-0.07	1.86	14	61
Denmark	3.36	0.96	0.70	0.14	-0.25	1.81	4	54
France	4.70	0.79	0.08	0.29	0.08	3.46	6	74
Germany	7.26	1.41	1.49	0.11	-0.23	4048	2	62
Netherlands	4.52	1.04	0.78	0.24	-0.15	2.61	5	58
Norway	3.47	0.89	0.13	0.24	-0.22	2.43	7	70
United Kingdom	2.38	0.51	0.50	0.29	-0.19	1.27	12	53

*All growth rates are percentage points per annum.
**Adjustments are for mean hours worked and changes in the age and sex composition of the labor force.

Source: Edward F. Denison, *Why Growth Rates Differ* (Washington, D.C.: Brookings Institution, 1967), Tables 21-1–21-20; reprinted in Mary Jean Bowman, "Education and Economic Growth," *Economic Factors Affecting the Financing of Eduction*, ed. Roe L. Johns et al., (Gainesville, Fla.: National Educational Finance Project, 1970), p. 63.

tal growth in European countries still recovering from World War II devastation.[44] A similar study by Correa examined changes in the growth rates of nine Latin American countries between 1950 and 1962 (Table 3.3). Argentina presents a picture roughly similar to that of the United States. In the other eight countries, education made a relatively minor contribution to the rate of national income growth.

Benson notes that analyses of past relationships between education and economic growth rates should not be regarded as predictors of future trends. High percentage contributions of education to income growth in the 1950s and early 1960s, which was fueled by population growth and growth in the educational system, may not be indicative of educational impact on growth rates in a society already well educated and providing for smaller numbers of students.[45]

Another noneconomic benefit of education that has been analyzed is the effect of public education on the distribution of personal income. During the sixties and seventies some policy makers, believing that education could be a vehicle for economic and social mobility, acted on the assumption that providing education for the poor would help to alleviate poverty by promoting income redistribution. During the seventies and early eighties, this contention was challenged by a number of writers who believed that education was simply not capable of meeting the expectations society had placed on it. Indeed, some of this group argued that education was instrumental in increasing the inequality of income distribution. Other studies,

TABLE 3.3 The Contribution of Education to National Income Growth in Latin America, 1950–62

COUNTRY	RATE OF GROWTH IN TOTAL NATIONAL INCOME	CONTRIBUTION OF EDUCATION	CONTRIBUTION OF EDUCATION AS A PERCENTAGE OF NATIONAL INCOME GROWTH
Argentina	3.19%	0.53%	
	16%		
Brazil	5.49	0.18	3
Chile	4.20	0.20	5
Colombia	4.79	0.20	4
Ecuador	4.72	0.23	5
Honduras	4.52	0.29	6
Mexico	5.97	0.05	1
Peru	5.63	0.14	3
Venezuela	7.74	0.19	2

Source: H. Correa, "Sources of Economic Growth in Latin America," *Southern Economic Journal,* 37 (July 1970), Table IX.

[44] Edward F. Denison, *Why Growth Rates Differ* (Washington, D.C.: Brookings Institution, 1967).

[45] Charles Benson, *The Economics of Education* (Boston: Houghton Mifflin, 1978).

however, support the proposition that education may promote economic redistribution by narrowing wage differentials. This issue is far from settled, and the capacity of the educational system to influence income distribution deserves to be assessed further.[46]

Although education improves a person's earning ability, education itself is not equally available to all. In fact, there is evidence that more education is available to the children of high-income families than to those of low-income families.[47] If schooling is measured in terms of education outputs, the evidence suggests that children from low-income and socially disadvantaged families do not perform as well as their middle- and upper-income classmates. According to the National Advisory Commission on Civil Disorders, "in the critical skills—verbal and reading ability—Negro students are falling further behind whites with each year of school completed."[48] Later studies reveal that the black-white achievement gap has narrowed but still exists.[49] The tendency of states to provide greater educational opportunities for high-income families is probably stronger in higher education than in primary and secondary education. In a study of higher education in California, Hansen and Weisbrod conclude:

> Some low-income persons have benefitted handsomely from the availability of publicly subsidized higher education. But on the whole, the effect of these subsidies is to promote greater rather than less inequality among people of various social and economic backgrounds by making available substantial subsidies that lower-income families are either not eligible for or cannot make use of because of other conditions and constraints associated with their income position.[50]

They found that a greater proportion of children from high-income families than from low-income families attended California's institutions of higher education; that those from high-income families tended to enroll in the more prestigious and expensive University of California whereas children of low-income families frequently attended two-year junior and community colleges; that students from high-income backgrounds stayed in school longer and thus were receiving state subsidies longer; and that because of their superior educations, students from high-income families could look forward to higher lifetime earnings than those from low-income families. Hansen and Weisbrod generalize their findings to other states:

[46]Elchanon Cohn, *The Economics of Education*, rev. ed. (Cambridge, Mass: Ballinger, 1979), p. 51.

[47]James W. Guthrie, George B. Kleindorfer, Henry M. Levin, and Robert W. Stout, *Schools and Inequality* (Cambridge, Mass.: MIT Press, 1971); and John I. Goodlad, *A Place Called School* (New York: McGraw-Hill, 1984).

[48]*Report of the National Advisory Commission on Civil Disorders* (New York: Bantam, 1968), p. 25.

[49]See, for example, Congress of the United States, Congressional Budget Office, *Educational Achievement: Explanations and Implications of Recent Trends*, August 1987, Washington, D.C. Congressional Budget Office.

[50]W. Lee Hansen and Burton A. Weisbrod, *Benefits, Costs and Finance of Public Higher Education* (Chicago: Markham, 1969), pp. 77–78.

> What we have found to be true in California—an exceedingly unequal distribu-
> tion of subsidies provided through public higher education—quite probably is
> even more true for other states. No state has such an extensive system of local
> Junior Colleges as does California, and for this reason, no state has such a
> large percentage of its high school graduates going on to public higher educa-
> tion. As a result we can be rather confident that California has a smaller per-
> centage of its young people receiving zero subsidy than do other states.[51]

In summary, public education provides a number of external benefits that, although difficult to measure, are used to justify public intervention in the organization and financing of education. Economic growth, social understanding, and political stability are likely outcomes of public education. Current methods of funding
and allocating education are not effective means for further reducing income
inequalities in the United States. Stated somewhat differently, if government intends
to use education to promote greater income equality, it may have to assess not only
the way it finances and rations education, but also the quality of education, especially in urban schools, and other social programs, such as those affecting housing, transportation, and health care, that along with education affect social mobility.
In higher education, a higher proportion of government support may have to be allocated directly to students, with those from low-income families receiving most of
the assistance. It should be remembered, as noted in Chapter 2, that equality is just
one of the goals deserving attention in public policy making.

ECONOMIC DETERMINANTS OF EDUCATION SUPPLY AND DEMAND

Assuming a system of free public education, a question remains: How much public
education is enough? Are there guidelines to assist the American people and their
representatives in deciding when to stop public spending for education—or when to
increase it? Ultimately, the decision as to how much education is enough is made
politically, a topic discussed in the last portion of this chapter and again, at length,
in Chapter 8. In this section we examine economic factors affecting education supply and demand.

Economists conceive of choices in several ways. One is in terms of foregone
opportunities. Another is from the perspective of individual decision makers;
economists assume individuals do things to improve their well-being. Third,
economists believe that everything worth having or doing is costly. It costs money,
takes time, or requires that something else be given up. Also, because individuals
make decisions to improve their situations, and because decisions involve costs,
people prefer less costly to more costly alternatives, other things being equal. Why?
Because the cheaper they can obtain some good or service, the more money they
have left to do other things they enjoy.

These assumptions can be formulated as a simple model of the supply of and
demand for education. Assume that people desire education. Education, whether it is
primary or secondary education, vocational education, community education, or

---

[51]Ibid., p. 78.

higher education, is something that people believe improves their well-being and consequently are willing to pay for.[52] In other words, a certain amount of education is produced, which, because it is costly, has a price. This supply of a certain quantity and quality of education is determined by the willingness of providers of goods and services to produce at a given price. In other words, at a certain teacher wage level, some segment of the work force will enter the education profession. Similarly, at some price level, textbook publishers will supply texts of a given standard. The aggregate of various inputs to education at their associated prices gives rise to a *supply curve*, a construct, like the *demand curve*, that helps explain how much education is produced and how much it costs.[53]

The relationship between demand and supply in education is illustrated in Figure 3.1. The demand curve, DD', depicts a relationship between price of education and quantity consumed. The demand curve slopes downward to the right, indicating that as the price of education falls, the quantity consumed increases. Similarly, the supply curve, SS', displays the relationship between price and the quantity that will be made available for consumption. The supply curve slopes upward to the right, indicating that suppliers will produce more and better education if purchasers are willing to pay higher prices. Assuming decisions about education supply are left to the private market, so that only the private benefits of education are considered, an equilibrium would be reached at S_1, where OA_1 of education would be produced at a price of A_1S_1 (or P_1).

Suppose now that the public or external benefits of education are sufficiently large that a community decides to increase the quantity of education being purchased from the private market. If it believed that education produced A_1A_2 of public benefits, then the price would have to be lowered to A_2D_1 (or P_3) to entice individuals to purchase that much education from private providers. In order to persuade suppliers to produce OA_2 of education they would have to receive a price of A_2S_2 (P_2), and the community would have to subsidize suppliers by the amount D_1S_2.

This simple model of the supply of and demand for education provides some useful insights into the way education is provided in American society. Clearly, more education is provided than would be purchased from private sources in the marketplace. This is not only because primary and secondary education is compulsory in the United States, but also because public schools are free. Families with school-age children pay no more than other citizens.

Problems in Determining Demand for Education

A major problem in analyzing demand for education is describing what education is. There are two general answers to the question. Education can be defined as either the amount of knowledge or education a student receives, or the amount of

[52]The question here is not how many students will demand education (because education is compulsory) but how much and what quality of education are demanded by a community.

[53]This discussion and that in the following section ignore the influence of public suppliers of funding for education and assume a direct connection between consumers and suppliers of goods and services. This separation of educational consumers and funding bodies is addressed on p. 66.

FIGURE 3.1 Education Supply and Demand

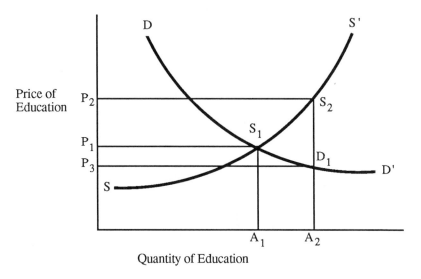

Quantity of Education

opportunity a student is allocated to become educated. This issue has already been discussed in Chapter 2 in terms of alternative measures of equal educational opportunity—that is, equal outcomes and equal access. For example, assume that a teacher spends an equal amount of time teaching two students, one who is precocious and another who is average. At the end of a period of instruction, the precocious child will probably be able to perform better. Deciding how much education each received depends on one's definition of education. If one uses an output definition of education, the precocious child has learned more. If educational access is the measure used, both have received the same amount. Which of the two definitions is appropriate depends on what is considered to be the educational demand that exists at the time.

Education is often measured differently depending on the level of education being discussed. If the measure is basic abilities such as how to read, write, and compute—skills a community might believe absolutely necessary for minimum citizenship—then it is important that every child achieve them, even if this requires additional resources for slower students. Here, opportunity to learn is an acceptable measure of educational output. Again, expectations differ at different levels of education. External benefits in primary education accrue to a community only when most students are literate and able to function responsibly. Higher education's external benefits, especially creation of new knowledge, accrue to a community even if only a few students are educated to a level leading to creation of new knowledge. What is important in higher education is to provide students with an opportunity to develop their full potential even though only those with ability and unusual motivation will eventually succeed in making major contributions.

SUPPLY OF PUBLIC EDUCATION

The supply of public education is closely related to the costs of education. The greater the costs, the less education provided. Direct education costs depend on many factors, including number of students to be educated, type of education they receive, distribution of students in a geographic area, number of years of education provided, and quality of education services. Total costs of education in the United States have increased dramatically, from less than $1 billion in 1930 to more than $260 billion in 1988. Much of the increase has resulted from increases in the number of students in school. There have been more school–age children, and they have stayed in school longer. Many younger and older people who were traditionally excluded from school are now receiving public educations. These include preschool children, handicapped children, pregnant girls, and many adults. In 1890, public school enrollments were less than 13 million. By 1990, this number will be approximately 41 million.[54]

School costs have been affected by changes other than increasing enrollment. Schools today are expected to provide many more services and a wider range of courses. These additional services and courses require more teachers and aides. Because personnel costs account for 85 to 90 percent of a school's budget, the more teachers, the higher the costs. Costs have also risen because of an effort to provide educational opportunities for exceptional students, who are usually taught in small classes and provided more individual attention. Again, these extra services are expensive; if additional public funds to cover them are unavailable, their provision can reduce the resources available for the regular school curriculum.

Educational costs are affected by students' geographic distribution. It costs more to teach students in sparsely populated areas because of high transportation expenses, small buildings, and small class sizes. As explained in Chapter 6, most state finance formulas provide extra funds for the added costs of operating small schools. Average costs are reduced when students are concentrated, although the optimal school or district size is probably smaller than most suppose.[55] Large school districts—those with more than 15,000 or 20,000 students—also have high average costs. The extra costs of large school districts may result from high administrative expenses, high costs for maintenance and security, and the expense of operating a school in a congested area.

The important point is that the supply of education, private or public, is affected by costs. Whenever a high-cost program is added to the school curriculum, the resources it utilizes are not available for another program. In this sense, the search for efficiency—the least expensive way of providing services—is directly tied to both educational opportunities and educational quality.

[54]Data in this paragraph are taken from U. S. Department of Education, National Center for Educational Statistics, *Digest of Educational Statistics* (Washington, D.C.: Government Printing Office, annual).

[55]James W. Guthrie, "Organizational Scale and School Success," *Educational Evaluation and Policy Analysis,* 1, No. 1 (Winter 1979), pp. 1–14.

POLITICAL DETERMINANTS OF THE PRICE AND QUANTITY OF PUBLIC EDUCATION

Economics is only a part of the calculus behind decisions affecting education supply and demand. Politics is also important because schooling decisions are ultimately made by voters and by public officials such as school board members and legislators. Unlike the marketplace, where consumers both decide how much they want and also pay for what they want, the political process is characterized by decision makers who are neither consumers nor principal providers of resources and by a separation of those providing resources and those benefiting from them.

The Dual Role of Citizens

Separating educational consumers and those who pay for education services leads to conflicting views on the supply of education. Some political analysts contend that a system of "free" public education results in relatively too many resources being devoted to public education. This, it is argued, is because elected officials tend to be more responsive to vocal, well-organized special interests than to the general public. This conclusion, however, overlooks the fact that many consumers of education are also taxpayers. As voters, they must decide not only how much education they want, but also how much they can afford. In this dual capacity a taxpayer is likely to give more weight to the immediate burden of additional taxes than to the longer-term benefits of additional education. This argument leads to the conclusion that too little education is provided in the public sector.[56]

Whether the equilibrium established by policy makers and taxpayers, who weigh both education benefits and costs, produces more or less service than what would be provided in the marketplace is also affected by other community characteristics. For instance, much depends on the proportion of families in a community with children, or, more exactly, the proportion of families having a direct interest in schools. If one assumes that school budgets require approval of a taxpayer majority, then public school services will be greater than educational services provided privately, as long as more than a majority favor additional school services.[57] Furthermore, as the proportion of families with a direct interest in schools declines, but remains more than a majority, the service level will increase. This occurs because, as the number of voters with a direct interest in schools declines to 50 percent of a community, the tax price of education also declines, thus leading to greater demand.

In other words, as the proportion of families having school–age children in schools or family members working in schools nears 50 percent, a larger share of the total cost of schooling is transferred to taxpayers lacking a direct interest in

[56]For an interesting analysis of the difficulties created when demand for a public service exceeds taxpayers' willingness to pay for it, see James M. Buchanan, "The Inconsistencies of the National Health Service," in *Theory of Public Choice,* ed. James M. Buchanan and Robert D. Tollison (Ann Arbor: University of Michigan Press, 1972), pp. 27–45.

[57]Private equilibrium above is the amount of service that would be provided if education were solely a private activity.

schools. This reduces the price and increases the demand of the majority of voters needed to approve the higher level of services. The relationship between per-pupil spending and level of services is illustrated in Figure 3.2.

The situation is different when the number of taxpayers receiving private benefits from education (those with children or grandchildren in school or with family members working in the schools) drops below 50 percent. In this case, provision of public schooling may be below the private equilibrium. The average voter now receives only external educational benefits and is likely to vote for a school budget that provides schooling to cover only minimum standards. Again, per-pupil expenditures or service levels are likely to increase as the proportion of families with a direct interest in schools declines further. This occurs because even the demand for external educational benefits is likely to increase as the tax price falls.[58]

This analysis of the effects of majority voting on school budgets overlooks many financial and organizational factors that smooth out the curves depicted in Figure 3.2. It does illustrate why large urban school districts often have difficulty passing school budgets. Typically, the proportion of families with school–age children is much lower in cities than in rural and suburban school districts. Consequently, it is difficult in urban areas to obtain school budget overrides or special levies because so few people have a direct interest. The result is that school tax rates in urban areas are often below those in other school districts even though urban areas contain many people who value education highly.

FIGURE 3.2 School Expenditures and Percentage of Families With School-Age Children

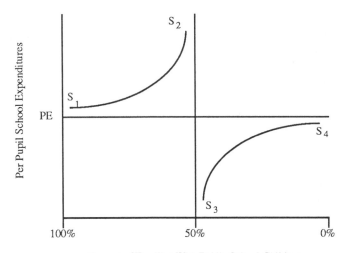

Percent of Families With Public School Children

---

[58] As the number of children declines, the average tax price of receiving the public benefits of education also declines, thereby increasing the demand for those benefits.

School Boards versus School Bureaucracies

Another political factor affecting the supply of public education is the relationship between school boards, which generally approve school budgets, and school bureaucracies. William Niskanen has analyzed this relationship and theorizes that legislative bodies, such as school boards, tend to approve budgets larger than those that would result from equating the marginal benefits of additional spending on schools with the marginal costs.[59] The following paragraphs translate Niskanen's argument into a school district setting.

A school district administration does not deal directly with consumers or taxpayers when it is preparing its budget. Instead, it offers a proposed set of school programs to a school board, along with a proposed budget. The school board, in turn, obtains money to support the budget from federal, state, and local revenues and from a few small fees and charges. The primary constraint facing school administrators is the size of the budget they receive. A less direct constraint is the proportion of personal income the public is willing to turn over to the school board for education. School administrators have few sources of funds—tuition is one—beyond those provided by the school board. Consequently, school board members' personal preferences are more likely to be considered in preparing the district's program and budget than are preferences of the community at large.

The relationship between the school board and school bureaucracy is not a typical superior–subordinate match, however. In fact, school administrators are well placed to dominate the relationship and obtain benefits for themselves in the process.[60] School boards, it is true, generally are elected, are legally responsible for all facets of school operations, and have authority to hire and fire superintendents. The power of the administration arises from its monopoly on the supply of educational services and the fact that the school board is legally bound to provide such services. The school board does not have the option of closing schools if the administration is ineffective. According to Niskanen, the bureaucracy's monopoly position gives it a clear advantage in bargaining with the school board:

> Under many conditions it gives a bureau [superintendent and administrative staff] the same type of bargaining power as a profit–seeking monopoly that discriminates among customers or that presents the market with an all–or–nothing choice. The primary reason for the differential bargaining power of a monopoly bureau is the sponsor's lack of a significant alternative and its unwillingness to forego the services supplied by the bureau. Also...the interests of those officers of the collective organization responsible for reviewing the bureau are often best served by allowing the bureau to exploit this monopoly power.[61]

[59]William A. Niskanen, Jr., *Bureaucracy and Representative Government* (Chicago: Aldine-Atherton, 1971).

[60]Harvey J. Tucker and Harmon Ziegler, *Professionals versus the Public: Attitudes, Communication and Response in School Districts* (New York: Longman, 1980).

[61]Niskanen, *Bureaucracy and Representative Government*, p. 25.

From the viewpoint of the school bureaucracy, school board preferences are summarized in a budget–output function. "Any point on this function represents the maximum budget the sponsor [school board] is willing to grant to the bureau for a specific expected level of output."[62] The budget–output relationship is such that the school board is willing to provide a larger budget for a higher level of expected output. As output increases, however, the amount of budget increase a school board is willing to provide decreases. This means that the school board's marginal budget–output function (or demand curve) declines as output increases.

Assuming that school administrators want as large a school budget as possible,[63] we can illustrate how the budget review process is likely to operate. According to Niskanen, the school administration will submit to the school board a budget that "maximizes the expected approved budget subject to the constraint that the approved budget must be sufficient to cover the costs of the output expected by the sponsor at the budget level."[64]

The expected level of output is illustrated in Figure 3.3. The school board's marginal valuation of the school district's services is represented by DD´. Assuming a marginal cost function SS´, the approved budget and output will be Q_1, the point that provides the maximum balanced budget. At this level of output, Q_1, the total budget preferred by the school board (the area ofeb) just covers the minimum total costs of producing the same output (the area ofda). The district will be providing services for which the marginal benefits to the school board, fe, are less than the marginal costs, fd, of providing those last increments of service, or at a level above what economists say is efficient—the level where marginal value equals marginal cost, Q_2. Bargaining between the school administration and the school board will continue, in other words, until all net benefits (acb) that would accrue from an optimal level of service are absorbed by the net costs (ced) of operating above the optimal level, Q_2.

Conclusion

This analysis of education supply and demand takes into account several peculiar features of the political decision-making process in public education. Determination of education price and quantity depends on definitions, on the interests of adults in educating their own and others' children, and on a variety of institutional factors through which education is financed and provided. This analysis emphasizes the dual role that citizens play both as consumers of education and as taxpayers, and concludes that the level of services provided by taxpayers is less than they would demand if someone else were paying the bills. The interaction between school bureaucracy and school boards also tends to produce a level of services greater than that which equates marginal benefits and costs.

[62]Ibid.
[63]For a defense of this assumption, see Niskanen, ibid., chap. 3.
[64]Ibid., p. 46.

FIGURE 3.3. Equilibrium Output of a Bureau

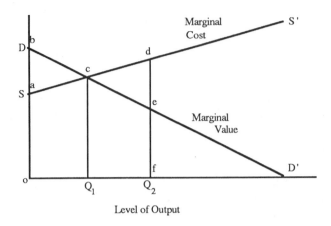

Level of Output

Source: Derived from William A. Niskanen, Jr., Bureaucracy and Representative Government (Chicago: Aldine Atherton, Inc., 1971), p. 47.

SUMMARY

In this chapter we have attempted to examine the role of government in education. In providing institutional programs from kindergarten through graduate school, government confers benefits on those in school as well as on many who are not. These private and public benefits of education provide justification and support for government financing and provision of education. They do not, however, give policy makers a clear rule for deciding when to spend more or when to stop spending for public education.

How much education is enough? The answer to this question is determined politically. This political process depends on the forces of education supply and demand. We have discussed factors affecting the supply–demand equation, noting in particular several political impediments to decisions that would optimize the supply of education from an economic perspective. Even if these impediments were removed, decisions on how much to spend for education would also be affected by purely external factors, such as changing population characteristics. In addition, many other developments are likely to affect education in the future. For example, since birthrates have declined most sharply among high-income, well-educated households, schoolchildren are likely, on the average, to be less well prepared for school than schoolchildren in the past. This will increase the need for more preschool education and more remedial and compensatory education. Also, an increasing elderly population in the United States will affect education in unforeseen ways. Senior citizens may demand selected education programs in the form of adult education. They may well demand that more resources be allocated for social services such as public transportation, welfare, and police protection, thereby decreasing reserves available to schools.

Education is financed largely out of public budgets. Consequently, education will be affected by the structure of public spending in the future. If, for example, defense expenditures were reduced as a result of new international treaties freezing or limiting production of military weapons, substantial sums of money might be released for which education could make a claim. If, on the other hand, international relations worsen and the arms race intensifies, education might lose more of its share of public monies. Somewhat more certain are the effects that large federal deficits and the underfunding of veterans benefit programs and state and local retirement programs will have on future allocations of public dollars. Billions of future dollars have already been legally obligated for paying the national debt and the costs of these programs, dollars that will not be available for education regardless of future schooling needs.

Prospects for major technological breakthroughs in the field of education are difficult to estimate. Many suggestions have been made for rearrangements in the processes, organization, and financing of education. Computers, video technology, and vouchers may change education as it is known today. These and other innovations may prove popular because of demonstrated success—or more likely because of the perceived failure of traditional arrangements to provide the quality of education the public prefers. Schools are remarkably impervious to change, however, and without a major crisis it is not unreasonable to expect schools in the future to look much as they do today.

chapter four

THE ORGANIZATION OF PUBLIC SCHOOLS

Knut Wicksell, a noted nineteenth-century political economist, wrote that the task of social theory is not to dictate what is equitable and efficient policy, but to specify institutional frameworks in which equitable and efficient policies are likely to be chosen. Chapter 2 examined the equity, efficiency and liberty implications of government involvement in education. Chapter 3 described the political and economic framework in which decisions affecting United States education financing are made. This chapter examines the formal organization of public education and the sources of the fiscal strain affecting it. A primary concern is the institutional framework of public education and how it can be changed to produce a balanced educational policy.

AN ECONOMIST'S APPROACH TO ORGANIZATIONAL ANALYSIS

This chapter views the organization of public education from the perspective of an economist. One of the trademarks of an economist is a predisposition to think about issues in terms of alternatives. There are many ways to organize public schools, and different organizational arrangements may create different educational experiences and outcomes. Organizations in themselves are neither good nor bad. They can, however, be evaluated in terms of their likely effects on desired outcomes. Much of economic analysis is concerned with questions of efficiency—whether a particular form of organization is more or less efficient than another. Economic concepts and analyses may also be used to ascertain the consequences of alternative organizational arrangements on the equity and responsiveness of public services.[1]

Several economic concepts are instrumental in understanding organizations. Foremost in the study of economics is the individual. Only individuals possess values, make choices, and take actions. One frequently hears that "the legislature enacted a bill" or "the school board decided to do something." In fact, even if involved in collectives, only individuals take actions. It is important to know which individuals are involved, how they arrived at their joint decisions, and what the consequences of their joint decisions are on themselves and on future decisions of the group. The focus throughout the chapter is on educational organizations as collections of individual decision makers and on constraints and incentives organizational arrangements provide them.

A related assumption is that individuals act with a purpose: to improve their well-being; to change from a situation that is less desired to one that is more desired. The assumption that individuals act with a purpose, or act rationally, does not mean they are selfish or are free to do as they like. It means that given a choice, they will choose to improve their situation, or avoid or reduce something they do not want. Organizations can be viewed as sets of opportunities and restrictions on the ability of people to improve their well-being. The following discussion emphasizes how current and alternative educational organizational arrangements allow individuals to improve their situations.

Equally central to economics is the notion that every action is costly. "There is no such thing as a free lunch," as economics professors have been known to warn their beginning students. Estimating the costs of alternative forms of action is an important step in any decisional process. Too frequently individuals unfamiliar with economic concepts assume that if private actions are too costly, government should assume the activity. This may be an overly simple view.[2]

---

[1] The centrality of alternatives to an economist is aptly described by James Buchanan:

The economist's stock-in-trade—his tools—lies in his ability to and proclivity to think about all questions in terms of alternatives. The truth judgment of the moralist, which says that something is either wholly right or wholly wrong, is foreign to him. The win-lose, yes-no discussion of politics is not within his purview. He does not recognize the either-or, the all-or-nothing, situation as his own. His is not the world of the mutually exclusives. Instead, his is the world of adjustment, of coordinated conflict, of mutual gain.

"Economics and Its Scientific Neighbors," in *The Structure of Economic Science: Essays on Methodology,* ed. Sherman Roy Krupp (Englewood Cliffs, N.J.; Prentice-Hall, 1966), p. 168. See also L. H. Tribe, "Policy Science: Analysis or Ideology," *Philosophy and Public Affairs,* 2, no. 1 (Fall 1972), 55–110; L. M. Mead, "Policy Science Today," *Public Interest,* no. 73 (Fall 1983), 165–70; and E. Stokey and R. Zeckhauser, *A Primer for Policy Analysis* (New York: W. W. Norton & Co., Inc., 1978).

[2] For an analysis of this point see James M. Buchanan, "Politics, Policy, and the Pigovian Margins," in *Theory of Public Choice,* ed. James M. Buchanan and Robert Tollison (Ann Arbor: University of Michigan Press, 1972), pp. 169-82.

Public activity entails two important costs that must be kept in mind. Because public choices, once made, are binding on every member of a community, they impose costs on those members of the community who disagree with the decision. These are the external costs of collective choice.[3] Public actions also impose decision-making costs—the time, energy, and resources needed to reach a joint decision.

The economic paradigm of social analysis is a useful way of analyzing school organization. This approach, however, is not without its critics.[4] Some believe that the model contains inescapable biases. In the case of public education, the model favors efficiency rather than equity, private good rather than public good. There is also a growing critique of analytical frameworks that attempt to separate facts from values.[5] Most quantitative and formalistic policy-analysis models, it is asserted, contain implicit value choices and normative implications. Finally, students of policy analysis contend that the economic model of organizational analysis may not provide adequate guidance on how to implement public policy.[6] It generally gives more information on what should be done to maximize policy makers' values than on how such policies are to be implemented by complex public organizations. Despite these reservations, an economic perspective facilitates identification of the structural components of educational organizations that contribute to many of their fiscal problems.

The next section of this chapter describes the organization of American schools and analyzes its important features. Subsequent sections examine organizational problems facing public schools and several major issues underlying proposals for restructuring public education.

PUBLIC SCHOOLS IN THE UNITED STATES

Primary and secondary education in the United States is by almost any measure a large endeavor. Approximately $170 billion was projected to be spent in 1988 to ed-

[3]The costs of collective action are analyzed in detail in James M. Buchanan and Gordon Tullock, *The Calculus of Consent* (Ann Arbor: The University of Michigan Press, 1962).

[4]See R. J. Bernstein, *The Restructuring of Social and Political Theory* (New York: Harcourt Brace Jovanovich, Inc., 1976); E. Bredo and W. Feinberg, eds., *Knowledge and Values in Social and Educational Research* (Philadelphia: Temple University Press, 1982); G. Burrell and G. Morgan, *Sociological Paradigms and Organizational Analysis* (New York: Plenum, 1979); B. Fay, *Social Theory and Political Practice* (London: Allen & Unwin, 1975); and J. D. Moon, "The Logic of Political Inquiry: A Synthesis of Opposed Perspectives" in *Political Science Scope and Theory*, ed. G. I. Greenstein and N. W. Polsby (Reading, Mass.: Addison-Wesley, 1975), pp. 83–109.

[5]See R. N. Bellah, "Social Science as Practical Reason," in *Ethics, the Social Sciences, and Policy Analysis,* ed. D. Callahan and B. Jennings (New York: Plenum, 1983), pp. 129–61; I. R. Hoos, *Systems Analysis in Public Policy: A Critique* (Berkeley: University of California Press, 1972); and J. J. Pruty, *A Critical Reformulation of Educational Policy Analysis* (Geelong, Australia: Deakin University Press, 1984).

[6]See J. Pressman and A. Wildavsky, *Implementation* (Berkeley: University of California Press, 1973); R. F. Elmore, "Complexity and Control: What Legislators and Administrators Can Do about Implementing Public Policy," in *Handbook of Teaching and Policy*, ed. L. S. Shulman and G. Sykes (New York: Longman, 1983); and D. Mann, ed., *Making Change Happen?* (New York: Teachers College Press, 1978).

ucate an estimated 41 million children in public schools. An additional $20 to $30 billion was projected to be spent to educate approximately 5.7 million children in 27,700 private primary and secondary schools.

Approximately 3 million teachers and other educational professionals serve the public school population.[7] Teachers' organizations are among the most organized and influential political lobbies in the nation. They constitute a major source of campaign funds at the state and local levels in many states, and compose one of the most active lobbies during most state legislative sessions. Many teachers serve on local school boards and in state legislatures. Educators and their families now account for a larger segment of our population than the historically powerful farm bloc.[8]

Governance

Responsibility for managing public education in the United States is decentralized and diffused. Public schools are governed within a federal structure in which local, state, and federal governments each have important and overlapping roles.

LOCAL SCHOOL DISTRICTS

For historical reasons and because of the belief that individual freedom can be best protected if government is in the hands of small, self-governing communities, states generally delegate major responsibility for operating and financing public schools to local school districts. They are the basic administrative unit in the organization of schools and are the means through which local communities control their schools.

Most school districts are units of special government, created and empowered by state law to administer public schools.[9] They have the power to tax, the right to enter into contracts, and the right to sue and be sued. Independent school districts are legally controlled by elected governing boards. These governing boards generally employ a superintendent to implement school board decisions. Despite the formal independence of most school districts, they have many informal ties with local governments. These ties are growing increasingly close as municipalities become aware of the importance of good schooling to their own survival .

School district relationships with state government are both legal and financial. State laws and regulations specify who shall attend schools, length of the school year, rules for establishing and altering district boundaries, required courses, and numerous other facets of local school operations. State governments also provide a substantial proportion of local school district revenues, accounting for 49

---

[7]These figures are derived from reports distributed by the Department of Education's National Center for Educational Statistics.

[8]The growing power of the educational lobby, particularly at the state level, is discussed in a number of books. See Harmon Ziegler and Michael Baer, *Lobbying* (Belmont, Calif.: Wadsworth, 1969); and Michael W. Kirst, *Who Controls Our Schools?* (Stanford, Calif.: Stanford Alumni Association, 1984).

[9]Approximately 10 percent of the school districts are fiscally dependent upon municipal governments and do not share all of the powers of their independent counterparts. Also, the approximately 1000 local districts in California do not have conventional taxing authority.

percent of total public school revenues in 1985.[10] The bulk of the remaining revenues is raised from local sources, but state laws specify the form of taxes school districts may use and in many states restrict the amounts raised from local sources.

Local school districts receive relatively little financial aid or other assistance from the federal government. Districts with children whose parents are employed in federal facilities or who live on federal property receive direct financial assistance through federal impact aid programs. Urban school districts also receive funds directly from the federal government for public housing programs. Federal funds accounted for only 6.5 percent of school district revenues in 1986, although in a few states (Mississippi, 18.10 percent; Alabama, 18.04 percent) they are much greater.[11]

THE STATE ROLE

State government is the focal point in educational policy making. In fact, education is the responsibility of the states or the people, since it is *not* one of the functions specifically delegated by the Constitution to the federal government. At the state level several groups have important roles in the governance of public schools. State constitutions, statutes, and considerable practical experience render state legislatures ultimately accountable for public education. The legislatures have final authority to create and empower school districts, counties, and in some cases regional agencies to provide educational services. Within legislatures, education committees generally are responsible for bills involving educational policy.

Most of the day-to-day administration of public education, and much of the staff effort needed by legislatures for policy making, is conducted by state education bureaucracies. Governors, state boards of education, chief state school officers, and state departments of education all participate in educational governance at the state level. The importance of each, however, varies among states.

Governors influence educational policy by heading a political party, developing legislative programs, and controlling the state budget. A chief state school officer or a state teachers' organization may recommend bills and have them considered by the legislature. Unless provision for the legislation is contained in the governor's budget, however, its chances of passage are slim. Finally, governors influence educational policy through their right to veto legislation and to appoint members of state boards of education.

A state board of education is accorded general supervision of public schools. In most states, members are unpaid, are appointed by the governor, and tend to have little influence in policy making.[12] The State Board of Regents in New York and the State Board of Education in California are exceptions: they play active roles in

---

[10]National Education Association, *Rankings of the States, 1985* (Washington, D.C.: 1985), p. 46, Table F-8, and NEA Research *Estimates*, computerized data bank.

[11]*Estimates*, Ibid.

[12]For an analysis of how state boards of education could strengthen their policy-making role, see Michael W. Kirst, "Strengthening and Improving Relationships between State Boards of Education," in *The Imperative of Leadership* (Denver: National Association of State Boards of Education, 1975), pp. 5–15.

educational policy making.[13] The state board of education delegates most administrative matters to the chief state school officer and state education department professional staff.

The top professional educator in each state is the chief state school officer. In more than half of the states, chief state school officers are appointed by the state board of education. In about twenty states, however, they are elected by a statewide constituency. The chief state school officer is the nominal top executive of the state education department and serves the state board of education much as a school district superintendent serves a school board. However, he or she is also expected to advise the legislature and governor on matters of educational policy. This advisory role is complicated in states electing their education executive, because the governor and the chief state school officer may be chosen by constituencies with conflicting expectations.

Administration of education in the state is conducted by the state department of education. Most state education departments are small and involved mainly in administering state education programs. State education bureaucracies in New York, Illinois, and California, however, are larger than those in most other states, and play active and influential roles in developing state education policy.

The state role in public education has continued to increase. State contribution to school funding increased from 16.5 percent in 1920 to more than 50 percent in 1986.[14] Not only has the state share of school revenues increased, but state officials are also more likely today to perceive that improved schools are essential for economic growth. Consequently, in the 1980s many states enacted sweeping legislation to force fundamental changes in the school curriculum, the length of the school year, and teacher education programs. Again, much contemporary educational reform is designed to improve the competitiveness of American industries in world markets and ultimately to foster economic growth.

THE FEDERAL ROLE

The federal role in public education has always been a relatively minor one, but is certainly not likely to disappear in the foreseeable future.[15] As we have seen, education was not one of the functions delegated by the Constitution to the federal government—there was no national system of public education—and thus it was reserved for the states and the people.[16] Even so, the federal government has always had a hand in public education and has not been reluctant to act vigorously whenever the national interest is involved. The Morrill Act of 1862 (establishing

[13]The role of the State Board of Regents in New York State is discussed in Stephen K. Bailey et al., *Schoolmen and Politics* (Syracuse: Syracuse University Press, 1962).

[14]National Center for Educational Statistics, *Digest of Education Statistics* (Washington, D.C.: U.S. Department of Education, 1986), and NEA Research *Estimates*, computerized data bank.

[15]The federal role is detailed in Chapter 7.

[16]Amendment X of the Constitution states, "The powers not delegated to the United States by the Constitution, nor prohibited by it to the States, are reserved to the States respectively, or to the people."

the land-grant colleges), the Smith-Hughes Act of 1917 (providing support for vocational education), and the Elementary and Secondary Education Act of 1965 (providing financial aid to low-income students) are just a few examples of major federal initiatives in public education.

Federal courts have also intervened in public schooling. No single judicial decision has affected public schools more than the 1954 Supreme Court decision mandating racial desegregation. Federal court rulings on student rights and rights of handicapped and non-English-speaking students have also led to changes in the administration of local schools.[17]

Since 1980, the federal government has withdrawn its support from a number of educational programs. Federal initiatives in bilingual education have been curtailed. Federal education policy shifted in the Reagan years from support of specific programs to unrestricted aid and bloc grants. Per-capita distribution has replaced redistribution as a primary basis for federal financial support of public schools. One effect of this has been a drop in federal aid as a percentage of total school expenditures from 8 percent in 1968 to just over 6 percent during the 1980s. On the other hand, federal influence has perhaps been enhanced by effective use of exhortation and admonition—the "bully pulpit."

Characteristics of Public School Organization

WEAK PLANNING

Public schools seldom engage in systematic planning. If it were not for their virtual monopoly condition, they might be severely damaged by this lack of foresight. The shortage of systematic educational planning is particularly evident at the federal level. The federal government reacts to crises. Witness, for example, its funding of science programs after the Russian Sputnik launching and the spate of 1980s reform proposals following release of unfavorable comparative data on the academic performance of American students. For the most part, there is no national educational policy that sifts down to local school districts.

Although states have legal responsibility for establishing and operating public schools, they have delegated most of the financial and operational responsibilities to local school districts. States legislatures do, of course, enact laws and issue regulations affecting local school districts, but they do not normally develop comprehensive education plans that guide allocation of state resources or development of program criteria. This situation may be changing slightly in the late 1980s as more state coordinating boards and departments of education begin preparing long-range strategy. What little ad hoc educational planning exists, however, is generally unrelated to other areas of social policy, such as housing, transportation, income maintenance, or land use. A flagrant example is the lack of coordination on both the state and federal levels between school integration plans and urban housing policies,

17On due process for students, see *Dixon v. Alabama Board of Education*, 194 F2d 150 (5th Cir, 1961); on the constitutional rights of exceptional children, see *Mills v. Board of Education*, 348 F. Supp 866 (D.D.C. 1972); on rights of non-English-speaking students see *Lau v. Nichols*, 483 F2d (9th Cir., 1973).

which tend to resegregate the areas targeted for integration. Then, too, school building programs seeking the cheapest land outside the urban fringe conflict with land-use plans to control dispersion of metropolitan populations. Part of the problem is that most state departments of education do not collect, analyze, or publicize data needed for educational planning. Even if such information were available, the political system contains few incentives for comprehensive, long-term planning of educational programs.

Most of what little coordination and planning occurs in public education takes place at the local level. Many large school districts have offices of planning and attempt to forecast needs and develop programs to meet them. Most districts, however, operate on a year-to-year basis. Compulsory attendance laws and designated attendance areas create monopoly conditions and thus eliminate many incentives for schools to respond to changing community preferences for education. What has occurred in the past largely determines the trend of future offerings.

DIVERSITY

A newcomer to American public education must be struck by the uniformity and, at the same time, the diversity of public primary and secondary education. Most districts are uniformly organized with school boards, superintendents, primary schools, secondary schools, principals, department heads, and classroom teachers. Whether you are in New York City or Amity, Oregon, classrooms, curricula, and the school day appear remarkably similar.

This semblance of uniformity is deceptive, for there are vast differences among school districts. The nation's largest school district, New York City, has almost a million students, whereas the average school district enrolls fewer than 3000 students. The median school district is smaller yet. Over 95 percent of the school children in Washington, D.C., are minorities, whereas in Portland, Oregon, minorities constitute approximately 25 percent of the school population.[18]

Diversity among school districts is particularly noticeable when finances are compared. These differences occur both among and within states. Table 4.1 provides 1985–86 data on the fiscal situation of public schools in the fifty states and the District of Columbia. The federal share of state educational costs varies from a high of 18 percent in Mississippi to a low of 3 percent in Wyoming. Since most federal aid is distributed according to the number of children eligible for handicapped programs, Education Consolidation and Improvement Act Chapter I programs, and impact-area programs, there is little a state or school district can do to increase the amount of federal aid it receives. A number of state governments provide more than two-thirds of local school costs—Alabama, Alaska, California, Delaware, Hawaii, Kentucky, New Mexico, and Washington. The state share of the fiscal costs of schools in Nebraska, New Hampshire, Oregon, and South Dakota, on the other hand, is less than a third of the total. Total school expenditure per child varies from

[18]National Center for Education Statistics, *The Conditions of Education* (Washington, D.C.: Government Printing Office, 1985), p. 27.

TABLE 4.1   Data Profile of Education in the States, 1985-86

	REVENUES PER PUPIL	% LOCAL CONTRIB- UTED	% STATE CONTRIB- UTED	SPENDING AS % OF NATIONAL AVERAGE	AVERAGE TEACHER SALARY	PUPIL- TEACHER RATIO
Alabama	$2,807	15.83	71.85	73.30	$23,500	18.97
Alaska	8,871	16.89	78.43	224.27	42,063	14.32
Arizona	3,243	33.08	59.02	75.98	25,972	18.01
Arkansas	2,946	28.31	61.34	70.97	20,386	16.83
California	3,947	23.42	68.99	96.90	31,269	22.86
Colorado	4,741	54.69	40.94	108.57	27,387	17.55
Connecticut	5,259	54.55	40.53	131.30	29,860	13.65
Delaware	5,003	23.55	68.74	121.33	27,467	15.09
D.C.	5,084	93.33	NA	134.84	33,801	13.13
Florida	4,125	38.59	53.41	100.22	23,833	16.23
Georgia	3,168	36.10	55.78	80.06	24,632	17.38
Hawaii	4,065	0.18	90.56	101.17	26,093	18.62
Idaho	2,699	30.44	62.73	67.40	21,476	19.60
Illinois	4,482	53.49	39.25	97.25	28,287	15.95
Indiana	3,783	38.26	57.57	84.85	25,191	17.51
Iowa	3,626	53.46	40.71	95.84	22,603	15.15
Kansas	4,454	50.83	44.59	105.14	23,427	13.83
Kentucky	3,131	20.98	68.58	76.64	22,467	17.75
Louisiana	3,531	35.60	53.57	83.90	20,054	17.24
Maine	3,542	41.21	51.07	89.87	21,257	15.54
Maryland	4,692	53.78	40.45	116.82	28,893	16.09
Massachusetts	4,882	50.71	43.71	124.67	28,615	14.13
Michigan	4,142	58.68	36.57	101.58	31,592	20.07
Minnesota	4,424	37.06	58.71	106.96	28,340	16.46
Mississippi	2,455	25.82	57.23	61.91	19,448	17.59
Missouri	3,594	54.47	38.91	84.73	23,468	14.97
Montana	4,725	41.89	50.17	106.01	24,198	14.24
Nebraska	3,452	66.79	28.11	88.23	21,797	14.33
Nevada	3,364	60.18	35.78	78.76	26,962	18.69
New Hampshire	3,609	91.22	4.98	83.66	21,869	14.30
New Jersey	6,008	52.44	43.19	148.71	28,718	14.30
New Mexico	3,756	10.58	75.14	91.37	23,976	17.45
New York	5,908	53.38	43.41	153.37	32,000	13.79
North Carolina	3,389	27.90	64.20	90.40	23,775	18.13
North Dakota	3,510	38.37	53.49	82.17	21,284	14.38
Ohio	3,920	48.70	46.32	95.27	26,762	17.07
Oklahoma	3,256	28.02	66.50	73.93	22,540	15.49
Oregon	4,327	67.31	27.94	110.73	26,691	16.23
Pennsylvania	4,783	49.67	45.30	111.95	27,429	15.33
Rhode Island	4,841	54.03	41.88	125.40	31,079	15.98
South Carolina	3,302	31.87	58.26	78.43	23,039	16.95
South Dakota	3,304	61.13	27.80	79.70	18,781	14.54
Tennessee	2,790	40.27	49.98	68.04	22,612	19.16
Texas	3,990	46.85	45.70	92.11	26,094	16.73
Utah	2,921	39.08	55.61	61.70	23,035	22.65
Vermont	4,246	58.17	35.61	95.47	23,085	13.09
Virginia	3,987	59.91	34.05	96.53	25,473	15.81
Washington	4,168	18.69	75.60	99.52	27,238	19.61
West Virginia	3,452	26.46	63.78	75.78	21,446	14.76
Wisconsin	4,684	56.19	39.83	114.08	28,206	15.45
Wyoming	6,863	59.45	38.11	146.13	28,230	13.33
U. S. Average	4,121	43.41	50.22	100.00	26,698	17.90

Source: National Education Association, *Rankings of the States, 1987* (Washington D.C., 1987).

a high of $8871 in Alaska to a low of $2455 in Mississippi. Average teacher salaries are more than twice as high in Alaska as in Arkansas, Louisiana, Mississippi, or South Dakota.

There is also considerable variation in tax structure among the fifty states. Some states, such as Washington, New Hampshire, and Florida, have no state personal income tax. Others, such as Oregon and Missouri, have no sales tax. State tax structures also vary in their progressiveness—that is, in the distribution of the tax burden according to individuals' income. Some states, such as New York, tax their citizens heavily for public services. Others, such as New Hampshire and Ohio, provide minimum public services, relying more on individuals to provide for their own needs. The willingness of states to tax themselves has a direct and strong bearing on support of public education. (See Chapter 5 for an extensive discussion of tax burdens.)

Within states there are also wide disparities among school districts in wealth, school tax rates, and revenues raised per pupil. Property taxes are a large source of revenues for public schools. Consequently, the property wealth of each school district largely determines its ability to finance public schools. Table 4.2 compares the 1968–69 assessed property valuation, tax rates, and expenditures per average daily attendance (ADA) in Beverly Hills and Baldwin Park, California, two districts made famous by the *Serrano* case described in Chapter 2.[19] Because property wealth per pupil was much lower in Baldwin Park than in Beverly Hills, parents in Baldwin Park had to tax themselves at two and a third times the tax rate of Beverly Hills to raise less than half the revenues per pupil. In many states the top 20 percent of school districts in terms of property wealth have four to five times as much property wealth per pupil as the districts in the bottom 20 percent. Revenues generated per pupil in these wealthy districts typically exceed those of property-poor districts by ratios of two to one or more. That revenues are unequal (although not as unequal as wealth) is the result of imperfect state attempts to equalize. State intervention in this facet of school financing is discussed more fully in Chapter 6.

TABLE 4.2 Wealth, Tax Rates, and Expenditures in Two California School Districts, 1968–69

DISTRICT	ASSESSED VALUE PER ADA	TAX RATE	EXPENDITURE PER ADA
Beverly Hills	$50,885	$2.38	$1,232
Baldwin Park	3,706	5.48	577

Source: Joel S. Berke, ed., *Answers to Inequity* (Berkeley, Calif.: McCutchan, 1974), p. 199. Reprinted by permission of the publisher.

[19]The 1971 California State Supreme Court decision in *Serrano v. Priest* is reprinted in *Answers to Inequity*, ed. Joel S. Berke (Berkeley, Calif.: McCutchan, 1974), pp. 179–205.

Means for measuring and enhancing resource equalization are described in Chapter 13.

Although it is common to speak of *the* system of funding and providing public schooling, this is far from accurate. There are fifty-one different systems of public education in the United States, with wide variations in the sources and amounts of revenue available to schools and districts within each.

WEAK CENTRAL MANAGEMENT

Public school management is often viewed unfavorably in the literature when compared with private enterprise. Public schools appear to have a "bottom-heavy" and weak centrally coordinated administration.[20] School boards and superintendents are described as being at the mercy of teachers' unions on issues of work rules and teacher discipline. The goals of schools are often unclear, as are the educational technologies necessary to achieve them.[21] School reward structures seldom foster excellence, and resources are frequently inadequate to meet the demands on schools.[22] Schools are described by organizational theorists as being *loosely coupled*.[23]

Management problems led to an unprecedented clamor for educational reform in the early 1980s. Starting with the previously cited *A Nation At Risk*, the reports of numerous commissions and committees called for a widespread overhaul of the teaching profession, public education incentive structures, and school administration. Most of these reports attempted to change schools from a process-oriented, role-based management structure to an outcome-oriented, goal-based one. During this reform period, student achievement and excellence replaced educational opportunity and equity as standards for assessing school management.

STRENGTH OF TEACHER UNIONS AND COLLECTIVE BARGAINING

Collective bargaining has produced many changes in the political economy of public schools. Thirty-two states now have laws permitting collective bargaining by teachers. More than 65 percent of all full- and part-time professionals work in school districts covered by collective bargaining contracts. Before unionization, teachers were poorly situated to challenge the dominance of professional administrators in educational decision making. With collective bargaining they gained a large measure of control over many facets of school operation.[24] The

[20]R. F. Elmore, "Complexity and Control: What Legislators and Administrators Can Do about Implementing Public Policy," in *Handbook of Teaching and Policy,* ed. L. S. Shulman and G. Sykes (New York: Longman, 1983), pp. 128–45.

[21]J. G. March and J. P. Olsen, *Ambiguity and Choice in Organization* (Bergen, Norway: Universitetsforiaget, 1976).

[22]R. Weatherley and M. Lipsky, "Street-level Bureaucrats and Institutional Innovation: Implementing Special-Education Reform," *Harvard Education Review,* 47, no. 2 (May 1977), 171–97.

[23]Karl E. Weick, "Educational Organizations as Loosely Coupled Systems," *Administrative Science Quarterly,* 21, no. 1 (March 1976), 1–19.

[24]See Lorraine McDonnell and Anthony Pascal, *Organized Teachers in American Schools* (Santa Monica, Calif.: Rand, 1979).

importance of this shift in the power of teachers is described by David B. Tyack, a prominent historian of American education:

> From the late 1950s, when teachers had little influence, to 1970, a powerful new alignment of forces took place in urban schools, one comparable in potential impact to the centralization of control in small boards and powerful superintendents at the turn of the century....at the very least, teachers were the group with the greatest power to veto or sabotage proposals for reform. No realistic estimate of strategies for change in American education could afford to ignore teachers or fail to enlist their support....[25]

The most important change accompanying teacher unionization has taken place in educational decision making. Prior to unionization, most decisions at the district level were made unilaterally by a district superintendent or staff member and were subject to ratification by a popularly elected school board. However, under most collective bargaining statutes, decisions affecting teachers' wages, benefits, and working conditions as well as many educational matters are now made bilaterally. On many issues it is mandatory under state laws that school managers and teacher representatives reach agreement in a contract.

The shift from unilateral to bilateral decision making reverses the intent of many early-twentieth-century reforms in education. Independent local school districts, nonpartisan election of school board members, and professional superintendents were purportedly created to insulate education from politics. Although education and politics were never completely divorced, the widespread practice of collective bargaining has dampened discussion of separation. Collective bargaining is, in many ways, the epitome of political decision making. It is a procedure whereby teachers can influence decisions by expressing themselves directly to management. Rather than having to resign in order to protest, teachers can now voice their dissatisfaction straightforwardly.[26] Public employees have transplanted from the private sector a political procedure for increasing their power in public organizations.

Despite approximately thirty years of experience with a variety of collective bargaining arrangements, educators agree little on their impact on schools, with respect either to costs or to formation of educational policy. Opinions, of course, vary widely. Sylvester Petro claims that

[25] David B. Tyack, *The One Best System* (Cambridge, Mass.: Harvard University Press, 1974), pp. 288–89.

[26] Hirschman coins the terms *exit* and *voice* to distinguish economic and political methods of registering complaints:

> The customer who, dissatisfied with the product of one firm, shifts to that of another, uses the market to defend his welfare or to improve his position, ... one either exits or one does not.... In all respects, voice is just the opposite of exit. It is a far more "messy" concept because it can be graduated, all the way from faint grumbling to violent protest; it implies articulation of one's critical opinions rather than a private "secret" vote in the anonymity of a supermarket; and finally it is direct and straightforward rather than roundabout. Voice is political action par excellence.

Albert O. Hirschman, *Exit, Voice and Loyalty* (Cambridge, Mass.: Harvard University Press, 1970), pp. 15–16.

among the numerous, grave, and perhaps critical threats to the survival of civil order in the United States, one more ominous than the rest stands out: the movement in all the states and in the federal government to compel collective bargaining between our governments and unions acting as representatives of government employees. Although this movement rests upon a series of incredible distortions and misrepresentations of fact, is propelled by premises, theories and arguments which cannot withstand serious examination, and creates chaos in every branch and sector of government where it takes hold, it is nevertheless gaining ground year by year, even day by day, in all our governments—federal, state, and local.[27]

Other critics are less apocalyptic about the consequences of collective bargaining. Nevertheless, they contend that the problems school districts face grow with its introduction. It takes more time, energy, and resources to make decisions. Furthermore, unionization may distort political decision making. School board members find it more difficult to be reelected following a long teachers' strike. Perhaps most worrisome to critics of collective bargaining is the possibility that unionization will limit the role of government in education. They worry that both the high costs of negotiated settlements and the dilution of public control over educational policy eventually may lead elected officials and the public to seek alternatives to public programs.[28]

Most observers, however, have come to accept the extension of collective bargaining rights to teachers. They contend that collective bargaining results from the growing impersonality of large school organizations and, if structured properly, can help improve American public education. In particular, they assert that collective bargaining can reduce unrest by establishing an agreed-upon procedure for resolving management–labor disputes. In addition, proponents believe students can learn how problems are solved in democratic political institutions by observing teachers and administrators resolving disputes through negotiations. A third benefit claimed for collective bargaining is that it will improve teacher morale. Today teachers are blamed for educational system failures over which they have little or no control. Collective bargaining promises school professionals greater influence over what is taught in classrooms, and this greater control could foster a renewed commitment to teaching. Finally, supporters of collective bargaining believe it, more than anything else, will force school districts to develop more effective management.

ORGANIZATIONAL SOURCES OF SCHOOL FISCAL PROBLEMS

Even to a detached observer, public education in the United States exhibits many signs of strain. Enrollments are growing in many states, yet governments are hav-

[27]Sylvester Petro, "Compulsory Public-Sector Bargaining: The Dissolution of Social Order," *Freeman*, 25, no. 8 (August 1975), 494.

[28]These and related concerns are discussed in Harry H. Wellington and Ralph K. Winter, Jr., *The Unions and the Cities* (Washington, D.C.: Brookings Institution, 1971).

ing difficulty raising added funds and building more facilities. Parents who perceive that their children are being discriminated against or inadequately educated continue to ask the courts to overturn state finance systems and state education laws. Educational problems seem particularly acute in urban school districts where educational achievement is low and household poverty is high. Teacher pay still has not recovered its early 1970s purchasing power and strikes plague many communities, creating new frustrations for working parents whose children are not in school.

What are the reasons for these apparent problems? Why has a long history of public education success been altered? Some argue that those in control made mistakes that could have been avoided. They point to incompetent public officials, administrators, or union leaders as the source of the problems. Educators often encourage this view by saying that schooling is a matter of people working with people, that if you have good (and better-paid) people, then the education system will be good.

Another view is that public education's difficulties can be attributed to the institutional structures through which schooling is provided, a problem that can be solved only by reforming educational institutions. The second explanation is more plausible than the first. One can find little evidence that educators are less competent or more foolish now than in the past, or that they are less concerned about their clients' welfare than professionals providing other public services. Even in the unlikely event that this were true, it would be difficult to guarantee that future educators would be more competent or wise. On the other hand, there are institutional reforms that can alleviate many of the strains facing public education.

Inadequate Local Taxes

It is frequently alleged that there is a serious fiscal imbalance in public education.[29] Local school costs cannot adequately be met with local property taxes. Yet the most productive sources of revenue, personal and corporate income taxes, are controlled by state and federal governments and are generally unavailable locally to meet rising school costs.

The fiscal imbalance argument is raised in support of perennial proposals to increase the state and federal share of local educational costs.[30] The fiscal imbalance between state and national governments was used in the 1960s as a justification for passage of federal revenue sharing.[31] It also underlay the proposal by former presi-

---

[29] An excellent analysis of the "fiscal imbalance" issue is contained in Wallace E. Oates, "Automatic Increases in Tax Revenues: The Effect on the Size of the Public Budget," in *Financing the New Federalism*, ed. Wallace E. Oates (Baltimore: Johns Hopkins, 1975), pp. 139–60. See also James M. Buchanan, *Public Finance in Democratic Process* (Chapel Hill: University of North Carolina Press, 1976), p. 65; and Michael Reagan, *The New Federalism* (New York: Oxford University Press, 1972), p. 38.

[30] The Advisory Commission on Intergovernmental Relations ranked state fiscal systems by the proportion of local school costs borne by the state. See John Shannon and Michael Bell, *A Preliminary 'Report Card' on the 50 State–Local Fiscal Systems* (Washington, D.C.: Advisory Commission on Intergovernmental Relations, 1975).

[31] This program was permitted to lapse in the 1980s when the federal budget deficit grew large.

dent Nixon for a national value-added tax to replace local property tax support of public schools.[32] In the 1970s the National Education Association proposed that the federal government fund one-third of the costs of public schools for the same reason.

Underlying the notion of fiscal imbalance in public schooling is the assertion that the demand for public schooling increases faster than the supply of funds from local property taxes. The typical argument is that education costs rise relatively rapidly, both because public education is labor-intensive[33] and because people demand more of it as their incomes rise. Consequently, school budgets rise more rapidly than inflation and more rapidly than growth of personal income. Property taxes, on the other hand, tend to increase more slowly. At a given tax rate, receipts from property taxes are proportional to increases in assessed property values. Since assessed valuation in many communities increases more slowly than educational expenditures, school tax rates have generally increased, and public resistance has been strong. The result is that the demand for increased school budgets grows more rapidly than property tax receipts. According to those who advance the fiscal imbalance argument, local school districts must turn to the more responsive sources of revenues at the state and national levels to recoup the deficit.

From the point of view of the rational taxpayer, this argument is illogical. It presumes that local taxpayers are willing to increase public school expenditures if they can be funded with more responsive state and national revenue sources, but will not support an expanded public school program if it requires raising local property tax rates. This suggests that people care more about their local tax rates than their total tax bill. It appears more reasonable to assume that it is the total tax price of public service that determines the levels of service demanded.[34] If it is the tax price of public education that determines demand, then it might be argued that the time and costs involved in enacting new tax rates tend to slow government responses to the increasing demand for public schooling. If this were so, the supply of public schooling would be too small.

On the other hand, taxpayers' apparent willingness to approve increased state and federal support for education, but to oppose higher property tax rates, may result from their being unaware of the real tax costs of greater state and national support. The *fiscal illusion*—that they are getting something for nothing—may result from ignorance[35] or from the belief that someone else pays the costs of better services when state and national taxes are used.[36] Fiscal illusion tends to produce an oversupply of public schooling.

[32] A value-added tax is like a sales tax that producers and distributors pay on the value added at each stage of production.

[33] Productivity gains in the private sector result largely from technological improvements. In education there are few inventions. Consequently, if teachers' salaries are to keep pace with private sector salaries, education unit costs have to rise faster than general prices.

[34] The tax price is the unit cost of a public service that is paid for from taxes.

[35] See Anthony Downs, "An Economic Theory of Political Action in a Democracy," *Journal of Political Economy*, 65 (April 1957), 135-50.

[36] Mancur Olson, Jr., *The Logic of Collective Action* (Cambridge, Mass.: Harvard University Press, 1965).

It is entirely plausible that resistance to local property tax increases may be a direct result of individual decisions that enough is being spent on public education. It is to be expected that as school costs rise, a point is reached at which a majority of voters is no longer willing to vote additional taxes for schools.[37] Voters may, of course, decide not to purchase additional education, for a number of reasons—a stronger desire for other public services, dissatisfaction with school services or government services in general, or changing economic conditions. Nonetheless, if school districts want to increase budgets, they must either increase the quality of the services they provide (thus increasing the tax price people are willing to pay for them) or reduce the tax price through internal efficiencies.

Interstate and Intrastate Differences in Fiscal Capacity

A second source of strain in the United States school finance system is the disparity in fiscal capacity among school districts within states, and the wide differences among states in per-capita income and property wealth. As noted in our discussion of the *Serrano* case, it is not uncommon for one district in a state to tax itself at twice the rate of another and produce less than half the revenues of its wealthier counterpart. Similarly, residents of Mississippi would have to tax their personal income at twice the rate of citizens in New York or Connecticut to have the same level of public service.

On equity grounds, most states attempt to equalize educational opportunities by providing more state money to poor districts than to wealthy ones. Chapter I of the 1981 Educational Consolidation and Improvement Act (ECIA) also distributes federal dollars to states in proportion to the numbers of students from low-income families. Despite these efforts, large variations in the fiscal capacities of districts and states remain.

District wealth and income disparity, besides being inequitable, creates problems of allocative efficiency.[38] From an efficiency point of view, underinvestment in education in some areas hurts the entire economy. When families migrate to wealthier districts so that their children can receive a better education, inefficiencies are compounded because the right to live wherever one chooses may motivate both high-wealth and low-wealth districts to reduce educational spending. When low-income families or families from low-income communities move to high-wealth school districts, the amount spent per child in the high-wealth district declines.

[37]Michael Boss, "Revolution or Choice? The Political Economy of School Referenda" (paper for the Department of Political Science, Indiana University, 1977).

[38]There is a lively debate among experts on the relationship between amount spent on education and quality of education received. For an analysis of the debate, see John E. McDermott and Stephen P. Klein, "The Cost–Quality Debate in School Finance Litigation: Do Dollars Make a Difference?" *Law and Contemporary Problems*, 38, no. 3 (Winter–Spring 1974), 415–35; David J. Armor, "School and Family Effects on Black and White Achievement: A Re-examination of the USOE Data," *Sociology of Education*, no. 2/3 (April/July 1983), 168–229; Eric A. Hanushek, "Conceptual and Empirical Issues in the Estimation of Education Productivity Functions, " *Journal of Human Resources*, 14, no. 3 (Summer 1979), 351–88; Richard J. Murnane, "Interpreting the Evidence on School Effectiveness," *Teachers College Record*, 83, no. 1 (Fall 1981), 19–36; and L. Stedman, "A New Look at the Effective Schools Literature," *Urban Education*, 20, no. 3 (October 1985), 295–326.

Given a normal demand curve for education, as quality declines, the demand for education at a given tax price also declines.

The possibility of migration also creates an incentive for low-wealth districts to underinvest in education because they assume educational services are available in higher-wealth districts at lower tax prices. Optimal levels of educational services would be more likely if states and the federal government redistributed resources to make the amounts of education available in school districts independent of district or state wealth.

The High Cost of Urban Education

A third source of strain is the deterioration of many urban school systems. Urban schools' problems are of long standing and are well documented—transient enrollments, poor academic performance, high levels of truancy, violence, and so on[39] Some of the problems are financial. It costs more to provide similar educational services in urban school districts than in suburban and rural settings. The higher costs of urban land, buildings, teachers, and maintenance mean less education per dollar spent. Second, cities have relatively large numbers of schoolchildren requiring expensive special education programs. These include low-income, English-deficient, and handicapped students. Also, a larger proportion of urban students opt for vocational training programs, which are more expensive than the traditional college preparatory programs. Third, competition for taxpayers' dollars is greater in the cities than elsewhere, making it more difficult to raise funds for schools.[40]

City schools also suffer from political or jurisdictional problems. Power in many state legislatures is split between urban, rural, and suburban legislators. The result can be policies unsympathetic to urban problems. Furthermore, states are reluctant to allow the federal government to assist cities without going through state agencies although, increasingly, federal programs contain "pass-through" provisions permitting direct assistance to cities.

RESTRUCTURING PUBLIC EDUCATION

Many suggestions have been advanced for adjusting the size of educational organizations to make them more efficient, equitable, and responsive. Proposals range from consolidating school districts to making individual schools the basic unit of school management. The problem is that research is inconclusive as to the optimum size of school districts. There is no consistent relationship between school

[39]James B. Conant, *Slums and Suburbs* (New York: McGraw-Hill, 1961); Walter I. Garms, James W. Guthrie, and Lawrence C. Pierce, *School Finance: The Economics and Politics of Public Education* (Englewood Cliffs, N.J.: Prentice-Hall, 1978), chap. 15; and Michael W. Kirst and James W. Guthrie, *Conditions of Children in California* (Berkeley: Policy Analysis for California Education, University of California, 1988).

[40]Factors in the higher costs of urban education are analyzed in depth in the Potomac Institute's *Equity for Cities in School Finance Reform* (Washington, D.C., 1973); and Betsy Levin, Thomas Muller, and Corason Sandoval, *The High Cost of Education in Cities* (Washington, D.C.: Urban Institute, 1973).

district size and costs of services provided or performance of students. For example, whereas large schools may have a per-pupil advantage in utility costs, their transportation costs may be greater per pupil than those of small schools or districts. Educationally, large schools and districts can usually offer more advanced sections of mathematics, science, and foreign language but are also more likely to have alienated and disinterested students who cannot adjust in larger organizations.[41] Bigger is not necessarily better, either financially or educationally. The remainder of this chapter attempts to shed some light on the issue of the optimal size of educational units.

The Size of Educational Units

The appropriate size of political units is one of the most frequently recurring issues in the theory of democracy. Political scientist Robert Dahl has written that determination of the optimal size for democratic political units involves an inescapable dilemma. The larger government is, the more it can regulate those environmental features its citizens want regulated. The larger the unit, however, and the more complicated its machinery, the less its citizens can participate in its decisions. Conversely, the smaller the unit, the greater the chance for citizen participation, but the more limited its range of environmental control. In centralized government, citizen participation is minimal; in decentralized government, it runs the risk of being trivial.[42]

Economists emphasize trade-offs in determining optimum unit size. A more centralized organization of public education, or any public service for that matter, reduces the disparity among the services provided by individual units. An egalitarian distribution of income requires a transfer from the wealthy to the poor. In a highly decentralized society, it is difficult to redistribute income. If a single small unit of government adopts a redistributive set of taxes and subsidies, it creates incentives for the rich to move out and for the poor to migrate into the community. Even if all members of a society believed in a more equal distribution of income, people would still tend to pass the burden of eliminating inequality to others.[43] Additionally, no individual community would likely undertake such a utopian goal, simply because of the migration problem. If communities begin with unequal resources, only centralized action can significantly reduce the inequalities.

Whereas pursuit of economic equality favors centralized government, pursuit of resource efficiency generally favors decentralized government.[44] The task of re-

---

[41]See James W. Guthrie, "Organizational Scale and School Success," *Educational Evaluation and Policy Analysis,* 1, no. 1 (Winter 1979), 1–23.

[42]Robert A. Dahl, "The City in the Future of Democracy," *American Political Science Review,* 61 (December 1967), 953–70.

[43]James M. Buchanan, *The Demand and Supply of Public Goods* (Chicago: Rand McNally, 1968), chap. 5.

[44]An exception is the case of a pure public good—one that is consumed jointly and in the same quantity by all consumers. For example, national defense or clean air benefits everyone whether a particular individual pays for it or not. Consequently, individuals will understate their preference for a public good, believing that someone else will provide it for them. Left to individuals or local government, in other words, pure public goods would be underproduced. See

source efficiency—allocative efficiency—is to match resource use with consumer preferences. Centralized government provides uniform service for its members. This may be efficient if the preferences of the individuals being served are similar. If they are different, however, centralized provision may be inefficient. Decentralized units of government, on the other hand, can provide a variety of service levels to match the particular preferences of a community. Decentralized government thus offers the prospect of increased efficiency through a greater range of services more nearly satisfying differing tastes of consumers—even though there may be diseconomies of small scale.[45]

Decentralized government may also increase efficiency by encouraging greater experimentation and innovation in the production of goods. Local control of schools is often supported on grounds that communities are good laboratories for new educational techniques. If a program fails, only a relatively few children are disadvantaged. If it succeeds, it can be copied by other school districts. Related to this argument is the claim that alternatives increase with the number of units producing a public service. When each community offers its own program of services, citizens have an opportunity to choose combinations of desired services by deciding where to live. One community may offer excellent schools and parks, another relatively more services for senior citizens. As this argument would have it, citizens are better off deciding their own priorities rather than acquiescing in a uniform level of services provided by a centralized government.[46]

Technical efficiency may also be enhanced in decentralized units because expenditure decisions are more likely to be made by the same people paying for them. A school district that must pay for construction of a new school is more likely to consider carefully the costs and benefits of a new building than it would if construction money were provided by state or federal governments.

Even assuming that the goal of equality can be pursued through transfer of funds from richer to poorer units of government, and that some degree of decentralization facilitates resource efficiency, one must still determine the optimal size of a consumer group. In determining the optimal size of a group that is to receive educational services, whether it be a classroom, school, or school district, we need to consider several factors.[47] First, by organizing in groups, people can obtain goods more cheaply. Unit costs are lower, all other things being equal, when there are twenty students per teacher rather than an individual tutor for each child. Similarly, per-pupil costs are likely to be less in a district with 1000 students than in a district

Paul Samuelson, "The Pure Theory of Public Expenditures," *Review of Economics and Statistics,* 36 (November 1954), 387–89; and John Head, "Public Goods and Public Policy," *Public Finance,* 17, no. 3 (1962), 197–219.

[45] Economies of scale are the declining per-unit costs of production arising from increases in the number of units produced.

[46] The option to "vote with one's feet" is known as the Tiebout hypothesis. See Charles M. Tiebout, "A Pure Theory of Local Expenditures," *Journal of Political Economy,* 64 (October 1956), 416–24.

[47] The following analysis draws primarily from Wallace E. Oates, *Fiscal Federalism* (New York: Harcourt Brace Jovanovich, Inc., 1972), chap. 2.

FIGURE 4.1 Determining Optimal Unit Size

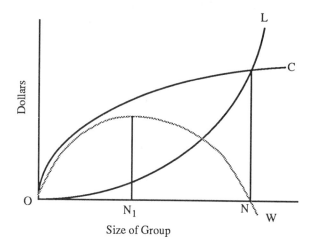

Size of Group

Source: Wallace E. Oates, *Fiscal Federalism* (New York: Harcourt Brace Jovanovich, Inc., 1972). p. 39.

with only 20 students. Curve *OC* in Figure 4.1 illustrates the aggregate cost savings from increasing the number of individuals who jointly consume a public good—that is, the lower-cost services resulting from joint consumption. Cost savings rise rapidly at first, as the first few members of a community join together, and then level off as the advantage of having additional people join the group is lessened. At *N*, all members of the community jointly consume the service.

There is, however, a welfare cost to joint consumption, because some members of the community have to consume other than their desired level. Such external costs increase with group size. The amount of welfare loss resulting from external costs, represented by curve *OL*, depends on the range of preferences represented in the group. If everyone prefers the same amount, the loss will be small and *OL* will lie closer to the horizontal axis. If there are wide differences in preferences, then the loss will be great and *OL* will rise more rapidly as group size increases. As expected, welfare loss increases as group size increases. This is because the influence of individuals on their own level of consumption diminishes as the number of people in the group increases.

Determining optimal group size for consumers of a public good, in other words, involves a trade-off between increased cost savings from joint consumption in larger groups (*OC*) and losses resulting from some individuals' consuming other than what they desire (*OL*). The curve *OW* in Figure 4.1 represents net welfare from joint consumption for each group size. The quantity *OW* is obtained by subtracting *OL* from *OC* and reaches a maximum at N_1, the optimal group size in the illustration. Increasing group size beyond that point will reduce net welfare from joint consumption.

This analysis, which has focused on the trade-offs between cost savings and welfare gains or losses from collective consumption, overlooks several other factors likely to affect optimum unit size. For example, the analysis ignores the possibility that the quality of service in one area may affect the welfare of individuals in another area. With migration, the quality of education in one district spills over into other districts. The smaller the units, the more difficult it is to internalize these externalities. Conversely, the larger the group, the greater the increase in individual welfare resulting from internalizing external costs and benefits. Since gains from internalizing externalities will increase with group size, curve OW in Figure 4.1 would move upward and N_1 would move to the right. The presence of interjurisdictional externalities increases the size of the optimal group for joint consumption.[48]

Studies of Cost–Size Relationships in Public Education

Many studies have been conducted on the cost–size relationship among different sizes of school districts, but most are poorly conceived and inconclusive. In general, they indicate that there are significant economies of scale up to approximately 1500 to 2000 students in a district and significant diseconomies of scale when districts comprise more than 20,000 students.[49] G. Alan Hickrod, in a study of the cost–size relationship among school districts in Illinois in 1974, found that the greatest efficiency was achieved in districts with approximately 2400 ADA.[50] However, fixation on any particular number should be avoided, since many factors, including the definition of the optimum size of school districts being used, affect the analysis. The most important considerations are what to do with unusually small schools and school districts, and what to do with extremely large ones. Per-pupil costs are generally higher in small school districts than in average-size districts. Some economists believe that small-district consolidation increases efficiency.[51] Others contend that the disadvantages of bigness more than outweigh the high costs of smallness and argue against further consolidation of small districts. Efficiencies probably can be gained by consolidating small districts, particularly those with fewer than 1000 students. The greatest efficiency gains, however, are likely to come from decentralizing those districts with more than 20,000 students.

[48]The problem of interjurisdictional externalities is just one complicating factor. The costs of collective decision making and congestion should also be considered when analyzing the most efficient size of an organizational unit.

[49]For bibliographies on school district size, see Robert E. Stephens and John Spiess, "What Does Research Say about the Size of a Local School District?" *Journal of State School System Development*, 1 (Fall 1967), 183–99; and Educational Research Service, *Size of Schools and School Districts*, ERS Information Aid No. 8 (Washington, D.C., 1971).

[50]G. Alan Hickrod, "Cost–Size Relationship among School Districts in Illinois, 1974" (Research Paper 2-HCYH-75, Center for the Study of Educational Finance, Illinois State University, 1975).

[51]Elchanan Cohn, *Economics of State Aid to Education* (Lexington, Mass.: Heath, 1974).

SUMMARY

Public education financing is affected directly by the organization of public schools. This chapter examines relationships between school organization and finance, emphasizing the federal structure in which educational choices are made and educational services provided.

Public primary and secondary education in the United States served an estimated 41 million children and consumed approximately $170 billion in 1988. Although states are becoming increasingly involved in school finance, collective bargaining, and school curricula, both provision and financing of public schools is still predominantly local. The federal role is a minor one, although important historically and symbolically in improving the educational opportunities of disadvantaged, handicapped, and non-English-speaking students, and significant recently for efforts to facilitate efficiency.

Public school organization nationwide is characterized by lack of planning, diversity, loosely coupled management, and increased strength of teacher unions. This seemingly ad hoc manner of operation creates numerous financial problems for schools. For example, local school districts constantly plead to state and federal governments to assume a larger share of their costs. Many educators believe that relief from heavy local property taxes for schools will reduce resistance to larger school budgets. The argument is based on the assumption that taxpayers and voters are less sensitive to higher state and federal taxes than to local property taxes. Another problem arises from the wide variations in property wealth among school districts. This creates numerous inefficiencies and inequities in public school finance. Finally, the plight of America's urban centers and urban school systems is intensified by state finance systems that do not adequately address the unusual educational problems of city schools.

The chapter concludes with an analysis of school district size. For most of the twentieth century, reformers asserted that consolidation of small schools and small districts would make schools more efficient and more equal. We challenge this conventional assertion, arguing that the costs of much consolidation outweigh its potential benefits. The goals of efficiency and equity may be better achieved by providing greater choice in and community influence over public schooling.

chapter five

PAYING FOR
PUBLIC EDUCATION

The fiscal side of school finance can be divided into three stages: generating, distributing, and spending money. This chapter is concerned with the generation of money for public education, and with the taxes primarily used to do so.

Education is supported chiefly by broad-based taxes (taxes based on a widespread condition), but other methods of financing are conceivable. User charges (known as tuition when applied to education) come to mind. If education is primarily a personal investment or a consumption good—that is, if it does not have a preponderance of favorable social consequences—it would appear that students or their families should bear the major burden. If, however, schooling benefits accrue mainly to society rather than to the individual, society should pay the cost through taxes. At present, public elementary and secondary schools of all states are tuition-free, supported primarily by local and state taxation. Thus, this chapter concentrates on taxation.

A number of states have dedicated a particular tax to education. However, these narrowly based tax sources have been found insufficient to meet the revenue needs of this largest single object of state and local governmental expenditure. As a result, educational finance has rested primarily on broad-based taxes such as income, sales, and property taxes. This chapter first defines some general characteristics of taxes and then describes how they apply to each of the three most general taxes. We then discuss the tax limitation movement and conclude with some alternatives to taxation for education.

CHARACTERISTICS OF TAXES

It is important to understand taxes' *bases; equity; yield; administration* and *compliance costs;* and *economic, social,* and *political effects.*

Basis

There are four bases, or criteria, for levying a tax: wealth, income, consumption, and privilege. These all involve money—the first three directly, the fourth indirectly.

A tax on *wealth* is based on the ownership of property. The most common example is the property tax, the amount of which is based on the amount of property owned. Another example is the federal estate tax, based on the size of a deceased person's estate. Note that the size of the tax bears no relation to the income generated by the property owned, but is based only on the value of the property.

A tax on *income* is based on the taxable income of individuals (or corporations). Taxable income is income after allowable expenses and deductions. One of the virtues of an income tax is that the amount of the tax is related to the income used to pay it.

A tax on *consumption* is usually called a sales tax, particularly if it applies to all or most sales. If it applies only to the purchase of a particular class of items (such as a tax on theater admissions), it is called an *excise tax.* Import duties on particular goods are also excise taxes. Many states have enacted *lottery* statutes. A lottery can best be viewed as a product sold by the state and an excise tax on that product. (The proportion of lottery revenues paid in prizes is the product, and the difference between total revenues and prizes plus operating expenses is the tax, which is conveyed to the state.)[1]

A tax on *privilege* is a tax levied on the right to engage in some sort of conduct regulated by government. It usually takes the form of *license fees.* These fees may be related directly to commercial gain, as in the case of a retail store license, a medical license, or a license to operate a taxicab. On the other hand, they may have no direct relation to money, as with a dog license, a driver's license, or a hunting license. The number of licenses required by state and local governments is large, and the money collected in fees is substantial.[2] Imposition of license fees is usually defended as being a regulatory function of government rather than a tax, with the li-

---

[1] Twenty-two states had lotteries as of 1985. In all of them, lottery revenue constituted less than 5 percent of total state revenue. Advisory Commission on Intergovernmental Relations, *Significant Features of Fiscal Federalism, 1985 Edition* (Washington, D.C.: Government Printing Office, 1986), p. 126, Table 75.

[2] Data on the amount of money raised by license fees are not available. However, in 1984 auto and driver's license fees raised $7 billion nationwide, about 3.5 percent of total state revenues. Advisory Commission on Intergovernmental Relations, *Significant Features of Fiscal Federalism, 1984 Edition* (Washington, D.C.: Government Printing Office, 1985), pp. 46-47, Table 31.

cense fees paying the costs of regulation. This is only partially true: fees are often much greater than costs. Governments also sell exclusive or semi-exclusive rights to engage in certain commercial activities within city or regional boundaries. These are called *franchises* or *concessions*. An example is a franchise granted to a cable television company.

Governments raise money by other methods that cannot strictly be called taxation. Higher levels of government transmit *intergovernmental aid* to lower levels. For example, both the federal government and state governments grant financial aid to local school districts. Governments charge *fees for service*. For example, a municipal government may operate an electric utility and sell power. Since a fee for service is a charge for a specific product, it cannot strictly be called taxation.

Equity

Since taxes are a burden imposed on all by the will of a majority, they should treat all in an equitable manner. This may conflict with other considerations, as indicated later, but it is a worthwhile goal. What should determine whether a tax is equitable?

First, the tax should treat equals equitably. For example, two individuals with the same amount of taxable income should pay the same amount of income tax. Two persons who own property of equal value in the same neighborhood should pay the same amount of property tax. This is a relatively simple criterion, and easy to judge. Most taxes are relatively equitable on this criterion; exceptions regarding the property tax will be discussed later.

Unfortunately for those establishing tax criteria, not all persons are equal. It is thus necessary to establish rules for tax treatment of unequals—a more difficult task. The most obvious criterion is that persons should pay in proportion to benefits received, or in proportion to their contribution to the cost of whatever is supported by the tax. For example, street improvements may be charged to adjoining property owners based on the footage of property fronting on the street. Charges are not necessarily in proportion to benefits received, for in most cases there is no way of measuring the benefit an improved street provides. A prime example of a tax based on the *benefit principle* is the National Highway Trust Fund, supported by gasoline taxes. The money in the fund is used to construct and maintain federally aided highways, and the amount contributed by each person, based as it is on a fixed amount per gallon of gas, is related to an individual's use of those highways.

Taxes based on benefit received or on contribution to cost seem so eminently reasonable that there is a temptation to endorse this principle as a basis for all taxation. Unfortunately, it is not that simple. It is often difficult to assess either benefits received or contribution to cost. Should police costs be charged to the person saved from robbery or murder, on the basis of benefit received, or to the felon, on the basis of contribution to the cost of the department? Or are there benefits to an average citizen from safer streets and homes that cannot be allocated on any strict accounting basis? There is general agreement that police expenses cannot be allocated on a benefit or cost basis.

What about national defense costs? There is a different problem here. No individual operating only out of logical self-interest would pay taxes for a pure public good such as national defense, because there is no easy way for governments to defend citizens who pay for national defense without also defending those who do not pay. This is known as the *free-rider* problem. In addition, there is no rational way of calculating either individual benefits from or costs of national defense. Allocation of taxes on this basis is not feasible. Rather, the total budget is decided on a collective basis through congressional action, and resources are generated through taxes based on criteria other than benefits received.

Welfare costs present yet a third problem. Here, individual benefits are clear— welfare payments to persons. However, the folly of charging individuals a tax equal to the amount of welfare benefits received is obvious. Welfare has income redistribution as its principal goal. Taxation based on benefit received would directly contradict this goal.

For these reasons, most taxes cannot be allocated on the basis of benefit received or contribution to cost. An alternative equity criterion must be found. That criterion is the *ability-to-pay principle*, discussed next.

PROGRESSIVE AND REGRESSIVE TAXES

Regardless of the basis for levying a tax (wealth, income, expenditure, or privilege), taxes are paid mostly out of income. In judging the equity of a tax by whether it is consistent with the principle of ability to pay, one must compare the amount of tax paid with income. Suppose it is found that, for a given tax, people with incomes of $10,000 pay an average of $100 in tax, and people with incomes of $20,000 pay an average of $200 in tax. Each income group is therefore paying an average of 1 percent of its income in tax. This is said to be a *proportional tax*. Whether such a tax is a property tax, a sales tax, or an income tax, the comparison is the amount of tax paid with the *income* of the payer of the tax. A proportional tax would, on the surface, appear to meet the ability-to-pay standard, for each person pays the same percentage of his or her income in tax. Next, suppose that those with $10,000 in income continue to pay $100 in tax but those with $20,000 pay $150. Now the lower-income group is paying 1 percent of its income, but the higher-income group is paying only three-quarters of 1 percent. Note particularly that although the higher-income group is paying more dollars, it is paying a smaller percentage of its income than the lower-income group. A tax with this characteristic is called a *regressive tax* (see Figure 5.1).

Finally, suppose that the $10,000 group continues to pay $100 but the $20,000 group pays $400. Those with higher incomes are paying 2 percent of their income, those with lower incomes only 1 percent. Such a tax is called a *progressive tax* (because the rates progress toward higher percentages at higher incomes).

Which of these types of tax (regressive, proportional, or progressive) comes closest to meeting the ability-to-pay criterion? In considering this, we must realize

FIGURE 5.1 Tax Characteristics

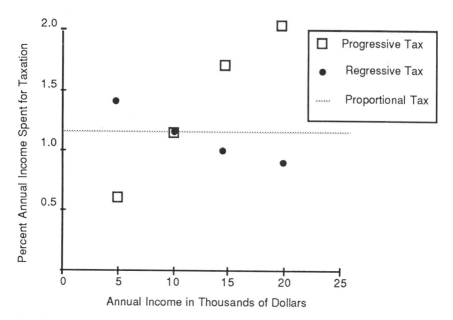

that there is a basic amount households need to maintain a minimum standard of living. Families whose incomes are at this subsistence level often spend all of their income for necessities and have nothing left to pay taxes. At the other end of the scale, extremely wealthy families find they are unable to spend all of their income on goods and services. They clearly have excess income, which could be used for investment or for paying taxes. Under these circumstances, it is evident that a regressive tax is not based on ability to pay and that actually a proportional tax is not either. A progressive tax, at least theoretically, leaves untouched the monies necessary for a minimum standard of living. However, there is no agreement on how progressive a tax must be in order to be equitable. If it is close to being proportional, it is probably unfair to poor people; if it is extremely progressive, it is probably inequitable to wealthy people. The broad band of disagreement between these extremes results partly from lack of consensus on how much necessities cost.

Another reason for belief in the equity of progressive taxation is an unwritten tenet in the American ethos that government should intervene to reduce extreme income inequalities. One way to do this is to tax a greater percentage of the income of the wealthy than that of the poor. On the other hand, many political conservatives would point out that it is the rich who invest in businesses and thus fuel the free enterprise system. Progressive taxes reduce the money available for such investment, decreasing general prosperity and incidentally the future income available to be taxed. An alternative way to redistribute income, used extensively in the U.S., is to make payments to low-income people through programs such as Aid to Families with Dependent Children (AFDC) and Medicaid. These *transfer payments* are discussed next in connection with incidence of taxation.

Impact and incidence. The discussion thus far has implied that the burden of taxation rests on those who physically pay the tax. This is not necessarily true. Business firms of all kinds are taxed, but ultimately, of course, individuals bear the burden of taxation. To discover whether a tax is progressive or regressive, one must determine upon whose shoulders falls the ultimate burden of the tax. The actual taxpayer—individual or firm—is said to bear the *impact* of the tax. Those individuals who ultimately experience the burden of a tax are said to bear its *incidence.*

Discovering the tax impact is a trivial matter, for it is easy to record who actually pays. Discovering the tax incidence is much more difficult. There are no firm guidelines, and economists can only make reasonable assumptions. For example, suppose a federal excise tax is levied on cigarette production. On which individuals does the burden of this tax ultimately fall? There are three main possibilities. The tax may be shifted forward to cigarette purchasers in the form of higher prices. It may be shifted backward to the cigarette manufacturer's employees in the form of lower wages. Or it may not be shifted, but remain with the owners of the manufacturing corporation (its stockholders) in the form of lower dividends. In economists' language, the burden may be borne by *consumption, labor,* or *capital.* What will happen in individual cases depends upon specific circumstances. *Not shifting the tax* is a last resort of a corporation, to be used when other strategies fail. To some extent manufacturers may be able to shift a tax backward (probably not by reducing wages but by reducing the work force, or by not granting a large increase the next time wages are negotiated). This may be possible where a tobacco company is the principal employer in a community, for workers are not apt to leave a company unless the difference between what they can earn there and what they can earn elsewhere is sufficient to offset the large economic and psychic costs of moving.

The chances of shifting a tax forward to the consumer are good. The demand for cigarettes is relatively *inelastic:* regardless of price, smokers continue to purchase approximately the same amount. As a result, manufacturers will promptly increase their prices by an amount sufficient to cover the tax. They know this will have little effect on the number of cigarettes sold. It would be different in the case of a tax on peas, for example, for the demand for peas is highly *elastic:* faced with a higher pea price, many people would shift to beans or carrots. Under these circumstances producers would be able to shift little of the tax forward, and the tax might ultimately be borne by owners in the form of a lower return on their investment.

Whether a tax is shifted backward or forward depends upon individual circumstances. However, the concern here is not with individual cases of shifting taxes. About the overall effect of tax incidence—whether it is progressive or regressive— there is no general agreement among economists. Assumptions must be made about what will happen on the average, and economists differ on which are the most reasonable assumptions. There is, however, a modest amount of agreement, which will be reported in our discussion of specific taxes later in this chapter.

There have been attempts to discover the progressiveness or regressiveness of the United States tax system as a whole. One example is a study by Joseph Pechman.[3] He calculates that for 1980, the sum of all federal, state, and local taxes in the United States had an incidence roughly proportional throughout a wide range of incomes, with most people paying approximately 25 percent of their incomes in taxes. Actual distribution of tax burdens depends upon one's assumptions about the extent to which certain taxes are borne by capital, labor, or consumption. Pechman computes tables based on a variety of assumptions, but there is surprisingly little difference among them. The table incorporating the most progressive assumptions indicates that the lowest income decile pays about 33 percent of its income in taxes. However, the second decile pays about 23 percent and the highest decile about 29 percent, with everyone else in between. The most regressive set of assumptions suggests that the lowest decile pays about 51 percent of its income in taxes, the second decile about 28 percent, the top decile about 26 percent, and everyone else between 25 percent and 27 percent. Regardless of assumptions, it does not appear that the wealthy manage to escape taxation. The top 1 percent of the population in income pays about 28 percent of its income in taxes under the most progressive assumptions, and about 22 percent under the most regressive assumptions.

As pointed out, it is generally impossible to assign benefits of expenditures from tax monies to individuals. The exception is cash payments to people for welfare, unemployment compensation, Social Security, and so forth. Economists call these *transfer payments* for they represent neither income nor expenditure in the economy as a whole. They simply involve taking money out of the pockets of some individuals and putting it into the pockets of others without the provision of goods or services. Pechman finds, not surprisingly, that the lowest-income groups receive more in transfer payments than they pay in taxes. Analyzing the effect of transfer payments across all income levels, he finds that the U.S. tax system is progressive in the total range of incomes if one uses the most progressive assumptions. If one uses the least progressive assumptions, the tax system is progressive for the lowest 70 percent of incomes, roughly proportional for the next 29 percent of incomes, and slightly regressive for the top 1 percent of incomes (see Table 5.1). Based on these data, the United States tax system as a whole may be relatively equitable.

This is not to imply, however, that the system is equally equitable in every state or community, or among particular individuals. Tax laws in each state are different, some states relying heavily on income taxes, others on sales taxes. The burden of the property tax varies substantially from one community to the next. Particular individuals must pay based on their liability for each tax, which may bear little relationship to their income. One can speculate on progressivity and regressivity only in overall terms, not in individual ones.

---

[3]Joseph A. Pechman, *Who Paid the Taxes, 1966–85* (Washington, D.C.: Brookings Institution, 1985), p. 48, Table 4-4. The most progressive assumption is Pechman's Variant 1c; the most regressive is his Variant 3b.

TABLE 5.1 Transfers and Taxes as a Percentage of Adjusted Family Income Less Transfers under Two Incidence Assumptions

INCOME DECILE[a]	MOST PROGRESSIVE ASSUMPTION			MOST REGRESSIVE ASSUMPTION		
	TAXES	TRANSFERS	TAXES LESS TRANSFERS	TAXES	TRANSFERS	TAXES LESS TRANSFERS
Lowest[b]	32.8%	98.3%	− 65.5%	50.8%	101.3%	− 50.5%
Second	22.6	58.3	− 35.7	28.3	54.7	− 26.4
Third	23.8	34.7	− 10.9	28.3	34.8	− 6.5
Fourth	25.1	23.7	1.4	28.4	23.7	4.7
Fifth	25.9	15.3	10.6	28.9	15.6	13.3
Sixth	26.1	10.9	15.2	28.6	10.5	18.1
Seventh	26.4	7.6	18.8	28.9	7.8	21.1
Eighth	27.4	5.7	21.7	29.8	5.5	24.3
Ninth	28.3	4.3	24.0	29.9	4.4	25.5
Highest	28.6	2.6	26.0	26.3	2.6	23.7
Top 5%	28.5	2.1	26.4	25.0	2.1	22.9
Top 1%	27.9	1.1	26.8	22.0	1.1	20.9
All classes	27.5	10.0	17.5	28.5	9.9	18.6

[a]Population arrayed in order of income.
[b]Includes only sixth to tenth percentiles.
Source: Joseph A. Pechman, *Who Paid the Taxes, 1966–85* (Washington, D.C.: Brookings Institution, 1985), p. 53.

Pechman also discusses the extent to which the U.S. tax system is changing in incidence over time. Table 5.2 presents his data for 1966, 1970, 1975, 1980, and 1985 (1980 and 1985 data are estimated). Under the most progressive assumptions, total taxes during the two decades have become less progressive for the bottom two deciles and the top decile, while remaining proportional over the remainder of the distribution. Under the most regressive assumptions, total taxes have remained proportional over all of the distribution except the top 5 percent, where they were more regressive in 1985 than in 1966. All in all, the picture for the total U.S. tax system is one of remarkable stability.

Yield

The yield of a tax is its ability to generate revenue. In evaluating a tax it is useful to compare its yield with those of alternative taxes and with the cost of administering the tax. Some taxes are incapable of large yields. For example, the dollar volume of paper clip sales is so small that even a 100 percent excise tax on pa-

TABLE 5.2 Effective Percentage Rates of Total Federal, State, and Local Taxes in Various Years

INCOME DECILE[a]	MOST PROGRESSIVE ASSUMPTION					MOST REGRESSIVE ASSUMPTION				
	1966	1970	1975	1980	1985	1966	1970	1975	1980	1985
Lowest[b]	16.8%	18.8%	21.2%	20.6%	21.9%	27.5%	25.9%	29.6%	28.9%	28.2%
Second	18.9	19.5	19.9	20.4	21.3	24.8	24.2	24.2	25.7	25.6
Third	21.7	20.8	20.5	20.6	21.4	26.0	24.1	22.2	24.6	24.6
Fourth	22.6	23.2	22.0	21.9	22.5	25.9	25.8	24.6	25.2	25.2
Fifth	22.8	24.0	23.0	22.8	23.1	25.8	26.4	25.3	25.8	25.3
Sixth	22.7	24.1	23.3	23.3	23.5	25.6	26.3	25.3	25.9	25.6
Seventh	22.7	24.3	23.6	23.6	23.7	25.5	26.2	25.5	26.0	25.4
Eighth	23.1	24.6	24.4	25.0	24.6	25.5	26.4	26.0	27.1	26.3
Ninth	23.3	25.0	25.3	25.7	25.1	25.1	26.1	26.3	27.2	26.1
Highest	30.1	30.7	27.1	27.3	25.3	25.9	27.8	24.2	24.9	23.3
Top 5%	32.7	33.0	27.6	27.5	25.2	26.6	28.5	23.4	24.0	22.4
Top 1%	39.6	39.0	28.5	27.5	25.5	28.9	30.9	21.9	21.7	21.2
All classes	25.2	26.1	25.0	25.3	24.5	25.9	26.7	25.5	26.3	25.3

[a]Population arrayed in order of income.
[b]Includes only sixth to tenth percentiles.
Source: Pechman, *Who Paid the Taxes,* p. 68, Table 5-2.

per clips would yield relatively little revenue. On the other hand, the federal individual income tax yields an amount sufficient to cover more than half of federal operating costs.[4] In general, the more broadly based a tax, the greater its potential yield. Thus, an excise tax is generally not capable of as great a yield as a general sales tax. The cost of administering a tax is discussed in the next section, and yield and administration costs are compared there.

ELASTICITY

Of interest in connection with a tax's yield is the rate at which yield increases if average personal income increases. A tax whose yield increases at a greater rate than that of incomes is said to be *elastic;* one whose yield increases at a slower rate is said to be *inelastic.* For example, suppose there is an excise tax on soap of one cent per bar. If individuals' average income increases, is the yield of this tax apt to increase, and if so, how rapidly? The demand for soap changes only slightly with changes in income. Even if the incomes of all people doubled, people would probably use only a little more soap. Thus, one would expect the tax yield on soap to increase less rapidly than incomes, and would thus term the tax *inelastic.*

[4]In 1984, federal individual income taxes raised $296 billion. Direct general federal expenditures, excluding Social Security and grants to states and localities, were $565 billion. Advisory Commission on Intergovernmental Relations, *Fiscal Federalism, 1985,* p. 40, Table 29, and p. 24, Table 14.

Measurement of elasticity can be formalized by defining *income elasticity of yield* as follows:

$$E = \frac{\text{percentage change in tax yield}}{\text{percentage change in personal incomes}}$$

If percentage change in tax yield is equal to percentage change in income, elasticity will equal one. An elastic tax has an elasticity greater than one; an inelastic tax has an elasticity less than one. Elasticity of yield of a tax on soap of one cent per bar might be expected to be low, perhaps in the neighborhood of 0.2.

On the other hand, the yield elasticity of the personal income tax has been in the range of 1.5, making it a remarkably elastic tax.[5] Elastic taxes are of significant advantage to governments in a period of expanding income, whether expansion is real, or caused only by inflation. The reason is that government tax income increases more rapidly than income in general, whereas government expenses (given a constant level of services) tend to increase at about the same rate as that of incomes in general. This means that in an expansion period the government has a continuing excess of income, which it may use to finance new programs. (This phenomenon began to change in 1985, with indexing of the federal income tax, but it is as yet too soon to know the extent of the change.) Ramifications of this phenomenon are discussed shortly in connection with the political effects of taxes.

In general, a progressive tax is an elastic tax and a regressive tax is an inelastic tax. This follows from the definition of a progressive tax as one that collects a higher percentage of a wealthy person's income than a less wealthy person's income. If incomes of all persons increase, a progressive tax will take a greater percentage of the incomes of all (as noted later in our discussion of the income tax). When average incomes increase, a progressive tax has an increased yield both from the increase in income (assuming no indexation) and from the increase in the percentage of that income that is taken. Thus, yield increases faster than increases in income. This connection should be clear in the case of the income tax. It is not as close and direct in the case of taxes not based directly on income, but it exists nevertheless.

Cost of Administration and Compliance

The cost of administering a tax is the cost to government of levying and collecting the tax. The cost of compliance is the cost to the taxpayer of complying with tax requirements. A federal tax of ten cents a pack on cigarette manufacture would have a relatively low cost of administration. The reason is that there are only a few cigarette manufacturers. It is easy to require these manufacturers to report monthly to the government the number of packs of cigarettes produced during the previous month. The number is multiplied by ten cents per pack, and a check for the total accompanies the report. At relatively low cost the government can audit to ensure correct reporting of the number of packs produced.

[5]Joseph Pechman, *Federal Tax Policy,* 3rd ed. (Washington, D.C.: Brookings Institution, 1977), p.12.

The cost of tax compliance varies greatly. Usually it should be low. Perhaps the tax with the lowest compliance cost is the property tax. Individual property owners receive a tax bill yearly or semiannually, and write checks for the amount. No additional effort is required. At the other extreme is the individual (or corporate) income tax. Careful sets of books must be kept, supporting evidence must be filed, accountants must often be hired to prepare tax returns, and occasionally time and expense are necessary in substantiating the return.

Economic and Social Effects

If a tax is designed only to raise money, its economic and social effects should be as neutral as possible. That is, imposition of the tax should not affect economic decisions made by people, nor should it affect social well-being. (Note that we are discussing the effects of the imposition of the tax, not the effects generated by spending that tax money for governmental purposes.) Some taxes have more substantial economic effects than others. An excise tax on a particular commodity will serve to increase its price (if the incidence of the tax is passed forward) or decrease profit (if it is passed backward). Either situation is apt to result in decreased consumption of the commodity—an economic effect.

An important alleged social effect of the property tax has been abandonment of low-rent housing in cities because property taxes (on top of other expenses) exceed rental income. This can happen when the assessed valuation of property is not changed to reflect reduced rentals obtainable on it. The result may be an increasing shortage of adequate housing for a city's poor. Of course, a tax may be levied mainly for its economic or social benefits. For example, an import tax is levied on foreign goods to protect a domestic industry. The fact is that most taxes have important social and economic effects. Federal taxation insufficient to cover federal expenditures leads to deficits and an increase in the national debt. If debt increases faster than economic expansion (as it did in the mid and late 1980s), the borrowing necessary to service that debt can result in higher interest rates. Higher interest rates, in turn, tend to discourage borrowing for expansion or capital construction. This can particularly affect an industry, such as housing, that is highly dependent upon debt financing.

Some states have higher taxes than others. New York consistently has had the highest total taxes, as a percentage of personal income, in the nation. Industries tend to move from highly taxed states. (This is, of course, only one reason industries move. Conversely, they are often held to their present location by investments in plants.)

Many of the economic effects of imposing taxes are unintended. Often, however, taxes have an intended social or economic effect. An excise tax on tobacco is intended, among other things, to discourage smoking, and an import tax on shoes is intended to protect a domestic industry. An income tax credit for installing home insulation is intended to encourage energy conservation. A problem with taxes designed for such specific effects is that they may, as a result, become less equitable. Balancing equity, yield, and desired economic and social effects is a difficult task. The social and economic effects of specific taxes are discussed in subsequent sections.

Political Effects

Taxes are at once the nemesis and the lifeblood of public officials. Without tax revenues they are unable to provide governmental programs that attract votes. However, officials' votes to raise taxes can be politically fatal. Consequently, in a period of increasing incomes, such as the one the U.S. has had for the majority of years since World War II, an elastic tax is favored by elected officials. When incomes increase, tax yield increases even faster, providing money for new programs without necessitating higher tax rates. Public officials can both have their cake and eat it. This has been generally true of the federal government's tax structure, which has had an elasticity greater than one. Many new federal programs have been undertaken in the last forty years, financed mainly by federal tax structure elasticity.

Many states have had a combination of taxes that on the whole is inelastic, forcing frequent increases of tax rates.[6] This is a no-win proposition for public officials, and it is understandable that they have been attracted to state income taxes, which are generally elastic. Forty states now have broad-based personal income taxes, compared with only thirty-three in 1960.[7]

Of course, elasticity is not a one-way road. An elasticity of greater than one implies that when income decreases, tax yield will decrease even faster. The United States economy has been blessed with more periods of expansion than of contraction, but a recession can be disastrous for a government that has based its operations on the expectation of ever-increasing tax revenues. An example is New York, where the halcyon days of the 1960s became the nightmare of the 1970s. Governmental commitments to new and extended programs had been made with the expectation that tax revenues would increase to cover needs. When recession hit, revenues were grossly insufficient. A state that had based much of its finances on borrowing against future revenues suddenly found its access to capital markets severely restricted. Some agencies and political divisions of the state were in even worse shape, with New York City seeking federal loan assurances and teetering on the brink of bankruptcy for years.

[6]For 1970, the Advisory Commission on Intergovernmental Relations listed eighteen states with tax structures of low elasticity (0.80 to 0.99) and twenty-three states with medium elasticity (1.00 to 1.19). Only 9 states had tax structures with high elasticity (above 1.20). The lowest was Ohio, with an elasticity of 0.80; the highest was Alaska, at 1.47, followed by Wisconsin, at 1.41. *Significant Features of Fiscal Federalism, 1976–77 Edition* (Washington, D.C.: Government Printing Office, 1977), Vol. II, p. 50, Table 32.

[7]In 1985, Alaska, Florida, Nevada, South Dakota, Texas, Washington, and Wyoming had no individual income tax. Connecticut, New Hampshire, and Tennessee had limited income taxes. Advisory Commission on Intergovernmental Relations, *Fiscal Federalism, 1985,* p. 78, Table 5.

COMPARISON OF TAXES

This section compares an important tax from each of the three principal bases (income, consumption, and wealth) according to the characteristics described in the previous section. Because the property tax, rightly or wrongly, is the tax most closely connected with education, it receives the most attention. Although important, the corporate income tax is not discussed separately.

Personal Income Tax

The federal personal income tax produces more revenue than any other U.S. tax. In addition, forty-three states have income taxes, and thirteen also allow local income taxes.[8] Although these state and local income taxes vary, they tend to be similar to the federal tax, and most of the remarks here will apply to them too.

The basis of the income tax, of course, is income. Since income is what people mostly use to pay taxes, this is important. The income tax is more nearly based on ability to pay than any other tax. However, does the federal income tax treat equals equally? That depends on how one defines equals. If equals are people who have the same net income, deductions, marital status, and number of dependents, then their taxes will be equal. Similarly, one can say that of two persons who differ only in amount of taxable income, the higher-income person will pay a greater percentage of his or her income in tax. The income tax is thus a progressive tax. However, each of these qualifications is important, for they mask differences among individuals that many think are used as loopholes to avoid taxation. Two individuals with the same gross income will not necessarily have the same taxable income. Some expenses, such as moving expenses, can be deducted from income. Some income is not included at all, most notably interest on municipal bonds.

Two individuals may have quite different deductions. One can increase deductions (and thereby decrease taxable income) by having large medical bills, by paying taxes (since local property taxes are deductible), by mortgaging one's house and paying interest (such interest is deductible), or by making charitable contributions.

There are, of course, many other deductions, exceptions, and adjustments to income, and all of them, at one time or another, have been referred to as loopholes. Whether they are in fact loopholes depends on one's perspective. A frequent complaint is that interest on municipal bonds is nontaxable. It is possible for a person to have an income of over a million dollars a year, all of it in interest on municipal bonds, and pay no income tax at all. Although this seems grossly inequitable from an individual point of view, it is defended as a subsidy of state and local governments by the federal government; the former can sell their bonds at a lower interest rate because the interest is nontaxable. If the decrease in interest received exactly balanced the tax that would have been paid, there would be no benefit to individuals. However, the decrease in interest received is equal to the taxes paid by the marginal purchaser. High-income taxpayers find that their reduction in income as a result of buying the bonds is substantially less than the tax they would have to pay if the

[8]Ibid., pp. 87–88, Table 58.

money were invested elsewhere. For example, suppose it were possible to purchase a corporate bond paying 8 percent interest or a municipal bond at 7 percent interest. If the individual purchasing the bond had a top (marginal) tax rate of 25 percent, one fourth of the interest on the corporate bond would be taken away. The individual would be receiving the equivalent of a 6 percent return on the corporate bond, compared with 7 percent on the nontaxable municipal bond.

Most other adjustments to income, deductions, and exemptions are also defended as being desirable on some economic or social basis, or simply on the basis of equity to the individual. There is some justification for each. The result, however, is a law so complex that it is difficult to state that it treats equals equally. It has been proposed that all of these adjustments, deductions, and exemptions be abandoned, with people simply taxed a flat percentage of their gross incomes. This proposition solves only part of the problem, by eliminating itemized deductions and complicated tax tables. However, individuals who operate a small business at home should not report gross receipts as income, for they have expenses connected with the business. But defining which expenses are legally deductible revives several of the original complications. Other examples could be drawn. Even so, it is possible that the income tax could be further simplified, and it is clearly the most complicated tax.[9]

Since individual income taxes are paid by persons who are usually unable to shift the burden to others, its incidence and impact are essentially identical. Thus its incidence can be measured more accurately than that of most other taxes. Based on the adjusted gross income of families (which is the usual basis for judging incidence), the income tax is definitely a progressive tax. This is true not only because the first $2540 of income per person is untaxed,[10] but also because the higher the income, the higher the tax rates. The personal income tax is generally conceded to be America's most progressive tax, and its progressiveness offsets the regressivity of many other taxes. The result, as mentioned, is a total U.S. tax system remarkably proportional across the majority of incomes. Estimated effective rates of the federal individual income tax for 1985 for deciles of population arrayed by income are shown in Table 5.3.[11]

The yield of the income tax is large and accounts for more than half of federal operating revenues. Many states also receive significant amounts of money from state income taxes. Nationally, the yield of state income taxes in 1985 was 1.9 percent of total personal income, or about 20 percent of the yield of the federal individual income tax.

As noted, there is a direct connection between progressivity and elasticity, particularly in an income tax. Thus, the nation's most progressive tax is also its

[9]The 1986 changes in the federal income tax, the most comprehensive changes in many years, did not make the tax much simpler, but they did eliminate some tax shelters that had been strongly criticized, and reduced the top tax rate.

[10]Single person under age sixty-five, 1987 rates.

[11]More recent data based on the 1986 amendments were not available at the time of writing. Note that the effective rate is obtained by dividing total tax by adjusted gross income, and is thus less than the marginal rate.

TABLE 5.3 Effective Rates of the Federal Individual Income Tax for 1985

INCOME DECILE[a]	EFFECTIVE TAX RATE
Lowest	1.1%
Second	3.0
Third	4.4
Fourth	5.7
Fifth	6.7
Sixth	7.4
Seventh	8.0
Eighth	9.3
Ninth	10.3
Highest	11.5
All deciles	9.0

[a]Population arrayed downward in ascending order of income.

Source: Pechman, *Who Paid the Taxes*, p. 69, Table 5-3.

most elastic tax. When national (or state) incomes increase, income tax yield increases faster, because additional income is taxed at higher rates. This was formerly true even if income increases were caused by inflation. As understanding of this phenomenon increased among nonspecialists, there came a demand for income tax *indexation*. The intent of indexation is to tie tax brackets to inflation rates so that inflation caused by income increases will not cause increases in percentage of income taken by the tax. The tax would still be elastic when real incomes increase, but inflation effects will be canceled out. President Reagan made indexation one of his goals in his first term, and the federal income tax was indexed starting in 1985.

The cost of administering the income tax is high, for the tax is complicated. Many examiners, auditors, and computer operators are necessary to verify the accuracy of returns and investigate questionable ones. However, the yield of the tax is so great that the cost of administration as a percentage of yield is acceptably low. It can be argued on economic grounds that government should hire additional examiners, for each examiner currently returns far more than his or her salary each year in additional taxes. On an economic basis, government should hire examiners until the last one just covers his or her salary in taxes recovered. (In economic terms, the greatest yield is realized from the tax when the marginal costs of hiring additional examiners just equals the marginal gain from so doing.) The reason government does not do this is that the large number of additional examinations of income tax returns might generate political resistance.

Income tax compliance cost is also high, for the taxpayer must account for income and deductible expenses, keep accurate records, and either spend time preparing the tax return or pay someone else to do it. (The psychic costs are also high when one is audited.) High compliance cost is one of the reasons for calls to simplify the income tax.

Social and economic effects of the income tax are many and varied. Some are unintended, such as the tax shelter for the unusually wealthy provided by the non-taxability of municipal bond interest. Many of the effects, however, are intended. Deductibility of charitable contributions is intended to encourage charitable giving; churches, hospitals, and colleges would have a more difficult time if the deduction were repealed. Deduction of interest on residential mortgages is intended to encourage home ownership. In addition to such specific economic and social effects, the federal income tax is used to influence the overall business cycle. Several times, in periods of inflation, a surtax has been added to the tax to reduce the amount of money in circulation and thus to dampen inflation; at other times there has been a temporary tax reduction to speed recovery from recession.

The income tax has been an elected official's dream because of its elasticity, which provides ever-increasing revenues without the necessity of increasing taxes. Not since World War II has there been a significant increase in income tax rates. However, the percentage of income that an average person paid in income tax increased substantially over that period because inflation put everyone in a higher bracket. So-called bracket creep resulted in higher effective tax rates over the past twenty years even though almost all of the changes made in the income tax during that period reduced nominal rates.[12] Table 5.4 displays the effective overall rate of the federal individual income tax as a percentage of income.[13]

Because it had not been necessary to increase nominal rates, there was little public outcry until the late 1970s when the high rates of inflation created calls for tax reduction and indexation, as mentioned. Interestingly, during a recession the federal government does not experience the same problems as states with elastic tax structures. The federal government can budget for a larger deficit rather than raising tax rates. States cannot usually run deficits.

TABLE 5.4   Effective Rate of the Federal Income Tax
            as a Percentage of Personal Income

YEAR	TAX RATE
1966	7.7%
1970	8.6
1975	8.0
1980	9.2
1985	9.0

Source: Pechman, *Who Paid the Taxes*, p. 66, Table 5-1.

[12]Nominal rates are those stated in the tax tables. Effective rates are obtained by dividing actual tax paid by actual total income from all sources, with no deductions.

[13]The 1985 indexation of the income tax should cause the effective rate to stabilize. The 1986 amendments should reduce the average effective rate.

General Sales Tax

Forty-five states have *general sales taxes*, and for some it is the principal source of state income.[14] In addition, thirty-one states allow local governments (usually counties and municipalities) to "piggyback" a local sales tax on the state tax.[15] The state collects both taxes simultaneously and rebates local proportions to appropriate government units. The basis of the sales tax, of course, is expenditures. All retail sales are taxed at the point of sale. To avoid double taxation, states do not tax sales from wholesaler to retailer. The retailers pay the tax to the state.

The *value-added tax (VAT)* used in many European countries is simply a general sales tax collected by a different method. Instead of all businesses involved in the manufacture and distribution of a product being exempt from the tax except the retailer, each business in the chain pays a portion of the tax. A wholesaler, for example, buys products from a manufacturer and pays the manufacturer a VAT based on the stated percentage of the sales price (that percentage approximates 20 percent or more in many countries, significantly higher than U.S. sales taxes). The wholesaler sells products to retailers at a higher price, and collects from those retailers VAT at the same rate. The wholesaler must then remit to the government the difference between the taxes collected from retailers and the taxes paid manufacturers. Thus, wholesalers pay a net tax based only on the value they add to products by performing wholesaling functions. VAT is similarly collected from each link in the chain of production and distribution. The total collected is equal to what would have been collected from a retail sales tax at the same rate.

Certain sales are usually exempted. Many states exempt food used for home preparation, on the basis that food is a necessity for poor people. Pharmaceutical drugs are also exempted in many states because such taxes would unnecessarily burden the sick. In some states services are not taxed, and in no state is there a tax on rent.

The sales tax treats equals equally, since people who spend the same amount pay the same amount of tax. (Actually, people who spend a greater part of their income on food and rent pay less tax, which is presumably desirable.)

The impact of the sales tax is on retailers, for they pay the tax to government. However, the incidence is almost entirely on the purchaser. Because of the general nature of the tax, it is not apt to cause shifts in consumer purchasing patterns. Not only are all retailers of the same product subject to the same percentage of tax, but most other products to which individuals might shift are also subject to the same tax. This means that retailers are apt to be subject to the same competitive pressures after imposition of the tax as before, and they do not suffer by shifting the entire tax to consumers. (Again, exceptions would have to be made regarding food and rent.) To evaluate the incidence of the sales tax, one can thus ask how individual expenditures compare with income. In general, poor people spend a greater percentage of their income than wealthy people. The sales tax is therefore regressive in

[14]Only Alaska, Delaware, Montana, New Hampshire, and Oregon had no general sales tax as of December, 1985. Advisory Commission on Intergovernmental Relations, *Fiscal Federalism, 1985,* p. 92, Table 62.

[15]Ibid., p. 90, Table 61.

spite of the exemptions for food, drugs, and rents, which constitute a large part of poor people's expenditures. Table 5.5 shows sales tax incidence as a percentage of income for population deciles.

The costs of administering and complying with the sales tax are low. Administration is less expensive than in the case of an income tax because it is easier to deal with a limited number of retailers than with a much larger number of individuals. The state must, of course, perform occasional audits to ensure that the sales reported are correct. The firm has a slight additional cost in the time taken to add sales tax to the price of the product (although the electronic cash registers now in common use automatically calculate taxes). It is not necessary to keep the money paid for sales tax separate; firms simply total all sales at the end of the month, multiply by appropriate sales tax rates, and send a check to the state.

The yield of state and local sales taxes is substantial. In 1985 sales taxes produced $125 billion nationwide. This was 36 percent of total state–local taxes, making the sales tax the most important revenue source below the federal level.[16] The economic and social effects of the tax may be rather small in most cases. The tax is paid in small amounts and on most products, and thus is not apt to exert much influence on purchases. There are geographic effects, though. The New York City sales tax is 4.25 percent (in addition to a state sales tax of 4 percent).[17] Although this does not cause casual shoppers to leave town to shop, major purchases may be made outside the city. Automobile dealerships have virtually been driven out of the city as a result of this tax, for the city sales tax on a $10,000 car is $425, and it is worth a drive to the suburbs to save that amount. The total sales tax on a $10,000 car purchased in New York City would be $825, and it is possible to purchase the

TABLE 5.5 Effective Rate of the Sales Tax, 1985

INCOME DECILE[a]	EFFECTIVE RATE
First	7.0%
Second	5.9
Third	5.0
Fourth	4.6
Fifth	4.3
Sixth	4.1
Seventh	3.9
Eighth	3.7
Ninth	3.3
Tenth	1.9
All deciles	3.4

[a]Population arrayed downward in ascending order of income.

Source: Pechman, *Who Paid the Taxes,* p. 80, Table A-4.

[16]Ibid., pp. 40–41, Table 29.
[17]As of 1984. Ibid., p. 99, Table 65.

same vehicle only a few miles away in Connecticut or New Jersey, where the tax would be $750 or $600, respectively. Similarly, residents of the Northwest are attracted to the north shore of the Columbia River, where they may live in Washington, with no income tax, and shop in Oregon, with no sales tax.

Sales tax elasticity has been estimated at around 1.0, which means that the yield of the tax rises at the same rate as personal income in a state. Since government expenditures have tended to rise faster than incomes, those states that rely on the sales tax have occasionally been forced to raise sales tax rates, a politically unpopular step.

Property Tax

The property tax is a principal financial support of the public schools in almost every state (Hawaii and New Mexico are notable exceptions). Just as the income tax is the principal revenue source for the federal government and the sales tax for the state governments, the property tax has been the mainstay of local government.

BASIS

The property tax is the most important example of a tax on the ownership of wealth. The only other significant example is the estate tax. However, the property tax does not tax all wealth. Wealth can be divided into *real property,*[18] *tangible personal property,* and *intangible personal property.* Real property consists of land and improvements firmly attached to the land. Such improvements are mostly buildings, but also include fences, power lines, and landscaping. Tangible personal property includes items of intrinsic value not attached to the land. Automobiles, clothing and furniture, and business inventories and machinery are examples. Intangible personal property consists of evidences of wealth having no intrinsic value of their own, such as bank deposits, stocks and bonds, and mortgages. Most real property is taxed, some tangible personal property is taxed, and almost no intangible personal property is taxed.

The Assessment Process. Before property can be taxed, its owner must be located and the value of the property established. This is the duty of the *assessor,* an elected or appointed official of the town, city, or county. Assessors prepare area maps of their jurisdictions, showing each separate parcel of land. Dimensions of the land, a description of its boundaries, and the owner's name are easy to obtain because all states require that any transfer of ownership of real property be recorded, usually by an official known as a *recorder.* These maps enable the assessor to ensure that every piece of real property in his or her jurisdiction is accounted for. Each piece of property is given an identifying number, and its owner of record is determined from the recorder's files.

[18]The term *real* comes from *royal,* for all land originally belonged to the king in England, whence come many of our legal terms.

The next problem is to assign a value to the property. This is an extremely difficult process and the source of many complaints. Usually only property subject to taxation will be valued. This means that streets, public buildings, and other governmental property will not be valued, nor will the property of churches and other tax-exempt private institutions. Tax-exempt property can be a large part of the total: in New York City approximately a quarter of all property is tax-exempt.

The usual standard is *market value*. This is generally defined as the sale price that would be agreed upon by a buyer and a seller both of whom were informed and who were not in collusion. The assessor's problem is to assign such a value to each piece of property. The easiest place to do this is a subdivision of similar houses where there are a number of sales during the year. It is easy to average these sale prices and assign the rest of the houses in the subdivision the same value, with minor adjustments for differences such as installation of a swimming pool. It is more difficult to assess the value of an older home in an area of homes of widely differing styles and sizes. More difficult yet is assessing a small business. Valued as a going concern, the business may be worth much more than if one were to sell the property for a different use. However, the assessor is to value property at its "highest and best" use, and this would normally be the present business use. Since small businesses change hands infrequently and tend to be quite different from one another, basing the valuation on a comparison of property sales may not be feasible. Frequently, an assessor will *capitalize* a business's *income*. That is, on assuming, for example, that a 10 percent profit on investment is reasonable, the assessor multiplies profit figures by ten to determine the assumed value of the business as an investment. The assessor may estimate profit figures using sales tax data: if the sales tax is 5 percent, sales are twenty times sales tax paid. If profit is normally 2 percent of sales (e.g., in a supermarket), the 2 percent is used to estimate profit.

Valuation of a large factory is even more complicated. The factory may be only one of many properties of a large corporation, and it may be impossible to obtain an accurate estimate of the profit of this one property. A third basis of valuation is frequently used in such cases—*replacement value less depreciation (RVLD)*. Each part of the factory (land, buildings, machinery, and inventories) is appraised for an estimate of the cost to replace it at today's prices. Appraisals are then reduced by depreciation based on an assumed useful life of the item. Machinery might have a useful life of only ten years, whereas a building might have a useful life of fifty years. Land is never depreciated, for its useful life has no limit (although a depletion allowance is made in the case of a mine, oil well, or quarry). The depreciated replacement values for various parts of the property are added to obtain a total property value. Utilities present yet another problem, because of their extensive distribution networks. An electric utility's power lines are of no value (other than salvage) except as they are parts of an overall distribution system. If the entire property of a utility in an assessor's jurisdiction consists of a few miles of high-tension line, it is difficult to value. For this reason, many states assess utilities themselves. Some states use a combination of capitalized earnings and RVLD to assess utilities. A utility system's total value is determined by the system's capitalized earnings. The parts of the system are valued on the basis of RVLD. The

RVLD of the part of the system within each assessor's jurisdiction is expressed as a percentage of the RVLD of the entire system, and the total value of the utility based on capitalized earnings is multiplied by this percentage to determine the value of the portion of the utility in each assessor's jurisdiction.

Another type of property that is difficult to value is farmland. Farmers who live some distance from centers of population may find that their farmland, based on its income-producing ability, has a value of only $500 an acre. Farmers on the outskirts of an expanding metropolitan area may find that their farmland, with exactly the same crop-producing ability, is valued by the assessor at $5000 an acre. This is because the assessor must value the land at its *highest and best use* (the use for which one could realize the highest sale price), and this is its use as subdivision land. The resulting taxes may be so high that the farmer is driven to sell the land to developers. In effect, the assessor has constructed a self-fulfilling prophecy. This appears unfair to a farmer who wishes to continue farming, but it is not unfair at all to the farmer who is only waiting for the best offer from subdividers. A solution to this problem has been adopted in a number of states. Farmers in these states can place their land in an *agricultural reserve*. They guarantee that the land will not be used for purposes other than agriculture for a specified number of years, in return for which the assessor must value the land based solely on its value for farming. If the land is sold during the agreement period for a different use, the owner is subject to back taxes based on the difference in assessment between that for farmland and that for its highest and best use.

Effects of assessment. This farmland example should serve to illustrate that the assessment process has important economic and social consequences. In the case of the highly taxed farmer, the economic consequence is that land near cities and suburbs is forced into housing developments sooner than it would be otherwise. Small farmers are forced out of businesses they expected to leave to their children. Land on the fringes of the city becomes less expensive to the developer than land closer to the city, encouraging sprawling development and involving considerable expense in terms of longer sewer and water lines, utility lines, roads, and travel time for residents. Of course, the economic and social consequences do not occur evenly, as is evident from developers' readiness to fight such special exemptions as that for farmland.

In California, golf courses were subject to the same kind of assessment adjustment described for farmland. They too are usually located near populated areas, and assessing them for their value as subdivision land was forcing them out of existence. However, there was no provision for paying back taxes if the land were converted from golf course use, and a large number of golf courses suddenly came into being as developers realized that this was a way of avoiding taxes on land they were holding for future development.

One of the greatest concerns about the economic and social impact of the property tax has been the adverse effect of the tax on poor people, who pay a larger share of their income in housing costs than do the wealthy. One way of remedying this, in use in all but two states, is the *homestead exemption*.[19] In Florida, for example, the first $25,000 of assessed valuation of an owner-occupied house is exempt from taxes.[20] This clearly favors individual ownership over rental housing. It is also a subsidy available only to those financially able to own a house, and not to those who must rent. The circuit-breaker (discussed later) is a more reasonable way of accomplishing the same purpose.

Assessing personal property. The description to this point has concentrated on processes by which a value is attached to all real property by an assessor. The assessor may also assess personal property, but the extent to which this is done varies widely from one state to another. One problem with assessment of personal property is discovering it in the first place. Real property transfers must be recorded, and construction of buildings usually requires a permit. Personal property, though, may be acquired and sold without public notice. Most assessors make little attempt to assess accurately homeowners' tangible personal property. If they assess it at all, they simply use a percentage of the value of the residence as the presumed value of the personal property in it. Of more importance is the *assessment of machinery and business inventories,* for the amounts involved are large.[21] This can lead to bizarre behavior. For example, in California the value of inventories used to be assessed as of the first Monday in March each year. In February, therefore, businesses attempted to reduce inventories to a minimum. Retail businesses held inventory sales. Oil companies ceased pumping oil from the ground and allowed their tanks to go dry. In general, each business attempted to sell as much inventory as possible and to buy as little as possible. On the day following assessment day, everyone scrambled to rebuild inventories.

Intangible personal property is an even greater problem, for stocks and bonds (which, along with bank deposits, constitute most intangible personal property) can be easily hidden in safety deposit boxes or stored outside an assessor's jurisdiction. The result is that, with the exception of bank deposits in a few states, little intangible personal property is assessed. In some states all personal property is exempt from assessment. An interesting consequence of this occurs in New York. In-ground swimming pools are assessed and taxed as real property; they are vastly outnumbered by above-ground pools, which are personal property and not assessed.

Determining actual assessments. Having attached a value, which is presumed to be a market value, to each piece of property, the assessor must assign an *assessed value.* The assessed value is, in most cases, a fraction of the market value. This is true even in those twenty-two states where constitutions or statutes require

[19]The two states are New York and Wisconsin. Advisory Commission on Intergovernmental Relations, *Fiscal Federalism, 1985,* pp. 117–22, Table 72 .

[20]Ibid.

[21]Forty-three states taxed business inventories and/or other commercial and industrial property as of 1981. Advisory Commission on Intergovernmental Relations, *Fiscal Federalism, 1984,* pp. 122-23, Table 73.

assessors to assess property at full market value.[22] The reason for *fractional assessment* is a practical one. Assessment, by its nature, is inexact. Because it affects their pocketbooks, people will protest if they believe that their assessments are too high. An assessment at *full market value* is much more open to public scrutiny than an assessment at some unknown fraction of market value. In addition, taxpayers who complain that their fractional assessment is higher than their neighbor's may be told by the assessor that the law requires a full market value assessment and may be asked if they wish their property valued at that. Courts in some states have supported assessors in this practice. There are more insidious reasons for fractional assessments. As pointed out, assessment of large properties (factories, for example) is extremely complicated. An assessor frequently does not have sufficient expertise to assess such properties accurately. In such a case, the assessed value of the property is frequently negotiated between assessor and property owner. Large property owners find it more difficult to convince a number of boards and councils to minimize taxes than to arrange privately with an assessor to set low assessments. There are clearly opportunities for illegal agreements.

The law usually requires all *classes* of property to be assessed either at full value or at the same percentage of full value. Again, this requirement is followed more in the breach than in the observance. Assessors know that individuals vote and businesses do not, for example. In San Francisco for many years, residences were assessed at less than 10 percent of full value while businesses were assessed at 50 percent of full value. In a few states fractional assessment at different rates for different classes of property is permitted or required. In Arizona, for example, producing oil and gas property is assessed at 100 percent of full value, railroads, mines, timber, and utilities are assessed at 34 percent, commercial and industrial property at 25 percent, agricultural and vacant land at 16 percent, and residential property at 10 percent of full value.[23] However, in most states these interclass differences exist in defiance of the law, which usually requires that assessments to be at 100 percent of full value, or that all property be assessed at the same fraction of full value. In the state of New York, many towns are reassessing as a result of a successful challenge of inter- and intraclass differences, the state's highest court having required that all property be assessed at full market value. The problem is that in many cities commercial and industrial property was previously assessed at a much higher fraction of its full value than was residential property (an *interclass* difference). When assessed values are elevated to full value, the result is a massive shifting of property taxes from commerce and industry to residences. To neutralize this transfer, cities in some states are levying taxes at different *rates* for industry than for residences. This is often known as *splitting the rate* or *splitting the role*.

[22]The twenty-two states are listed in Advisory Commission on Intergovernmental Relations, *Significant Features of Fiscal Federalism, 1982–83 Edition* (Washington, D.C.: Government Printing Office, 1984), pp. 109–10, Table 70.

[23]*Fiscal Federalism, 1982–83*, p. 111, Table 71. The ratio of assessed valuation to market value of residential property ranged, in 1981, from 80 percent in Virginia and Kentucky to 4 percent in Montana. The average nationwide is about 36 percent. U.S. Bureau of the Census, *1982 Census of Governments: Taxable Property Values and Assessment–Sales Price Ratios* (Washington, D.C.: Government Printing Office, 1984), CG82(2), Table 11.

Calculating the tax rate. After an assessed value has been attached to each piece of property, an assessor's obligation is complete. The responsibility for adopting budgets then falls to general governments, such as cities and counties; special governments, such as school districts and mosquito abatement districts; and enterprise districts, such as port authorities and other taxing entities. The budget of a governmental unit less its income from other sources leaves an amount to be raised by property taxes. This amount, divided by the assessed valuation of the property within the geographical boundaries of the unit, provides the tax rate to be applied to that property. For example:

Budget	$15 million
Other income	$10 million
To be raised by taxes	$5 million
Assessed valuation	$250 million
Tax rate	0.020

This tax rate is customarily expressed in one of several ways, depending upon the state: twenty mills (a *mill* is one-tenth of a cent, and this means twenty mills—two cents—per dollar of assessed valuation), $20 per $1000 of assessed valuation, $2 per $100, or 2 percent.

It is not possible, however, simply to add the tax rates for each of the governmental units within the assessor's jurisdiction to obtain the total tax rate for that jurisdiction. Each unit usually covers a different geographical area, but there is much overlapping. The overlapping boundaries create areas in which the total tax rate differs from that of adjoining areas. *Within* each area, however, the tax rate is the same for all property. Each of these areas of uniform tax rate is known as a *tax code area*. A typical county in some parts of the United States may have hundreds of such tax code areas. On the other hand, there are a few places, mostly in the South, where all government functions have been consolidated under a single county government, with the tax rate the same countywide. An example is Dade County, Florida, which operates everything within its boundaries except the school district (including the municipalities of Miami and Miami Beach); the school district is *coterminous* with (occupies the same geographical area as) the county. The same tax rate applies to all property in Dade County.

Fractional assessment creates a number of problems, discussion of which has been delayed until now. First, of course, if different properties (or different classes of property) are valued by an assessor at different percentages of market value, they will be unevenly subject to the property tax. If, however, an assessor values *all* property within the jurisdiction at the same percentage of market value, there appears to be no difficulty. A low total assessed value would simply mean a higher tax rate, since the tax rate is obtained by dividing budgeted tax needs by assessed valuation. In reality, however, there are two main problems. First, in many states school districts have statutory maximum tax rates. By assessing property at less than market value, an assessor is limiting the access of school districts to the full tax amount they would otherwise be able to levy. Second, states allocate aid to school districts based on the wealth of the district. An underassessed district creates the illusion of a poor district entitled to more state aid. In the past this has led to *competitive underassessment* among districts in some states. A solution to the intergovernmental aid problem is a state *board of equalization,* which determines for each school district and other government units the ratio of assessed to full value, enabling state aid to be based on full value. Although this is now done in most states, it does not solve the problem of differences in assessment ratios *within* a district.

In addition to fractional assessment of all property and different assessment rates for property of different classes, there is the problem of *intraclass* discrepancies. Identical properties are often assessed quite differently. This results in part from the subjectivity inherent in appraisal. Part of the problem, though, is that many assessors revalue property infrequently. Assessors are understaffed and revalue only that property that comes to their attention, either because of a sale or because a building permit has been issued. This means that the new owner of an old home may find the assessment roughly equal to 90 percent of the home's value, whereas the long-time owner of an identical home next door, not reassessed for thirty years, may have an assessment less than 50 percent of the home's market value. These kinds of intraclass differences are particularly visible and trigger unhappiness over the property tax.

In spite of complaints about assessment practices, only a few states have made major improvements through state action. Examples are Oregon, Maryland, Arizona, and Florida. In Arizona, for example, there is an independent Department of Property Valuation empowered to regulate assessment standards and local assessors. Each Arizona assessor's office is provided with a set of assessment manuals so that an assessor may conform with requirements for statewide uniformity. The State Department of Property Valuation has also provided a uniform system numbering and mapping parcels, along with uniform tax code area maps and uniform procedures for handling exemptions under Arizona statutes. No assessor may establish or change any valuation without approval by the department. Electronic data-processing equipment is used extensively wherever possible. Current sale prices are stored in the computer, which notes any deviation of appraised value below 80 percent or above 96 percent of the sale price. County assessors are provided with printouts so they can review and update appraisals to bring tax rolls into conformity with standards.

EQUITY

The first concern of equity is whether equals are treated equally. The property tax is probably weaker in this respect than most taxes. The problem, of course, lies in assessment practices. The inter- and intraclass discrepancies in assessments previously described mean that properties of equal value in the same tax code area may pay quite different taxes. In addition to these assessment problems, tax exemptions diminish the equity of the property tax as well as its revenue-raising capacity.

INCIDENCE

Consideration of whether the property tax treats unequals equitably involves the tax's incidence. It is a trivial matter to discover the impact of the tax, for tax bills are individually addressed, but analyzing incidence is another matter.

One school of economists views property taxes as regressive, perhaps the most regressive of the major taxes. Another group believes the property tax is progressive. The arguments will be summarized only briefly here. Those interested in further discussion should consult the literature in the field.[24]

Most economists agree that property taxes on land fall on the owner of the land at the time the tax is initially levied or increased. The tax cannot be shifted because under equilibrium conditions the only way to increase price is to increase demand or decrease supply. The landowner has no control over demand, and there is no way that supply can be decreased in the aggregate, because the supply of land is almost perfectly inelastic.

Wealthy persons, who have more disposable income than poor people, own proportionately more land. Since the incidence of property taxes on land falls entirely on landowners, this portion of the tax is presumably progressive. However, property taxes paid are deductible items on the income tax, and wealthy property owners benefit more from this provision than do poor property owners because they have higher *marginal tax rates*. Thus, the net effect is not as progressive as might appear at first.

Taxes on improvements (and on personal property) can be divided into three categories. The first is owner-occupied housing. Again, all agree that the burden of this tax falls entirely on the owner-occupant, who is both capitalist and consumer; there is no one to whom to pass the tax liability. Since this was already true for the land on which owner-occupied houses stand, the incidence of the property tax on these properties is exactly the same as the impact. (One should not be confused by the existence of mortgages into thinking that banks own much housing stock. The individual who owns the house, and has merely borrowed money with which to purchase it, must pay the taxes, not the bank.) The incidence of the property tax on single-family owner-occupied housing tends to be regressive because wealthy people spend a smaller proportion of their incomes for housing than do poor people.

The analysis is more difficult in the case of rental housing, for it is not clear to what extent the burden of the tax can be conveyed to the tenant in the form of higher rents, and to what extent it must be absorbed by landlords in the form of a diminished return on investment. One view has all of the property tax on rental *housing* (not land) passed forward to the renter. Since poor renters pay a greater proportion of income in rent than do rich people (and assuming for the moment that property taxes are a relatively constant percentage of rents), the incidence of the

[24]A summary of the controversy is contained in Joseph A. Pechman and Benjamin A. Okner, *Who Bears the Tax Burden?* (Washington, D.C.: Brookings Institution, 1974), pp. 25–43. Book-length presentations are Dick Netzer, *Economics of the Property Tax* (Washington, D.C.: Brookings Institution, 1966); and Henry J. Aaron, *Who Pays the Property Tax?* (Washington, D.C.: Brookings Institution, 1975). Netzer's book presents the regressive view, Aaron's the progressive.

property tax on rental housing must also be regressive. The other view is that in the short run the supply of housing is almost as inelastic as the supply of land. This means that it will be impossible in the short run for landlords to pass the property tax forward to renters.

This second group of economists notes in addition that even if the property tax on rental housing is passed forward to the renter it may not be regressive, because property taxes are not a constant percentage of rents, as the first group assumes. The proportion of rent that represents a return to capital in low-rent housing is considerably smaller than it is in high-cost housing. Most of the rent in inexpensive housing pays for current costs of the housing, including taxes.

Third, the second group points out that it is an illusion that truly poor families pay high property taxes. Among those with unusually low incomes are a disproportionate number who have low incomes only temporarily. Examples are young couples who can reasonably expect to increase their incomes rapidly, retired persons who have accumulated substantial wealth even though their current income is low, and individuals who have been able to offset income against business expenses or otherwise reduce their adjusted gross income. This group of economists argues that one should not use current income as the measure in judging regressivity, but *permanent income*. They define permanent income as that income that individuals expect to earn on the average over the long term. They argue that when permanent income is used, even the tax burden on owner-occupied housing is progressive.

Finally, the more regressive view of the incidence of the property tax on commercial and industrial buildings and business machinery and inventories is that the tax is passed on to consumers in the form of higher prices for goods purchased. The more progressive view is that these taxes are borne by owners of capital.

It is not at all clear which group of economists is more correct. Anyone who reads carefully the analyses of both sides is struck by the number of assumptions that must be made because of lack of data. Economists are fond of making assumptions; doing so simplifies conditions and renders them more amenable to analysis. Unfortunately, it also abstracts from reality, and often it is difficult to determine the extent to which an assumption is justified, or how it will upset the conclusion if it is not correct. Pechman's analysis of the incidence of the property tax is presented in Table 5.6. It is clear that the two views display a different picture of the burden of the tax.

Progressive assumptions present a property tax that is clearly progressive. Regressive assumptions display a property tax that is regressive for the lowest 20 percent of the population in income, but proportional for all other deciles. It appears that the most one can say at present is that it is by no means certain that the tax is onerously regressive. It should not be condemned solely on that account.

If the property tax is regressive, its greatest burden is on poor people. The *circuit-breaker,* a way of selectively reducing this burden, has been adopted in one form or another by many states. The circuit-breaker excuses all or a portion of the property taxes a family pays on its residence above a specified percentage of its in

TABLE 5.6   Effective Property Tax Rates as a Percentage of Income, 1985

	TAX RATES	
POPULATION DECILE[a]	PROGRESSIVE ASSUMPTIONS	REGRESSIVE ASSUMPTIONS
First	0.7%	3.3%
Second	0.7	2.5
Third	0.9	2.1
Fourth	0.9	2.1
Fifth	1.0	2.1
Sixth	1.2	2.1
Seventh	1.3	2.1
Eighth	1.3	2.2
Ninth	1.7	2.3
Tenth	3.3	2.3

[a]Population arrayed downward in ascending order of income.

Source: Pechman, *Who Paid the Taxes*, p. 80, Table A-4.

come. For example, the law might provide (as in Michigan) that 60 percent of the excess of taxes over 3.5 percent of family income will be forgiven. Suppose a family has an income of $20,000 and pays property taxes of $1000. Three and a half percent of its income is $700, and the excess of property tax is $300. Sixty percent of the latter is $180. The family would report this fact on its state income tax return and deduct the $180 from the income tax. If the deduction exceeded the tax, the state would refund the difference. The circuit-breaker is applied to rental property also; it is assumed that 17 percent of rental payments constitutes property taxes paid.[25] The circuit-breaker has been adopted in one form or another by thirty-two states in the exceedingly short time since its appearance in Wisconsin in 1964.[26] The reason for its popularity is that it is a tax exemption tailored to the income of the taxpayer. Thus it is less costly to the state than a homestead exemption, which benefits rich and poor homeowners alike in dollar terms. However, the circuit-breaker has drawbacks. It tends to benefit the most those who spend a high proportion of income on their homes, including those with higher incomes who choose to invest in extravagant homes. Another problem is the assumption that a uniform percentage of rent is property tax, for this is patently false even if we agree that landlords pass the entire burden of the property tax on to tenants. Yet this notion too—that the incidence of the property tax is upon renters—has come under challenge, as indicated in the previous section.

[25]Advisory Commission on Intergovernmental Relations, *Fiscal Federalism, 1985*, p. 112, Table 71.

[26]Five states adopted circuit-breakers in the 1960s, twenty-six in the 1970s, and one thus far in the 1980s. Ibid.

YIELD

The property tax is a potent generator of revenue. In 1985, property taxes were 12 percent of total taxes at all levels (federal, state, and local), 29 percent of combined state–local taxes, and 75 percent of local taxes. Almost $100 billion is raised each year in property taxes nationwide.[27] In New York State alone, the property tax raised more than $10 billion in 1983. This is more than was raised by any other tax in this most highly taxed state.[28] However, property taxes have trended downward after hitting a high point in 1970. Much publicity has been given to tax limitation initiatives such as Proposition 13 in California and Proposition 2 1/2 in Massachusetts. But many other states have also lowered their effective property tax rates. The result, shown in Table 5.7, is that rates in 1985 are only 60 percent of rates in 1970.

The property tax has usually been thought of as an inelastic tax. The reasoning is that assessed values do not tend to increase as rapidly as personal incomes, mainly because assessments are not constantly updated. The result is that a constant tax rate will produce revenues that do not increase as rapidly as incomes. However, the analysis is not that simple. It is not necessary to assume a constant tax rate. Government demands for money have increased faster than incomes. Those governments that depend heavily on the property tax (that is, almost all local governments) have been forced to increase property tax rates, and they have been surprisingly successful in doing so, as we can see in Table 5.8. From 1902 to 1922, property tax receipts increased from 2.9 percent of GNP to 4.5 percent. From 1932 to 1948 property taxes remained remarkably constant in dollars, raising between $4 billion and $5 billion per year. They jumped to 7.7 percent of GNP in 1932 as the depression hit while tax receipts remained almost the same. A long period of prosperity (interrupted by several minor recessions) began in 1946 and continued for twenty-five years. During this time, property tax yields in dollars increased eightfold and yield as a percentage of GNP rose steadily from 2.4 percent to 3.4 percent. The yield declined to about 2.5 percent of GNP in 1980, reflecting the property tax limitation measures adopted by some states, and has remained at about

TABLE 5.7 Effective Property Tax Rates as a Percentage of Income

YEAR	RATE
1966	3.0%
1970	3.3
1975	2.8
1980	2.0
1985	2.0

Source: Pechman, *Who Paid the Taxes*, p. 66, Table 5-1.

[27]Calculated from data in ibid., pp. 40–41, Table 29.
[28]Ibid., p. 232.

that level since. The property tax, then, has shown a remarkable characteristic in this century: it is elastic in periods of prosperity, increasing in yield faster than the economy, yet inelastic during depression, decreasing in yield scarcely at all even when the economy takes a terrible beating. From the point of view of governments that depend upon the property tax, this *revenue resilience* is the best of all possible worlds. From the point of view of the taxpayer, particularly the one with no children in school, the picture is, of course, not as rosy, and this is undoubtedly the reason for some of the tax limitation movements.

COSTS OF ADMINISTRATION AND COMPLIANCE

The administrative cost of the property tax is usually low when expressed as a percentage of yield. Part of the reason for this, however, is that in most states assessments are poorly carried out. Proper assessments might double or triple the cost of administration. The general effect of this would be to improve the equity of the tax (by reducing inter- and intraclass discrepancies), but it would probably not improve the yield in most cases. The reason is that property tax yield is determined by local government revenue needs, which are translated into a tax rate. Evasion of formally levied property taxes is rare, for governments can collect unpaid back taxes by seizing the property and selling it. There is significant evasion of taxes through abandonment of property in a few cities, such as New York, but it can be argued that the assessed value of the property was too high in such cases, for the property was obviously abandoned as worthless.

The cost of compliance is probably lower for the property tax than for any other major tax. Property owners receive a tax bill and pay it in one or more installments. The time and effort involved in doing so are nil.

ECONOMIC AND SOCIAL EFFECTS

As should be evident from the foregoing discussion, the economic and social effects of property taxes are important. There is no general agreement among economists on overall or specific effects of the tax, but many would agree with the following ideas.

First, the property tax is, in effect, an excise tax on consumption of housing, as noted by Netzer.[29] In other words, although it is a tax on ownership of a particular kind of wealth (primarily real property), to the extent that it is levied on residential housing it has an effect similar to that of a sales tax on expenditures associated with home ownership. If the average property tax, expressed as a percentage of average expenditures for housing, is greater than general sales tax rates, the result will be to discourage consumption of housing—that is, people will choose to live in smaller, less expensive houses. This is not necessarily bad. Americans are the best-housed people in the world, and it may not be necessary or desirable to encourage overall increases in housing consumption. There may be specific instances

[29]Dick Netzer, "Property Taxes," *Municipal Finance,* 44, no. 2 (November 1971), 36.

TABLE 5.8 Federal, State, and Local Taxes as Percentages of
Gross National Product, Selected Years, 1902–84

YEAR	FEDERAL TAXES	STATE AND LOCAL TAXES	
		TOTAL	PROPERTY TAXES ONLY
1902	2.1%	3.6%	2.9%
1913	1.6	4.0	3.3
1922	4.6	5.4	4.5
1932	3.1	10.6	7.7
1940	4.9	7.8	4.4
1948	15.4	5.4	2.4
1956	15.9	6.4	2.8
1964	14.7	7.8	3.3
1970	15.2	9.0	3.4
1978	13.2	9.6	3.2
1980	13.3	8.5	2.5
1982	13.2	8.7	2.6
1984	11.3	8.8	2.5
1985[a]	11.7	8.9	2.5

[a]Estimated

Sources: 1902–1940: Advisory Commission on Intergovernmental Relations, *Financing Schools and Property Tax Relief: A State Responsibility* (Washington, D.C.: Government Printing Office, 1973), p. 16; 1948–1984: Advisory Commission on Intergovernmental Relations, *Fiscal Federalism, 1985*, p. 43, Table 31.

where high taxes discourage housing, primarily in city ghettos, but this is a result mostly of assessed values that are unreasonably high considering the returns on landlord investment. Proper assessment can correct these abuses.

Second, that property taxes are higher in some places than in others has an effect on the value of property. An interesting example occurred in Rochester, New York, in the mid 1970s. Several small "free" school districts existed there, the result of an agreement many years before that brought some valuable industrial property from these districts into the city, in exchange for which the city agreed to educate students of the small districts at no cost in perpetuity. As a result, free-district residents paid no school taxes. A house in a free school district would sell for about $10,000 more than its identical counterpart across the street in the city school district. The cost of borrowing the money needed to make this additional $10,000 investment was approximately equal to the school taxes paid by the owner of the house in the city. When the legislature abolished these districts by annexing them to others, the free-district homeowners suffered a loss of roughly $10,000 in the value of their homes. This is an example of what is called *capitalization theory.*

The effect of the property tax is incorporated (capitalized) into the value of the house.[30]

This problem is not confined to such unusual situations, however. In most states there are *tax islands*—school districts with large concentrations of industrial or commercial property and few students. The burden of school expenses is low and the total assessed value of the property in the district high, resulting in a low tax rate. This encourages location of more industry, exacerbating the situation. Perhaps the most egregious example is Teterboro, New Jersey, with an assessed value in 1986 of $195 million and only one pupil. Businesses locating in these tax islands effectively escape most school property taxation, which is typically more than half of the total property tax bill.

It has been proposed by many that commercial and industrial property be taxed by the state for schools at a uniform rate, thus leaving only the residential tax base available for local discretion. Presumably this would have several desirable results. Businesses would not be able to escape taxation by locating in tax islands. Decisions on business location would be made on bases other than avoidance of taxes. Furthermore, local taxes would be paid only by those who decide on rates: local voters. In spite of its attractiveness, this proposal has not yet been adopted by any state. This is partly because of the political power of industries situated in tax islands. Also, the short-range problems attending the proposal seem to outweigh its long-range benefits. For one thing, the necessary statewide tax rate would in many cases be more than industry is currently paying in large cities. In other words, large cities, whatever their other problems, are to some extent tax islands with regard to schools. That industry could relocate in suburbs without incurring a tax penalty might hasten the exodus of industry and commerce from the city, decreasing employment opportunities and increasing urban decay.

A third effect of property taxes springs from *exemption* of certain types of property, such as government buildings, streets, churches, hospitals, private schools, and other nonprofit agencies. Exemption seems desirable since there is no point in government taxing itself, and encouragement of religious and charitable institutions is considered important by most people. However, exemption can result in a serious problem for cities (especially state capitals) and school districts having large concentrations of these properties.

There are a number of other economic effects, but it is possible that to some extent they merely balance the effects of other taxes. Netzer has noted, for example, that the federal income tax encourages consumption of housing because it allows deductions of property taxes and of interest paid on mortgages. Sales taxes are never applied to rents. Both of these taxes, then, tend to encourage spending on private housing, although property taxes may act as a deterrent to home buyers.[31]

The social effects of the property tax are also important, although it is often difficult to differentiate these effects precisely. A combination of factors, among

[30]See Aaron S. Gurwitz, "The Capitalization of School Finance Reform," *Journal of Education Finance,* 5, no. 3 (Winter 1980), 297–319.

[31]See Netzer, *Economics of the Property Tax,* p. 69.

them lower taxes at the time suburban land was being developed, have contributed to the urban sprawl that has rendered the United States a nation of commuters. Resistance to property taxes has affected schools more than other arms of government; the long-range effects of possible poorer education for many children are yet to be felt.

THE TAX LIMITATION MOVEMENT

In June 1978, California enacted Proposition 13. This state constitutional amendment was placed on the ballot through a voter initiative and overwhelmingly approved by two-thirds of California's voters. It provided that total property taxes for all purposes were limited to 1 percent of assessed value. The assessed value of a piece of property could not be increased more than 2 percent per year unless the property was sold; it could then be increased to reflect the selling price. No property tax could be levied above the 1 percent limit, and other taxes could be levied or increased only by a two-thirds vote of the people. The effect was to limit drastically the ability of the state of California and its political divisions to raise money through taxes. The 1 percent property tax, divided among cities, counties, school districts, and other political entities, was not nearly sufficient for the operation of these governments. The state was forced to "bail out" local governments. In general, each government was given a budget that was 90 percent of the previous year's budget. Property tax proceeds were divided among local entities, and differences between property tax receipts (and other revenues) and their approved budget were subsidized by the state. The effect was the same as it would have been if the state had levied a 1 percent property tax and then provided full support for all local governments. California schools are now, in effect, fully state-supported; the effects of this are discussed in the next chapter.[32] Here, the concern is with the effect of the tax limitation movement that Proposition 13 exemplifies.

Tax or *expenditure limitations* have been adopted in nineteen states. All but two adopted these limitations between 1976 and 1980.[33] There was fear among those who operate local governments that the fever would spread nationwide and severely limit government services, but it now appears that the movement has abated. After an initial flurry lasting about three years, no additional substantial limitation measures have been passed. However, in those states with such limitations, public officials have had to learn to live with a completely different set of spending constraints.

There are other kinds of tax limitation. Indexation of the income tax, mentioned earlier, is a way of limiting tax elasticity in response to inflation. Elected officials who want to spend a greater share of the national (or state) income must

---

[32]Interestingly, after a decade of Proposition 13's effects, a few school districts in California had experienced such high turnover of expensive properties that their property tax revenues enabled them to support their schools without the state subsidy, even though their property tax rate did not exceed the constitutional limit of 1 percent.

[33]Advisory Commission on Intergovernmental Relations, *Fiscal Federalism, 1985,* pp. 148–53, Table 92 .

vote for higher tax rates when indexation is in effect, instead of waiting for inflation to provide the boost.[34]

Of course, there are positive and negative features of tax limitations. On the positive side, limitations stem governments' gradual tendency to absorb a larger share of personal income. That government takes a particular share of income is not, in itself, bad. The problem is merely to decide how much and which services to furnish privately and which publicly. Tax rates in rural communities are often low because many services furnished by government in a city (street cleaning, fire protection, garbage collection) are provided by individuals or volunteers in rural areas. However, services furnished by government are available whether or not an individual wishes them. Decisions on what is to be furnished are made collectively. Those who dislike this complain of creeping socialism. There is also serious concern, both in the United States and abroad, about the effect of high taxes and broad provision of governmental services on incentives for individuals to work.

On the negative side, tax limitations are by their nature general and often ignore the special needs of certain governmental jurisdictions. In California, where a second-wave tax limitation statute has limited the amount that school districts may spend, districts expanding rapidly find there are only limited funds available for new construction.[35] Some areas of the state are rapidly increasing in population and find it difficult to raise sufficient money to build the necessary schools.

Tax limitation statutes also intentionally limit the ability of citizens at the local level to increase taxes to finance new governmental expenditures. By doing so, they have limited choice.

ALTERNATIVES TO TAXATION FOR EDUCATION

In those states with strong tax limitation statutes, citizens have naturally examined the possibility of supplementing financing for schools from sources other than taxation. There are modest possibilities.

One alternative is *tuition*. However, this is not possible for school-age children under the constitutions of most states. State constitutions usually specify that all children of the state shall receive a "free" education. It is usually possible to charge tuition for adult courses, but these, generally small in number, are often eliminated under a stringent tax limitation statute. In some states, it may be possible to charge schoolchildren for textbooks (a common practice at the high school level a generation or two ago), but current laws in most states prohibit this also.

It is possible in most states to charge for certain specific services not considered part of the normal educational process, such as transportation to out-of-town football games and provision of certain after-school activities. Another tactic is to deed the school grounds to the city for joint use by schools and the community. The city is then responsible for maintenance. The city may not be suffering as

[34]As of 1985, ten states had indexed their income taxes. Ibid., p. 91, Table 61.

[35]This second wave has resulted from the 1979 Gann Initiative, which limits government spending to an amount determined by changes in population and personal income.

much from a tax limitation statute as the school district because it has other sources of income.

A district with surplus buildings and property can rent space or lease land to others. Of course, it could also sell the surplus property. (These and other alternatives are described in Chapter 10.) Large school districts can perform functions for smaller surrounding districts for less than it would cost the smaller districts to do so themselves, but the fee for performing those functions would be greater than the marginal additional cost to the large district. Examples are the furnishing of computer, purchasing, and warehousing services. These services could also be furnished to private schools in the area, which would increase the efficiency of operation of the schools. A possibility in some high-income districts is to form a private foundation. The foundation solicits contributions from parents of schoolchildren and community residents and then distributes the money to the school district. In the city of Piedmont, California (a high-income community completely surrounded by Oakland), such a foundation provides approximately 10 percent of the district's revenues. Another possibility, tried in a number of communities, is to persuade a business firm to "adopt" a school as a special project, furnishing money for needed items and encouraging its employees to volunteer services for the school.

In some parts of California, population is increasing rapidly. Subdivisions are being built to accommodate thousands of families, and school districts find it impossible to generate sufficient capital to build needed schools. The state legislature permits local school boards to levy a fee on developers for each house built, with the receipts used to construct schools.

SUMMARY

The American system of public education is the largest single enterprise of state and local government. Even nationally it is rivaled only by defense and welfare expenditures. Supporting the costs of education is a system of general taxes, consisting primarily of local property taxation supplemented by state grants-in-aid, mainly from sales and income taxation. The percentage of each tax used for school support varies from one school district to the next, and from state to state.

This chapter has identified and explained five characteristics of taxes:

1. The *basis* of the liability for payment of the tax. The basis is wealth (as in the property tax), income (the income tax), expenditure (the sales tax), or a privilege conferred by the government (license fees and franchises of various kinds).
2. The *yield* of the tax—that is, its capability for raising money. A property tax has an inherently greater yield than a tax on theater admissions.
3. The *costs of administration and compliance,* usually expressed as a percentage of the yield.
4. *Economic and social effects.* Although a tax ought to be free of unintended economic and social effects, unfortunately the most important taxes are not.
5. *Political effects.* Each of the major taxes also has important political effects that must be taken into account.

In connection with the basis of taxes, the equity of taxes was also discussed. Equity requires that equals be treated alike, and in general that unequals be taxed based on ability to pay. Progressive taxes are more equitable than regressive taxes, which cost low-income persons proportionately more than those with high income. When assessing tax equity, it is not sufficient merely to examine the impact of the tax (those who initially pay it); one must examine the incidence of the tax—who ultimately pays. Determining incidence is a complicated economic exercise. There are two schools of thought regarding property tax incidence, one determining it to be progressive, the other concluding that it is regressive. The three most important taxes (personal income, sales, and property) were compared on the basis of these characteristics. Each tax has advantages and disadvantages. One of the major problems of the property tax is in determining the value of property through the assessment process. This process was described in detail, and potential solutions to some of the problems of assessment were discussed.

The property tax raises more money than any other specific tax for schools, and it is the only tax of which citizens regularly have an opportunity to express their disapproval—by voting on school budgets and for school board members. These facts, plus inequities in assessing property that lead to inequities in taxation, have made the property tax appear to be the most unpopular tax. However, a careful analysis of this tax, and a comparison of its characteristics with those of the income and sales taxes, reveals that some of this antipathy may be misdirected.

More important, the property tax is not likely to be abandoned as a source of school support in the foreseeable future, for the simple reason that it raises such a massive amount of money. To find a comparable revenue source would be politically difficult, since the only taxes sufficiently broadly based to provide the necessary money are the sales and income taxes. In most states these taxes would have to be doubled, tripled, or quadrupled to match the amount now provided for schools by the property tax.

There is a great deal to be said for a balanced tax structure involving taxes based on income, wealth, and consumption, for those who manage their affairs in such a way as to minimize one tax can be covered by another. Those who espouse a single tax (whether it be an income tax or a land tax) tend to ignore this. In addition, the higher a particular tax, the greater the incentive to find ways to evade it.

All of this suggests it is unwise to abandon the property tax as a principal means of support for public schools. However, ways should be sought to improve its operation. This chapter provides suggestions for improvement, including proper assessment practices to prevent inter- and intraclass inequities in taxation, and circuit-breakers to relieve the excessive burden of property taxation on low-income individuals and families.

The chapter closes with a discussion of the tax limitation movement which has made it difficult or impossible to increase taxes in some states, and some possible ways for school districts to raise revenue when taxes are insufficient.

chapter six

DISTRIBUTING STATE EDUCATION DOLLARS

In financing public schools, states have been concerned with equity, adequate provision, and efficiency of education. There has been a lesser concern with choice. The emphasis on these values has shifted over time. However, there has been more formal attention to equity.

EQUITY

The goal of school finance that is labelled *equity* is more commonly expressed as *equality of educational opportunity*. This expression recognizes that it is not possible to educate all students to the same level, for they have different preferences and innate abilities. There are many possible definitions of equal educational opportunity, but in practice the concept has been limited to mean assuring equal dollars per student or assuring enough money to provide comparable programs for students when their different needs and the costs of providing them have been taken into account. To meet this second goal, one must take into account three separate kinds of inequalities among school districts—differences in *wealth*, in *educational need*, and in *educational cost*. Separate remedies are appropriate for each, and the three must be combined in constructing a school finance program that is truly equitable. Each will be discussed in turn.

Wealth Equalization

Throughout U.S. history, we have relied heavily on property taxes to support the public schools. Although this was equitable among local taxpayers (ownership of property, at one time, was an accurate measure of ability to pay taxes), it was inequitable among communities. A property-rich community with a lower tax rate could finance a better education than could a property-poor community with a higher tax rate.

The situation is illustrated in Figure 6.1, the first of a series of illustrations of wealth equalization systems presented in this chapter. The horizontal axis of the chart represents community wealth expressed in dollars of property value per pupil. The numbers on this scale are purely arbitrary, used to illustrate the concept. The vertical axis represents dollars of expenditure per student. Assume that the communities of the state differ in wealth per pupil, but that they all decide to make an equal sacrifice in providing education, by levying a property tax at a rate of fifteen mills.[1] There is no other revenue available to schools besides receipts from this tax. The line *OP* extending diagonally upward from the origin represents receipts from this tax for districts of different wealth. For example, at a tax rate of fifteen mills, district A with $100,000 of property value per pupil will raise $1500 per pupil (fifteen mills means $0.015 per dollar of property value; $100,000 x .015 = $1,500). District B, with property value of $200,000 per pupil, will raise $3000 per pupil at the same tax rate. In other words, the amount raised is directly related to community wealth, and when there are variations in wealth, districts that levy the same tax rate raise widely differing sums per pupil.

Several points are of note here. One is that the range in value of property per pupil among districts within a state is usually much wider than illustrated in this

FIGURE 6.1 No State Aid

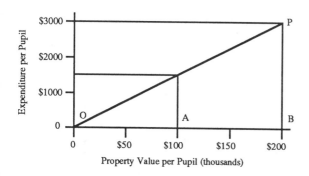

Property Value per Pupil (thousands)

---

[1] A mill is an old English coin, no longer in use, the value of which is a tenth of a cent, or $0.001. A tax rate of fifteen mills ($0.015) is a tax of 1.5 cents (fifteen mills) per dollar of assessed valuation. This is equivalent to a rate of $15 per $1000 of assessed valuation, $1.50 per $100 of assessed valuation, or 1.5 percent.

figure. It might range from approximately $10,000 per pupil to over $500,000 per pupil. Thus, the range in amounts raised per pupil by the property tax is great. At a tax rate of fifteen mills, the $10,000 district raises $150 per pupil and the $500,000 district raises $7500 per pupil. On the other hand, the range can be deceptive. The vast majority of the districts in the state might typically have property values per pupil ranging from, say, $50,000 to $200,000. Even so, this means a range of four to one in ability to raise money through taxes. (See Chapter 13 for additional information about such disparities.)

The concept of tax rate representing equal sacrifice is an abstract one. If houses are worth $100,000 on average in district A, and $200,000 in district B, a tax rate of fifteen mills will mean that householders in district A will pay $1500 in school taxes and those in district B will pay $3000. Presumably, differences in home values represent differences in homeowners' wealth, and in their ability to pay taxes, although it is not that straightforward. Homeowners in district B do pay more money in taxes, although their tax *rate* and presumably their sacrifice is the same.

Remember, these are averages. In district A there may be two homeowners, each with two children in school, one of whom owns a home with a value of $40,000 and the other with a home valued at $100,000. The first pays $600 in taxes at a fifteen-mill tax rate, the second pays $1500, yet the children of both receive the same education. And, of course, the homeowner who has no children also pays taxes, even though he receives no direct benefit from the schools. The principle involved here might be expressed as "from each according to his ability; to each according to his needs."[2]

We discuss property value here without distinguishing between *full value* and *assessed value*. Although taxes are levied on assessed value, our illustrations assume uniform assessment rates—that is, the assessment of all properties at full value.

Finally, others besides homeowners pay taxes. Commercial and industrial enterprises also pay, usually at the same rate. This means that our two communities, A and B, (with property values of $100,000 and $200,000 per pupil) might actually have houses of equal value. The difference might result from a substantial industrial base in the second town. In that case, the homeowners in both towns would pay the same amount in taxes but the school district in the second town would have twice as much to spend per pupil. This would seem to be particularly egregious, although it could be argued that the presence of industries in a town makes it a less desirable place to live.

There are three implicit philosophies behind the variety of wealth equalization strategies used by states. That they are seldom made explicit has rendered discussion of their pros and cons less clear than it should be. The first of these philosophies might be called the *minimum provision philosophy*. Its proponents assert that there is an interest by the state as a whole in seeing that every child is provided with at least a minimum of education. This could be thought of, perhaps, as the amount necessary to make young people employable and to make them capable of intelli-

[2]Karl Marx, *The Communist Manifesto*.

gently making choices in a democracy. This minimum education should be guaranteed by the state, through some mechanism, to all students, regardless of the school district in which they live. Any additional education is thought of as a benefit to the individual student, or to the community. This additional education may be provided as a local luxury by the community to the extent it sees fit, unsubsidized by the state.

The second philosophy might be called the *equal access philosophy*. Its advocates contend that there is an interest on the part of the state in seeing that all school districts have equal access to money for education, but that each community should have the right to decide the amount of education to provide. Whereas the first philosophy emphasizes equality of provision, this philosophy puts it emphasis on equality of access to funds.

The third philosophy is more comprehensive, and might be called the *equal total provision philosophy*. Its supporters claim that all public education must be provided to all students in the state on an equal basis.

We turn now to the most common types of programs of state aid to education designed to promote equality, starting with those that adhere to the first philosophy. It should be emphasized that these are idealized programs. None of them exists in any state in its pure form.

MINIMUM PROVISION PHILOSOPHY

Flat grant program. When states began to appropriate money to local communities to assist with the cost of schooling, intergovernmental grants took the form of equal amounts of money to each community, regardless of its number of children or its ability to raise money locally. Subsequently, funds were distributed on the basis of equal dollars per pupil to each district. At the turn of the twentieth century, thirty-eight states distributed so-called flat grants using a school census as a basis for apportionment. Other states used enrollment or average daily attendance.[3] Since the school-census basis (a count of all school-age children in a district) provided districts with state money whether or not children attended school, it provided no incentive for districts to retain children in school.

Ellwood P. Cubberley, in 1906, was the first to write persuasively of the problems of school finance.[4] He was concerned with the manner in which flat grant formulas favored cities, where school districts could afford to operate schools longer, and where larger class sizes were possible. School costs were higher in rural areas, where it was frequently necessary to employ a teacher to instruct ten or fewer children. Cubberley's solution was to allocate to each district an amount for each teacher employed. This, of course, still did not equalize wealth. Cubberley's plan can best be described as another variety of flat grant, with the teacher as the unit of measurement instead of the child. Today, no state depends primarily on flat grants

[3] Ellwood P. Cubberley, *School Funds and Their Apportionment* (New York: Columbia University, Teachers College Press, 1906), p. 100.
[4] Ibid.

as a means of financing its share of educational cost. The last state to rely upon such a method, Connecticut, adopted an equalizing plan in 1975.

Figure 6.2 illustrates the operation of a flat grant program. The chart is very similar to Figure 6.1. The only difference is that the state provides a flat grant of $1000 per pupil. This is shown by the horizontal line at $1000. Each district receives this much regardless of its wealth or the rate at which it decides to tax. Now assume that each district decides, *nevertheless*, to levy a tax at a rate of fifteen mills. The result is the total amount of money available per student shown by the sloping line. District A now has $2500 per pupil to spend; district B has $4000. The amount district B has is shown by the vertical line *BOP* to consist of the portion *BO*, which is the $1000 flat grant, and the portion *OP*, which is the $3000 raised by taxes. The absolute difference in expenditures is exactly the same as before:—$1500 per student. However, the *ratio* of expenditures has lessened. Without the flat grant, district B spends twice as much as district A. With the flat grant, it spends only 60 percent more ($4000/$1500 = 1.60).

The flat grant approach adheres to the first philosophy in assuming that a specific minimum of schooling should be guaranteed to every citizen. It assumes further that the state in its wisdom can determine the costs of this minimum education and will allocate that dollar amount as a flat grant. Schooling in excess of this minimum is held to benefit only the individual recipient or the community in which he or she resides. It is therefore a local luxury to be indulged in as each community sees fit, but not to be subsidized by the state. Under this philosophy, the flat grant is a satisfactory wealth equalizer. It does not equalize for differences in need or cost, but that is a different matter, to be discussed later. Since the amount of the flat grant is presumed to be sufficient to cover the education level the state believes to be minimally necessary, and, furthermore, since it is provided to all students equally and is raised by taxes levied at a uniform rate on all residents of the state, there is nothing inherently unequal about it.

FIGURE 6.2 A Flat Grant Program

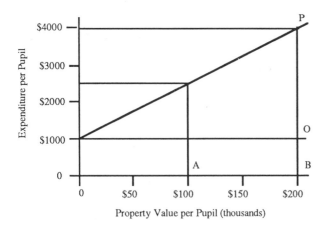

Property Value per Pupil (thousands)

Foundation program. One practical problem with flat grants is that states seldom have sufficient revenue to provide an adequate amount per student. For example, Connecticut, in the last year in which it used the flat grant (1975), provided $235 per student (plus some categorical aids); average expenditure per student in Connecticut at the time was $1507.[5] The reason states typically cannot find the necessary money is that they have allocated use of the property tax exclusively to local communities. It is rare to find a statewide property tax. A solution to this problem was described in 1923 by George D. Strayer and Robert M. Haig. In a report to the Educational Finance Inquiry Commission, based on a study of New York State, they proposed a system that has the effect of capturing a portion of the local property tax for state purposes, without that being openly evident.[6] Their proposal has since become known as the *foundation program*, or the *Strayer-Haig plan*. Just as with the flat grant, the state specifies a dollar amount per student to which each school district is entitled. Implicitly, this is the amount of money that is necessary to guarantee a minimally adequate education. The state requires each district to levy a property tax at a fixed rate (called *required local effort*) and provides only the difference between the amount raised by that tax and the guaranteed expenditure level. Thus, a property-poor district will raise very little with the tax at the specified rate, and the state will provide generously. A district richer in property will raise almost as much as the dollar guarantee and will receive little equalization aid from the state. A very rich district will raise more than the guarantee and will receive nothing from the state.

If the state requires each district to levy a property tax at a specified rate in order to receive state money, and counts the proceeds of that local tax as part of the guarantee, the required property tax is, in effect, a state tax. If the required local tax rate is relatively high, a substantial amount of money will be raised. This, combined with state money, enables the legislature to establish a guarantee level sufficient for a minimal education. Some states do not require the district actually to levy the tax at the specified rate, calling it instead a *computational tax*. It is then a device used only in determining the amount of state aid. A few property-poor districts may then levy a lower tax than this, raising less money per child than the guarantee and subverting the intent of the equalization plan.

Foundation program operation is illustrated in Figure 6.3. The horizontal line *LE* depicts the dollar amount of the foundation guarantee, supposedly representing the cost of a minimal program. The section labelled *Required Local Effort* is the amount raised by the local property tax at a required rate of ten mills. The section labeled *State Aid* is supplied by the state, at a foundation level of $2000. For district A, the required local effort (RLE) raises little money, and the state contribution is high. District B raises most of the guarantee locally, and district C raises more than the guarantee and receives nothing from the state. The solid sloping line at the top is the total amount that would be raised if all districts chose to levy an optional

[5] Marshall A. Harris, *School Finance at a Glance* (Denver: Education Commission of the States, 1975), p. 1.

[6] George D. Strayer and Robert M. Haig, *Financing of Education in the State of New York* (New York: Macmillan, 1923), pp. 173-74.

local tax at the rate of five mills, in addition to the required tax. District B can raise more than district A, and district C can raise more then district B. The line becomes steeper at point M because districts beyond that point already raise more than the guarantee by using only the required rate, thus making the total amount they collect that much higher. That is, the slope of the line OK is ten mills, the slope of the line LM is five mills, and the slope of the line MN is the sum of those, or fifteen mills.

It may be argued that it is unfair that some districts, because they happen to be rich in property, have more money to spend from levying the required tax rates than do property-poor districts. If the required tax is indeed a state tax, then the amounts raised above the guarantee should be returned to the state to be used elsewhere. This concept is called *recapture,* and the effect of it is shown by the dashed lines in Figure 6.3. District C would raise, at the required rate, the amount shown by the line CF. It would return to the state the amount EF, leaving it exactly as much as every other district. Because of this, if it levied an additional optional tax at the same rate as the other districts, it would raise the amount EG. With recapture on the 10 mills of RLE, the amount raised by districts at a fifteen-mill tax rate are shown by the line LMGP.

The underlying philosophy of the foundation plan is the same as that of the flat grant: the state should provide for an adequate minimum educational program, defined as a specified number of dollars per student, and districts may raise money above that guarantee if they wish, as a local luxury, without help from the state. A system such as this, including recapture, would provide complete wealth equalization if the underlying philosophy were accepted. States, however, have been unwilling to employ the recapture concept. To do so is to admit publicly that the required property tax is a state tax rather than a mechanism open to local option. In addition, the amount of taxes *exported* from a local district is highly visible. Recapture has been attempted in only a few states, and repealed in some of those.

FIGURE 6.3 A Foundation Program

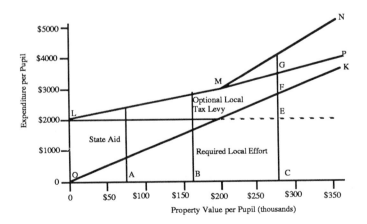

An alternative, of course, would be to simply levy a statewide property tax at the RLE rate, and use the proceeds to finance a flat grant system. Looked at this way, one can see that the flat grant is simply a special case of the foundation program, in which the required local tax rate is zero.

As with the flat grant (and indeed with all school finance schemes), there are practical problems with the foundation plan. The plan assumes that the foundation amount is the amount necessary for a minimally adequate education, although there is no way of determining this with accuracy. Because of the additional money made available through required local effort, at least this guarantee may be set higher than it would be with the flat grant. However, there is still no substitute for setting it politically, and controversy will always occur over whether it has been set sufficiently high.

Another problem is the *minimum grant* that usually accompanies a foundation program. The reason for this grant is that it is not only unpopular to recapture excess tax money generated by districts, it is even unpopular to grant them nothing. As a result, each district receives at least a minimum dollar amount of state aid per pupil regardless of its wealth. Since this minimum aid flows only to the wealthy districts, it is obviously disequalizing.

EQUAL ACCESS PHILOSOPHY

Percentage equalizing. Flat grants and the foundation plans have a similar philosophical underpinning: the state has an interest in seeing that each student receives a minimum education, and it undertakes to guarantee this on an equal basis. Percentage equalizing has a different philosophy. Essentially, it defines equity as equal access to money for education, and it also holds that the amount of education to be purchased by a community should be determined by that community.

With percentage equalizing, each district determines the size of its own budget, and the state pays a share of that budget determined by the district's *aid ratio*. The aid ratio is defined by means of a formula usually written in the form

$$\text{Aid ratio} = 1 - f\frac{y_i}{\bar{y}}$$

where

y_i is the assessed valuation per pupil of the district,
$\bar{y}$ is assessed valuation per student of the state as a whole, and
f is a scaling factor that is usually set somewhere between 0 and 1.

For example, if property value per pupil of the district were $20,000 and that of the state $80,000, and the scaling factor were 0.5, the aid ratio for the district would be

$$1 - .5 \times \frac{20,000}{80,000} = .875$$

This means the state would provide 87.5 percent of the budget of the district, with the district expected to raise the remaining 12.5 percent from local taxes. If the district had instead an assessed valuation of $80,000 per pupil (the state average), the aid ratio would have been 0.5, and the state would have provided half of the district's budget. It is easy to see that with this particular scaling factor, when a district's assessed valuation becomes twice that of the state, the aid ratio becomes zero. Above that point it becomes negative, the implication being that the district should instead send some tax money to the state. This is recapture, as discussed in connection with foundation plans, and it has proved no more popular in percentage-equalizing states than in foundation states.

Just as the flat grant is a special case of the foundation plan, the foundation plan can be thought of as a special case of the percentage equalizing plan in which the budget to be participated in by the state is set at a particular figure instead of being allowed to fluctuate.

Adoption of percentage equalizing was first urged by Harlan Updegraff and Leroy A. King in 1922, about the same time Strayer and Haig were recommending the foundation plan.[7] However, it was popularized by Charles S. Benson in 1961, and most of the eight states that enacted it did so shortly thereafter.[8] It is interesting that the Strayer-Haig plan became part of the school finance plan of the majority of states, whereas percentage equalizing was never widely adopted. However, a plan with a new name—power equalizing—but an identical purpose evolved in 1970, and its concepts were adopted by many states.

Power equalizing. Power equalization is a wealth equalization concept described by John E. Coons, William H. Clune, and Stephen D. Sugarman in their book *Private Wealth and Public Education.*[9] They concern themselves not with equalizing expenditures per pupil, but with equalizing the ability of local districts to support schools. They argue strongly for the virtues of *subsidiarity,* by which they mean making decisions at the lowest appropriate level of government feasible. This implies that decisions on school expenditures should be made by the local district. (Indeed, the three authors argue that these decisions should even be made by the individual family, leading to a concept called *family power equalizing.*) Coons, Clune, and Sugarman put forth their Proposition 1, which states that public education expenditures should not be a function of wealth, except the wealth of the state as a whole. This argument formed a substantial part of the legal reasoning exhibited in *Serrano* and other school-finance equal-protection cases.[10]

The philosophy behind power equalizing is the same as that behind percentage equalizing: the ability to raise money should be equalized, but the decision as to how much money to raise should be left to the local district. Under power equaliz-

[7]Harlan Updegraff and Leroy A. King, *Survey of the Fiscal Policies of the State of Pennsylvania in the Field of Education* (Philadelphia: University of Pennsylvania, 1922), chap. 2.

[8]Charles S. Benson, *The Economics of Public Education* (New York: Houghton Mifflin, 1961), pp. 242–46. Prior to the publication of this book, only Wisconsin and Rhode Island had plans that were percentage equalizing in form.

[9]John E. Coons, William H. Clune III, and Stephen D. Sugarman, *Private Wealth and Public Education* (Cambridge, Mass.: Harvard University Press, Belknap Press, 1970).

[10]See the discussions of *Serrano* and other equal-protection suits in Chapters 2 and 8.

ing, the state establishes a schedule of tax rates, with an amount per pupil guaranteed to a district for each level of tax. Such a schedule might look like this:

TAX RATE (MILLS)	GUARANTEED REVENUE PER PUPIL
5	$1000
10	$2000
15	$3000
20	$4000

(The guarantee at other intermediate tax rates is obtained by interpolation.) This schedule is the simplest power equalizing schedule, and amounts to a guarantee of a specified number of dollars per pupil per mill levied.

However, power equalizing is more general than percentage equalizing because it is not necessary to have the linear schedule implied by the guarantee of an amount per mill per student. For example, it would be possible to have a large guarantee per mill for the first ten mills, and a much smaller guarantee for mills in excess of ten. This would tend to move districts toward a levy of ten mills, where the high marginal increase in revenue per student would suddenly decrease. A few states (Michigan is an example) did this, but most states enacting power equalizing have adopted the simple linear schedule.

Coons, Clune, and Sugarman were influential. By 1984, eighteen states had adopted some form of power equalizing as an important feature of their school finance system.[11]

Guaranteed tax base. A third name for plans based on the equal access philosophy is the *guaranteed tax base*, or GTB. The state guarantees each district the same assessed valuation per student. The district calculates the tax rate necessary to raise its budget, using as an assessed value for the purposes of calculation the guaranteed valuation per pupil times the number of pupils. It then levies this calculated rate against the actual assessed valuation. The state compensates for differences between the amount actually raised and the amount that would be raised at the guaranteed valuation.

At this point it should be emphasized that percentage equalizing, power equalizing (with a linear schedule), and GTB plans are mathematically identical.[12] They are simply different ways of saying the same thing, emphasizing different aspects of the general idea of equal access to funds. They are illustrated in Figure 6.4. This chart could represent a percentage equalizing plan with a factor f of 0.5 and an average state assessed valuation of $100,000. Alternatively, it could represent a

---

[11]*School Finance at a Glance, 1983–84*, (Denver: Education Commission of the States, 1984).

[12]A proof of the equivalence of percentage equalizing and a guaranteed valuation per pupil is given in Walter I. Garms, James W. Guthrie, and Lawrence C. Pierce, *School Finance: The Economics and Politics of Public Education* (Englewood Cliffs, N.J.: Prentice-Hall, 1978), pp. 194–95. A proof of the equivalence of power equalizing and percentage equalizing is given in pp. 198–99 of the same volume.

power equalizing plan with a guarantee of $200 per pupil per mill of tax. Finally, it could represent a GTB plan with a guarantee of $200,000 assessed valuation per pupil. There is no difference in operation among the three plans. Figure 6.4 shows the results of two different tax rates. The solid lines and upright type show a tax rate of ten mills; the dashed lines and italic type reflect a tax rate of fifteen mills. The actual tax rate of a particular district, of course, could be any amount, but the principle is the same. Note that in each of the two instances, lines representing state aid and local effort are graphically the same as those in Figure 6.3 for the foundation plan. District A receives $2000 per pupil at a ten-mill tax rate, and $3000 per pupil at a fifteen-mill rate. At the ten-mill rate, it provides $750 from local taxes and the state provides $1250. At the fifteen-mill rate, the district raises $1125 and the state provides $1875. District B provides much more from its own taxes, and the state aid is much less, but it receives the same total amount per pupil at each tax rate as does district A. District C raises more money from its own taxes than is guaranteed by the state, and receives no state aid.

Like the others, these plans have suffered from practical problems. One is that since the emphasis is on the district deciding the size of its own budget, there should be no restriction on the size of this budget. However, to guarantee that the state will share in any budget, no matter how large, is a frightening prospect for lawmakers and state officials, who fear wholesale raids on the state treasury. Consequently, the state usually limits the expenditure per student that will be equalized by the state. As long as this limit is substantially above the average expenditure, there is little cause for concern. Frequently it is set much lower. Then most districts simply are guaranteed the maximum state guarantee per student. This is the

FIGURE 6.4   Percentage Equalizing, Power Equalizing, and Guaranteed Tax Base Plans

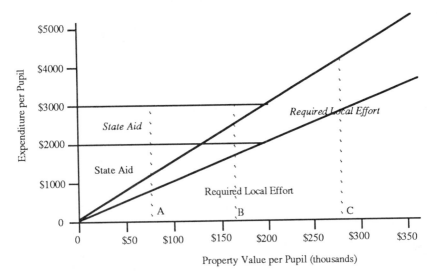

equivalent of a foundation plan with a guarantee at that level and a required local tax rate equal to the tax rate associated with that guarantee under the plan in use.

A second problem with equal-access plans, one that they share with foundation plans, is that some districts might get no equalization money at all (or, worse, be forced to contribute to the state instead). This has been politically unpalatable, and the remedy has been to see that all districts receive some state aid, either by specifying a minimum amount per pupil to which each district will be entitled, or by specifying a minimum aid ratio.

EQUAL TOTAL PROVISION PHILOSOPHY: FULL STATE FUNDING

The third philosophical position on equalization was first espoused by Henry C. Morrison, in 1930.[13] It was brought forward again in 1967 by Arthur C. Wise as a legal position from which to argue for increased wealth equalization within a state.[14] According to this position, education is a state responsibility and must be made available to all the state's children on an equal basis. There would be no geographical variation in school expenditure. It does not, however, preclude adjustments for differing educational needs or differences in the cost of producing education of equivalent quality. It does mean that, *other things being equal*, students will be recipients of equal monetary provision. The only means by which this can be accomplished operationally is for the state to mandate the expenditure level, and equity demands that the expenditures be supported by statewide taxation. Therefore, this method of financing the schools has become known as *full state funding*, or *full state assumption*.

Full state funding does not necessarily imply state operation of the schools, but merely a state guarantee of equal amounts of money per pupil to each district. However, it has been clear in states that have de facto or de jure full state funding that the result is substantially greater state control.

Only one state, Hawaii, has de jure full state funding. Education has been operated by the state since statehood, and there are no local districts. However, other states have approached full state funding as a de facto position, even though their school finance system is nominally quite different. New Mexico and Florida have foundation plans with low required local effort. Almost all of the districts in the state raise less than the state guarantee through the required local effort, and thus receive state equalization aid. Both states have rigid restrictions on optional extra millage. The result is a system in which all of the schools in the state are funded on the same basis, as if there were a full state funding scheme in effect.

California is an interesting case, which will be discussed in more detail later. As we saw in Chapter 5, California's Proposition 13, passed in 1978, limited property taxes to 1 percent of property value for all purposes. With few exceptions, each school district's share of these taxes is less than is necessary to run the district,

[13]Henry C. Morrison, *School Revenue* (Chicago: University of Chicago Press, 1930).

[14]Arthur C. Wise, *Rich Schools, Poor Schools* (Chicago: University of Chicago Press, 1967).

and the state makes up the difference. There is little possibility of an optional local levy. However, the state does not guarantee districts the same amount of money per student. Rather, guaranteed revenue per student for each district is based on what it actually spent in 1977–78, adjusted for inflation. The effect is full state assumption without equalization (although, as will be shown later, there have been significant advances toward equalization in California).

An interesting way of distributing money in a full state assumption scheme has been suggested by Jay Chambers.[15] He has developed a *resource cost model*, which separates education into homogeneous programs. For each program, experts determine the required inputs: teachers, aides, supplies, and so forth. For each district, a cost is developed for each kind of input. The district is then provided by the state with the amount of money necessary to buy inputs for the programs required for its students. This is, then, a method for providing equitably for educational provision within a system of full state funding, taking into account differences in needs and costs.

Full state assumption would appear to solve most of the problems previously discussed in connection with the other formulas. The marks of a true full state funding plan are that all educational funds are raised by statewide taxes (which could include property taxes) and that the money is spent equally on similarly situated students. Disallowing any local supplementary aid eliminates the tax and expenditure discrepancies that haunt practical application of the other plans. However, such a high degree of equity has a price. The legislature, having provided all education revenues from state sources, will want to see that the money is spent judiciously. It is almost inevitable that full state assumption will bring increased state control over education. In Florida, for example, where de facto full state assumption was enacted in 1973, the state at the same time enacted a requirement that most of the funds generated by the presence of students in a school be spent on those students in that school. Since students in different programs (the mentally retarded, the physically handicapped, those pursuing career education, etc.) generated different amounts of state money, this requirement mandated a school-by-school, program-by-program accounting system, with auditing by state officials. The result is a dilution of local school officials' initiative.

WHICH PHILOSOPHY IS BEST?

Most individuals implicitly hold one or another of these three different philosophical positions on equity, without carefully analyzing it. Naturally, one's views affect which of the plans is judged as equitable.

The philosophy of equal total provision—that the state should furnish on an equal basis all public education in the state—is the most egalitarian. Not only is all funding equal, but all taxation is also equal, since the source of funds is statewide taxes. The minimum provision philosophy equalizes expenditures and taxation only for that portion of expenditures deemed necessary for a minimum adequate program.

[15]Thomas B. Parrish and Jay G. Chambers, *An Overview of the Resource Cost Model (RCM)* (Stanford, Calif.: Associates for Education Finance and Planning, 1984).

Expenditures for other purposes are unequalized. The difference between minimal provision and equal total provision is actually one of degree. Full state funding does not equalize any educational services furnished outside the public schools, whether by private schools or by individual tutors. However, there is a great difference between equalizing all of the many things that the public schools offer and equalizing only a minimum program.

The equal access philosophy is quite different. Power equalizing, percentage equalizing, and the GTB make no attempt to equalize expenditures on education. They simply equalize access to the funds for those expenditures. One could think of the equalizing of expenditures as *student equity*, and the equalizing of access to funds as *taxpayer equity*. Full state funding does both; the foundation plan does both (but to a limited extent); and power equalizing is concerned only with taxpayer equity. The distinction is an important one. Most of the school finance lawsuits have raised the constitutional issue of education as a state function that must be furnished on an equal basis to all. It seems much easier to find a plan providing student equity that meets this criterion than one that provides only taxpayer equity.[16]

Need Equalization

The foregoing discussion of wealth equalization contains the "other things being equal" assumption—that all students are alike in their need for education. This is manifestly untrue. Many students have unusual learning problems that require costly special teaching methods. The mentally retarded, emotionally disturbed, blind, and deaf are only a few such categories. In addition, many normal children can benefit from a program that is more expensive. This is particularly true in the area of career or vocational education. Fortunately, these differences in needs can be incorporated into a wealth-equalizing scheme as part of a comprehensive state aid plan. The ways in which this is done can be categorized as *entitlement, reimbursement,* and *organizational schemes*.

ENTITLEMENT SCHEMES

These schemes entitle a school district to an amount of aid that is specified in advance, independent of the actual costs to the district of operating programs for students with special needs. (Of course, the amount is presumably related to the average cost of such programs.)

Weighting systems. Imagine a foundation plan that guarantees a given number of dollars per student. Implicit in such a plan is that all students should have the same basic amount spent on them. If one wishes to spend different amounts on students with special needs, one can do this by counting each such person as more than one student. For example, educable mentally retarded students might be weighted 1.5 compared with the 1.0 weighting of so-called normal students.

[16]See Chapter 8 for a more detailed discussion of the legal positions involved in these lawsuits.

Weighting presumably represents the ratio of the cost of providing a basic special program to that of providing a basic normal program. Usually the normal student in the middle elementary grades is weighted 1.0 and all other weights are related to this standard. The sum of all weighted students is obtained, and this weighted student count is used as the basis for calculating state aid. Simply by substituting weighted students for actual students, one can use this method with any of the wealth equalizing plans that have been discussed. This means that practically, as well as conceptually, it is possible to separate need equalization from wealth equalization.

Weighting schemes assume that the cost of a special program bears a fixed cost relationship to the cost of a normal program. This is assumed to be true both within districts and among districts. The state compensates districts on this basis, but without otherwise dictating the content of programs.

If a weighting plan for need equalization is to be equitable, it is necessary to have an accurate determination of the program costs for special categories of students relative to the program costs for normal elementary students. This constitutes a major difficulty in using weighting plans. Because we do not yet have an agreed-upon technology for educating each category of student, it is impossible to agree on the extra cost involved. Even if it were possible to agree on the technology, local district cost-accounting methods are undeveloped.

Another difficulty with pupil or program weights is that they need frequent revision in order to remain consistent with actual cost differences. But this is where circular reasoning enters the argument, for this year's weights will depend on the amount spent last year. However, the amount spent this year will depend on the money available, and therefore on the weights used.

If the specified weight allocates a state aid amount more than the per-pupil cost of a special program, school districts will tend to misclassify students into special programs, and then use the unneeded funds for other programs, including those for normal students. This happened in Florida, where several small rural districts placed the majority of their students into either mentally retarded or vocational programs. The remedy for such abuses is state quotas, which can be unfair if they prevent enrollment in special programs of students who actually need special assistance. Another remedy is state auditing of student placements.

Approximately twenty-two states use weighting schemes in their state aid programs. In Florida, there are thirty-three separate programs, with weights that vary widely. A few examples are as follows:

PROGRAM	WEIGHT
Grades 1–3	1.234
Grades 4–9	1.00
Grades 9–12	1.116
Educable mentally retarded	2.30
Deaf	4.00
Hospital and homebound, part-time	10.00
Vocational education	1.17 to 4.26

Flat grants for special programs. About ten states fund one or more special programs through a flat grant of a specified number of dollars per pupil in the program. The implicit philosophy is that the excess cost of educating a child in such a program is that specified number of dollars in every district.

Individually calculated entitlements. The imprecision of weighting and flat grant schemes means that some districts receive more and others receive much less than they need for special programs. Computers have made it possible to calculate an entitlement for each program for each district in a state. For example, in California, such a system operates for special education. Each student who may be entitled to a special education program is examined and an individual education program (IEP) established for him or her. The program, in other words, is tailored to the student. Special education and related services are provided by a local plan area, which may consist of a single district or a group of districts that have agreed to cooperate to provide the required full range of services. By summing the IEP requirements of the children in the local plan area, the district(s) can establish a need for personnel and other services. Entitlement for instructional personnel is based on the number required and the average costs of their salaries and benefits in the local plan area. To this is added an entitlement for support services (including administration, supplies, maintenance, etc.), based on a ratio of such costs to the costs of instructional personnel in the local plan area. The result is a total entitlement for special education. From this is subtracted any federal aid to which the local plan area is entitled. The remainder is provided by the state. (Remember that California is a state that has de facto full state assumption of educational costs.)

REIMBURSEMENT SCHEMES

Reimbursement schemes compensate districts for actual costs of providing for special needs. Districts account for special program expenditures, deduct state-defined costs of educating normal students, and receive state reimbursement for all or a portion of the extra costs. Approximately seventeen states have excess cost reimbursements for instructional programs.

A major advantage of this approach is that districts are reimbursed only for the actual *excess cost* of the programs; this eliminates the previously mentioned misclassification incentive. Another advantage, particularly from the legislature's view, is that money is restricted to categories for which the grants are given. This necessitates state definition of types of reimbursable expenditures, a cost-accounting system, and a reliable state audit, all of which are restrictions on district freedom.

Another advantage of the excess-cost system is that the amount granted is tailored to a district's expenditure pattern. This is better than the assumption, as in a weighting system, that costs in all districts are the same proportion of normal costs.

A disadvantage of the excess-cost system, if the state pays all or most costs, is that there is little incentive for districts to operate an efficient program. This often leaves the state with the necessity of specifying a maximum dollar limit on the amount of aid per student to be granted. This may be unfair to high-cost districts, while providing no brakes on the expenditures of a low-cost district.

Another disadvantage is that districts are not reimbursed until expenditures have been made, reports submitted to the state, and expenditures audited. Often a district is hard-pressed to find money to start a new program because of this delay.

ORGANIZATIONAL SCHEMES

A third manner of providing services for special students is to assign special-program responsibility to an *intermediate education district*. The main advantage of the larger district is organizational. Because of economies of scale, intermediate districts can afford to provide programs for handicapped students that individual districts might find too costly because of the few students in the district with that handicap. A disadvantage is that it is not practical to use this approach for all special programs. Students must be transported from their usual schools, and this inhibits mainstreaming. Also, additional transportation costs may outweigh the economies of scale gained by concentrating handicapped children in one place. Finally, local district authorities may fear loss of control over an important part of the education of their children.

OVERVIEW

There is a place in a well-designed school finance system for each of these methods of need equalization. Weighting is heavily dependent upon arbitrary cost factors, inviting misclassification of students or a failure to offer specific programs. It is probably best used where there is little or no possibility of either type of subversion—for example, when weights are used for various levels of education. That weights are arbitrary (e.g., high school students may be weighted 1.25) is not important from an equity standpoint (as it would be for special programs), because all students experience each level of schooling.

Certain special programs, such as those for the multiply handicapped or severely mentally retarded, are probably best handled by an intermediate education district, state schools, a consortium of school districts, or private contracting. These services usually require a large investment in tools and equipment, and such an arrangement can spread these costs over a large pupil population.

Districts should also be allowed to contract with intermediate education districts for special programs. Such services will then be offered by an intermediate district only if it can convince local officials that it can offer better services or operate at lower cost than they can. The state would offer aid through weighting or other entitlement methods to local districts for special students who are, say, blind. The district would use this money either in operating its own program or in contracting with the intermediate district, whichever it found more effective or less expensive.

Most special needs should be handled through programs providing reimbursement for excess costs. Such programs offer little incentive to misclassify students into programs or not to offer the programs, as there is with weighting. Districts can spend different amounts to meet needs without being rewarded or penalized. The biggest problem is that the state must establish a maximum allowable reimbursement to prevent districts from operating needlessly expensive programs. An alternative is to reimburse only a percentage of the excess cost, which gives the district a stake in how much is spent.

Alternatively, these special needs can be handled through an individually calculated entitlement program such as that described earlier. Such a system appears to provide reasonably adequate safeguards against improper classification of students, and there is an incentive toward efficiency in that the district does not receive more money if it spends more, or less money if it economizes.

Finally, there can well be special needs that the state will simply ignore in its financial scheme, or for which it will perhaps pay a small fixed amount per pupil, allowing districts to provide for them out of money to which they are entitled for regular students. This would be the case for experimental or inexpensive programs.

Cost Equalization

Equalization may be needed to balance differences among districts in the cost of providing educational services of similar quality and kind. There are several reasons for cost differences. They divide rather well into two categories: (1) differences in the amount and cost per unit of supplies and services that must be purchased by the school district, and (2) differences in the amounts districts must pay to attract and retain employees of comparable quality.

Supplies and services may differ in cost for various reasons. The school district in a mountain area may have to pay a large annual bill for snow clearance. The mountain district may also use more fuel for heating and find that its unit cost for fuel is higher. A sparsely settled rural area may be unable to avoid small classes and high busing costs. Land cost for school sites is much higher in cities, as is the cost of vandalism. In general, extra costs tend to be higher in rural and highly urbanized districts, and lower in suburban districts.[17]

Salaries constitute 70 to 80 percent of the average school district's budget. Thus differences in the costs of hiring and retaining employees of equivalent quality are even more important than differences in the cost of supplies. There may be differences in the cost of living among districts, resulting from variation in rents or housing prices, food, and so on. More important, however, are differences in the attractiveness of a school as a place to teach and a community as a place to live.

It is easier to recognize cost differences than it is to measure and subsequently compensate districts for them. All states compensate districts for costs of necessary bus transportation in some manner. This is because such costs vary so widely. Usually compensation is on a cost-reimbursement basis. A district records the transportation cost of eligible students. Record keeping for such purposes is usually complicated. In fact, accounting for the transportation reimbursement—a small part of total state payments—is frequently more complicated than all the rest of the district's cost accounting combined. The state then reimburses the district for a portion of these transportation costs. In New York, state reimbursement is ninety percent of

[17]See Garms, Guthrie and Pierce, *School Finance,* chap. 15, for a description of city schools' financial problems.

costs. There is clearly little incentive for New York districts to economize on transportation costs. In Florida, on the other hand, each district's transportation costs are estimated by means of a regression equation, with density of population used to predict a district's transportation expenditure. The district is paid this estimated cost. If it manages to transport students for less than the estimate, it may use the extra funds for other purposes. If it spends more than the estimate, it must make up the difference from its own sources. This approach encourages efficiency in operating transportation systems. Florida's is an entitlement approach, whereas New York uses a reimbursement system.

States also subsidize cost differences for *necessary small schools*—schools that must exist because transportation distances to larger schools would be too great. Students may be weighted, with those in the smallest schools given the highest weightings. These students are counted like those weighted for need differences. Alternatively, small-school students may be treated separately, with a special formula specifically for them.

As we have noted, the major cost variation is in the salaries necessary to attract teachers and other employees of equivalent quality. Some states have dealt with this problem by using a state salary schedule, not for paying teachers individually but for placing the teachers of a district in order to determine the amount of state aid to be received. Teachers are each placed in the column and step of the schedule appropriate to their training and experience, the total teacher salaries that would be paid if the teachers had been on the state salary schedule is determined, and this amount is used in making an adjustment to the amount of state aid to be received by the district. In effect, this compensates a district that has more teachers near the high end of the schedule for that fact, while not compensating it for paying higher salaries than the state schedule.

Whether this is an equalizing measure or not depends on whether one views placement of teachers on a salary schedule as something under district control. The general principle of cost equalization is that districts should be compensated for differences in cost that they cannot control, but not compensated for discretionary differences. If a district has declining enrollment, it cannot hire new teachers (except to replace some of those who retire or leave), and the teaching staff each year tends to move farther up the salary schedule. The district has little current control over this. On the other hand, if there is expanding enrollment the district hires teachers, and it has a good deal of control over whether it hires experienced teachers or those near the beginning steps of the schedule. State aid confers greater help on districts that hire experienced teachers. Since wealthy districts are more able to hire expensive teachers in the first place, this kind of state aid may be antiequalizing.

Florida adjusts a district's state aid entitlement by cost-of-living differences. Each district's foundation aid level is adjusted by a cost-of-living index. Districts with lower costs of living have lower foundation levels. A cost-of-living index is a poor indicator of the actual cost differences in hiring employees of comparable quality, for differences in the attractiveness of the district as a place to work and live are also important to teachers. Nevertheless, it is a more effective way to compensate for differences in cost than the state salary schedule approach.

The most sophisticated attempt to adjust for differences in cost has been Jay Chambers's *cost-of-education index*.[18] This approach involves gathering information on all of the items that would result in cost differences among districts. Some of these items would be the result of conscious choices made by the district, such as the choice to have fewer pupils per classroom. Others would be outside the control of the district, such as the amount of snow that must be cleared. A schedule is prepared in which those items of cost not under the control of the district are shown at their actual cost to the district, and those under control of the district are shown at the state average cost. The total cost of operation of the district is computed on this basis. This would be the total cost if the district were in its current situation but made average decisions. State aid is based on this.

One of the principal troubles with the Chambers approach is that many costs represent items that are not completely under district control. Although the district cannot control the amount of snow that falls, it can decide the extent and frequency of snow clearance. The major item, of course, is teacher salaries, and the extent to which this is controlled by the district depends, among other things, on the rate at which it can hire new teachers. Some districts have little control over teacher costs, others have a great deal. Collective bargaining brings other problems. It is not clear how much control a district has over the salary costs that are arrived at through collective bargaining, and this probably varies greatly from district to district.

A second problem with the Chambers approach is that it requires massive amounts of data, from each district in the state. The procedure itself is sufficiently complicated that it is difficult to explain to legislators and laymen.

Another area of frequent attempts at cost equalization is that of *declining enrollment*. Here, the problem is short-term. Typically, such declines result in one or two fewer students in each class; this makes consolidation of classes difficult. A district continues to use the same number of teachers and classrooms, resulting in an increase in per-student cost. Over time a district can make reductions, remedying the short-term problem. In economists' terms, this is the result of marginal costs being substantially less than average costs. This works on the up side too, with a few additional students not increasing district costs very much, but state aid formulas have always given districts as much help for additional students as for existing ones. However, there are cries for help when enrollment declines.

Approximately half the states have tried to provide additional aid to districts suffering enrollment declines. One alternative is to permit a district to choose either the previous year's or the current year's enrollment as a basis for claiming state aid. The growing district uses the current year's enrollment figure; districts with decreasing enrollments use the previous year's figure. A variation allows districts to use either current enrollment or a moving average of the previous three, four, or five years. Either method provides temporary relief for a district faced with enrollment declines, but does not put off the day of reckoning indefinitely.

A different approach, used in a few states, is to offer a *save-harmless* provision, which guarantees the district no less total state aid than it received the year

[18]Jay G. Chambers, "The Development of a Cost of Education Index," *Journal of Education Finance*, 5, no. 3, (Winter 1980), 262–81.

before. If the district has declining enrollment, this could be thought of as the equivalent of counting "phantom students." If the save-harmless provision disappears after a short time, the effect is similar to that of the plans just discussed. If it continues indefinitely, as it has in New York, it can result in districts being paid on the basis of enrollment many years before, even though current enrollment is less than half of that.

ADEQUATE PROVISION

From 1940 to 1970, the major concern of state school finance officials was to provide the resources necessary to meet the rapidly increasing demands on schools. Not only were enrollments burgeoning, but also the public was demanding more services. Programs such as vocational education increased the average cost per student at the same time that the number of students was increasing rapidly. The result was that state governments were under persistent pressure for new money. There was also concern with efficiency and equality during this time, but those goals often had to be subordinated to a continuing need to finance expansion.

This period of growth was accompanied by a labor shortage as well as a money shortage. Teachers were in short supply, and the economic system responded, as is typical, by increasing the price, thus encouraging more people to enter the profession. Teacher salaries increased faster than salaries of workers in general. Some saw this as an increase from grossly inadequate salaries to a decent living wage, while others believed the new salary levels exorbitant.

These increased labor costs were added to the other costs incurred from the growing numbers of students and expanding program demands. Average cost per student increased tenfold, from $100 in 1940 to $1000 in 1970; total elementary-secondary public education costs increased eighteenfold, from $2.26 billion to $40.27 billion during the same period.

Legislatures have usually tried to promote efficiency in the schools by enacting expenditure restrictions. From 1940 to 1970, previous expenditure restrictions were relaxed or eliminated, either by the legislature or by direct vote of the people. For example, many states had tax rate limitations, but local elections to permit school districts to tax above this limit regularly passed by large margins.

Legislation increasing costs seldom increased equality. Although most states had equalization programs—and most were spending more on education than ever before—these higher disbursements did not lessen expenditure inequalities within states.

Large increments of state money were injected into education in the 1950s and 1960s, and this was generally matched or exceeded by increases in local revenues. Most of the state money and almost all of the local money were in the form of additional *general aid*, money that could be used for any district purpose (as opposed to *categorical aid*, which can be used only for specified purposes).

In addition to general aid, states provided categorical aid for a variety of special programs, such as education of mentally retarded and physically handicapped children. Several states even attempted to alleviate environmental handicaps such as poorly educated parents or poverty and ghetto living conditions.

Other categorical aids went for construction of many badly needed new schools, particularly in suburbs in the fast-growing states. These suburbs frequently were unable to raise enough money locally, and state assistance became crucial.

During the late 1960s and the 1970s, there was considerably less emphasis on adequate provision. The strongly felt need to improve our educational system that arose with Sputnik in 1957 had spent itself as the U.S. achieved its goal of putting a man on the moon. The concern was instead with equity—with seeing that all pupils had an equal chance to acquire an appropriate education. Even so expenditures per pupil rose more rapidly than the economy grew. Between 1965 and 1980, expenditures per pupil went up from $515 to $2291—a 345 percent increase including inflation, and a 70 percent increase in constant dollars.[19] During this same period, the national income per capita went up 42 percent in constant dollars.[20] One reason for the rapid increase in expenditures per pupil was the rapid decline in the number of pupils during this decade and a half. Marginal cost in education is considerably less than average cost, because an additional student or two does not require an additional teacher. For this reason, a decline in pupils translated into an increase in cost per student. In addition, attempts to improve equity usually were accomplished by *leveling up*—increasing money for the low-spending districts while taking nothing away from the high-spending. Thus, a rapid increase in expenditures per pupil accompanied attempts to improve equity. However, it is not clear that the increase in expenditures per student resulted in a more adequate education. In many cases, teachers taught smaller classes but continued to use the same techniques.

With the early 1980s came an increasing concern with adequate provision. The realization that test scores had been declining for some time pervaded the national consciousness, drawing increasing cries for school improvement. A series of reports in 1983 highlighted the problem and provided a rallying point.[21]

The new push for more adequate schools did not manifest itself in the form of additional general aid for the schools. Instead, there were attempts to deal directly with the problems of improving the schools, by increasing "time on task," lengthening the school day and the school year, improving the curriculum, providing special assistance to teachers, reducing class size in the early grades, and employing a wide variety of other tactics. Of course, these cost money, and the money was usually provided in the form of categorical grants—money that could be used only for

[19]Calculated from data from U.S. Bureau of the Census, *Statistical Abstract of the United States, 1985* (Washington, D.C.: Government Printing Office, 1984), p. 131, Table 207, and p. 475, Table 789.

[20]*Ibid.*, calculated from p. 433, Table 717, and p. 6, Table 2.

[21]At least 15 reports critical of U.S. education were issued within a year. Prominent among them were Mortimer J. Adler, *The Paideia Proposal* (New York: Macmillan, 1982); Ernest L. Boyer, *High School: A Report on Secondary Education in America* (New York: Harper & Row, Pub., 1983); John I. Goodlad, *A Place Called School: Prospects for the Future* (St. Louis: McGraw-Hill, 1983); and National Commission on Excellence in Education, *A Nation at Risk: The Imperative for Educational Reform* (Washington, D.C.: Government Printing Office, 1983). For a summary of the facts and viewpoints of these reports, see Education Commission of the States, *A Summary of Major Reports on Education* (Denver, 1983).

specified purposes. In some cases the new programs were mandated by the state, whereas in others the categorical money was held out as an incentive for the districts to institute the new programs.

EFFICIENCY

Efficiency has long been a goal of those who finance education. It is expressed as a desire to obtain adequate education for as little money as possible. The goal is laudable, but difficult to attain. The problem is that there is little agreement on what education is to accomplish, how it is to be accomplished, and how accomplishments are to be measured. In the past, those concerned with school efficiency merely advocated imposing spending limits, theorizing that educators having a restricted amount of money will use it more wisely. During the postwar period of rapid school expansion the goal of efficiency was muted, but the enrollment decline in the 1970s, coupled with a continued rapid rise in expenditures per student, prompted reinstitution of limits. In the 1980s, legislatures have adopted a more active role by providing categorical money as an incentive for school improvement. Districts must often apply for the money, supplying detailed plans to the state education department for spending it.

Spending Limits

Spending limits have usually taken the form either of restricting the amount of money available to a district or of making money available in the form of categorical aid, which must be spent on programs considered desirable by the legislature, rather than leaving expenditures to local discretion. Restrictions on amounts of money have taken the form of *tax rate limits*, *annual budget votes*, or *expenditure or revenue limits*.

TAX RATE LIMITS

The most common form of restriction is the tax rate limit. Until recently, most states outside the Northeast (where budget votes are the norm) had such limits. The tax rate limit is a maximum rate that may be applied to a district's assessed valuation to raise money for school purposes.

These limits have numerous flaws. If a uniform limit is applied across the state (the usual situation), districts that have the same full valuation of property per pupil but different assessment ratios (see Chapter 5 for a discussion of the assessment process) will raise different amounts of money per pupil. These differences have led to state boards of equalization, which adjust local assessed values to a uniform assessment rate for school purposes.

Even if the tax rate limit is based on full valuation rather than assessed valuation, there are vast differences in the amount of money per pupil that can be raised by different districts levying the tax at the allowed limit. This is because there are great differences in the amount of property value per pupil among districts.

Even though general state aid programs are designed to alleviate these differences, they usually are inadequate for this purpose. The result is that districts must levy taxes at a rate above the limit. States usually provide for districts to raise their tax rate limit by a vote of the people in the district. In addition, for certain special purposes they may provide for a school board to levy taxes above the tax rate limit without a vote of the people. Such *override* taxes are often used for special education, for free or subsidized meals for needy children, and for community services.

ANNUAL BUDGET VOTES

Annual votes on the school district budgets have long been a custom in the northeastern states. The school board proposes a budget, indicating total estimated expenditures, the revenue expected from all sources other than local taxes, and (by subtraction) the amount to be raised from local taxes. Theoretically, this direct vote should be a useful mechanism for adjusting expenditures to voters' desires. However, it sometimes does not work, partly by design of the school board. Even voters who want to inform themselves thoroughly before voting usually find it extremely difficult and thus may not be able to vote intelligently. The information furnished to the voters typically does not compare the coming year's proposed expenditures with the current year's actual, does not put expenditures in per-pupil terms, and does not adequately explain proposed changes.

Also, elections are sometimes delayed until autumn, which threatens voters with a delayed school opening if they do not pass the budget. New York law provides that a district that fails to pass a budget election can operate on an "austerity" budget. This budget is austere only in excluding auxiliary programs of particular interest to parents: interscholastic athletics, non-required transportation, and school lunches. On the other hand, whatever the district agrees to pay the teachers as a result of collective bargaining is automatically included in the budget, and taxes are raised to pay these salaries. Thus the budget is austere for the public but not necessarily for educators.

DIRECT REVENUE OR EXPENDITURE LIMITATIONS

The failure of tax rate limits or budget votes to provide meaningful limitations on school district expenditures has led some states, to adopt more direct controls. Typically, the state limits the amount each district can spend per student. This is the most direct form of control and, if established uniformly on a statewide basis, would result in equal expenditures per pupil statewide. However, it is neither politically possible nor desirable to establish such uniform limits. Some districts have higher costs per student for providing the same amount of educational services, for reasons that are beyond their control. These include high costs for transporting pupils, for heating and snow removal, and for salaries of personnel in high-wage areas. Such districts would have insufficient money if the limit were uniform statewide.

The political justification for permitting disparity is as follows. Establishing a uniform limitation would either result in some districts being forced to reduce their expenditures drastically (if the limit were established only slightly above the median expenditure), or constitute no real limitation (if established near the level of the highest-spending district). As a result, when legislatures institute such limitations, they usually set each district's current rate of expenditures as its ceiling and provide for a yearly increase to allow for inflation. There may be a provision that allows low-spending districts a greater inflationary increase than high-spending districts, thus gradually squeezing the expenditures of the districts together. Such a provision is made for purposes of equity, however, rather than efficiency.

Categorical Aid

The limits discussed above have represented a confession by the legislature that it does not know how to make the schools efficient, but that it hopes school professionals will find ways to do so if sufficiently motivated. It is unlikely that these limits will promote efficiency. The bureaucratic imperative is toward expenditure expansion, not cost containment. Faced with a shortage of funds, school professionals will often make decisions designed to encourage citizens to open their pockets (such as curtailing interscholastic athletics) rather than trying to find ways to operate more efficiently.

Recognizing revenue or expenditure limitation flaws, many legislatures have opted to decide which are the priority areas for spending money on education, and then to provide funds for these specific purposes. Much of the recent increase in school funds has been provided through this mechanism. Such categorical programs take away local discretion and substitute decision-making at the state level. It is difficult to establish regulations at the state level that accommodate all the different local situations. Whether categorical aid, with its accompanying restrictions, contributes to efficiency is open to question, but at least it forces districts to concentrate more on areas considered high in priority by the legislature.

CHOICE

The three main values affecting public school policy noted in Chapter 2 are equity, efficiency, and liberty or choice. Most of the history of public education has been one of narrowing choice. By delegating local communities, or school districts, responsibility for education, states initially gave these communities wide latitude to choose the kind, amount, and quality of education to be provided. The first compulsory attendance laws began to circumscribe this freedom of choice. No one argues that this restriction of choice was bad. As noted, these three goals tend to conflict with one another, and each must be balanced against the others. Compulsory attendance is a restriction of freedom in favor of equity and adequacy.

However, as states have given more aid to local school districts, they have tended to exercise more control. Nowhere has this been clearer than in California, which in 1978 escalated from a local contribution of more than half of the total expenditure to a situation where the state in essence funds all education. School boards have found that their freedom to make decisions about most matters has been greatly circumscribed. It is clear that the legislatures have not necessarily been cavalier. They believe that they must exercise a prudent concern for the public funds they are granting to school districts. But the result has been a movement of control to the state as the proportion of school expenditures furnished by the state increased during the 1970s and 1980s.

Local school districts have also restricted the freedom of choice of parents and children. Most school districts tell parents what school their child will attend, which teacher he or she will be taught by, which subjects will be taught, and which textbooks will be used. In the elementary schools in particular, parents have little choice regarding the education of their children.

It need not necessarily be this way. Some school districts allow parents to send their children to any school in the district, or to one of several others besides that in their attendance area (subject, of course, to the availability of space). It is not clear, aside from bureaucratic convenience, why all school districts do not do this. But this is only a beginning. There have been a number of proposals to increase choice in the public schools.

Vouchers and Tuition Tax Credits

This is an idea of sufficient significance that it is discussed both here and in Chapters 14 and 15. The *voucher plan* was first proposed by Milton Friedman in 1955.[22] It is a radical concept in that it proposes dismantling the present system of publicly operated schools. It is conservative in an economic sense in relying on the private market rather than on government. Friedman described his plan thus:

> Governments could require a minimum level of education which they could finance by giving parents vouchers redeemable for a specified maximum sum per child per year if spent on "approved" educational service. Parents would then be free to spend this sum *and any additional sum* on purchasing educational services from an "approved" institution of their own choice. The educational services could be rendered by private enterprises operated for profit, or by nonprofit institutions of various kinds. The role of the government would be limited to assuring that the schools met certain minimum standards such as the inclusion of a minimum common content in their program, as it now inspects restaurants to assure that they maintain minimum sanitary standards.[23]

Voucher proponents assert that the plan has a number of advantages. Parents would be allowed to place their children in schools of their choice, instead of being forced to use schools and teachers for which they might have no enthusiasm. The injection of a greater amount of private enterprise would make schools more efficient and promote a healthy variety. Salaries of teachers would become more responsive to market forces. On the other hand, there might be more segregation by economic class, and probably also by race, than at present. The few public schools that remained might become the dumping ground for pupils private schools were unwilling to accept.

---

[22]Milton Friedman, "The Role of Government in Education," in *Economics and the Public Interest*, ed. Robert A. Solo (New Brunswick, N.J.: Rutgers University Press, 1955).
[23]Ibid., pp. 127–28 (emphasis in original).

In fact, an equivalent of the voucher plan operated in higher education for more than thirty years. The G.I. Bill, enacted immediately after World War II, provided a higher education subsidy for any veteran who could gain entrance to a postsecondary program. It paid full tuition, regardless of the tuition being charged by the institution, and subsistence for the veteran and his family. It has been widely regarded as one of the most successful federal programs in the field of education, and many veterans who otherwise would not have gotten additional education became college graduates. On the other hand, there were serious problems in the form of private for-profit schools that sprang up just to educate veterans. Audits showed that their curricula were inadequate and their instructors incompetent, and that they granted degrees without requiring the veterans to complete prescribed courses. Fortunately, the majority of the veterans went to established schools that furnished a reasonable education. Nevertheless, the potential for abuse is present when the free market is allowed to operate unfettered. Reasonable audits of performance must therefore be made.

In any case, voucher plans have not been accepted in elementary-secondary education. Far from being adopted in any state, the system has not even had a real trial on an experimental basis. For several years during the 1960s and early 1970s the Office of Economic Opportunity and the U.S. Office of Education attempted to promote a trial of a voucher system somewhere in the United States. The closest they came was a limited experiment in the Alum Rock School District, near San Jose, California, involving no private schools. The results were, at best, inconclusive.

Tuition tax credits constitute another proposal for helping to subsidize private schools. The family sending its children to private school would be allowed a credit equal to their tuition on its federal income tax return. Note that this is a deduction from the *tax*, not from income, and is thus of more value to the family. The notion is more fully discussed in Chapter 7.

Family Power Equalizing

Coons, Clune, and Sugarman recognized a problem with their proposed system of power equalizing. Although it met their criterion that the amount spent on a child's education should not depend upon the wealth of his or her neighbors, expenditures might still depend upon the *decisions* of those neighbors. A rural family desiring and willing to pay for an excellent education for its children might find its neighbors preferring low taxes and low school expenditures. To remedy such forced inequity, Coons, Clune, and Sugarman proposed *family power equalizing*.[24] In this modified voucher plan, several levels of educational quality would be available in a community's schools. Each family would then be free to choose the level of quality it wanted for its children, and would be taxed accordingly. Children would attend the school whose per-pupil expenditures were linked to their parents' choice of tax rate. Family power equalizing has had no warmer political reception than Friedman's voucher plan, and it seems highly unlikely that it will be implemented.

[24]Coons, Clune, and Sugarman, *Private Wealth and Public Education*, pp. 200–242.

Magnet Schools

The public schools have been understandably reluctant to forego control over education, as is implied in the Friedman voucher plan. There has also been no observable inclination to adopt a scheme of differential taxation as suggested by Coons and colleagues. However, many districts (particularly those in large cities) have allowed and encouraged an option within public schools. They have established *magnet schools*. Each such school emphasizes some different feature of education. One may concentrate on the arts, another on science and mathematics, a third on "basics" and firm discipline. Parents are allowed to apply to these schools for their children. The concept has been widely discussed in districts faced with the alternative of busing to promote racial desegregation.

Magnet schools have much to recommend them if they are operated well. A major problem is that they tend to be feasible only in large districts containing a large number of schools. The usual balkanization of school districts in the suburbs makes such schemes difficult. The private schools envisioned in the voucher plans would not suffer from this problem because they draw pupils without regard for district boundaries. In rural areas, however, all of these plans to increase choice are limited by population sparsity, which makes it difficult to establish special schools, public or private. Telecommunications may alleviate this difficulty in the future, allowing instruction of pupils in widely scattered locations.

COMPREHENSIVE STATE SCHOOL FINANCE PLANS

Each of the plans described above is only a part of a general school finance plan for a state. The overall plan should foster adequacy, equity, efficiency, and choice. Because these goals tend to conflict with one another, each is usually compromised to some extent in order to foster the others. In addition, school finance plans are designed in the political arena, and this results in accommodations to powerful actors, whether they be school districts or politicians. Finally, there is usually a wide variety of districts in the state—in size, special needs, and unusual situations—and the plan needs to make reasonable accommodation to these. The result is an overall school finance plan of fearsome complexity. It is not at all unusual to find no more than a handful of people in the state who understand the entire plan, and most of these are in the state education department. Such complexity makes it easy for inequity and inefficiency to creep in generally unrecognized.

SUMMARY

This chapter has discussed state financing mechanisms for promoting the values of equity, efficiency, and choice while also providing for adequate amounts of education. It has also mentioned ways of accomplishing this objective that have been proposed but not implemented.

Equity has had the most formal study. Three philosophical positions on equity have been expressed. The first, minimum provision, assumes that the state's duty is to ensure that all children have equal access to a minimum educational program. All additional education is a local option, not aided by the state. The types of state programs used to implement this philosophy are the flat grant and foundation programs.

The second philosophical position is that the state should guarantee to all districts equal access to money for education, while leaving it up to each district to decide how much education to provide. Finance schemes for implementing this philosophy have been called percentage equalizing, power equalizing, and the guaranteed tax base.

The third position is that the state should both provide and finance an equal education to all students. This has come to be known as full state assumption.

In addition to attempting to equalize differences in district wealth, states have attempted to recognize differences in students' needs. Some students (mentally, physically or environmentally handicapped, bilingual, etc.) require a more expensive education. Districts having higher concentrations of these pupils face higher average per-pupil costs. States attempt to equalize this burden through entitlement plans, cost reimbursement plans, and the creation of intermediate districts to educate these children.

Finally, there has been some modest attempt to correct for differences in the cost of providing equivalent educational services among districts. Some districts have high transportation costs because of sparse population, whereas others, in the cities, suffer from high labor costs. The most common attempts to correct these inequities have been embodied in special formulas for reimbursing districts for bus transportation or for costs of necessary small schools. In addition, cities are often given special aid through a combination of means.

There has been little sophisticated work on making the schools more efficient. One of the problems is that there is little agreement on the goals of the schools, or on how to achieve those goals. As a result, legislatures have usually tried to restrict the amount of money the schools receive, hoping that educators will determine ways to be more efficient by doing with less. Restrictive mechanisms used by legislators include tax rate limits, expenditure limits, and budget votes.

There has been little done by legislatures to increase choice. There have been proposals for voucher plans, tuition tax credits, and family power equalizing. In addition, local districts have established magnet schools, often with some aid from the state.

chapter seven

FEDERAL EDUCATION POLICY

The United States is nearly unique among the world's nations in not having a national system of schooling.[1] Nevertheless, since 1785 the federal government has played an important role in influencing the direction of America's state and local public education systems. Federal school-aid dollars generally constitute between 6 and 8 percent of elementary and secondary expenditures. This is not much money when viewed against the sizable backdrop of the nation's total school spending (see Chapter 1). However, the purposes for which federal funds are distributed, the legitimacy that high-level national officials are able to impart to proposals, the intense public visibility surrounding federal actions, and the sweeping legal mechanisms available for enforcement often enable federal officials and programs to exert influence far in excess of that derived from the actual dollar amounts involved. It is for this reason that policy makers, professional educators, and members of the public, whether or not they are directly involved in operating such programs, need to understand federal education policies and their constitutional foundations, legal basis, historic development, social objectives, operational principles, and political dynamics. These are the topics covered in this chapter.

[1]Australia, Canada, and West Germany also operate decentralized education systems, though nowhere nearly as dependent upon local school authorities as is the case in the United States.

CONSTITUTIONAL FOUNDATIONS

The United States Constitution does not explicitly grant citizens the right to an education, nor does it establish a national system of schools. These facts are surprising to many members of the public.[2]

The absence of any provision explicitly concerned with education or schooling appears to have been a conscious choice by the eighteenth-century framers of the Constitution. Notes compiled by James Madison during the Philadelphia Constitutional Convention suggest that members discussed establishing a national university but made no formal proposal to provide the federal government with a role in lower education.

Others in attendance considered learning to be important, and several luminaries of the period, such as Thomas Jefferson[3] and Benjamin Franklin,[4] had expressed their views on education in other settings. Thus, omission of the words *schooling* and *education* from the Constitution was not simply a casual act. It is unlikely that even Alexander Hamilton, who advocated strong central authority, espoused a large education role for government. Rather, the Jeffersonian view that less government is better probably pervaded the convention's thinking about education as well as other matters.[5]

In the eighteenth century, education was not yet firmly established as a local government function, let alone an undertaking important for a national authority. In many colonial settlements, schooling was significant primarily for allowing individual interpretation of biblical scriptures. Even when technical knowledge began to assume greater importance in people's economic lives, education arrangements continued to be more private than public. It was only in the mid nineteenth century that state-enacted compulsory attendance laws triggered the present models of public schooling.[6] Thus, those attending the 1787 Constitutional Convention had little experience with government provision of education, and their negative reaction to King George III and the strong British monarchy prejudiced them against granting a

[2] A 1987 national poll revealed that 70 percent of the public thought the Constitution granted the right to an education. *San Francisco Chronicle,* February 13, 1987, p. 7.

[3] See, for example, Jefferson's "Bill for the General Diffusion of Knowledge," proposed to the Virginia Assembly in 1779; reprinted in *Thomas Jefferson, Revolutionary Philosopher: A Selection of Writings,* ed. John S. Pancake (Rootbury, N.Y.: Barron's Educational Service, 1976), pp. 212–21.

[4] See Franklin's "Proposals Relating to the Education of Youth in Pennsylvania," reprinted in *Background Readings for the July 20–21, 1965, White House Conference on Education* (Washington, D.C: U.S. Department of Health, Education and Welfare, 1965) pp. 5–8.

[5] See Jefferson's December 20, 1787, letter to James Madison on the subject of the new federal constitution, in *Thomas Jefferson,* ed. Pancake, pp. 84–88.

[6] James W. Guthrie, Diana K. Thomason, and Patricia A. Craig, "The Erosion of Lay Control" in National Committee for Citizens in Education, *Public Testimony on Public Schools* (Berkeley, Calif.: McCutchan, 1975), pp. 76–121; and William Landes and Lewis Solomon, "Compulsory Schooling Legislation: An Economic Analysis of Law and Social Change in the Nineteenth Century," *Journal of Economic History,* 32, no. 1 (1984), 54–91.

national authority the right to control such a potentially influential undertaking as schooling.

The U.S. Constitution's Tenth Amendment specifies that "the powers not delegated to the United States by the Constitution, nor prohibited by it to the States, are reserved to the States respectively, or to the people." This provision reflects social contract theories of government, which were intensely important to the constitutional framers.[7] The right to individual self-determination was held to be an inalienable quality of each human being, one that should be ceded to representative governing bodies only with strict limitations. Hence, the Tenth Amendment explicitly asserts that the national government is to be imbued only with those powers expressly granted to it. All other authority is to be held by the states or by individuals unless specifically denied by the Constitution. The Tenth Amendment's ending, "or the people," makes clear that the citizenry is the ultimate source of governing authority.

The effect of the absence in the Constitution of a proclamation of express national responsibility for education and schooling, when coupled with the language of the Tenth Amendment, is to cede *plenary* (ultimate) legal authority for public education to state government. Each state constitution contains an education clause explicitly acknowledging the authority of the state in education and schooling.

As a consequence of these federal and state constitutional arrangements, the federal government has no widespread specific responsibility for operating education programs. (Direct federal administration of institutions such as the armed service academies, the Gallaudet College for the Deaf in Washington, D.C., and the Overseas Dependent Schools are limited exceptions.)

Despite this limited authority, the federal government has had a history of influence in education. In the mid twentieth century, federal authorities inaugurated numerous education programs that presently provide services throughout all fifty states, the trust territories, thousands of local school districts, and schools. It is unlikely that even a single American public school is presently untouched by federal education policy. Given the absence of explicit constitutional authority, what is the legal basis for such undertakings? There are several answers to this question.

LEGAL BASIS FOR FEDERAL INVOLVEMENT

The federal government's constitutional authority to finance and regulate education programs is derived from implied powers contained in several sections of the U.S. Constitution. Over the two centuries since ratification, numerous judicial interpretations of constitutional provisions have expanded the scope of the federal government's education authority. These implied powers have been reinforced by court decisions regarding the general welfare clause and other parts of the First

---

[7] See *Social Contract: Essays by Locke, Hume, and Rousseau,* ed. Sir Ernest Barker (Oxford: Oxford University Press, 1947).

Amendment and both the due process and equal protection clauses of the Fourteenth Amendment.

The First Amendment

GENERAL WELFARE CLAUSE

Article 1, Section 8, Clause 1, of the Constitution is commonly referred to as the general welfare clause. It states, "The Congress shall have power to lay and collect taxes, duties, imposts and excises, to pay the debts and provide for the common defense and general welfare of the United States." For a century or more following adoption of the Constitution, this was a controversial provision. Proponents of a limited national government, such as James Madison, desired a narrow interpretation whereas advocates of a strong central government, such as Alexander Hamilton, argued for a broad view of the clause. In the 1930s, U.S. Supreme Court decisions substantially altered the nature of the debate. In a case involving New Deal legislation sponsored by the Roosevelt administration, the nation's highest court ruled that Congress had authority to interpret the general welfare clause as long as it did not act arbitrarily.[8]

The Court also held that the clause could be interpreted differently from time to time as conditions necessitated redefinition of the nation's general welfare.[9] Debate has since shifted to whether or not a particular policy proposal is useful, instead of whether Congress possesses the authority to implement it. Consequently, federal education programs are viewed as falling within the implied constitutional authority of Congress. This is not to assert everybody always agrees on the wisdom of a particular legislative proposal or a new federal education program. Contemporary education initiatives can still provoke heated debate at the federal level.

CONTRACTUAL OBLIGATIONS

Article 1, Section 10, of the Constitution has been judicially interpreted so as to allow the federal government to restrict the ability of states and local boards of education to impair the obligations of contracts. The Supreme Court has held that "a legislative enactment may contain provisions which, when accepted as a basis of action by individuals, become contracts between them and the state or its subdivision."[10] The constitutional provision regarding contractual obligations and the legal principles derived from it have also been applied to controversies between teacher unions and school boards over tenure rights and retirement agreements.

SEPARATION OF CHURCH AND STATE

The First and Fourteenth Amendments provide a constitutional base for federal control over the relationship between religion and public school funding. The

---

[8]*United States* v. *Butler,* 297 U.S. 1, 56 Sup. Ct. 312.

[9]*Helvering* v. *Davis,* 301 Dr. S.619, 57 Sup. Ct. 904.

[10]*State ex rel Anderson* v. *Brand,* 313 U.S. 95.

First Amendment specifies that "Congress shall make no law respecting an establishment of religion, or prohibiting the free exercise thereof." The Supreme Court has held that the First Amendment was intended to create a "wall of separation between church and state."[11] Consistent with this view, both state and federal courts have struck down repeated state efforts to provide direct financial subsidies to religious schools.

The U.S. Supreme Court has evolved a three-pronged test to determine whether a sectarian school aid plan violates the wall of separation: (1) the statute must have a secular legislative purpose, (2) the statute's "primary effect" must neither advance nor inhibit religion, and (3) the statute and its administration must avoid excessive government entanglement with religion.[12] The application of these criteria has served generally to discourage state aid to church-related elementary and secondary schools. The 1983 Supreme Court decision in *Mueller* v. *Allen* approved a Minnesota statute providing a state income tax deduction for school fees, both public and nonpublic.[13] Advocates of federal aid to religious schools took this to be a signal that the Court was increasingly disposed toward their cause. However, a 1985 decision in a New York case, *Aguilar* v. *Felton,* suggests that the signal is mixed. Provision to church-related schools of federally funded compensatory education authorized by Chapter One of the Education Consolidation and Improvement Act was severely restricted by this decision.[14]

Regardless of *Mueller* and *Felton,* the long-term consequences of which are not yet easily predictable, the issue of federal aid to nonpublic schools has long been and undoubtedly will continue to be heated (see Chapter 1 on this topic). Negative decisions, however, have not extended to private *higher* education, in respect to which the courts have ruled a wider variety of government aid plans to be constitutional. The relatively greater intellectual maturity of college students is a crucial distinction for the courts.[15]

The Fourteenth Amendment

The Fourteenth Amendment, adopted in 1868, was one of three constitutional amendments intended to free the slaves. It stretched the mantle of the first ten amendments to protect the civil liberties of citizens from state encroachment.[16] The Fourteenth Amendment contains two clauses of particular importance to federal au-

---

[11]*Illinois ex rel McCollum* v. *Board of Education,* 333 U.S. 203; and *Everson* v. *Board of Education,* 330 U.S. 1.

[12]*Lemon* v. *Kurtzman,* 403 U.S. 602, 91 Sup. Ct. 2105, 1971; and *Leeman* v. *Sloan,* 340 f. Suppl. 1356, 1972.

[13]*Mueller* v. *Allen,* 54 U.S. L.W. 5050.

[14]*Aguilar* v. *Felton,* 53 U.S. L.W. 5013.

[15]For more on this topic see Richard E. Morgan, *The Politics of Religious Conflict: Church and State in America* (New York: Pegasus, 1968); and Chester E. Finn, Jr., "The Politics of Public Aid to Private Schools," in *The Changing Politics of School Finance,* ed. Nelda H. Cambron McCabe and Allan Odden, Third Annual Yearbook of the American Education Finance Association (Cambridge, Mass.: Ballinger, 1982), pp. 183–210.

[16]Michael W. LaMorte, "The Fourteenth Amendment: Its Significance for Public Educators," *Educational Administration Quarterly,* 10, no. 3 (Autumn 1974), 1–19.

thority over education, the so-called *due process clause* and the *equal protection clause*. The latter served as the basis for one of the most significant reforms ever undertaken in American public education—the overturn of dual school systems for whites and blacks, which evolved and were supported statutorily in seventeen southern states and the District of Columbia.

EQUAL PROTECTION

In 1954 the U.S. Supreme Court issued a school desegregation decision[17] that overturned the "separate but equal" doctrine, which had dominated U.S. race relations since the 1896 decision in *Plessy* v. *Ferguson*.[18] In *Plessy* the Court had let stand an 1890 Louisiana statute segregating the races on railway cars as long as, presumably, the facilities were equal. In *Brown* v. *Board of Education*, by far the most noted of the desegregation cases, the Court stated:

> We conclude that in the field of public education the doctrine of "separate but equal" has no place. Separate educational facilities are inherently unequal. Therefore, we hold that the plaintiffs and others similarly situated for whom the actions are brought are, by reason of the segregation complained of, deprived of the equal protection of the laws guaranteed by the Fourteenth Amendment.

The *Brown* decision, in conjunction with implementation decrees and numerous lower-court decisions, was resisted, sometimes violently. The eventual result, however, was a dismantling of the de jure racially segregated school systems that had long characterized public schooling in the South. More subtle discriminatory mechanisms that contribute to de facto segregation have not lent themselves so easily to legal remedy.[19]

The equal protection clause has also been used as the basis for a constitutional challenge to school finance arrangements in many of the fifty states. Chapter 8 explains the legal logic and practical consequences connected with this judicial reform strategy. Suffice it to state here that the practical outcome, though not wholly unsatisfactory, has been nowhere near the legal success of the school desegregation suits. Indeed, reform efforts in racial desegregation and school finance simultaneously display the power and limits of the federal government's ability to influence public education. Because of the complexity of the United States' multi-tiered and many-faceted system of government, the results of these efforts have not been nearly as successful as advocates had hoped, or as devastating socially as opponents had feared.

---

[17]*Brown* v. *Board of Education,* 347 U.S. 483, 74 Sup. Ct. 686.

[18]163 U.S. 537, 16 Sup. Ct. 1138.

[19]On this point see J. Harvey Wilkinson, *From Brown to Baake* (Oxford: Oxford University Press, 1976); Gary Orfield, *Must We Bus?* (Washington, D.C.: Brookings Institution, 1978); David L. Kirp, *Just Schools* (Berkeley: University of California Press, 1982); and Raymond Walters, *The Burden of Brown: Thirty Years of School Desegregation* (Knoxville: University of Tennessee Press, 1984).

DUE PROCESS

The Fourteenth Amendment's due process clause states, "nor shall any State deprive any person of life, liberty, or property, without due process of law." This clause also provides a major legal vehicle through which the federal government can influence public education. Generally, the due process clause must be weighed against society's need to protect itself.

Though continually being redefined judicially, so-called police powers are inherently within the authority of government at all levels. For example, teachers and other school employees are not free simply to do or teach whatever they would like if such actions jeopardize society's need to protect itself. Courts have generally enforced the Smith Act, which makes it a crime punishable by fine and imprisonment to advocate the forceful overthrow of the government. These rulings have established a limitation regarding what can be taught in public, as well as private, schools. As Morphet, Johns, and Reller state,

> those who insist that the federal government should have no control whatsoever over the curriculum of public schools seem to be unaware of the inherent police powers of the federal government relating to matters of national concern.[20]

The federal government's ability to influence America's system of schooling is not limited to its legal authority. Influence is also possible through means such as financial inducement, demonstration projects, dissemination of information and research findings, evaluation efforts, and moral persuasion. These are discussed in subsequent sections of this chapter.

EVOLUTION OF FEDERAL EDUCATION PROGRAMS

In 1785, even before ratification of the Constitution by all the original colonies, central government policy on education was being made. The Land Survey Ordinance of that year, as well as the better-known Northwest Ordinance, enacted two years later, provided for several sections of land in each township within newly formed territories to be reserved for support of public schools.[21] The significance of these provisions is difficult to deduce retrospectively. At the least, they served as precedents for subsequent federal policies regarding education. Their influence may have been even greater in that the authorization of land for public purposes that would otherwise have been ceded to private use perhaps reinforced whatever frontier desire existed for schooling.

---

[20] Edgar L. Morphet, Roe L. Johns, and Theodore L. Reller, *Educational Organization and Administration* (Englewood Cliffs, N.J.: Prentice-Hall, 1982), p. 204.

[21] See Roald F. Campbell, Luvern L. Cunningham, Raphael O. Nystrand, and Michael D. Usdan, *The Organization and Control of American Schools* (Columbus, Ohio: Chas. E. Merrill, 1980), pp. 26–27.

Regardless, over the two centuries subsequent to these early enactments, various federal government branches and agencies have initiated and implemented a wide variety of education programs.[22] The general justification for such activities is to meet national needs likely to be neglected by states acting independently or to introduce economies made possible by central authority management. Imagine, for example, that the nation's supply of highly skilled scientists or individuals possessed of a keen ability to speak languages other than English was so short as to jeopardize national defense or the nation's balance of international trade. It is unlikely that individual states would enact programs to meet such shortages. These are national needs, and on several occasions Congress has enacted and funded programs to solve problems such as these.

Similarly, some functions risk diseconomies if performed by smaller units and beg to be undertaken more efficiently by a central authority. Data collection and research and development activities are good examples. The congressional provision establishing the Department of Education[23] in 1867 made prominent mention of the agency's role in collecting useful statistics for sustaining and improving the nation's schools. This task, though performed unevenly over time by the federal education authority, nevertheless falls naturally to a central government. States and smaller units of government are not well positioned to gather and analyze information from across the nation. Hence, the present-day cabinet-level Department of Education systematically collects, analyzes, and publishes information on education in the United States.

In 1966 the federal government funded a controversial effort to assess the national performance of students and school graduates—the National Assessment of Educational Progress (NAEP). Initially this undertaking was contracted by the Department of Education to the Education Commission of the States (ECS), in Denver, Colorado. At that time, appraisers of performance were prohibited from making state-by-state comparisons. In 1983 the NAEP was moved to the Educational Testing Service (ETS) in Princeton, New Jersey. In 1987 a highly visible national study panel chaired by Tennessee governor Lamar Alexander and Spencer Foundation president H. Thomas James issued *The Nation's Report Card,* a report that recommended massive changes in governance and procedures for the NAEP. The panel proposed, for example, that state-by-state test score comparisons be undertaken.[24]

This massive achievement-assessment program, costing $5 million to operate in 1988, tests thousands of students throughout the nation. It is not an endeavor that individual states could easily organize or afford to operate for the entire nation. It falls more naturally to the federal government to conduct such an undertaking.

---

[22]See generally Carl F. Kaestle and Marshall S. Smith, "The Federal Role in Elementary and Secondary Education, 1940–1980," *Harvard Education Review,* 52, no. 4 (November 1983), 393.

[23]In 1867 the title *Department* did not connote cabinet ranking, as is the case currently.

[24] Lamar Alexander and H. Thomas James, *The Nation's Report Card* (Cambridge, Mass.: National Academy of Education, 1987).

OBJECTIVES OF FEDERAL EDUCATION POLICY

In attempting to meet otherwise unaddressed national needs and to perform functions that logically fall to a central authority, the federal government has generally oriented its education efforts toward fulfilling two major value objectives, enhancement of educational productivity and equalization of educational opportunity. Here again we can see the repeated significance to American public policy of the commitment to equality and efficiency described in Chapter 2. We turn now to a number of federal education endeavors within each of these categories. There are now far too many federal education programs to provide a detailed description of each. Hence, the programs we have selected for discussion are notable for their dollar magnitude, a precedent they established, or an important idea they embodied.

Enhancement of Educational Productivity

The value of efficiency makes a good beginning here because the first major federally sponsored education programs were intended to expand the supply of school activities crucial to national economic development.

LAND GRANTS AIDING HIGHER EDUCATION

One of the federal government's largest economic assets during the nation's first century was the vast amounts of undeveloped land under its control. In 1862 Congress passed the first Morrill Act, named after Senator Justin S. Morrill of Vermont, the bill's major proponent.[25] This statute allocated 30,000 acres of federal land to each state for each of its two senators and each of the representatives to which it was then entitled. Income from the sale or rental of these lands was to be used for establishing agricultural and mechanical arts colleges. These "A & M" colleges were to contribute to the new nation's supply of artisans and technicians. Such institutions were also to instruct students in military science and tactics.

Each state benefited from this program. Not all recipients have been public institutions, however. Cornell University in Ithaca, New York, and the Massachusetts Institute of Technology in Cambridge, Massachusetts, are both examples of prestigious private institutions that have received aid from the proceeds from Morrill Act lands. So-called land-grant colleges received additional aid upon passage of the Second Morrill Act of 1892 and the Hatch Act of 1897. In 1966 Congress passed a Sea Grant program providing colleges and universities with added federal funding to expand marine research. In 1987 the Reagan administration proposed to provide land-grant institutions with added funding to conduct research in electronics and other high-technology areas.[26]

---

[25]Morrill's first effort was enacted by Congress in 1858, only to be vetoed by President Buchanan. Morrill's "Reply to President's Veto of Land Grant Bill" is an articulate justification of federal encouragement of education. This speech is reprinted in *Background Readings*, pp. 21–22.

[26]Though subject to declining funding in the 1980s, there have also been several major federal programs offering financial support to college students.

Though these aid programs were directed at colleges and universities, they have also been important for elementary and secondary education in that they abetted the precedent of federal assistance for education. Subsequent legislation has been directed at assisting lower education.

VOCATIONAL EDUCATION TO ASSIST INDUSTRY AND DEFENSE

In the early twentieth century, as the United States moved toward World War I, Congress, concerned about the availability of enough skilled workers to supply both American industry and the war effort, passed the Smith-Hughes Act of 1917. The statute appropriated federal funds to states to establish secondary school programs in agricultural and industrial trades and homemaking. States were required to match the federal funds. This act established a precedent for matching grants that has become a major lever used by federal officials to induce program cooperation by state and local agencies.[27]

The federal government's initial concern for vocational education has been strongly sustained. Congress enacted the George-Reed Act in 1929, the George-Elzey Act in 1935, the George-Dean Act in 1937, and the George-Barden Act in 1946. The 1963 Vocational Education Act, promoted by President John F. Kennedy, established a different direction for vocational education, a direction that has been pursued with systematic reauthorizations. By the mid 1980s, Congress was annually appropriating approximately $1 billion for vocational preparation at the secondary level. States and other agencies provide even more funds, but federal programs have acted as an incentive for establishment of a complex vocational training system.

During the Great Depression of the 1930s, Congress established several antipoverty programs containing significant educational components. Frequently, vocational training was a prominent feature of these undertakings. For example, the Civilian Conservation Corps (CCC) and the National Youth Authority (NYA) both provided vocational training for unemployed depression youth. In 1965, as part of the Johnson administration's War on Poverty, the Federal Job Corps was established to enable out-of-school and out-of-work youth to gain job skills. Depression-era education programs were operated directly by federal agencies such as the War Department (now the Defense Department) and the Federal Security Agency, an ancestor of the present-day Department of Education. The Job Corps was operated by a variety of private organizations under direct contract to the now-defunct Office of Economic Opportunity. Compared with programs in surrounding local school districts, these federally funded and operated vocational training endeavors were unusually expensive, costing up to twenty times as much per enrollee as public school vocational training. Local and state public school officials insisted that they could perform the same function more efficiently. Such complaints, along with changing

---

[27]See "Debate on Smith-Hughes Vocational Education Act" (1917), reprinted in *Background Readings*, pp. 47–49.

economic conditions, eventually terminated these poverty-relief efforts, and virtually nothing of them remains today.[28]

In 1957 the Soviet Union launched the first successful earth-orbiting satellite, Sputnik. The event rocked America's sense of technological superiority. U.S. public education served as a convenient scapegoat for popular frustration and disappointment. The nation subsequently regained its poise and launched a massive federal program that resulted in moon landings and other space successes of the 1960s and 1970s. Education also benefited, with enactment of the 1958 National Defense Education Act (NDEA). This statute utilized federal matching funds as an incentive for local school districts to upgrade instruction in science, mathematics, and foreign language. Higher-education institutions also participated, through expanded financial support for college students entering the fields of science and math teaching. The NDEA was successful in helping schools meet the intensified public expectations for American scientific and technological supremacy.

In the 1960s the National Science Foundation (NSF) funded fellowships and advanced training programs for science and math teachers at many colleges and universities. The NSF also funded a number of science and math curriculum-revision projects that substantially influenced secondary school instruction.[29]

In the early 1980s, the mass media and professional periodicals began reporting increasing shortages of qualified secondary school math and science teachers.[30] Fear of losing a competitive economic position in international sales of high-technology products and techniques motivated President Reagan in 1985 to propose and Congress to enact the Education for Economic Security Act, embodying many of the same purposes as the 1958 NDEA.

RESEARCH AND DEVELOPMENT

There is less financial incentive to engage in research when potential results may advantage a host of others besides the initiating agency. Under such conditions, a tempting strategy is to wait and hope to piggyback on the research funded by another. Educational research and development can be viewed in this light. Why should one state expend its scarce resources on basic research on, for example, human learning when there is no reasonable way to restrict useful results to its boundaries? Under such circumstances, there is likely to be an underinvestment in an activity that might otherwise enhance educational efficiency and the productivity of the entire economy. To avoid such a condition, the federal government has long supported educational research and development.

[28]Henry J. Aaron, *Politics and the Professors* (Washington, D.C.: Brookings Institution, 1978); Charles Murray, *Losing Ground: American Social Policy 1950–1980* (New York: Basic Books, 1984).

[29]Paul E. Marsh and Ross A. Gortner, *Federal Aid to Science Education: Two Programs* (Syracuse, N.Y.: Syracuse University Press, 1963).

[30]James W. Guthrie and Ami Zusman, "Teacher Supply and Demand in Mathematics and Science," *Kappan,* 64, no. 1 (September 1982), 28–33.

In 1954 Congress passed the Cooperative Research Act, which authorized federal funds for educational research in institutions of higher education. This statute was administered by the U.S. Office of Education, one of several agencies constituting what was then known as the Department of Health, Education and Welfare (HEW). In 1965 the main features of the Cooperative Research Act were incorporated into Title IV of the Elementary and Secondary Education Act (ESEA). The latter act substantially expanded the amount of federal money available for education research. Additionally, it established twenty regional educational laboratories and twelve university-based research and development centers. The aim was for new ideas to be developed in the R & D centers and transformed into practical applications and distributed to school districts by the regional educational laboratories. This research, development, and dissemination strategy was patterned after a highly effective model utilized by U.S. agriculture.

In 1975 federal education-research functions were transferred to the new National Institute of Education (NIE), then within HEW and subsequently a part of the Department of Education. By the late 1970s, however, federal expenses accrued from the war in Vietnam, large outlays for domestic social programs, and diminished political affection for public schools had reduced education research appropriations. Several of the R & D centers and regional laboratories were closed, and funding for the remainder was insufficient to support large-scale research projects. Though the NIE continued to be the major funding source for education research throughout the 1970s and early 1980s, its institutional impact was minimal in many areas, and there were even serious suggestions for its dissolution.[31] By 1985 the NIE had been folded back into the Department of Education and was known as the Office of Educational Research and Improvement (OERI).

As with the surviving vocational education programs, all recent federally sponsored education efforts rely heavily on existing institutions and structures—state agencies, local school districts, and colleges and universities—for delivery of services. The direct delivery approaches seen in the CCC, NYA, and Job Corps are no more popular politically in the 1980s than they were a half century earlier. Whether this attitude will be altered over time is unpredictable. Regardless of the delivery mechanisms involved, however, the federal government is likely to have an interest in using education to enhance national economic efficiency and productivity far into the future.

In the 1980s the Department of Education began to play an intensified role in advocating more productive schools. One of the strategies entailed comparing individual states on measures of performance and resource inputs.

Equalization of Educational Opportunity

Expanding the services available to groups of previously underserved students is a relatively recent federal education function. Except for late nineteenth- and early twentieth-century efforts to provide for the education of various Native American groups, it was not until the second half of the twentieth century that major federal

---

[31]Chester Finn, "What NIE Cannot Be," *Kappan,* 64, no. 6 (February 1983), 407–10.

programs began benefiting groups of students for whom full educational access had not been available. However, since the U.S. Supreme Court's decision in *Brown* v. *Board of Education,* both the executive and the legislative branches have been more attentive to claims for equal educational opportunity by racial minorities, children from low-income households, handicapped students, and non-English- and limited-English-speaking students. All of these groups, though not to the same degree, have been the focus of relatively recent federal education programs.

THE EDUCATION CONSOLIDATION AND IMPROVEMENT ACT (ECIA)

In 1981 Congress accepted a Reagan administration recommendation and consolidated many existing education programs into two major statutory provisions of the ECIA. Chapter One of this act continues the major feature of the 1965 ESEA—federal funds for compensatory education for students from low-income families. Appropriations under this authority constitute the largest federally sponsored lower-education program. Funds are distributed to states based on a formula that takes into account the numbers of school-age children from low-income households. States, in turn, distribute Chapter One funds to counties and local school districts. Districts are responsible for spending compensatory education funds in a manner consistent with federal regulations and guidelines. Chapter One funds generally are used for elementary programs designed to enhance pupils' reading and arithmetic achievement. However, it is possible to utilize funds for other purposes, such as secondary remedial instruction, counseling, field trips, instructional materials, and, under limited circumstances, personal and health items such as eyeglasses.

Funding for compensatory education is classified as *categorical aid* because it can be used by local school districts only to provide added educational services to a specified category of students—in this case those who qualify because of their low-income circumstances. Local and state officials sometimes are restless about the relatively rigid spending requirements of the act, and federal audit requirements are stringent.[32] Evaluations of Chapter One programs are mixed, with a slight weighting toward the favorable end of the continuum.[33] Regardless, the programs appear to have gained enough of a political constituency that it would take unusually fierce federal budgetary pressure to eliminate it.

Chapter Two of the ECIA consists of a *block grant* comprising thirty-two previously enacted education programs. Funds are allocated to states based on a student population formula. Each state thereafter establishes a plan based either on school district enrollment or on measures of student need. Local districts are free to spend funds in whatever fashion they decide best meets their needs for added services.

Chapter Two's enactment was politically controversial. Many local and state education officials had long sought consolidation of federal categorical aid programs

[32]For proposals to relax regulations see Michael W. Kirst, "The Federal Role and Chapter I: Rethinking Some Basic Assumptions" (paper prepared for Research and Evaluation Associates Inc., Washington, D.C., 1986).

[33]Stephen P. Mullin and Anita A. Summers, "Is More Better? The Effectiveness of Spending on Compensatory Education," *Kappan,* 64, no. 5 (January 1983), 339–47.

into a limited number of the so-called block grants, wherein states and districts would be permitted greater discretion over spending. Interest groups comprising the educators and others who were benefiting most directly from the categorical aid resisted consolidation for fear their particular programs would lose ground to local spending priorities under a block grant. In 1981, when the Reagan administration initially proposed deregulation and consolidation, several major programs were discussed for inclusion, among them special education and compensatory education. The eventual compromise was to preserve the categorical integrity of major programs and to combine many smaller authorities. ECIA Chapter Two was the result.[34]

THE EDUCATION FOR ALL HANDICAPPED CHILDREN ACT

Throughout the 1960s and the early 1970s increasing political pressure was brought to bear on state legislatures to correct injustices to handicapped students. Many states were not providing school services for severely handicapped students, and other states were underfunding such programs. Following several important state court cases in which it was held that handicapped children also deserved equal protection of the law,[35] state legislatures as well as Congress enacted programs to ensure better schooling for the handicapped.

Public Law 94-142, the Education for All Handicapped Children Act (EHCA) of 1976, was one result. This federal statute, funded by annual appropriations of approximately $1 billion, distributes funds to states and ultimately to local districts for education services to various categories of handicapped schoolchildren. In accepting funds, states and districts must agree to follow a rigorous set of federal regulations in educating eligible students. Many local school officials express annoyance at the high level of distrust implied by the unusually legalistic procedures. Advocates for the handicapped reply that past abuses speak poorly for the integrity of local education officials and contend that firm federal regulations are altogether necessary to ensure that handicapped students are treated fairly.

THE EMERGENCY SCHOOL AID ACT

From 1955 through the 1960s judicial pressure was exerted upon southern districts to dismantle dual school systems. Throughout much of this period the Justice Department and the HEW Office of Civil Rights, both within the executive branch, also attempted to pressure school districts to undertake racial desegregation. Beginning in 1968, the Nixon administration attempted to dilute judicial and executive branch mandatory desegregation pressures and proposed to substitute more federal inducements for voluntary desegregation of local school districts. Proponents

---

[34]See Richard Jung and Michael W. Kirst, *Beyond Mutual Adaptation, Into the Bully Pulpit: Recent Research on the Federal Role in Education,* 86-ESPI-1 (Stanford, Calif.: Stanford Education Policy Institute, 1986). For research information about the effects of establishing this block grant program see Elchanan Cohn (ed.), *Federal Block Grants to Education* (Oxford: Pergamon Press, 1986).

[35]For example, *PARC* v. *Commonwealth,* 834 F. Sup. Ct. 1257 (ED Pa. 1971), 343 F. Sup 279 (ED Pa 1972); and *Mills* v. *Board of Education,* 348 F. Sup 866 (DCC 1972).

of racially integrated schools were skeptical of such a strategy, but Congress in 1972 nevertheless enacted the Emergency School Aid Act (ESAA).

The intent of this legislation was to assist local school districts in racially integrating schools by providing federal funds for in-service training of teachers, employment of teacher aides and instructional specialists for desegregated class-rooms, or whatever else local school officials reasonably contended would assist their districts in voluntarily desegregating schools. Appropriations for this statute reached their peak in the late 1970s, totaling approximately $300 million. Funding decreased thereafter and the entire authority was one of the thirty-two acts combined in 1981 to form Chapter Two of the Education Consolidation and Improvement Act. Local districts do not appear to utilize Chapter Two funds to the same extent or for the same purposes that they used ESAA funds.[36]

BILINGUAL EDUCATION

Increasing immigration, particularly from Spanish and Asian nations, began to challenge the resources of selected local school districts after midcentury. The children of many of the new Americans had only limited, if any, ability to speak and read English. Ironically, these youngsters were compelled by statute to attend schools whose medium of instruction, English, was for them unintelligible. In San Francisco, site of a heavy influx of non-English-speaking Asians, students and their parents filed suit against the school district in order to receive language assistance in school. The case, *Lau* v. *Nichols,*[37] eventually was decided in favor of the plain-tiffs. Based on Section 601 of the 1964 Civil Rights Act, the U.S. Supreme Court found that non-English-speaking students were discriminated against and mandated that the school district provide multilingual instructors and other educational assis-tance to these children.

The legal precedent became established that school districts were responsible for assisting limited- and non-English-speaking students. To defray the added costs of such services, several state legislatures enacted categorical school aid programs and Congress added Title VII to the Elementary and Secondary Education Act. The latter provision allocates funds, through states, to local school districts for bilingual instruction. Federal appropriations were never large, reaching a high of $100 mil-lion in 1979. By 1986 there was only a trickle of federal aid for this purpose.

Enhancement of Liberty

The federal government's concern for education has historically focused on the value of efficiency. The various manpower training acts have been consistent with this direction. Concern for equality is a more recent, though a more intense, activity if measured in dollar appropriations. Since World War II, the value of choice, or liberty, has received relatively less attention from the federal government. Congress enacted the Service Man's Readjustment Act, PL 78-346, which provided financial

[36]"How States Are Spending Their Block Grants," *School Finance News,* 2, no. 7 (April 7, 1983), 3.
[37]483 f2d (9OR., 1973); 94 S. C7. 786 (1974).

assistance to veterans who wanted to acquire postsecondary schooling (PL stands for "Public Law"). This statute, the G.I. Bill (described in detail in Chapter 6), was the forerunner of voucher plans in that federal funds went to the individual and he or she decided upon the institution to attend. However, the aid was for postsecondary schooling, and so no intense questions of aid to nonpublic schools were provoked.

In the 1980s the Reagan administration proposed a *tuition tax credit* plan, which would benefit both elementary and secondary as well as postsecondary institutions.[38] Controversy over such an arrangement has been more intense than that concerning the G.I. Bill. Tuition tax credits expand choice by permitting households to deduct all or a portion of *non*public tuition payments from their federal income taxes. The allowable dollar amount is a credit against federal income taxes owed, not simply a deduction from income. Such a plan is favored by many private school officials and parents of private school children. Conversely, many public school advocates view the plan with alarm. Opponents fear that such federal subsidies will undermine public schools, and they allege that the plan will violate First Amendment prohibitions of aid to religious schools.[39]

Prior to 1983, tuition tax credit proposals had passed in the U.S. Senate on six separate occasions. In 1979 the House of Representatives enacted a tuition tax credit plan by a narrow margin, but President Jimmy Carter's threat of a veto, given Democratic control of the Senate at the time, was sufficient to stifle the bill. President Reagan's administration again proposed such a plan, but the prospect of huge federal budget deficits in the 1980s dampened prospects for congressional approval.[40] Aside from economics and politics, however, the constitutionality of such a plan is perhaps enhanced by the U.S. Supreme Court's decision in the previously mentioned case of *Mueller* v. *Allen*.

Another mechanism for enhancing choice in education is the use of vouchers. Voucher plans are described in greater length in subsequent chapters. Suffice it here to mention that people have been advocating federal vouchers for several decades, and there was even a small federally funded voucher experiment in the 1970s. Reagan administration voucher proponents repeatedly proposed that Chapter One of the ECIA be revised to empower compensatory education funds to be allocated to households of low-income students so that they can decide as consumers how best

---

[38]James S. Catteral, "Tuition Tax Credits: Issues of Equity," in *Public Dollars for Private Schools*, ed. Thomas James and Henry M. Levin (Philadelphia: Temple University Press, 1983), chap. 8; Linda Darling-Hammond and Sheila Natrajaj Kirby, "Public Policy and Private Choice: The Case of Minnesota," in *Public Dollars for Private Schools*, ed. James and Levin, chap. 10; Martha Jacobs, "Tuition Tax Credits for Elementary and Secondary Education: Some New Evidence on Who Would Benefit," *Journal of Education Finance*, 5 (Winter 1980), 233–45; and Tim Mazzoni, "The Politics of Educational Choice in Minnesota" (paper delivered at the annual conference of the American Education Research Association, Washington, D.C., April 1987).

[39]See James S. Catterall, *Tuition Tax Credits: Fact and Fiction* (Bloomington, Ind.: Phi Delta Kappan Educational Foundation, 1983); and David A. Longanecker, *Public Costs of Tuition Tax Credits,* Institute for Research on Educational Finance and Governance, School of Education, Stanford University (Stanford, Calif., 1982).

[40]See Elizabeth J. Whitt, David L. Clark, and Terry A. Astuto, *An Analysis of Public Support for the Educational Policy Preferences of the Reagan Administration* (Charlottesville: University Council for Educational Administration, University of Virginia, 1986).

to remedy their education deficit.[41] Impediments to direct public assistance to private schools, such as those triggered by the U.S. Supreme Court decision in *Felton*, have been used as an added reason for making the changes previously cited. Congressional enthusiasm for voucher proposals, however, has not been high.[42]

On balance, the tuition tax credit ideas previously described have proved to be a more attractive mechanism for the federal government to enhance education choice. Tuition tax credits could encourage education choice and not necessitate the federal administrative overhead of a voucher plan. In that tuition tax credit plans have not yet succeeded, it is unlikely that vouchers soon will either. Indeed, as long as federal revenues substantially trail projected expenditures for existing programs, no major new education initiative is likely to develop. The possible exception is in those areas where education can be connected more easily with either improvement of the economy or with national defense.

It is an unusual categorization that neatly encompasses every item, and the one in use here is no exception. Whereas much of the federal government's education activity can be described as having been undertaken in pursuit of efficiency or equality, other provisions fall outside of this framework. One of the most significant is the so-called Impact Aid Program.

At the outset of World War II and again in the early 1950s with the Korean War, local officials frequently found their school districts faced with virtually unmanageable growth problems. Nearby military bases and other federal installations would expand quickly, and public schools often would have to absorb hundreds of additional pupils in a short period. Worse, federal installations were not subject to local taxation. To compensate for this condition, Congress enacted in 1940 and subsequently renewed the Lanham Act, P.L. 81-874. This *in lieu of* tax statute compensates local districts for loss of property tax revenue resulting from the "impact" of federal activity. Hence the funds have come to be known as *impact aid*. Local school districts annually conduct a census among pupils to determine eligibility. Thereafter they can use the funds as though they were general revenues. There is also a modest amount of impact aid for school construction purposes, which is authorized by P.L. 81-815. Table 7.1 displays the full range of federal programs related to lower education operated by the U.S. Department of Education in 1988.

There exist numerous federal education-related endeavors administered by departments other than Education. For example, the Department of Agriculture administers an enormous lunch and breakfast program that provides school districts with funds, nutritional advice, and surplus foodstuffs. Overseas Dependent Schools are federally operated for children of Americans stationed in foreign nations. The now defunct Office of Economic Opportunity (OEO), which did not belong to a de-

[41] For details see *Education Week,* 6, no. 24 (March 11, 1987), 10.

[42] This is not necessarily the case with public opinion. See Richard F. Elmore, *Choice in Public Education* (New Brunswick, N.J.: Center for Policy Research in Education, 1986); and Laura Hersh Salganik, *The Fall and Rise of Educational Vouchers,* The Johns Hopkins University Center for Social Organization of Schools, Report No. 307 (Baltimore, 1981).

TABLE 7.1 U.S. Education Department Budget for FY1986 and FY1987

	BUDGET (IN THOUSANDS)	
PROGRAM	FY1986	FY1987

COMPENSATORY EDUCATION FOR THE DISADVANTAGED
Grants for the Disadvantaged (Chapter One):

Grants to local educational agencies	$3,062,400	$3,453,500
State agency programs:		
Migrants	253,149	264,524
Handicapped	143,713	150,170
Neglected and delinquent	31,214	32,616
State administration	34,076	37,107
Evaluation and technical assistance	5,020	6,246
Migrant education:		
High school equivalency program	6,029	6,300
College assistance migrant program	1,148	1,200
TOTAL, compensatory education programs	3,536,749	3,951,663

IMPACT AID
Maintenance and operations:

Payments for 'a' children	490,941	533,000
Payments for 'b' children	124,410	130,000
Special provisions (Section 2)	21,054	22,000
Disaster assistance	29,570	10,000
Construction	16,747	22,500
TOTAL, impact aid	682,722	717,500

SPECIAL PROGRAMS
Improving school programs (Chapter Two):

State block grants	478,500	500,000
Secretary's discretionary fund:		
Inexpensive book distribution	6,699	7,800
Arts in education	3,021	3,337
Alcohol and drug abuse education	2,871	3,000
Law-related education	1,914	3,000
National Diffusion Network	10,240	10,700
Discretionary projects	2,921	1,500
Other special programs:		
Science and mathematics education	43,066	80,000
Traning and advisory services (Civil Rights, Title IV)	22,968	24,000
Follow through	7,177	—
Territorial teacher training assistance	1,914	2,000
General assistance for the Virgin Islands	4,785	5,000
Ellender fellowships	1,627	1,700
Women's educational equity	5,742	3,500
Magnet schools	71,775	75,000
Excellence in education	2,392	—
Leadership in educational administration (LEAD)	7,177	7,177
TOTAL, special programs	674,789	727,714

BILINGUAL EDUCATION

Bilingual programs	90,862	99,161
Training grants	32,121	33,564
Support services	9,991	10,370
Vocational training	3,527	—
Emergency immigrant education	28,710	30,000
TOTAL, bilingual education	165,211	173,095

TABLE 7.1 (continued)

PROGRAM	BUDGET (IN THOUSANDS) FY1986	FY1987
EDUCATION FOR THE HANDICAPPED		
State assistance:		
State grant program	1,163,282	1,338,000
Preschool incentive grants	28,710	180,000
Early intervention initiative	—	50,000
Special-purpose funds:		
Deaf-blind centers	14,119	15,000
Severely handicapped projects	4,785	5,300
Early childhood education	22,968	24,470
Educational technology and materials	—	3,500
Secondary and transitional services	6,316	7,300
Postsecondary programs	5,264	5,900
Innovation and development	16,080	18,000
Media services and captioned films	16,676	15,000
Regional resource centers	6,029	6,700
Recruitment and information	1,062	1,200
Special education personnel development	61,154	67,730
Special studies	3,089	3,800
TOTAL, education for the handicapped	1,349,534	1,741,900
REHABILITATION SERVICES AND HANDICAPPED RESEARCH		
Basic state grants	1,145,148	1,281,000
Supported employment	—	22,100
Service projects:		
Special demonstration programs	19,332	18,400
Recreational programs	2,105	2,330
Migratory workers	957	1,058
American Indians	1,340	1,500
Projects with industry	14,547	16,070
Helen Keller Center	4,115	4,600
Client assistance	6,412	7,100
Independent living:		
Comprehensive services	10,527	11,830
Centers	22,011	24,320
Services for older blind people	4,785	5,290
Training	25,838	29,550
Innovation and expansion	8,613	9,000
National Institute of Handicapped Research	41,983	48,500
Evaluation	1,723	2,110
TOTAL, rehabilitation services and handicapped research	1,309,436	1,484,758
VOCATIONAL AND ADULT EDUCATION		
Vocational education:		
Basic grants	748,738	815,000
National research and data programs	9,570	11,000
Consumer and homemaker education	30,273	31,633
State advisory councils	6,986	7,500
Community-based organizations	7,178	6,000
Bilingual vocational training	—	3,686
Adult education	97,579	105,981
TOTAL, vocational and adult education	900,324	980,800
TOTAL, ALL PROGRAMS	8,618,765	9,777,430

Source: *Education Week*, November 5, 1986, pp. 16-17.

partment but reported directly to the president, operated numerous important education programs. (The remains of these efforts have been shifted to the Department of Education.) The significance of these other efforts should not go unnoticed.

MAKING AND IMPLEMENTING FEDERAL EDUCATION POLICY

The Iron Triangle

Conventional wisdom holds that federal policy for almost any endeavor, not simply education, is a consequence of political interactions among the three components of the iron triangle—the education agencies of the executive branch, congressional committees, and interest groups. The idea for a new piece of legislation may arise from any of these groups or from a large number of other sources, such as a new book, a study supported by a philanthropic foundation, a journalist's article, or an academic research project. Once an executive branch agency or a member of Congress is interested in sponsoring the idea, drafting the concept in bill form is relatively easy, either by counsel in an executive branch agency or by the Legislative Drafting Service in the House or Senate.

Identifying potential supporters of an idea and then negotiating the compromises that may be necessary before important factions agree to support a bill may be difficult. The more important a bill, then the more groups likely to be affected, the larger the federal appropriation involved, and the greater the likelihood of controversy. Many more bills are defeated than enacted. In many cases an idea must be submitted repeatedly over a number of years before eventually proving sufficiently understood and popular to be adopted. Also, whereas an idea may stem from many sources and be initiated by any one component of the triangle, conventional wisdom holds that eventually the other two components must also agree before passage will occur. Brokering the multifaceted agreements necessary to ensure enactment of a bill is an art form seldom fully appreciated by the public.[43]

Implementation

Conventional high school civics textbooks explain that policy is made by the legislative branch and implemented by a politically sanitized executive branch agency. This is but another form of the frequently promulgated myth that a clear distinction can be made between policy making and policy administration. In fact, political conflicts left unresolved in the enactment process almost inevitably are reflected in efforts to implement legislation. Consequently, administering federal edu-

[43] Alternatives to the iron triangle concept of policy formation are presented by Michael Kirst and Gail Meister in *The Role of Issue Networks in State Agenda Setting,* Project Report 83-80Al, Institute for Research on Educational Finance and Governance, School of Education, Stanford University (Stanford, Calif., 1983).

cation policy is far from a mechanically simple, politically sterile, technocratic undertaking.[44]

Once an education bill has been approved by both houses of Congress, it is often necessary to convene a *conference committee,* composed of members from both House and Senate, to resolve differences between the two houses' versions of the bill. Assuming presidential approval, the bill is then a public law and is numbered as such. For example, Public Law 94-142 denotes the 142nd bill to become a statute in the ninety-fourth session of Congress. Thereafter, the specified administering agency within the executive branch is responsible for drafting regulations to implement the new statute.

Regulations are necessary because it is not generally possible in the enactment phase to write the statute so that it will cover every practical contingency connected with implementation and administration. Also, the political dynamics of enactment frequently necessitate a degree of ambiguity and vagueness. The higher the abstraction, the greater the probability that political agreement can be reached. "Accomplish good and avoid evil" is an admonition so vague as to be vapid. However, few oppose the principle. As soon as legislation becomes specific, detailing which groups will get how much money for what purposes, the prospect of political conflict increases. Thus, to dampen controversy and attract a greater number of supporting votes, authors of legislation sometimes leave the wording deliberately vague, and it is up to those who draft regulations to tidy up the rules of administration. If the statute is ambiguous, interest groups may lobby as assiduously to influence regulations as they did to influence the initial legislation itself.

An education bill is likely to fall within the administrative province of the Department of Education. This cabinet-level department was created in 1978 upon the recommendation of President Jimmy Carter. Previously, the U.S. Office of Education (USOE) as well as the National Institute of Education (now the Office of Educational Research and Improvement) were agencies within the Department of Health, Education and Welfare (HEW). The latter is now the Department of Health and Human Services (HHS), reflecting the separation of Education.

Department of Education legal counsel are responsible for drafting regulations. In this process, they pay particular attention to the *legislative history* of a bill. This is derived from committee hearing records and committee reports in both the House and the Senate. Whatever debate accompanied passage of the bill on the floor of each house also becomes part of the legislative history, as does the conference committee report, if any. From such records the intent of the bill is more fully deduced and prescriptions for administration are drafted that are intended to guide the actions of state and local officials as they implement the legislation. Regulations specify purposes for which the federal funds can be used, state and local plans that

---

[44]See Stephen K. Bailey and Edith K. Mosher, *The ESEA: The Office of Education Administers a Law* (Syracuse, N.Y.: Syracuse University Press, 1967); Hugh Davis Graham, *The Uncertain Triumph* (Chapel Hill: University of North Carolina Press, 1984); and James R. Jones, "The Role of Federal Government in Educational Policy Matters: Focus on Finance," *Journal of Education Finance,* 10, no. 2 (Fall 1984), 238–55.

may be required by the Department of Education, and rules by which local projects will be audited.

Regulations, once drafted, are submitted to appropriate congressional committees for approval. Also, they are published and distributed in the *Federal Register* to gain the reaction of educators and others in the field. When the approval process is complete, regulations are inserted in the *Federal Administrative Code* and carry the weight of law. Often, *guidelines* are provided to assist state and local officials in interpreting regulations and the statute itself. Federal guidelines are typically written in straightforward language and provide examples of procedures and programs to assist local administrators.[45]

Appropriation

To this point, explanations have focused on procedures concerned with enacting and implementing *authorizing* legislation, the substantive bill that specifies the purposes of the federal education program and authorizes funds to be spent. The actual dollar amount Congress will allocate to purposes for which spending is authorized is established through the *appropriations* process. This endeavor is a virtually separate legislative track involving interaction with executive branch budget officials and relying heavily upon the Congressional Budget Office and appropriations committees and subcommittees in both the House and the Senate. It is not sufficient for policy makers, professional educators, and members of the public merely to have a sophisticated understanding of the dynamics of authorization politics. Knowledge of appropriation politics, which is characterized by a separate political culture, is also necessary. A thorough reading of a book such as *The Politics of the Budgetary Process* by Aaron Wildavsky is useful in gaining a comprehensive view of this important area.[46]

GAINING ADMINISTRATIVE COMPLIANCE

Federal officials are anxious that education funds be spent in compliance with statutes and regulations. Inducing compliance is a topic that has been addressed by experts in public administration.[47] A few of the strategies utilized by the federal government are listed here. Keep in mind that the United States bureaucracy is multi-tiered, with each layer wanting to guard its historically evolved prerogatives.

---

[45]Regulations are not devoid of controversy. See David L. Kirp and Donald N. Jensen, *School Days, Rule Days: The Legalization and Regulation of Education* (New York: Falmer Press, 1987).

[46]Aaron Wildavsky, *Politics of the Budgetary Process* (Boston: Little Brown, 1984).

[47]For example, Paul Berman and Milbrey McLaughlin, *Federal Programs Supporting Educational Change: Implementing and Sustaining Innovations,* Vol. 8 (Santa Monica, Calif.: Rand Corporation, 1978); and Michael S. Knapp et al., *Cumulative Effects of Federal Education Policies on Schools and Districts* (Menlo Park, Calif.: SRI International, 1983).

The major strategy pursued with education programs is to require state and local agencies to submit in advance a plan for the use of federal funds.[48] The plan must comply with guidelines for the legislation involved. Thereafter, it is assumed that local administrators will operate in a manner consistent with the submitted plan. Periodically, a local or state agency may be audited, either by state officials, the Auditor General of the Department of Education, or the General Accounting Office (GAO) of Congress. The purpose of an audit is to ensure that program spending is consistent with locally submitted plans and with federal regulations.[49]

Another stratagem is to require local or state matching of federal funds. The reasoning is that the requirement of a mix of monies will commit local officials to the success of the federally subsidized endeavor as if it were wholly their own. Yet another strategy is to empower local clients or program recipients to pressure local districts to ensure compliance. There are at least two expressions of this strategy. One is to be found in P.L. 94-142, wherein parents of handicapped youngsters can request a "fair hearing" with local officials and even be represented by an attorney in the process. Such an adversary process is intended to protect clients' statutory rights and to provide them with a lever for gaining local district compliance. Somewhat more subtle is the creation of school-site advisory councils and parent advisory councils such as are recommended or required by a number of federal and state program regulations. The idea here is that parents—presumed program benefactors—will advise and appropriately oversee the actions of local education officials.

There have been a few examples of education agencies violating federal legislative intent. On balance, however, the overwhelming experience has been for local and state officials to attempt to operate federal programs honestly and effectively.[50]

NATIONALIZING INFLUENCES ON AMERICAN EDUCATION

Despite the United States' relatively decentralized education system, there exist a number of dimensions on which schools in one part of the nation are similar to those in another. This homogeneity extends beyond what would be necessary simply to instruct students of a similar age and grade. Moreover, this similarity is a

[48]Such plans generate a great many reports. See, for example, Mary Bankston, "Organizational Reporting in a School District: State and Federal Programs," in *IFG Policy Perspectives,* report of the Institute for Research on Educational Finance and Governance, School of Education, Stanford University (Stanford, Calif., 1982).

[49]A more extensive treatment of this topic is provided by Stephen N. Barro in "Federal Education Goals and Policy Instruments: An Assessment of the 'Strings' Attached to Categorical Grants in Education," in *Federal Interest in Financing Schooling,* ed. Michael Timpane (Santa Monica, Calif.: Rand Corporation, 1978), pp. 229–86; and Henry M. Levin and Man C. Tsang, *Federal Grants and National Educational Policy,* Project Report No. 82-18, Institute for Research on Educational Finance and Governance, School of Education, Stanford University (Stanford, Calif., 1982).

[50]Twenty years of analysis of federal education program implementation are reviewed and synthesized by Allan R. Odden, *Education Reform and Services to Poor Students: Can the Two Policies be Compatible?* (Berkeley, Calif.: Policy Analysis for California Education, 1987).

function of influences far greater than those exerted by federal officials. These additional nationalizing influences are extragovernmental.

For example, the use of test results by an overwhelming proportion of colleges and universities to determine admission eligibility renders the Scholastic Aptitude Test (SAT) and the American College Test (ACT), along with college admissions standards, major determinants of U.S. secondary school curricula. Regional accreditation agencies operating throughout the United States influence secondary school curricula, instructional procedures, and libraries. Textbook publishers generate greater profit potential the larger the market they serve; hence their desire to publish texts that are widely attractive, regardless of the values of a particular section of the nation or the tastes of local decision makers. Nationwide organizations such as the American Association of School Administrators (AASA), the National School Board Association (NSBA), the National Education Association (NEA), and the American Federation of Teachers (AFT) can influence state and local practices through their nationwide communication channels, which cut across local and state boundaries.

The Bully Pulpit

Throughout the Reagan administration years, the federal government influenced American educational policy as much or more through its efforts at moral and rhetorical suasion as through programmatic means. Perhaps no president since Theodore Roosevelt had been so successful in motivating the public and other elected officials to act in accord with his advice and admonitions. Reagan administration education managers repeatedly identified an educational dimension about which the public had intense concern and thereafter, through speeches, television news conferences, pamphlets,[51] and commission reports,[52] suggested actions that state and local governments should take to rectify errant conditions. In assessing his first term in office, President Reagan stated:

> If I were asked to single out the proudest achievement of my administration's first three and one-half years in office, what we've done to define the issues and promote the great national debate in education would rank up near the top of the list.[53]

The primary posture of the Reagan administration's education policy was that education was not a federal obligation but should be a responsibility of states and local school districts. The federal role, in their view, was to be restricted to collecting and distributing information, dispensing funds authorized by previous congresses, and advocating change through exhortation—the "bully pulpit," as it has

---

[51]See, for example, *What Works: Research about Teaching and Learning* (Washington, D.C.: U.S. Department of Education, 1986).

[52]See, for example, National Commission on Excellence in Education, *A Nation At Risk,* (Washington, D.C.: Government Printing Office, 1983).

[53]Ronald Reagan, "Overview of Education Reform Issues," in *A Blueprint for Education Reform,* ed. C. Marshner (Washington, D.C.: Free Congress Research and Education Foundation, 1984), p. 2; quoted in Jung and Kirst, *Beyond Mutual Adaptation,* p. 23.

come to be known. By these means, the federal government during much of the 1980s came to set the agenda for education throughout the states and localities without enacting a major new education program. Indeed, this influence was exerted even though the purchasing power of federal financing for education was eroding.[54]

SUMMARY

Unlike most other nations, the federal government in the United States does not play a paramount role in education. State governments are the prime policy makers, and the federal government funds programs, governed by state education agencies and operated by local school districts, intended to promote equality of educational opportunity and greater school productivity. Federal education support began in the eighteenth century, but did not result in significant financing until the mid twentieth century with enactment of major bills such as the National Defense Education Act (1958), the Elementary and Secondary Education Act (1965), the Education for All Handicapped Children Act (1976), and the Education Consolidation and Improvement Act (1981). Federal funds for education approximated $18 billion in 1986, divided almost equally between K–12 programs and higher education. Funding for the latter is devoted generally to student aid. Federal judicial decisions such as that in *Brown* v. *Board of Education* (1954) have also influenced U.S. education.

[54]See David L. Clark and Terry A. Astuto, *The Effects of Federal Education Policy Changes on Policy and Program Development in State and Local Education Agencies* (Charlottesville: University Council for Educational Administration, University of Virginia, 1986).

chapter eight

THE POLITICS OF
SCHOOL FINANCE

Decisions regarding public school financing are political. They are made by individuals in accord with the rules and procedures constituting United States political institutions. Citizens may affect educational financing by voting for school board members and state legislators, or by voting on school-related initiatives and referenda. They may petition school agencies and speak at public hearings. Judges influence policies by ruling on the legality of governmental actions. Legislators may enact educational programs and impose taxes to pay for them, subject to the rules of the legislative process and voters' willingness to elect them to office. Governors and educational executives propose programs and taxes and control educational financing by the way they implement programs. The purpose of this chapter is to explain the political dynamics of educational finance decisions.

In general, legal political actions available to individuals are prescribed by constitutions and institutional rules known to everyone. Adherence to predetermined rules increases the predictability of political behavior and makes it possible to reach collective decisions. Another distinguishing feature of political decisions is that they usually require agreement among many political actors, and once agreements are reached they are binding on all members of the community, including those who disagree with the decisions. In other words, government can enforce decisions once they are made.

POLITICAL BARGAINING

Political decision making is best described by comparing it to private decisions. When an individual decides what to eat, what car to buy, or where to live, he or she is engaged in a market exchange with another party. Usually, market decisions involve only two parties, and the consequences of those decisions impinge only on those directly involved. An exchange, called a sale, takes place if both parties believe they will benefit. A restaurant would rather have money than the food offered at that price, and the customer would rather have lunch than the money. The decision rule in most market transactions, in other words, is unanimous consent. All parties to an exchange generally agree to the terms of the exchange or there is no sale.[1] Sometimes when someone is particularly persuasive it is said that he or she got a "steal." Nevertheless, if both parties do not believe they are benefiting, at least marginally, no exchange takes place.

Likewise, political decisions result from an exchange process, called bargaining, whose purpose is to produce mutually beneficial outcomes.[2] Bargaining requires that something of value be ceded in order to obtain something else that is more valued.

Situations and Resources

Political bargaining, however, is more complicated than market decision making, for several reasons. One reason is the variety of situations in which bargaining takes place and the variety of political resources employed to influence decisions. Someone who wants a car approaches a car owner and attempts to arrive at a price at which the owner is willing to sell. An owner may be a private individual, a used-car salesman, or a new-car distributor. Generally the possibilities are few and there are only a few types of financial instruments a seller will accept. In politics, many techniques and resources are available to influence decisions. For example, parents who want a better reading program for their child can petition the school principal, the school board, the state legislature, or even the federal government. They can use their votes to try to elect school board members and legislators sympathetic to the need for better reading programs. They can seek support from other parents and interest groups. They can threaten legal action or a recall campaign if other tactics fail. They may even find grounds for legal action. There are many ways and tactics for influencing political decisions.

Levels

A second reason political decisions are more complicated is that there are several levels of decision making in politics. There are "constitutional" decisions that

---

[1] For a discussion of the unanimity rule in both market and political decisions, see James M. Buchanan and Gordon Tullock, *The Calculus of Consent* (Ann Arbor: University of Michigan Press, 1962), pp. 85–96.

[2] Bargaining is the subject of numerous political science books. For a general discussion of political bargaining, see Joyce M. Mitchell and William C. Mitchell, *Political Analysis and Public Policy* (Chicago: Rand McNally, 1969), pp. 437–66.

may have nothing to do with educational finance but that establish rules by which educational finance decisions are made.[3] For example, many states require school district voters to approve budgets that exceed the previous year's budget or utilize a higher tax rate. Or, states may earmark certain revenue sources for education or prohibit the use of specific taxes for education. In addition to constitutional decisions, politicians make policy decisions. Finally, administrators make operational decisions which implement policy decisions and frequently determine the manner in which educational resources are allocated. These operational decisions—who gets what within the totals available for a program or a district—produce some of the most intense bargaining in education.

Purposes

Third, different bargaining strategies have different purposes. Litigation, for example, is usually designed to establish limits on policy makers' behavior. Courts may declare that a statewide property tax is illegal, or that state funds may not be used in a manner discriminatory to certain students. Referenda, of course, usually establish only general policy guidelines or limitations. Most of the bargaining required to arrive at specific programs for financing schools occurs in state legislatures or local school district board rooms. This is where much of the fine tuning of school programs and budgets takes place.

Agreement

The most complicating characteristic of political decision making, however, is the need to obtain agreement, not just between a buyer and a seller but among many people, usually a majority. In referenda this may mean thousands, hundreds of thousands, or even millions of people. In a state legislature, a decision may require the approval of a hundred or more legislators. On some issues it is easy to obtain majority support. A resolution to commend someone for an outstanding achievement usually passes easily because everyone favors achievement and words of commendation are almost always politically costless. But finding majority support for a new school finance program or tax reform program is always difficult, because citizens in various legislative districts will be affected differently and legislators will attempt to negotiate the most beneficial programs for their districts.

Components

What then does political bargaining involve? It requires that individuals involved in making political decisions be able to persuade others of the merits of their proposals and, in most cases, be able to convince them to settle for less than they really want. Persuasion and compromise are necessary because

[3]James M. Buchanan, *Public Finance in Democratic Process* (Chapel Hill: University of North Carolina Press, 1967), pp. 287–93.

1. people have different ideas about what should be done and how to do it;
2. in most democratic political institutions no one group has sufficient power to impose its views on all others; and
3. political officials generally share the belief that in most situations some solution to a problem is better than none.[4]

Persuasion, negotiation, and compromise, in other words, are characteristic ways that democracies solve political problems and maintain civic peace.

Politicians who are unwilling to compromise on difficult issues stand properly accused of failing in their political responsibilities. George Bernard Shaw, remembering his own political career, argued for the necessity of compromising when he attacked a fellow Labour candidate for Parliament, Joseph Burgess, for being unwilling to do so:

> When I think of my own unfortunate character, smirched with compromise, rotted with opportunism, mildewed by expedience, . . . dragged through the mud of borough council and Battersea elections, stretched out of shape with wire-pulling, putrified by permeations, worn out by 25 years pushing to gain an inch here, or straining to stem a backrush, I do think Joe might have put up with just a speck or two on those white robes of his for the sake of the millions of poor devils who cannot afford any character at all because they have no friend in Parliament. Oh, these moral dandies, these spiritual toffs, these superior persons. Who is Joe anyhow that he would not risk his soul occasionally like the rest of us?[5]

In summary, this chapter focuses on the political bargaining processes that produce public decisions. Since public schools are financed largely from local and state sources, the following discussion is limited to the kinds of political bargaining that occur within districts and state legislatures over the financing of public schools.

LOCAL VOTERS AND EDUCATION POLICY

Although constitutions hold the state responsible for providing public education, most states delegate a major portion of this responsibility to local school districts. Approximately 40 percent of the funds for primary and secondary education are raised by local school districts, and local school boards are largely responsible for the planning, operation, and control of public schools.

School districts are highly constrained in their actions, however, particularly with regard to school financing. The federal government places many conditions on grants to school districts. Similarly, state legislatures and state education departments have constructed a complex superstructure of regulations to which local districts must adhere in operating local school programs. In the 1970s many states en-

---

[4]William C. Mitchell, *Public Choice in America* (Chicago: Markham, 1971), p. 126.
[5]Quoted in Hesketh Pearson, *GBS* (New York: Harper & Brothers, 1942), p. 156.

acted collective bargaining laws that further constrained local school officials' autonomy.

Local school districts are also affected by events over which they have little or no control. The Supreme Court's decision in *Brown* v. *Board of Education*, linking race and education policies, has had a profound effect on local school decisions. The Russians' launching of Sputnik created a wave of interest in education and led to increased federal funding of science programs. The report of the National Commission on Excellence in Education, *A Nation at Risk,* spawned not only a rash of legislation designed to improve schools but also a flood of other committees and commissions, each with its own ideas on how to improve educational programs. However, despite the vagaries of national events, the day-to-day decisions required in America's public elementary and secondary schools are made at the district level.

Determining the Community's Educational Needs

PROFESSIONALS' VIEWS

Decisions affecting the amount and mix of educational services in a local district emerge from interactions among many groups. One important group is the professional educators whose livelihoods depend on public willingness to support schools. As with advocates of other public services, professional educators generally argue that more programs and funds are needed. Their advocacy of new and bigger programs needing greater financial support is tempered only by calculations of what is politically feasible. If they seek too much, their claims may be disregarded entirely and they may end up with nothing.

POLICY ANALYSTS

Another important group is the policy analysts who provide supposedly objective estimates of educational needs and their costs. Analysts on the superintendent's staff or analysts hired as consultants by school districts project school enrollments and estimate the costs of providing alternative packages of services for the students expected to attend district schools. Typically, analysts begin with the basic education program, usually the program a district already offers, and then examine the costs and benefits of proposed additions. They employ a variety of research techniques designed to provide policy makers with the best estimate of educational need.

CITIZENS

Decisions regarding the "need" for education, however, are ultimately made by citizens of the community served by a school district.[6] School board members may support teachers' goals or have great confidence in a district's analysts, but their goals and analyses are worth little without local citizen approval. Educational deci-

---

[6]For a more extended discussion of varying definitions of educational need, see James M. Buchanan, "Taxpayer Constraints on Financing Education," in *Economic Factors Affecting the Financing of Education,* ed. Roe L. Johns et al. (Gainesville, Fla: National Education Finance Project, 1970), pp. 266–71.

sions, particularly regarding finance, are made by community members who elect school board members or approve school district budgets.[7] Individual voting decisions of citizens can be manipulated or ignored only within narrow limits. School board members failing to recognize this are unlikely to be reelected. Educational professionals who divorce school policy from community preferences will find many of their plans rejected.

Once the central role of citizen-voters in educational decision making is recognized, there is no one correct answer to the question of how much education is enough. The answer emerges from many individual calculations of benefits and costs. This answer is expressed by votes in school board elections or on school finance referenda, or in arguments presented by concerned citizens in public meetings, or is communicated informally to policy makers. Rationalizations of educational advocates and estimates of policy experts enter into public decisions as part of the information citizens use to make judgments. The most important information, however, is every individual's own perception of the benefits and costs of proposed educational programs. This is why it is often easier to obtain funding for a new football stadium or gymnasium than for a school library or music wing. Athletics provide private benefits for many community members whereas a library or music building benefits mostly those in school.

Translating Citizen Preferences into Education Policy

Individual estimates of education need are translated into policy decisions through an important mechanism—electoral processes. Equal educational services are generally available to all school-age residents in a district regardless of individual preferences for education. Costs are imposed largely on property owners in proportion to property value and not in relation to their consumption of education. A property owner with no children pays the same as an owner of comparable property with five schoolchildren. Although citizens cannot directly affect the "supply" of education through their purchases of education (as they affect the supply of cars when they buy a car, for instance), they can do so by voting in school elections.[8]

This does not mean that voters' knowledge about how much education they want or how much it will cost is exact. On the contrary, taxpayers' attitudes are often imprecise and subject to campaign influence. Voters have to be somewhat sympathetic toward schools, or at least interested in them, however, if school advocates' campaign messages are to be effective. Much electoral advertising is designed to provide voters with information about the benefits and costs of the measures to be voted upon. Some of it, though, is designed to change opinions through persuasion. For example, a local chamber of commerce may argue that a proposed school budget should be passed because efforts to obtain new businesses depend upon continued public school excellence.

---

[7]Ibid., p. 270.

[8]Some states and communities require more than majority approval of school tax and bond levies. For instance, Washington State requires that 60 percent of voters approve budgets and that the number of ballots cast be at least 40 percent of those cast in the previous general election.

There are clearly limits to the flexibility of voters' attitudes, however. Ultimately, if only subjectively, voter-taxpayers estimate tax costs (the tax liability of a proposed educational budget), the resultant tax price per child served in the program, and the quantity of education preferred at the estimated tax price. On the basis of these estimates, they decide whether to vote for or against school levies.

Suppose that all voters in a school district can be arrayed according to the quantity of education that each prefers (quantity here is the amount per pupil at each individual's estimated tax price per unit).[9] One possible array is illustrated in Figure 8.1. Q_s is the proposed school budget being voted upon. Q_m is the amount preferred by the median voter-taxpayer. Voters lying between O and Q_s along the array believe that the proposed budget would produce an oversupply of education at the required tax price. They prefer less education than is proposed and can be expected to vote against the budget because it is too large. However, since most districts reduce their budget requests if the budget is rejected at the polls, those to the right of Q_s are likely to vote in favor of the proposed budget for fear they would be offered even less if it were defeated. This hypothetical array of voters, therefore, is likely to approve the proposed budget, or any budget not greater than Q_m, which would receive just a majority vote.[10]

As is clear, there is no direct way for one individual to change the supply of education through voting. Median voter preference, however, is one measure of a community's collective preference for education, assuming, of course, that a community agrees that such a decision should be made by a majority of voters.[11] Median preference expresses the maximum amount of education that will be approved under majority rule.

The median preference may be close to the optimal supply of education for a community. Most voter-taxpayers are likely to be partially disappointed with any proposed education program. They will prefer either more or less than is offered. If, however, the degree of disappointment is measured by differences between their preference and what is being offered, then aggregate dissatisfaction in a community is minimized if the supply is established at the median preference.

Bell-shaped distributions of the education supply curve reflect both voter response to varying tax costs of education and the varying tastes of different individuals for education. Analyses of voter preferences among school districts must be care-

[9]The following analysis draws heavily on Michael Boss, *The Supply and Tax-Cost of Education and the Vote*, CASEA Technical Report No. 13 (Eugene, Ore.: Center for the Advanced Study of Educational Administration, 1973).

[10]Taxpayers who do not vote are ignored. Presumably, such voters expect that the utility of attempts to adjust supply and tax cost through voting is less than the expected cost of voting. This assumption is discussed at length in Anthony Downs, *An Economic Theory of Democracy* (New York: Harper & Brothers, 1957).

[11]Analyses of the *median voter* model of local fiscal decisions are found in Theodore Bergstrom and Robert Goodman, "Private Demands for Public Goods," *American Economic Review*, 63 (June 1973), 280–96; and Noel Edelson, "Budgetary Outcomes in a Referendum Setting," in *Property Taxation and the Finance of Education*, ed. Richard Lindholm (Madison: University of Wisconsin Press, 1974), pp. 192–227.

FIGURE 8.1   Array of Individual Preferences for Education

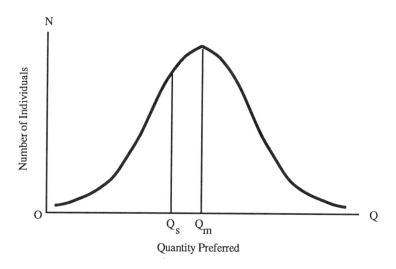

Quantity Preferred

Source: Michael Boss, *The Supply and Tax-Cost of Education and the Vote*, CASEA Technical Report No. 13 (Eugene, Oreg: Center for the Advanced Study of Educational Administration, 1973), p. 6.

ful to distinguish between quantities of education chosen because of different tax costs of education and quantities chosen because of different preferences (or tastes) for education. Both are frequently related to personal characteristics such as income and education.

Another implication of the median voter model is that a large percentage of favorable votes in a budget election is not a good indicator of a community's satisfaction with the education being proposed. A vote of 75 percent in favor may mean that most of the 75 percent believe too little education is being offered. Districts whose budgets receive votes of barely 50 percent in favor are more likely to be providing nearly optimal levels of education.

The Taxpayers' "Revolt"

If the preceding description of the voter-taxpayers' role in local school district fiscal decisions is correct, then what meaning can be ascribed to that episodic phenomenon, the so-called *taxpayers' revolt*? The term has been used to describe at least three different situations:

1. voters turn down tax referenda more frequently than in the past, for any of several reasons;

2. voters reject tax referenda because conditions surrounding school budget referenda have changed;

3. voters reject tax referenda merely because their attitudes toward public schools have changed so much that they would vote against referenda they would have approved in the past.[12]

These possibilities are illustrated in Figure 8.2, which depicts two patterns of community voting in response to proposed tax rates. Schedule A represents voter response under one set of conditions; schedule B represents response under another set. A shift along schedule A indicates a change in demand for education resulting from a shift in tax rates; a shift from schedule A to schedule B indicates a change in demand for education because of factors other than tax rate.

To simplify the discussion, we show only the effects of a proposed increase in school tax rate. The first interpretation of a taxpayers' revolt is shown by a shift from a higher point to any lower point on either vote-tax schedule. A decline in the proportion of yes votes from 2 to 5, from 4 to 2, or from 2 to 3 would each be regarded as a revolt. This view assumes that the purpose of referenda is to ratify decisions made by school board members and professional educators. Since voters are expected to approve budgets, any decline in their willingness to do so is interpreted as a revolt. This view of referenda is a curious distortion of their original purpose, which was to increase citizen participation in governmental decision making.[13]

FIGURE 8.2 Alternative Views of Voting Behavior in Local School Tax Referenda

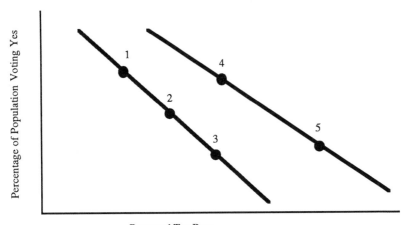

Source: Arthur J. Alexander and Gail V. Bass, *Schools, Taxes and Voter Behavior* (Santa Monica, Calif.: Rand Corporation, 1974), p. 50.

[12] Arthur J. Alexander and Gail V. Bass, *Schools, Taxes and Voter Behavior: An Analysis of School District Property Tax Elections* (Santa Monica, Calif.: Rand Corporation, 1974), p. 49.

[13] Frederick M. Wirt and Michael W. Kirst, *The Political Web of American Schools* (Boston: Little, Brown, 1972), p. 97.

In the second way of viewing the taxpayers' revolt, a higher rate of budget rejections is explained by voters' responding to a different set of conditions than in the past. A shift from one point on either tax-vote schedule to a lower point on the same schedule (from 2 to 3, or from 4 to 5) would reflect such a situation, since the preferences schedule has remained the same and only the proposed tax rate has increased. A variety of factors besides the proposed tax rate illustrated in Figure 8.2 might account for declining support for school budgets even when underlying attitudes toward public education (represented by vote-tax schedules A and B) remain unchanged. Alexander and Bass examined over fifty variables in a study of school taxes and voter behavior in California in the 1950s and 1960s and found that the proposed tax rate and its change accounted for most of the decline in voter support for school budgets.[14] In other words, the higher the proposed percentage tax rate increase, the lower the percentage of school budgets passed. This suggests that voters are willing to support gradual but not rapid increases in school costs.

Boss took the analysis one step further in his study of school referenda in Oregon.[15] He developed a simple mathematical model to estimate a community's demand for education. Application of the model to school budget elections in Oregon from 1963 to 1970 indicates that while the collective demand for education in Oregon increased continuously, the supply of education increased even more rapidly. As school boards set proposed supplies of education nearer estimated levels of collective demand for education, instances in which the proposed supply exceeded the actual demand increased, resulting in budget defeats. These defeats, Boss concluded, are part of the normal and desirable operation of a democratic system of public finance.

What constitutes too high a tax rate or too much education is not always clear. In New York State, for instance, school expenditures and school tax rates are almost always higher than in any state but Alaska. In Arizona expenditures are much lower, yet in both states voters must believe they are receiving about the right amount of education at the prevailing tax price, or they would elect officials willing to provide the "correct" amount of education. An important determinant of how much is enough seems to be how much similar and neighboring districts are spending or taxing themselves for schools.[16] The larger the difference between a district's proposed tax rate increase or per-capita school expenditure and that of lower-spending neighboring districts, the greater the voter turnout and the greater the likelihood of voters rejecting referenda.

These studies suggest that voters use school budget referenda in part to correct local school officials' fiscal policies. Districts that increase tax rates too quickly, or that offer more education than a community prefers, suffer higher proportions of budget defeats. Referenda may play a useful role in correcting school officials' fiscal decisions. To the extent that citizens should control educational decisions, a local

[14]Alexander and Bass, *Schools, Taxes and Voter Behavior,* p. 65.

[15]Boss, *Supply and Tax-Cost,* pp. 9–23.

[16]Jack W. Osman and W. Norton Grubb, "Adjustments from Disequilibrium in Local Finance: School Referenda in California" (paper from The Childhood and Government Project, University of California at Berkeley, 1975).

referendum on school budgets is an appropriate mechanism for ensuring that local voters obtain the education they want.

The term *taxpayers' revolt* appears appropriate only to describe a situation in which voters reject tax referenda they would have approved in the past. A shift from 4 to 2 in Figure 8.2 would indicate such a change. There is little evidence that a major shift in public attitudes toward public schools has occurred. Public opinion polls reveal that most parents continue to be satisfied with the performance of their children's schools,[17] and localities continue to approve larger school budgets.

There are a number of factors, however, that will constrain the future ability of local districts to raise school taxes. The growth in the United States in the proportion of older people, to whom property taxes are often particularly onerous, may affect school budgets. This effect could be particularly strong because a larger proportion of older people than younger people go to the polls.[18] The present massive federal debt may eventually diminish local districts' ability to fund increasing levels of school services. Large increases in the costs of other local government services, such as health care, are likely to compete with rising school costs for taxpayers' marginal dollars. All of these factors, however, are rational grounds for limiting the rise in educational expenditures. Older people and families without children value other public services more than education. To the extent that they reflect a shift in median preference away from additional school expenditures, referenda are serving to adjust the mix of public services to conform to a community's preferences.

Shifts of a second type—for example, from vote-tax schedule B to schedule A—can also result from school officials' actions related only indirectly to citizen demand for education. One instance is forced consolidation of school districts, an action shown to create hostility among unwilling constituents and to reduce citizen willingness to support future school budgets.[19] Forced busing, violence in schools, and poor performance of high school students on national achievement tests are also likely to erode the public's confidence in schools and their willingness to spend more for education.

It is more difficult to predict voter reaction to the tendency of policy makers to use schools as instruments for social change. Since World War II schools have been expected to promote racial integration and wealth redistribution. The role of social reformer for schools may conflict with their knowledge-transmission role. To the extent that voters in a community expect schools to transmit only local values to students, they may resist shifts in the educational program toward broader social reforms. The renewed 1980s emphasis on academic achievement and intellectual rigor may dampen the social reform agenda for public schools, at least for a while.

---

[17]In the 1976 Gallup Poll of the public's attitudes toward public schools, 50 percent of those with children in public schools gave schools an A or B rating. *Kappan,* 58, no. 2 (October 1976), 14–22. In 1987, 56 percent gave schools an A or B rating. *Kappan,* 69, no. 1 (September 1987), 17–30.

[18]Philip K. Piele and John Stuart Hall, *Budgets, Bonds and Ballots* (Lexington, Mass.: Heath, Lexington Books, 1973), pp. 44–47.

[19]L. A. Wilson II, "A Partial Model of Citizen Response to School District Consolidation" (paper for the Department of Political Science, University of Oregon, 1974).

In summary, the politics of school finance at the local level are tied closely to the behavior of local citizens. The ultimate constraints in many school districts are the willingness of local voters to support school budgets and, indirectly, the necessity of school board members to win elections. When school boards seek to expand education too rapidly, or to extend public schools' role beyond that desired by the community, voters are likely to express dissatisfaction at the polls. During the late 1960s and early 1970s, local voters rejected increasing numbers of school budgets and bond requests largely because they believed the benefits of additional schooling did not outweigh the additional costs involved. Rather than a revolt against public schools per se, this was simply an instance of voter participation in decisions affecting the supply of public education.

STATE SCHOOL FINANCE REFORM

During the last half of the 1960s and the early 1970s, school financing became a major policy issue in most state legislatures. There was a variety of reasons for the upsurge of interest in educational finance. Most of them had to do with rising costs and falling enrollments.

During the 1950s and 1960s, public education grew rapidly in the United States. Expansion created serious problems when the flow of new dollars to public education was slowed in the 1970s. Conflicts emerged as to how much and where to cut educational costs. Such conflict should not have been unexpected. Political theorists have observed that revolutions are most likely to occur when rising expectations, fostered during a prolonged period of growth, suddenly become unrealizable because of an economic downturn.[20] When public education's period of growth came to an end—because of declining enrollment and increasing voter resistance to school budget increases—competition for scarce educational dollars produced open conflict among the many interests involved. Coalitions of educational administrators and teachers, who had cooperated to secure additional funds for education, began to splinter. School board members and legislators who had previously supported increases for education were confronted by a larger and increasingly vocal constituency demanding more efficiency and accountability in the use of educational funds.

Since states are legally responsible for public schools, it was only a matter of time before conflicts over educational finance percolated up to state legislatures. Much of the pressure on the legislators for reform came first from educators seeking new sources of funds for public schools. These educators chose to interpret taxpayers' resistance in school budget and bond elections as a repudiation of the method of financing schools rather than as a rejection of the need for greater school spending. Consequently, they urged legislatures to shift more local school costs onto state taxes. Simultaneously, taxpayers, confronted with rapidly rising costs for all local services, wanted the local property tax burden reduced or shifted to other tax sources.

[20]James C. Davies, "Toward a Theory of Revolution," *American Sociological Review*, 27, (February 1962), 5–19.

Since a large part of local property taxes is used to support schools, school financing became an integral part of debates over the appropriate tax structure underlying all state and local services.

Curtailment of educational expenditures also highlighted inequalities in the existing methods of school financing. As long as all school district budgets were growing, most parents and school officials were satisfied with the resources available to them. When resources became tight, however, educators began to ask if all districts were experiencing similar shortages. They discovered that there was a wide range of tax rates and expenditure levels among school districts in most states.

Awareness that property-poor districts often had to tax themselves at two or three times the rate of property-rich districts in order to raise only a portion of the revenues per student led to a series of legal challenges to the constitutionality of prevailing methods of financing public education. In California, Minnesota, Texas, New Jersey, Wyoming, Kansas, Connecticut, and Idaho, judges held that existing finance arrangements violated education or equal protection clauses in state constitutions. In effect, school finance reformers, unable to achieve their major purposes through conventional legislative and executive branch channels, began to use litigation to further their political purposes. This litigation is too complicated to review completely. A summary of some of the more important cases follows.

School Finance Litigation

SEEKING A REASONABLE REMEDY: McINNIS V. OGILVIE

This case resulted in one of the earliest decisions handed down in an equal protection suit applied to school finance.[21] The plaintiffs—children from a property-poor Illinois school district—requested, as a remedy for the inequity they alleged, that public school revenues be re-allocated in proportion to student "needs." Plaintiffs' position was ultimately denied; among other reasons, the court ruled that no standards could be developed that would make a decision judicially manageable. The court could not construct a sufficiently objective measure of a child's or group of children's educational "needs." In effect, the court affirmed equality as an abstract value but refused to accept equal treatment or equal outcomes as definitions of educational equality.

Counsel for plaintiffs in subsequent equal protection cases modified their position on remedy in order to avoid the *McInnis* problem of unmanageable standards. They sought to persuade courts to adopt the so-called *principle of fiscal neutrality*. This standard, referred to as Proposition 1 by Coons, Clune, and Sugarman[22] and suggested also by Arthur Wise,[23] holds that "the quality of a child's schooling shall not be a function of wealth, other than the wealth of the state as a whole." This is

[21]*McInnis* v. *Ogilvie*, 394 U.S. 322 (1969). Originally *McInnis* v. *Shapiro*, 293 F. Supp. 327, 331 (N.D. Ill. 1968).

[22]John E. Coons, William H. Clune, Stephen D. Sugarman, *Private Wealth and Public Education* (Cambridge, Mass.: Harvard University Press, Belknap Press, 1970).

[23]Arthur Wise, *Rich Schools, Poor Schools* (Chicago, University of Chicago Press, 1970).

essentially a negative yardstick. It does not prescribe what a state school finance system should be; rather, it specifies what it should not be. Where courts have invoked fiscal neutrality, legislatures are free to redesign school finance arrangements in whatever manner appears reasonable. The only judicially imposed constraint is that the reform system not exhibit disparities related to school district and, presumably, household wealth. Coons and his colleagues and Wise attempted to design a judicially manageable principle that, while furthering the value of equality, would not unduly infringe on liberty.

LIMITED FEDERAL ROLE IN REMEDY: RODRIGUEZ V. SAN ANTONIO

In 1973, the United States Supreme Court, in a five-to-four decision,[24] overturned a federal district court ruling in a Texas school finance suit similar to *Serrano*. The plaintiffs were students and residents in a property-poor school district. They questioned the legality of the Texas school finance system and cited state officials for violating the U.S. Constitution's equal protection clause. However, the highest court failed to concur. The Court majority, in the absence of a specific constitutional reference, concluded that education did not constitute a "fundamental right." Thus, the state was not obligated to demonstrate a "compelling interest" in defense of the fiscal disparities that accompanied its school finance plan. The Court held that the Texas distribution plan was legal as long as it complied with a "rational basis test." This meant simply that, as long as the state had a reasonable justification for its system of distribution of school dollars, it would be permitted to stand. In applying this test, the Supreme Court stated that existing interdistrict expenditure disparities were balanced against state interests in maintaining local control. Though acknowledging that the Texas school finance arrangements might be unjust, the Court concluded that they were not unconstitutional. A measure of inequality, even though distasteful, was permitted in order to protect a measure of efficiency and liberty.

Plaintiffs' position in *Rodriguez* was found wanting on two other grounds. The Court held that students of property-poor school districts were not sufficiently homogeneous to constitute a *suspect classification*. Such students were not uniformly from low-income households, nor were they of any particular racial or ethnic group. Also, the Court was not persuaded that expenditure disparities resulted in damage to students. In the Court's view, the evidence was insufficient to conclude that state-imposed minimum expenditure levels throughout Texas had failed to assure children an adequate level of schooling. In effect, the Supreme Court accepted "equal access to minimally adequate resources" as a definition of equal educational opportunity.

In 1986, the Supreme Court issued a decision in *Papasan* v. *Allain*,[25] a Mississippi case, that curtailed the scope of *Rodriguez*. In this case the Court made clear that although there was no equal protection mandate to redistribute local property tax revenues to gain spending parity, such logic did not necessarily apply to

---

[24]*San Antonio Independent School District* v. *Rodriguez*, 36L. Ed. 2d 16, 93 S.Ct. 1278.
[25]*Papasan* v. *Allain*, No. US106, SCT 2932 (1986).

state education funds. If certain facts are held to be present, then states may have to distribute their contributions in an equitable manner.

Despite this more recent judicial clarification, the *Rodriguez* decision brought to a close, at least for the short run, any hope of a national school finance reform strategy based on the federal Constitution. If reform was to take place nationwide, it would have to occur state by state.

STATE EDUCATION CLAUSES ARE IMPORTANT: ROBINSON V. CAHILL

Five weeks following the United States Supreme Court's decision in *Rodriguez,* the hopes of school finance reformers received a boost from the New Jersey Supreme Court ruling in *Robinson* v. *Cahill.*[26] This decision, the most pervasive school finance reform ruling to that time, declared New Jersey's distribution formula to be in violation of the state constitution's education clause. That clause charges the legislature with providing a "thorough and efficient" system of education.[27] When provided with testimony regarding funding and school service disparities then present throughout the state's local school districts, the New Jersey Supreme Court found that the state education clause was being violated and mandated that the legislature redefine and comply with the constitutional directive "thorough and efficient."

The case is significant for at least two reasons. It emphasized that school finance reform could take place on state constitutional grounds even though the judicial avenue to nationwide reform had been closed, at least in the short run, by the decision in *Rodriguez.* However, the *Robinson* ruling also demonstrated that a court mandate is not always sufficient. The New Jersey legislature did not immediately comply with the judicial edict. Legislative action would have inevitably raised taxes, lowered expenditures in high-spending school districts, or both. These alternatives apparently were judged as politically more costly than whatever gains would have accrued from achieving greater equality. Eventually the court temporarily closed New Jersey's public schools in order to force legislative compliance with its ruling.[28] The matter was sufficiently unresolved that by 1986 plaintiffs had returned to court and were again challenging state compliance efforts.[29]

INTRADISTRICT DISPARITIES: HOBSON V. HANSEN

The cases discussed so far adjudicated problems of *inter*district disparities. Julius Hobson, a Washington, D.C., resident and school board member, noted the fact that even within the same district, schools serving predominantly white populations appeared to have a disproportionate share of high-paid teachers and sup-

[26]*Robinson* v. *Cahill,* 62 N.J., 473, 303 A.2d 273 (1973).

[27]New Jersey Constitution, Article VII, Section 4, paragraph i.

[28]Details of state executive and legislative branch efforts to comply with *Robinson* are recounted by Richard Lehne in *Quest for Justice* (New York: Longman, 1978).

[29]*Abbott* v. *Burke,* Docket No. C-1893-80 (Superior Court of New Jersey, Chancery Division—Mercer County).

plies. Consequently, he filed suit against the Washington, D.C., school district, alleging racial discrimination in the distribution of school services.[30]

In defending itself, the school district claimed it had no specific policy accounting for discrimination. Senior teachers—those highest on the salary schedule—held the prerogative of transferring to and working in the school of their choice. Many chose to teach in white neighborhoods. When they invoked their collectively bargained transfer privilege, they carried with them their higher salaries. The result was an educationally unjustifiable expenditure disparity. In his ruling, Judge Skelly Wright held that the "arbitrary quality of thoughtlessness can be as disastrous and unfair to private rights and the public interest as the perversity of a willful scheme."[31] Wright ruled that the school district had to redistribute resources, particularly teacher salaries, in an equitable manner. The district attempted to comply but encountered extraordinary technical difficulties in the process.[32]

By 1970 the original plaintiff, Julius Hobson, had become convinced that substantial disparities persisted. He filed a second suit,[33] and in 1971 Judge Wright issued an even stronger opinion. This case coincided with the discovery of *intra*district resource disparities in many large school districts throughout the nation. Attention focused on the problem prompted the U.S. Office of Education[34] to issue so-called *comparability* regulations, demanding that school districts distribute resources equitably in order to remain eligible for federal funds. The *Hobson* decisions and comparability policy reinforced the "equal access to minimal resources" view of equality of opportunity, but simultaneously permitted a more liberal definition of equality. The court ruling demands simply that minimal school services be distributed at least equally. An educationally justifiable reason for shifting added resources so as to favor one or another group of students is permissible. This latter condition edges closer to the previously described "equal treatment" definition of equality of education.

A final note. Difficulties in attempting to comply with *Hobson* provoked the Washington, D.C., schools to decentralize many budget decisions.[35] The central school board came to ensure an equal dollar distribution per pupil. Thereafter, decisions regarding the best use of money have been made largely by those at school sites.[36] This method of budgeting gives promise of promoting equality, expanding choice, and inspiring efficiency. (School site management is described in detail in Chapter 9.)

[30]*Hobson* v. *Hansen,* 269 F. Supp. 401 (1967) (known as *Hobson I*).

[31]Ibid., p. 497.

[32]See Joan Baratz, *A Quest for Equal Educational Opportunity in a Major Urban School District: The Case of Washington, D.C.,* a report prepared for D.C. Citizens for Better Education by the Education Policy Research Institute of the Educational Testing Service (Princeton, N.J., 1975).

[33]*Hobson* v. *Hansen,* 327 F. Supp. (D.D.C., 1971) (known as *Hobson II*).

[34]Elevated to department status in 1977.

[35]*Hobson* implementation difficulties are analyzed in Donald L. Horowitz, *The Courts and Social Policy* (Washington D.C.: Brookings Institution, 1977), chap. 4.

[36]See Baratz, *A Quest for Equal Educational Opportunity.*

As suggested, courts are by no means the only branch of government concerned with resolving conflicts among forces advocating actions consistent with equality, efficiency, or liberty. It is difficult to conceive of a government regulation or a piece of programmatic legislation that does not in some way involve a compromise between two or more of these values. Indeed, many believe that to arrive at means for greater equality and greater efficiency so as to provide each individual with greater liberty and to do so in a fashion that minimizes conflict is the purpose of a government. Governing education is no exception.

THE LEGAL ARGUMENT IN RETROSPECT

What can be said regarding equal protection and school finance reform? After more than twenty years of judicial efforts to overturn unequal state financing arrangements, the following principles appear to have emerged. Assuming a factual base of funding and taxing disparity either among schools in a district (intradistrict) or among districts within a state (intrastate), we can draw the following conclusions:

- The disparity must be addressed legally as a state issue. The U.S. Supreme Court decision in *Rodriguez* suggests that federal courts will be reluctant to invoke a U.S. constitutional standard.
- The evidence to date has not persuaded the U.S. Supreme Court that either a *fundamental interest* or a *suspect classification* is involved in school financing.
- Thus, states need possess only a *rational basis* for their financial arrangements and need not meet the more stringent test of a *compelling interest*.
- State interest can be triggered based on state constitutional grounds—either an *equal protection* or an *education* clause.
- A reasonable remedy must be sought.
- Irrationally allocated interdistrict resources are subject to court-ordered redistribution.

The courts did not, however, provide solutions. The task of finding constitutional remedies to court rulings, and to possible rulings in states where litigation was being pursued or threatened, fell to state legislatures. The most difficult problem facing legislators was to reform state school finance systems so that the quality of a child's education was not unduly influenced by the wealth of the school district, and at the same time to control or even cut back educational spending. Equalizing educational resources would not have been so difficult had additional state dollars been available for poor districts. Nor would budget tightening have been so difficult if everyone's budget had been squeezed by the same amount. Combining reform and retrenchment was politically explosive, however. These two issues became the underlying themes of what has come to be known as the school finance reform movement.

The Reform Movement

Following the 1971 California Supreme Court decision in *Serrano* v. *Priest*, cases were filed in most states challenging the constitutionality of state finance laws. The U.S. Supreme Court's ruling in *Rodriguez* v. *San Antonio* slowed the search for court remedies, but many cases were still pursued on the grounds that state constitutional provisions had been violated. In response to these cases and to public demands for property tax and school finance reform, many states created state school finance commissions to propose alternative state finance arrangements. In those states providing for the initiative and referendum, some groups put measures before the voters to limit the use of property taxes for schools and to restrict educational spending.[37]

Court actions and citizen concerns moved school finance reform onto the agendas of most legislatures during the 1970s. For the most part, however, significant reform did not occur until the economic recovery of the 1980s. There are several reasons for the slow response among legislatures.[38] One is the repeated attempts to seek reform through the courts. The judiciary is greatly limited in its ability to develop and administer public policy. Judges, for the most part, are not experts on educational finance. Nor do they have the staff, resources, or time to develop a comprehensive understanding of state finance systems and alternative financial arrangements for accommodating the many values pursued in the financing of public schools. Consequently, courts have tended to respond to observed inequities in the distribution of funds by mandating legislative reform, but without setting clear guidelines. For example, in the oft-cited *Serrano* decision, the California Supreme Court held that "the quality of education may not be a function of wealth other than the wealth of the state as a whole," but did not say how the state should meet this negative standard. Similarly, the New Jersey Supreme Court in *Robinson* v. *Cahill*, while requiring the state to define the scope of educational opportunity specified in New Jersey,[39] did not specify how its decision should be implemented. The courts' decisions, in other words, have not appreciably narrowed the alternatives available to state legislatures. Without specific judicial guidelines, legislators must engage in the tedious process of constructing a politically feasible school finance law.

Even if courts were capable of mandating specific school finance remedies, which they are not, they are poorly equipped to administer any such program. There are few actions they can take except negative ones, such as closing down schools or calling in the police, to gain compliance. They cannot enact new taxes, impose expenditure limitations, or create new distribution formulas, all of which are measures reserved to state legislatures.

Reliance on litigation has also retarded movement toward school finance reform because it gives legislatures an excuse for inaction. The judicial process is

---

[37]State constitutional referenda to revise school finance systems are described in Donna E. Shalala, Mary F. Williams, and Andrew Fishel, *The Property Tax and the Voters,* Occasional Paper No. 2, Institute of Philosophy and Politics of Education, Teachers College, Columbia University (New York, 1973).

[38]Reasons for the failure of states to reform their school finance systems are discussed in Michael A. Cohen, Betsy Levin, and Richard Beaver, *The Political Limits to School Finance Reform* (Washington, D.C.: Urban Institute, 1973); and Arnold J. Meltsner and Robert T. Nakamura, "Political Implications of *Serrano,*" in *School Finance in Transition,* ed. John Pincus (Cambridge, Mass.: Ballinger, 1974), pp. 257–85.

[39]Paul L. Tractenberg, "*Robinson* v. *Cahill:* The Thorough and Efficient Clause," *Law and Contemporary Problems,* 38, no. 3 (Winter–Spring 1974), 330.

slow. *Serrano* was filed in 1969. A final decision in the case was not handed down until 1976. But that decision did not end the courts' involvement in the case. In 1986 the California Supreme Court again agreed to review a case brought to show that the California legislature's response to Proposition 13—the state's law limiting property taxes—fails to meet the court's earlier ruling in *Serrano.*

The problem is that while a case is before the courts the legislature can postpone action pending clarification of the legal points being adjudicated. Then, if the court rules against plaintiffs for any reason, the legislature can argue that the court has given the existing system a clean bill of health.

Another reason for legislative inaction on school finance reform is that legislators simply cannot agree on what is wrong with schools. Some legislators believe educators' complaints of inadequate resources. Many legislators also contend that accountability, educational standards and requirements, student assessment, and teacher preparation are more important educational issues, and that reforms in these areas would either solve schools' financial problems or at least provide better guidelines for reforming school finance. These issues also receive support from influential business advocates and from citizen groups.

A third reason for legislative inaction is the difficulty of estimating the impact of reform proposals on individual taxpayers and individual school districts.[40] State tax structures and educational finance systems are extremely complex. Even the best estimates are based on uncertain assumptions regarding future state revenues, enrollment growth or decline, and likely rate of school-cost inflation. This lack of knowledge or fear of the unreliability of official estimates impedes the development of political coalitions supporting school finance reform.

A fourth reason for legislative reluctance is that reform proponents are weak whereas opponents are politically influential. Support for reform comes from four sources: the school lobby, parents and taxpayers in low-wealth school districts, school finance experts, and business leaders. None of these groups, with the possible exception of business leaders, has been particularly successful in mobilizing support for school finance reform.

In most states the school lobby consists of organizational representatives, administrators, school board members, and the larger school districts. These groups are joined on specific issues by organizations such as the League of Women Voters, civic associations, and occasionally by progressive business groups. Despite its size and diversity, the education lobby has not been a cohesive or influential force for school finance reform.

The diversity of the education lobby has tended to divide it on important educational finance legislation. School board members and local administrators often disagree with teachers over local control, accountability, collective bargaining, and tenure. Large differences among districts in size, wealth, and educational needs also contribute to conflict. School board members and administrators in wealthy urban

---

[40]See Walter I. Garms, James W. Guthrie, and Lawrence C. Pierce, *School Finance: The Economics and Politics of Public Education* (Englewood Cliffs, N.J.: Prentice-Hall, 1978), chap. 12, for a discussion of the technical difficulties surrounding school finance reform proposals and a description of computer simulation techniques for managing these complexities.

districts stand on one side of the political fence on issues of equalization, categorical aid, and shifts in the tax structure, while their colleagues in poor suburban and rural districts are on the other.

The school lobby suffers from other problems that reduce its effectiveness. Many elected officials distrust the narrow set of concerns that educators bring to the legislature. In testimony before legislative committees, educators are sometimes inclined single-mindedly to support measures for increased education funding and to oppose legislation for educational reform or additional controls. Likewise, research provided by educational organizations is often one-sided. This tendency toward narrow self-interest, along with the fact that the educational lobby is one of the best-financed pressure groups in most states, often makes public officials wary of educators' advice, even though large campaign contributions often provide educators ready access to legislators.

Parents and taxpayers in low-wealth districts stand to gain the most from school finance reforms, but are poorly organized. Effective participation in the political maneuvering surrounding an issue as complex as school finance requires knowledge and time. Administrators and school leaders in poor districts (many of which are also small) are occupied in operating their schools and may not have the time to become informed or to send representatives to state capitols. Furthermore, school finance complexities make it extremely difficult to mobilize public interest in reform. Many local voters cannot believe that proposed reforms will actually provide promised benefits. Finally, poor districts cannot rely on support from either the wealthy districts that would lose as a result of school finance reform, or the majority of moderately wealthy districts that would neither gain nor lose. Middle districts prefer the certainty of the existing system to the uncertainties of a new formula that offers them little. Rather than supporting comprehensive reform, they are more likely to seek minor adjustments that offer specific benefits.

A third group advocating reforms consists of school finance experts. Such experts are found on the staffs of state education agencies and legislative committees, and occasionally in universities. They collect and analyze data on current systems of school finance and place various reform proposals before legislative committees. Their problem is that they can provide little or no political support for the proposals they espouse.[41] They frequently are estranged from the education lobby, which may resent their interference in issues for which it claims proprietary rights, and they find it difficult to communicate with school district officials, who may not understand the intricacies of their statistical models and their formulas. Their best chance of promoting school finance reform is to link themselves to an influential legislator in hopes that he or she can provide the political support necessary to enact the experts' recommendations.

Influential business leaders in some states have been able to mobilize support for significant school reform. The California Round Table is one such group, and similar associations have been effective in Washington, Minnesota, and Texas. Specific interest groups such as the American Electronics Association have been

---

[41]An excellent discussion of the role of experts in public policy making is found in Guy Benveniste, *The Politics of Expertise* (Berkeley, Calif.: Glendessary Press, 1972).

active in school finance reform. The interest of business leaders in school finance reform is in the quality of the students graduating from public schools. To be competitive in an increasingly interdependent world economy, businesses in the United States need well-educated employees. When business leaders have been successful in influencing recent education reforms, as in California and Texas, they have usually tied school finance reform to educational reform. They advocate programs for increasing financial support for schools if convinced that additional resources will produce better-educated students.

Opponents of reform are usually less numerous but more zealous in guarding the privileges they receive from existing finance systems. Most state school finance laws favor large businesses, farmers, and parents and taxpayers in wealthy school districts. School finance proposals designed to provide equal educational opportunity increase resources for poor districts at the expense of wealthy taxpayers or taxpayers in wealthy districts. The more comprehensive a reform—that is, the more equitable a proposed system and the more districts to receive equalization—the greater the potential cost to wealthy districts.

Despite their lack of numbers, those speaking for wealthy school districts are particularly well positioned to oppose reform. In the first place, reform almost always requires additional state funds. Therefore, opponents can often count on the help of well-organized interests opposed to tax increases, such as taxpayers' associations, state industrial associations, the Farm Bureau, and state Grange organizations. Large public utilities and manufacturers often have their own lobbies which can be counted on to oppose new taxes on business or proposals to take funds away from relatively wealthy cities where they have offices.

Opponents of reform can also rely on the support of legislators representing wealthy suburbs and cities. Urban interests may not have a majority in the legislature, but reapportionment has given them sufficient strength in most states to block measures they oppose. This veto power comes also from urban representatives holding key committee and leadership positions. Furthermore, it is much easier to block a bill than to ensure its passage. The supporters of a bill must guide it through a succession of committee, floor, and conference votes, winning majority support at each stage. Opponents need only break a chain of favorable votes once. Even if they fail in the legislature, opponents have a reasonable chance of obtaining a governor's veto, since governors are always under pressure to dampen government costs. Finally, there is a good possibility of overturning a reform by referring it to the people.[42]

Opponents usually have the advantage of agreeing on their objectives. They oppose proposals that will cost them more in taxes but will reduce the flow of state dollars to their districts. Proponents, however, must build coalitions of groups, each wanting something slightly different. Divisions typically found among school finance reform proponents are seldom found among opponents.[43] If there is any

[42]Meltsner and Nakamura, "Political Implications of *Serrano*," p. 265.

[43]See Lawrence C. Pierce, "The Politics of School Finance Reform in Oregon," in James A. Kelly, ed., *Remaking Educational Finance: New Directions for Education*, No. 3 (Autumn 1973), pp. 113–31, for an analysis of how division defeated a major reform proposal.

law in politics, it is that comprehensive reform requires virtually undivided support from a large and influential coalition. School finance reform proponents have frequently had support from influential leaders both in the educational community and in state government. They have had difficulty, however, building sufficient support to allow specific proposals to pass the many hurdles to legislative enactment.

Policy Issues

Hundreds of school finance plans have been proposed in every state. Few have been enacted. An analysis of the bills before any legislature reveals that finance plans revolve around a limited number of basic issues, such as the scope of state responsibility, reapportionment, local control, equalization, and property tax relief. Each side of each issue has its supporters and opponents. Only by understanding these issues and being able to identify the actors likely to support each side, is it possible for legislators to build a plan with sufficient support to become law. Political decisions require agreement of at least a majority of legislators at each stage of the legislative process. In practical terms, this means that more than a majority of legislators is needed to enact legislation, since a minority of opponents has numerous opportunities to defeat it. No one group can produce a large plurality. Consequently, if a reform proposal is to have any chance of passing, it must involve compromises and trade-offs among the interests favoring each of the basic issues.

THE SCOPE OF STATE RESPONSIBILITY

An overarching issue confronting school finance reformers is the scope of state responsibility in education. This issue has two components. First, how much public education should be provided by each level of government? The education lobby will in general support more education at every level of government. However, the proponents of higher and lower education are often political adversaries over each sector's rightful share. Legislators also must balance funds for education with those required for other public services, such as prisons, welfare, and highways, as well as stay within publicly acceptable boundaries of taxation. Consequently, they must decide, explicitly or implicitly, the total amounts to be spent for education.

States may delegate to local school districts the decision on actual dollar amounts available for schools by allowing them to ask local voters how much they prefer to spend. Or a legislature may determine school spending levels, leaving little or no local option. States such as Florida have a local required tax with only minor discretion for local boards to add to the required levy. After the defeat of many special local levies in the state of Washington, the legislature assumed most of the costs of funding public schools and placed severe limitations on special levies. Similarly, the passage of Proposition 13 in California resulted in state-controlled funding of public schools. In general, the education lobby will oppose limitations on school expenditures or taxes, while many taxpayers, representatives of business, farm groups, and senior citizens will favor them.

A second issue is the proportion of total revenues to be provided by the state. Almost every reform proposal and reform group holds that the state should assume a larger responsibility for public school funding. This position follows almost necessarily from a desire to provide more equal funding. Since property wealth per pupil varies widely among districts, and since school districts must rely on property taxes to support local shares of school costs, expenditure equalization can take place only if the burden of school support is shifted to the state. Larger state funding of schools is strongly supported by county and municipal governments, which argue that schools' seemingly insatiable appetite for funds leaves them too few property tax dollars for necessary county and local services.

Agreement on the need for a larger state share has not, however, produced agreement on where to obtain needed additional funds. Increasing state funding requires that the state allocate surplus revenues to public education, that other state programs be cut, or that state taxes be increased. The first possibility is the easiest and probably explains why a number of states passed school finance reforms in the early 1970s, when inflation had created surpluses and federal revenue sharing funds could provide extra resources for public schools. The reform movement also revived in the mid 1980s, when economic expansion increased state revenues. Diversion of funds from welfare, highways, or health programs is unlikely, since demand for those services often grows even faster than that for education. Increasing state taxes provokes opposition from many groups, even some of those who openly support the need for a larger state share of educational costs.

Since school finance proposals calling for full state funding of schools entail major new state taxes or large increases in existing taxes, they are enacted infrequently. Only the temporary closing of New Jersey's public schools in July 1976 by the state's Supreme Court finally forced that state's legislature to enact a modest state income tax favored by the court. In May of 1985, Oregon attempted to enact a sales tax as an alternative to the local residential property taxes that had traditionally supported schools. The proposal was soundly defeated at the polls. The state share of educational costs is likely to increase gradually as pressures for greater equalization increase and as surplus state funds become available. The price for additional state funding, however, will be paid in controls over growth of educational expenditures, since legislators are all too aware that school districts are more likely to increase expenditures than to reduce local taxes.

REAPPORTIONMENT

Reapportionment of state legislatures is a second element in the drive toward school finance reform.[44] Legislators, for the most part, will vote their constituents' interests on school finance matters. They will support proposals to reduce taxes and support distribution formulas that increase state grants to their districts. Since alternative school finance plans have different impacts on different types of districts, legislative reapportionment changing the balance of votes among urban, suburban, and rural districts affects the fate of many school finance proposals.

[44]Cohen, Levin, and Beaver, *The Political Limits to School Finance Reform,* pp. 23–28.

The process of legislative reapportionment following the U.S. Supreme Court decision in *Baker* v. *Carr*[45] has changed the pattern of representation in many states. This case is the famous "one-man-one-vote" judicial decision requiring that representative districts contain equal population. Whereas rural representatives used to be dominant, today urban and suburban communities are more heavily represented. However, the increased numbers of urban and suburban representatives have not enhanced school finance reform. Reapportionment has often given wealthy cities veto power over proposals to redistribute resources from rich cities to the poorer countryside.

The increasing representation of urban areas has also helped change the legislature's definition of equal educational opportunity. Urban members emphasize the importance of providing adequate funds to meet the needs of different kinds of children. Instead of focusing on providing equal resources for children, they sometimes support plans to equalize the results of public education.

LOCAL CONTROL

The most frequently raised argument against school finance reform is the fear that it will result in a loss of local control.[46] This contention often exasperates reformers, who claim that local control is a myth.[47] Legal responsibility for public education rests with states. They have the power to regulate almost every facet of public education, even though most states delegate important responsibilities to local school districts. Furthermore, reformers argue, local control is a privilege enjoyed only by relatively wealthy school districts that can afford enrichment programs and other luxuries in addition to the programs required by state education codes. Poor districts tax themselves to the limit of their ability in order to meet minimum state requirements, and therefore cannot afford optional programs. Finally, school finance reformers sometimes suspect that local control is actually a euphemism obscuring educators' efforts to maintain their professional domination of educational decision making.

There is more to the doctrine of local control than critics are willing to admit, however. Local school districts—despite their lack of legal authority—are still the basic unit of educational management. Many program and personnel decisions are made by local school boards and administrators. Parents and taxpayers are also able to influence these decisions through their periodic votes for school board members and their participation in school budget and bond elections.

Many educators fear that school finance reform will weaken local control. Proponents of reform refer to a study by the Urban Institute showing no consistent correlation between percentage of state funding and degree of local school district

---

[45]*Baker* v. *Carr*, 369 U.S. 186 (1962).

[46]Fred S. Coombs, "The Effects of Increased State Control on Local School District Governance" (paper presented at the annual meeting of the American Educational Research Association, Washington, D.C., April 1987).

[47]Meltsner and Nakamura, "Political Implications of *Serrano,*" pp. 278–79.

autonomy.[48] Those who want to protect local control point to the deeply held belief that control follows dollars. They need only describe the regulations tied to most federally funded programs to emphasize their point. Believers in local control also contend that as a general principle government should leave decision making and administration to the smallest unit of government competent to handle them.[49] Coons, Clune, and Sugarman refer to this as the *principle of subsidiarity.* This argument places the burden on reformers to show that the state can manage schools better than local districts can.

Whether fact or fiction, the doctrine of local control has broad legislative and popular support. Attempts by legislators to restrict local spending or redistribute local tax dollars among districts have to contend with this doctrine.

ACCOUNTABILITY

A fourth issue affecting proposals to reform school finance is *accountability.* During periods of rapidly rising school expenditures, taxpayers and their legislative representatives often demand demonstrable results in return for additional educational funding. Demands for accountability may be used to oppose school finance reform. "If increasing educational funding makes no difference in the performance of schools, why should we support new educational programs or impose new taxes on our constituents?" Accountability sometimes becomes an important political argument against increased support of public education.

Demands for greater accountability are also a direct challenge to the doctrine of local control. To the extent that local control serves to protect the hegemony of educators over educational decisions, accountability moves in the opposite direction by increasing political supervision of public school programs. On one hand, legislatures themselves are taking a more direct role in the operation of schools. Instead of providing funds and leaving education program decisions to local officials, legislators are likely to support specific programs that have proved effective. The 1980s reform efforts in many states are explicit in describing new regulations and programs.[50] On the other hand, legislatures are enacting legislation to increase citizen influence over educational decisions. Open-meeting laws, state assessment programs, and efforts to devolve educational decisions upon the school site are all intended to increase public schools' responsiveness to the citizens they serve.

Correlates of Reform

That school finance reform has been difficult to accomplish should not be surprising, for it frequently requires major alterations in existing institutions and in

[48]See Betsy Levin and Michael A. Cohen, *Levels of State Aid Related to State Restrictions on Local School District Decision–Making* (Washington, D.C.: Urban Institute, 1973).

[49]For a thoughtful defense of local control in education, see Coons, Clune, and Sugarman, *Private Wealth and Public Education,* pp. 14–20.

[50]See Thomas B. Timar, "Managing Educational Excellence" (Ph.D. dissertation, University of California, Berkeley, 1986); and William Chance, *The Best of Educations: Reforming America's Public Schools in the 1980's* (Olympia, Wash.: Catherine T. MacArthur Foundation, 1986).

long-practiced patterns of citizen behavior. Machiavelli warned of the difficulty of creating new institutions in his advice to new rulers:

> They should observe that there is nothing more difficult to plan or more uncertain of success or more dangerous to carry out than to introduce new institutions, because the introducer has as his enemies all those who profit from the old institutions, and has as lukewarm defenders all those who will profit from the new institutions. This lukewarmness results partly from fear of their opponents, who have the laws on their side, partly from the incredulity of men, who do not actually believe new things unless they see them yielding solid proof. Hence whenever those who are enemies have occasion to attack, they do it like partisans, and the others resist lukewarmly; thus lukewarm subjects and innovating prince are both in danger.[51]

Many states have attempted to reform their systems of school finance, and from their successes and failures it is impossible to discern in general which strategies are most likely to be effective. As we have seen, the task of school finance reformers is to develop a proposal that can obtain enough support to be enacted by the legislature, signed by the governor, and approved by voters. Since supporters of school finance reform are often politically weak and fragmented, they must create a coalition of supporters.

In general, the tactics of building winning coalitions are well known and practiced in most state legislatures. Major provisions are added to a proposal to attract potential supporters; those elements likely to mobilize opposition are deleted or disguised. This requires bargaining with powerful interests and, as mentioned, a willingness to settle for less-than-ideal solutions. Once the basic proposal has been constructed so as to accommodate the major interests required for enactment, sponsors of the proposal enter into negotiations with other possible supporters to gather additional support, and with opponents to weaken their opposition. Minor provisions are added and deleted, and promises of future support are traded off against promises not to oppose the bill openly at some stage in the legislative process. Success in formulating a reform proposal that is attractive to a winning coalition comes from understanding the underlying policy issues involved and how those issues affect different groups of constituents.

PRECONDITIONS

Those who have observed the politics of school finance reform agree that several conditions greatly favor passage of reform legislation.[52] First, states passing

---

[51]Niccolò Machiavelli, "The Prince," in *Machiavelli: The Chief Works and Others,* trans. Allan Gilbert, Vol. I. Copyright 1965 by Duke University Press.

[52]A good example of a participant-observer view of the correlates of school finance reform is Joel S. Berke, "Strategies and Tactics for State School Finance Reform," address to the National Symposium on State School Finance Reform, Washington, D.C., November 26, 1973 (Syracuse, N.Y.: Syracuse University Research Corporation, 1973). See also Susan Fuhrman, "School Finance Reform in the 1980's," *Educational Leadership,* 38, no. 2 (November 1980), 122–24; Susan Fuhrman, "The Politics and Process of School Finance Reform," *Journal of Educational Finance,* 4, no. 2 (Fall 1978), 158–78; and Joel Sherman et al., "National Setting for

school finance reforms usually have a history of attempts to change the methods of financing schools. Reform frequently comes about gradually through an evolutionary process rather than suddenly in response to specific events. Berke describes how this process occurred in Kansas:

> Kansas was a state in which, since the 1970 session of the legislature, there has been an alternation of standing committees and interim committees (during the off season of the legislature) studying and considering change in the educational funding system. Finally, in the legislative session of 1973, a reasonably significant piece of legislation, a modified power equalizing approach, was passed. When you trace this progression forward you can see the proposals and counterproposals developing, closure slowly coming about, and a continuing of legislative personnel and staff working on the effort.[53]

Similarly, successful reform efforts in Minnesota, Florida, and California emerged only after years of study and consideration and the rejection of numerous proposals.

School finance reform is also sufficiently unpopular and complex that some outside event is often necessary to rouse a legislature to build support for a reform proposal. In a number of states, legal opinions have activated public and legislative concern for school finance reform and even forced a legislative response. Court decisions in themselves are unlikely to produce an acceptable school finance package. Nevertheless, they may act as a catalyst for change. *Serrano* v. *Priest* in California not only forced changes in that state but also became a major theoretical justification for reform efforts in other states. Governor Thomas McCall frequently talked about the "*Serrano* principle" in his unsuccessful effort to win voter approval of a full state funding program in Oregon.

Of course, there are other external events that influence school finance reform. The availability of revenue sharing funds for two entitlement periods in fiscal 1972–73 made it easier for several states to pass reforms that year. We have seen that widespread voter rejection of school district special levies forced legislative action in the state of Washington. Special school finance meetings convened by the Education Commission of the States, the National Conference of State Legislatures, and the National Educational Finance Project produced new ideas that found their way into successful reform proposals. In most cases these external events are gratuitous. Nevertheless, reformers may consider whetting the public appetite for reform by filing lawsuits and encouraging voter initiatives designed to increase a sense of urgency for reform.

Political leadership is a third precondition for reform.[54] Successful proposals require bargaining and compromise. Consequently, supporters in the legislature must be willing to expend the effort to build a winning coalition. Governors in some states, such as North Carolina, Tennessee, and Florida, have played an

---

for School Finance in the 1980s," *Journal of Educational Finance,* 8, no. 3 (Winter 1983), 343–59.

[53]Berke, "Strategies and Tactics," p. 3.

[54]Ibid., pp. 4–5.

important role in educational finance reform, particularly when they have been elected on platforms calling for such measures. Private commissions and state education departments, on the other hand, seldom have been sufficiently close to legislative cloakrooms to be effective. Since school finance proposals are complicated, and the opportunities numerous for a proposal to be derailed, having leadership in both houses of the legislature is important. Support of both presiding officers is also helpful. Most important, though, is the attention and guidance of committee chairpersons in both houses who are well informed and willing to stake their political careers or reputations on the outcome of specific proposals. School finance reform needs all the help it can get from any source, and there are inevitably able people from universities and educational organizations who perform useful services. The point is that their efforts are likely to fail if they do not have the assistance of powerful insiders—legislators who have the respect and political resources needed to persuade uncommitted colleagues to cooperate.

Finally, school finance reforms almost always coincide with the availability of surplus funds that would allow the state to increase expenditures in low-spending districts *without recapturing funds from high-spending districts.* For example, California's reforms that followed voter passage of Proposition 13, the property tax limitation, were made possible in large part by the presence of a $7 billion surplus in the state's general fund. Similarly, the Maine legislature was able to use three years of state revenue-sharing money to ease the burden in the first few years of its financial reform program. However, with the national recessions of 1973–74 and 1980–82 state surpluses evaporated, and with them the possible passage of many reform bills. When resources for education are scarce, reform is more difficult and less frequent. The politics of school finance reform is the politics of more.[55] Those who would lose much from reform usually have adequate incentives and resources to block it.

STRATEGIES OF REFORM

Reform of any kind is difficult, as Machiavelli warned. Reform of a state's school finance system is particularly difficult because so many resources, both physical and human, are involved and because educational finance reform by itself is seldom sufficiently attractive to pass. Consequently, careful attention must be given to developing and packaging a finance proposal.

Perhaps the most important consideration is the necessity of packaging school finance reform with more popular measures. Usually, proponents combine finance reform with educational reform or property tax relief, both of which are clearly popular with legislators and local voters. The combination of finance reform and property tax relief involves an interesting set of trade-offs. Property tax relief means there is less money provided to schools locally. This means in turn that the state must assume part of the costs of maintaining current school programs, leaving

---

[55]For added analysis of the relationship between resources and reform, see James W. Guthrie and Julia Koppich, "Exploring the Political Economy of Educational Excellence," in the *1988 Yearbook of the Politics of Education Association* (forthcoming), chap. 3.

less available for equalization. The greater the extent of property tax relief, the less is available for equalization, and vice versa.

School finance reform may also be tied to programs providing greater accountability. This is the approach Texas governor Mark White and Governor Lamar Alexander in Tennessee proposed in the early 1980s. Again, however, trade-offs are involved. Accountability will weaken support for school finance reform among teachers. Accountability, on the other hand, may be necessary to win the support of conservative legislators and the public.

Successful packaging of a reform proposal also requires a trade-off within the legislature itself. Urban legislators may demand specific categorical programs in return for their support of significant equalization provisions. Urban school districts are benefited when students enrolled in school rather than those in attendance are counted. Whether to use average daily membership (ADM) or average daily attendance (ADA) may become an important issue in legislative bargaining. In Utah, for example, disagreement on this issue was resolved in a most predictable way. The legislature finally settled the conflict between urban and suburban interests by adding ADA and ADM, and then dividing by two.[56]

Political bargaining and compromise can become excessive and jeopardize reform goals. Given the uncertainties of the political process, some legislators tend to strive for everyone's approval of their proposals. Legislation designed for such a comprehensive coalition becomes unreasonably costly, since every interest's special program must be added. Furthermore, these so-called Christmas tree bills provide legislators and voters with more specifics to vote against. Finally, such bills, in trying to satisfy too many interests, often are costly and obscure the original goals.[57]

A second strategic consideration is the scope of the proposed reform. In general, it is best not to aim too high. Large, comprehensive changes excite strong opposition from those whose interests are jeopardized. Modesty in the reformer's goals also reduces the risk of mistakes. Incrementalism minimizes chances for major mistakes and provides policy makers with time to correct small errors.

Policy makers should carefully consider the consequences of proposed reforms on the public. The ultimate voice in determining whether a program is successful is the public's voice. The public pays the necessary taxes and experiences the effects of the proposed changes. In general, the amount of difficulty state government can expect in implementing school finance reforms is a function of the scope of the proposed changes, the proportion of the population whose behavior would be changed, and the significance of the changed behavior to those being controlled.[58] The corollary of this proposition is that the more modest the changes, the smaller the number of people involved, and the less sensitive the issues included, the more likely the public is to accept a proposed change.

[56]Berke, "Strategies and Tactics," p. 5; and Timar, "Managing Educational Excellence."

[57]William H. Riker, *The Theory of Political Coalitions* (New Haven: Yale University Press, 1962), pp. 32–33.

[58]Mitchell, *Public Choice in America*, p. 342.

Finally, legislators should pay particular attention to rewards for compliance and penalties for noncompliance. Often public policies fail because rewards and penalties are inadequate. A graduated system of positive and negative sanctions—providing large and increasing rewards for those whose behaviors are most important, and large and increasing penalties for behaviors policy makers wish most to discourage—may work. Most important, however, is to recognize that people generally do not like to be told what to do. School finance reforms that impose strict controls and limitations are bound to be unpopular. Free choice and voluntary compliance should always be considered.

SUMMARY

School finance reform ultimately requires the support of local citizens and members of state legislatures. Local citizens, through their votes for school board members and their ballots in local school budget and bond elections, participate in decisions affecting the kind and quality of education provided. The first part of this chapter examined procedures through which citizen preferences are translated into educational policy.

Special attention has been given to the meaning of *taxpayers' revolt*. Rejection of local school budget and bond proposals may reflect a majority belief that additional educational spending benefits are outweighed by the additional costs involved, rather than the more widely accepted view that the public has become disillusioned with government and with schools in particular.

School finance reforms in state legislatures must overcome a wide variety of problems created by the many competing values and interests that surround school finance proposals. Legislative inaction often results from complex legal maneuverings in courts, disagreement over problems needing to be resolved, uncertainty about the results of proposed solutions, and widely divergent and competing interests.

On occasion, when direct political action has failed to produce finance reform, advocates have pursued a more indirect political approach—litigation. This chapter reviewed major school finance court cases and the legal principles flowing from them.

The chapter concluded with a discussion of the correlates of state school finance reform. In the legislature, the main task is to develop a proposal that can gain sufficient support to be enacted by a legislature, signed by a governor, and perhaps approved by the voters. This requires a package of provisions that appeals to a majority but does not arouse intense opposition among strong interests. In general, reforms take time; enactment often occurs only after years of unsuccessful efforts. External intervention by state courts may, in some cases, initiate school finance reform processes. Equally important, however, will be the political backing of governors and legislative leaders, and the availability of surplus revenues so that most local school districts can benefit from a new method of distributing state funds.

Building a successful reform proposal requires unusual legislative skill and a keen appreciation of the public's interests and attitudes regarding education and taxes. The more comprehensive the change, the more people who are affected, and the greater the change required, the greater the opposition proponents can expect. Resistance to change will be reduced in proportion to how much free choice citizens are given and how much the plan relies on voluntary compliance.

chapter nine

PLANNING AND BUDGETING

American education can benefit from greater managerial attention to systematic planning and budgeting. Schooling directly affects the lives of millions of individuals and annually absorbs hundreds of billions of dollars. An undertaking of such magnitude deserves careful scrutiny of future endeavors and assessments of past performances. This chapter explains the purposes and utility of educational planning and outlines planning processes. It also illustrates forecasting techniques useful for education executives, explains budgeting procedures, and describes the relationship between resource allocation and planning.[1]

Planning and evaluation represent obverse sides of a chronological coin or complementary points in a cycle of organizational activities. Planning is the systematic determination of future allocation of resources. It shares many features with rational decision making. It differs primarily in three ways:

1. The planner or planners may not in fact be the individual or team of individuals responsible for implementing the plan. In short, planners are not necessarily executives or decision makers.

[1]The authors wish to acknowledge the assistance of Richard Pratt in the preparation of this chapter. Also, portions of this chapter are adapted from James W. Guthrie and Rodney J. Reed, *Educational Policy and Administration: Effective Leadership for American Education* (Englewood Cliffs, N.J.: Prentice-Hall, 1986).

2. Planning is oriented toward a time horizon beyond the immediate present.

3. Planning involves systematic efforts to reduce uncertainty, to convert unknowns to statements of probability. A decision maker concerned with an immediate condition may not have the luxury of being able to assign reasoned estimates to alternative scenarios. Planning can mitigate the risks involved in having to make instant decisions.

Evaluation is more concerned than planning with the immediate present or, even more likely, with past events. Evaluation involves assessing the outcomes of one or more events, making judgments regarding effectiveness, and providing information that can shape future decisions.

Planning and evaluation are two major stages in a cycle of events aimed at enhancing an educational organization's ability to serve its clients—pupils, parents, and the public. The full cycle involves planning for future events, implementing or executing a plan, and evaluating outcomes.

Budgeting is a practical bridge between planning and evaluation. Figure 9.1 illustrates the relationships among planning, budgeting, and evaluation. Budgeting is an important component of planning and evaluation. Budgets represent the financial crystallization of an organization's intentions. It is through budgeting that a school or school district can decide how to allocate resources so as to achieve organizational goals. Ideally, resources are expended consistent with an organization's overall plans, and evaluations of programs and activities subsequently inform the next cycle of planning and budgeting. Budgeting is not simply a technocratic process that is always totally rational and devoid of political considerations. However, planning and evaluation are meaningless unless they can influence an organization's resource allocation. Budgeting is the process of allocating an organization's resources. This chapter describes budgeting and its place in planning and evaluation. In some ways budgeting is a component of a larger organizational activity, planning. Thus, the chapter begins by describing planning; it then explains budgeting.[2]

PLANNING

Planning is a management function that should occur at all levels within an educational system. As decentralized as education is in the United States, even federal officials should concern themselves with broad trends and the provision of incentives for states and local districts to act in the national interest. State officials should be concerned with matters such as enrollment projections, teacher supply and demand, and capital needs. In addition to these state concerns, local officials are regularly engaged in planning new buildings, alterations in the curriculum, changes in attendance boundaries or bus routes, implementation of new student grading policies, or the launching of school-site parent advisory councils.

[2]As important as program evaluation is, space is not devoted to it in this chapter.

FIGURE 9.1   The Planning–Budgeting–Evaluation Cycle

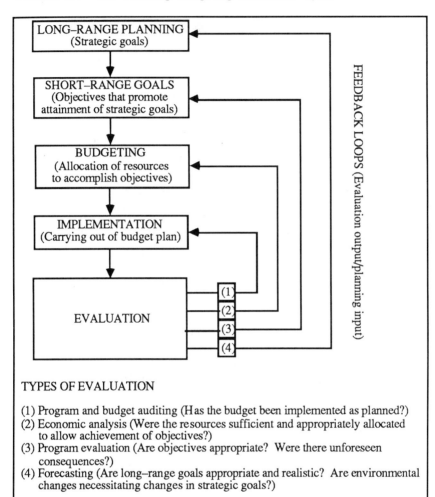

TYPES OF EVALUATION

(1) Program and budget auditing (Has the budget been implemented as planned?)
(2) Economic analysis (Were the resources sufficient and appropriately allocated to allow achievement of objectives?)
(3) Program evaluation (Are objectives appropriate? Were there unforeseen consequences?)
(4) Forecasting (Are long–range goals appropriate and realistic? Are environmental changes necessitating changes in strategic goals?)

Some anticipated undertakings may occur often enough to make detailed planning unnecessary. An elementary principal with twenty years of administrative experience in a stable enrollment district may have opened school successfully for so many fall semesters that he or she has reduced the process to a routine. Experience can substantially inform future activities, and such a principal may need only review previously developed lists in order to refresh his or her memory regarding the necessary steps. If an anticipated undertaking is already covered by routine, then there is seldom a need for elaborate forecasting. Planning at this level can become trivial. At the opposite end of the spectrum, undertaking racial desegregation in a large school district can involve complexity akin to a major construction project's deployment of personnel and supplies. Success will be difficult under any circumstances; the absence of systematic long-range planning for an undertaking of such complexity virtually assures its failure. What is the educational planning process?

The Process

The purpose of planning is not simply to institute change. Change will occur whether or not there is a plan. Rather, a prime purpose of planning is to reduce uncertainty and focus organizational activities so as to utilize resources efficiently. Through systematic long-range planning it may be possible for an organization to reduce the amount of time involved in delivering a service, produce greater pupil achievement or parent satisfaction, induce greater client participation, and so on for a number of goals. There is no one comprehensive planning process or set of techniques that universally guarantees efficiency and effectiveness. Rather, depending upon the goals sought and the organization involved, one or another planning mode may be appropriate. National manpower, industrial, agricultural, and educational planning is favored by some socialist governments. American values generally do not accept such centralization, favoring instead planning by private-sector organizations and subunits of government . Such planning can become highly disaggregated. Indeed, much planning is left to households or even to individual citizens. However, capitalism and freedom are not arguments against planning. The question is the appropriate level of planning and decision making, not planning versus no planning.

Planning can be conceived of as *strategic* or *managerial*. The distinction is one of abstraction. A strategic plan for one level of operation may be regarded as managerial for another. A strategy is a plan for achieving a large-scale objective. A tactic is one of several steps in a strategy. Managerial plans comprise tactics. We can illustrate the general meaning of these terms with examples.

STRATEGIC PLANNING [3]

A nonprofit hospital increasingly loses patients. Rising medical costs and competition from outpatient clinics and neighborhood surgeries have reduced revenues. The board of directors requests top-level administrators to prepare a strategic plan for recapturing the hospital's share of the medical market. After examining available demographic and medical service information, the administrators conclude that several patient populations in the region are underserved. The hospital's board of directors adopts a strategic plan to enhance its client population and increase its market share by providing new services to the elderly as well as opening new programs in weight loss and sports medicine. Having settled upon such a strategy for becoming more competitive, the board instructs management to undertake the detailed tactical planning necessary to implement such a strategy.

[3]For added information on this topic, see James W. Guthrie and Guy Benveniste, *Strategic Planning in Education: Achieving and Maintaining an Effective Organization* (New York: Allyn & Bacon, in process).

MANAGERIAL PLANNING

A school board becomes uncomfortably aware that an increasing proportion of district students are scoring low on standardized tests. The board directs the superintendent to assess the situation and develop a strategic plan for elevating pupil achievement.

An analysis of student performance throughout the district reveals two major problems. One is that the district's secondary school curriculum is no longer appropriately "aligned." What the district expects to be taught—the so-called *standards of achievement*—what the teachers are conveying in their classes, what is covered by tests, and what district criterion-referenced tests are measuring are not coinciding sufficiently. (Chapter 14 contains a more extensive explanation of *curriculum alignment.*) Second, low student performance is concentrated at a few schools where teachers' absenteeism, turnover, and formal grievances have increased over the last several years. In these schools, curriculum problems have been compounded by low employee morale and inadequate administrative leadership.

The superintendent and staff explain these findings to the board and recommend a two-pronged plan in which (1) a major realignment of the district's secondary school curriculum is begun the following summer (a project that should proceed in stages, subject-matter area by area, and that may well take several years), and (2) a systematic assessment of the leadership at low-performing schools and, where necessary, a buttressing or replacement of principals. The board agrees with the two procedural strategic objectives—curriculum alignment and strong school-site leadership—and turns to the central administration for the managerial planning and operational procedures necessary to implement them.

Whether strategic or managerial, whether done by a school district or another organization, planning processes are remarkably similar. A problem must be identified. In our two examples, it is the loss of clientele, or market share, and lowered "output." Subsequent analyses must be undertaken to identify possible causes of the problem. Efforts must then be made to generate possible solutions. An assessment of the likely costs and effects of solutions should be made. Where a solution depends upon events or actions outside an organization's immediate control, an effort should be made to judge the probability of such events taking place. Finally, having assessed alternatives and their associated probabilities, planners should rank the solutions. Having agreed on a solution, they can perform the detailed planning necessary for its implementation. Planning follows a paradigm similar to problem solving or decision making. Planning techniques can help rationalize the process and reduce uncertainty.

Techniques

There are many useful planning techniques, such as *PERT, linear programming, queuing theory, computer simulation,* and *cost-benefit analyses* and *present-value discounting* as components of budgeting. We will discuss the first four of these, devoting the most attention to queuing theory.

PERT (PLANNING, EVALUATION, AND REVIEW TECHNIQUE)

PERT was initially developed for use with the Polaris missile program in the 1950s as a technique for managing large-scale multistage military projects. The stages of a large project are interdependent; for example, completion of step B may require prior completion of step A. Development of a PERT chart requires an analysis of each of the steps required for project completion. This means more than simply identifying the necessary steps and putting them in order. It also means assessing the resources needed for each step. Resources translate into three things: money, knowledge, and time. An important component of PERT is the *critical path*. This is the sequence of activities that allows the least room for delay and that therefore requires special attention. The critical path determines the minimum amount of time necessary for project completion.

LINEAR PROGRAMMING

This technique is used in planning resource allocation where one factor is to be optimized (made as large or small as possible) while the others are held constant or maintained within certain limits. It is useful mostly where there is a single clear goal, where the technology for achieving the goal is agreed upon, and where all of the factors and constraints involved in goal achievement can be quantified. Some manufacturing processes exhibit these characteristics, but education seldom does.

QUEUING THEORY

A queue is a waiting line. It can comprise either people—such as people waiting at a bus stop or students in line at a cafeteria—or things, such as equipment waiting for repair or jobs waiting for a computer run. Queuing theory addresses the question of whether lines are too long or waiting periods excessive. It applies to situations involving the following conditions: (1) the elements in the queue arrive at random time intervals, and the arrival of each element is independent of the arrival of all the other elements; (2) the service time for each element in the queue is independent of the service time for any other element and is not affected by the length of the queue; (3) the queuing system is in equilibrium (i.e., has been in operation long enough to allow the laws of probability on which the theory is based to take effect); (4) the elements in the queue are served on a first-come-first-served basis; (5) the elements in the queue do not leave until they have received service; and (6) the average number of elements arriving in the queue during a unit of time is less than the average number of elements that can be served during the same unit.

As an illustration of queuing theory, suppose a school district operates on a five-hour day, would like its computers to serve 1900 students daily, and would like to restrict the average waiting time to gain access to a computer to less than four minutes.

First, assume the average length of a computer session is half an hour. This means that 200 terminals, at half an hour per session and five hours per day, have an average service capacity of 2000 students per day. This capacity exceeds the expected use of 1900 students per day, thus satisfying the sixth of the conditions just outlined. Now if students were allocated to specific periods on a computer, there would be no waiting and queuing theory would not apply. Remember that one of the other conditions of the theory is that each person's arrival at a queue is random and independent of any other person's arrival. If students choose their own times to use computers, then one must expect that occasionally there will be excess demand (that is, users will outnumber terminals) and that some students will have to wait their turn. Average waiting-line length can be calculated with the following formula:

$$E(W) = \frac{A^2}{S(S-A)}$$

where $E(W)$ is expected waiting time, A is arrival rate of students per day, and S is service rate, or number of students per day the system is able to accommodate. Thus,

$$E(W) = \frac{1900^2}{2000(2000-1900)} = 18.05 \text{ students}$$

This formula is based on probability theory and has no simple intuitive explanation. It is not necessary to go into its derivation here.

If the average queue length is 18.05 persons, then those who join it must, on average, wait until 18.05 persons ahead of them have been served before acquiring their turn. Therefore, average waiting time, $E(T)$, is

$$E(T) = \frac{E(W)}{A} = \frac{18.05}{1900} = .012 \text{ days} = 3.6 \text{ minutes}$$

at five hours per day.

Thus it has been established that 200 terminals will serve 1900 students per day with the desired average waiting time of less than four minutes. Notice that the decision makers in this example would have started with the desired value for $E(T)$ and worked backwards to obtain the needed number of terminals.

This is a simple example that requires only manual calculation. In fact, many queuing problems can be solved by hand. The computer can be an advantage, however, in more complex problems, such as those involving more than one service center. It can also be advantageous if decision makers would like to solve problems using different values. For instance, we would solve the problem in this example by recognizing each school as a service center with its own expected arrival rate. In addition, decision makers may want to analyze how much money they could save (by purchasing fewer computers) if the average waiting time were extended to ten minutes.

Queuing theory can be used in a number of situations in a school setting, but it has limitations. Perhaps its most serious drawback is that it deals only in averages. It cannot determine expected waiting times in individual cases, or even maximum waiting times, which may be more important in some cases. For example, queuing theory may specify that the *average* wait in a cafeteria line is ten minutes. This may seem fine until experience shows that the *maximum* wait is twenty-five minutes, giving some students virtually no time to eat if we assume a thirty-minute lunch period.

Queuing theory is a planning technique that can inform decision making, but it should not be misunderstood as actually making decisions. Its utility extends beyond supplying "objective" data—it also uncovers basic assumptions that are not directly amenable to quantification, but that executives must decide. One assumption in our example is that average waiting time should be less than four minutes. As queuing theory yields more precise information on the relationships between number of terminals and waiting time, decision makers can make fairly accurate estimates of the cost of reducing waiting time or the savings made by lengthening it. This involves placing a dollar value on waiting time, which in the absence of a market system must be established arbitrarily. In this case, queuing theory helps us identify the value of student time in quantitative terms.

COMPUTER SIMULATION

Models impute order to reality by positing relationships between things and events. Models need not be complex or sophisticated. Most people have mental models that allow them to give meaning to everyday experiences and to make predictions about future events. In negotiating a teacher pay scale with a school board, one might use a mental model of school board characteristics, past behavior, and current budget constraints to predict the achievable, and plot strategy accordingly.

Computer simulation attempts to accrue information about a process or phenomenon through the use of models. A model may be *representative,* in which case it reflects reality and allows a user to learn about and understand the phenomenon under study. An example of a representative model is a computer-simulated cockpit, which allows a pilot-trainee to learn how to fly under lifelike conditions but without ever leaving the ground. Other models may be *predictive.* These must also be representative, in the sense that they resemble actual processes, but they are programmed to provide users information regarding possible outcomes given different circumstances. The atomic chart is a representative model, but it has also served as a predictive model in that it has allowed scientists to project characteristics of undiscovered elements (and, in fact, even to predict that such elements exist). The field of economics utilizes many predictive models. Policy makers use economic models to predict the effects of a tax increase on consumer demand and hence inflation and employment.

Models may be *deterministic* or *stochastic.* In a deterministic model, identical inputs always produce identical outputs. In the simulated cockpit, if the pilot follows correct procedures and if the equipment is functioning properly, a smooth landing will always result. In a stochastic model, static relationships between inputs and outputs do not hold because random events are present. Policy makers cannot predict the effects of a tax increase with absolute accuracy because too many random events could affect the outcome. Stochastic models incorporate statistical procedures that simulate these random events. Most models in education, such as educational production functions, are stochastic. Because models incorporate large numbers of variables and relationships, simulations are almost always done by computer. Computer simulation cannot be described in terms of simple formulas or processes, and its complexities are beyond the scope of this chapter. Computerized spread sheets (explained in Chapter 12) are a form of simulation useful for developing models applicable to many school-related financial activities.

BUDGETING

It is through budgeting that an organization aligns its resources with its purposes.[4] Also, the budget process is the concrete, practical link between *planning*, the forward-looking portion of an organization's management activities, and *evaluation*, which focuses systematically on past performance.

School finance and administration textbooks commonly describe budgeting in the context of business practices. This book abandons such a convention for three reasons. First, as mentioned in the preceding paragraph, budgeting is more usefully viewed as a component of management's planning and evaluation activities. In addition, a budget should represent a plan for direction of an organization's total discretionary resources, such as time, personnel, and physical resources—not simply money.

Also, the budget process must be understood as a political activity. Resource allocation is not simply a technocratic undertaking. Once resource decisions have been made regarding matters such as goals, personnel, salary levels, and supplies, keeping accurate records, though by no means simple, is a technical activity. However, prior to that point, budget decisions may involve bargaining. Depending upon their value orientation—for example, equality, efficiency, or liberty—various school constituencies may desire different organizational outcomes. Parents may prefer smaller classes, teachers may reasonably prefer higher salaries. Science cannot easily be invoked to resolve such conflict. Bargaining, ideally conducted in good faith with an organization's purposes and welfare in mind, may have to be the mechanism for resolving such differences. Once a bargain has been struck, its fiscal consequences should be represented in the budget. In this sense, a budget is a political document. It is the concrete representation of the political compromises that have been made.

Fundamental Assumptions

For budgeting to be most effective, three critical conditions should exist—*annualarity, comprehensiveness,* and *balance.*[5]

---

[4]For added information on budgeting see Aaron Wildavsky, *The Politics of the Budgetary Process* (Boston: Little Brown, 1984.)

[5]The authors are grateful for Aaron Wildavsky's explanations of these assumptions.

ANNUALARITY

A budget, an organization's resource allocation plan, is intended to cover a fixed period, generally a year. This need not be a calendar year, beginning January 1 and ending the subsequent December 31. Indeed, few school districts utilize a calendar year. The budget year is generally known as a *fiscal year*. The fiscal year for the majority of U.S. school districts begins July 1 and concludes at the end of the following June, in the next calendar year. However, some districts utilize a fiscal year that coincides with the academic year or with their state's legislative appropriations cycle.[6] The fiscal year for school districts is usually specified by the state.

Regardless of the precise period, or even if it is a two-year period, the important principle is that there is a previously agreed-upon span of time over which resource allocation and financial administration occur. Also, in order to be maximally useful, the fiscal year should not be altered frequently. Select a fiscal year and stay with the decision. Otherwise, public confidence, record keeping, and fiscal analyses are jeopardized.

COMPREHENSIVENESS

An organization's budget should encompass all fiscally related activity, on both the resource and the expenditure sides. A budget may contain a variety of funds and accounts, such as instruction, administration, maintenance, and transportation. It may well keep track of expenditures in more than one way—that is, by function, such as physical education, as well as by object of expenditure, such as instructional salaries. What is important is that all revenues received by an organization, regardless of source or purpose, and all that an organization spends, regardless of source or purpose, be encompassed by the budget and the budget process. If a budget is not comprehensive, organizational resources may be accrued or utilized for purposes outside its leaders' control. This may or may not be illegal. It certainly is inefficient.

BALANCE

This is a third critical budget assumption. What is received by way of resources must not exceed what is spent. This is not to assert that all organizations must always live within their immediately available resources. Certainly resources can be borrowed and paid back later. Borrowing money to construct a long-lasting building makes good sense (as illustrated in Chapter 10). The point is that a budget assumes explicit organizational acknowledgment of resources and obligations, and the two must match. If they are out of balance, again an organization is out of control.

---

[6]The federal government's fiscal year begins October 1 and concludes September 30 of the subsequent year.

The Budget Cycle

Budgeting contains four important, sequential, and recurring components. The first, *budget development*, is oriented toward the future; it embodies a concern for what will or should be. *Budget administration* is concerned with the present and focuses on proper financial procedures and approvals. *Accounting* (or *bookkeeping*) is oriented toward the immediate past, toward what happened and to what degree it was consistent with projections. The fourth component, *cost analysis*, takes a longer view of the past; it involves an assessment of past actions and an appraisal of their effectiveness relative to costs.

The first of these, budget development, should be aligned with an organization's planning cycle. The fourth, cost analysis, should be aligned first with the evaluation portion of the cycle and subsequently with the planning phase of the cycle. The following explanation concentrates on these two components. The purposes and operation of budget administration and accounting are discussed more generally.

The term *budget cycle* reflects the repetitive pattern to the activities of organizations and the life of its constituents. Such a pattern facilitates looking toward the future and assessing the past. An organization's budget cycle begins, ends, and then, as is the nature of cycles, begins again. The four components of budgeting—development, administration, accounting, and analysis—are arrayed sequentially in this cycle, but they overlap. All four activities may be, indeed should be, occurring simultaneously, though each may well be focused upon a different fiscal year.

For example, in August or September of any particular year, a school district's staff might well be engaged in current-fiscal-year budget administration activities, such as preparing payrolls and approving purchase orders for the forthcoming spring semester's instructional supplies. This is budget administration. Accounting staff might well be closing the record books on the recently completed school year. They would be summing expenditures for different categories and setting records in order for an annual audit. This is bookkeeping. Evaluation staff members might well be engaged in data collection and analytic procedures involved in appraising results of an instructional innovation that was tried during the just-ended school year. They might be undertaking these cost analyses in order to inform the superintendent whether or not the innovation should be continued or terminated. Last, officials may be engaged in developing the budget for the school year beginning the following September.

BUDGET DEVELOPMENT

This is the forward-looking phase of budgeting, the time when decision makers agree, even if implicitly, on an organization's mission and objectives for the forthcoming fiscal year. The decision makers must also agree on assumptions crucial to budgeting—for example, what the average class size will be, how many days during the year the school district will operate, what the average size of schools will be, and thus how many school buildings the district will operate. Will the district need to open new schools or close old ones? What will district revenues be from various sources—local, state, federal, and philanthropic? These and dozens of related decisions must be made in as orderly and reasonable a fashion as the political process permits. Education decision makers often neglect formal discussion of such important topics. Under such circumstances, decisions are made by default; inertia prevails. This is a pity. When appropriately conducted, decisions regarding such important preconditions are described in a *budget assumption letter*. This document is distributed to appropriate budget process participants and guides the framing of their budget proposals.

To facilitate budget planning, organizations generally design a so-called *budget development calendar* (Table 9.1). It typically is the responsibility of a district's budget officer to develop such a calendar and gain its approval by the superintendent and school board. Thereafter, the budget officer is responsible for seeing that factual items and necessary analyses are supplied early enough to mesh with appropriate calendar target dates.

A complete budget development calendar is guided by chronological events, such as state-legislated approval dates, actions by the legislature on appropriations, expiration of collective bargaining agreements with employees, and the school academic calendar. Such important dates are specified in the left-hand column of the calendar in Table 9.1.In addition to critical dates, a complete budget development schedule makes clear crucial items of information, or assumptions about crucial information. For example, budget participants need to know what projected enrollments are for the forthcoming school year, what revenues are expected to be, what salary increases, if any, are to result for employees as a consequence of bargaining, and what the size of the teacher work force is to be. Often this information will be contained in the previously mentioned budget assumption letter.

The budget development schedule should also specify the participants in the decision process. These are listed in the right-hand column of Table 9.1. The district illustrated here has a highly centralized budget development process. To be sure, principals and other employees participate in budget decisions. Indeed, the committee frequently referred to on the calendar comprises representative employees. However, even though employees participate in developing the budget, the result is still a centralized school district plan. It is possible to allocate substantially greater budgetary discretion to school sites—to have a decentralized budget. The dynamics of this arrangement are described later in this chapter.

It is during the budget development phase that the results of prior analyses should be taken into account. Planning techniques such as those illustrated earlier in this chapter can inform this part of the budget cycle. Also it is at this point in planning the next year's resources that a decision should be reached regarding expansion of what has been appraised and found effective and termination of what is

TABLE 9.1   Budget Development Calendar

DATE	EVENT	PARTICIPANTS
Wed. 1/19 7:00–10:00	Preliminary budget development discussion with Board.	Superintendent Business Office
Mon. 1/24 3:30–5:00	General Orientation Meeting; preliminary budget development discussions.	Budget Committee Principals Union Reps
Wed. 1/26 1:00–5:00	Workshop to review base budget parameters (revenue, expenditures, staffings, etc.); begin to develop and balance preliminary budget.	Committee
Fri. 1/28 1:30–5:00	Continue 1/26 session.	Committee
Mon. 2/7 3:30–7:30	Review/discuss preliminary budget recommendations.	Committee Principals
Tues. 2/8 3:30–7:30	Review/discuss preliminary budget recommendations.	Committee Union Reps
Wed. 2/16 7:00–10:00	Presentation of preliminary budget with Board.	Board Superintendent
Wed. 2/23 7:00–10:00	Continue 2/16 regular Board meeting. NOTE: LAST DATE FOR ACTION ON LAYOFFS, if necessary (to effect legally required notice to employees by 3/15)	Board Superintendent
March–April	General Group and Board workshop discussion sessions on program budget planning, e.g., Special Education, Elementary and Secondary Instruction, Operations and Maintenance, Instructional Support Services, others. Dates and specific budgets for review to be determined.	All Board

IF PRIOR LAYOFF ACTION TAKEN, FOLLOW-UP WOULD BE:

DATE	EVENT	PARTICIPANTS
Thurs. 4/7 2:00–8:00	Refine preliminary budget; develop tentative budget. Review recommendation regarding layoffs.	Committee
Mon. 4/11 3:30–7:30	Review/discuss refined preliminary budget.	Committee Principals

TABLE 9.1   (continued)

DATE	EVENT	PARTICIPANTS
Tues. 4/12 3:30–7:30	Review/discuss refined preliminary budget.	Committee Union Reps
Wed. 4/20 7:00–10:00	Board action on final layoff notification (by 5/15), if necessary.	Board Superintendent
Wed. 4/27 7:00–10:00	FINAL DATE FOR BOARD ACTION ON LAYOFF (to effect notice by 5/15, if necessary)	Board Superintendent

IF NO PRIOR ACTION TAKEN, CONTINUE HERE:

DATE	EVENT	PARTICIPANTS
Tues. 5/17 and Tues. 5/24 2:00–8:00	Tentative Budget workshop. Complete education plan and tentative budget recommendations for Board approval	Committee
Thurs. 6/2 3:30-7:30	Review/discuss Tentative Budget Recommendations.	Committee Union Reps
Mon. 6/6 3:30–7:30	Review/discuss Tentative Budget Recommendations.	Committee Principals
Wed. 6/8 7:00–10:00	Board workshop/discussion of Tentative Budget Recommendations.	Board Superintendent
Wed. 6/15 7:00–10:00	Board to adopt Tentative Budget.	Board Superintendent
Fri. 7/1	LAST DAY TO FILE ADOPTED TENTATIVE BUDGET WITH COUNTY. Must indicate date, time, and location of public hearing on Final Budget.	Business Office
Thurs. 7/7 9:30–2:30	Review, discuss, complete Final Budget Recommendation—group effort.	Committee Principals Union Reps
Wed. 7/13 and Wed. 7/27 7:00–10:00	Board Workshop/discussion sessions on Final Budget Recommendations.	Board Superintendent
On or before 8/1	County shall review and return filed Tentative Budget. County may accept changes in the date, time, and location of public hearing on Final Budget.	Business Office
Wed. 8/3 7:00–10:00	Board to hold public hearing and adopt Final Budget.	Board Superintendent
Wed. 9/7	LAST DATE TO HOLD PUBLIC HEARING, ADOPT AND FILE FINAL BUDGET.	Board Superintendent Business Office

judged ineffective. This is where the evaluation portion of the cycle begins to inform planning and budgeting.

BUDGET ADMINISTRATION

Once various components of an organization have agreed on planned resource allocations for the forthcoming fiscal year, it becomes crucial to ensure that resources are indeed allocated in accord with the agreement, and that expenditures are consistent with the budget. This is the function of the organizational members responsible for budget administration. Here are found employees with titles such as Comptroller, Bursar, and Business Manager. Regardless of their label, their overall responsibility is to approve or to see that approval has been obtained for requests for spending. The purpose of this is to ensure that spending requests are consistent with agreed-upon budget plans. For example, payroll departments, purchasing officers, maintenance supervisors, and shipping and receiving departments as well as line administrators all have a role to play in seeing that resources are received and distributed in keeping with the district's overall resource allocation plan—its budget.

ACCOUNTING[7]

Assuming that resources are allocated in an approved manner, it still is necessary to maintain records of such transactions. This is done for three reasons, the first of which is to ensure that over time particular functions do not receive more resources than intended. Accounting procedures can keep track of accrued actual expenditures by budget category, as well as *encumbrances*—resources that have already been obligated though not yet spent.

The second reason records are kept is to enable the organization, after the fact, to ensure compliance with the spending plan. To this end, bookkeeping records are utilized by auditors—people who review spending actions to report compliance, or lack thereof, with the budget. An organization, if sufficiently large, may have both internal and external auditors. At least annually, most states require school districts to have an external audit of their books to ensure spending compliance not only with district budgets but also with state and federal regulations.

The third reason for financial record keeping is that the organization can subsequently use the information as the basis for financial analyses such as cost-effectiveness analysis or appraisals of equity. These analytic endeavors depend crucially upon records being kept accurately and in a useful form. Generally, the more abstract the level of aggregation, the less useful the data. For example, a single entry such as "Salaries" typically is of little use to analysts. How many individuals were being paid? How much were they paid? To do what? For how long? These questions imply the kinds of bookkeeping categories more likely to permit studies of efficiency and equity.

[7]For more on this topic, see Malvern J. Gross, Jr., and William Warshaner, Jr., *Financial Accounting Guide for Non-Profit Organizations,* 3rd ed. (New York: John Wiley, 1983).

School districts generally adhere to a uniform accounting code. In 1957, the United States Office of Education published *Financial Accounting for Local and State School Systems: Standard Receipt and Expenditure Accounts*.[8] This was intended as a guide to state and local education agencies in keeping their financial records. This document and its successors[9] have been widely beneficial. By encouraging local and state agencies to adopt a standard form of record keeping, they have facilitated research across geographic boundaries as well as over time. Each state now has a uniform accounting manual patterned after the federal model.

Budget approval and accounting are typically considered together as budget administration. They are separated here simply for purposes of explanation. However, each differs from the fourth component of the budget cycle, evaluation.

COST-EFFECTIVENESS ANALYSIS [10]

Cost-effectiveness analysis and cost-benefit analysis are similar methods of examining the economic value of one or more alternatives. In cost-benefit analysis, the dollar amount of all benefits flowing from an alternative is compared with the dollar value of all costs associated with that alternative. A major problem with cost-benefit analysis is that it is often difficult to assign monetary values to benefits. (How much is it worth in dollars for a child to learn to read faster?) In cost-effectiveness analysis, two or more alternatives are examined, each of which is presumed to offer the same benefit; the intent is to discover the least-cost alternative. This eliminates the problem of assigning monetary values to benefits.

It might seem unnecessary to provide a special name for a procedure as easy as adding up costs. However, the procedure is not as simple as it may appear. The problem is that costs often occur at widely different times, and that a dollar today is not worth the same as a dollar several years from now, *even* if there is no inflation. An intelligent person given the choice of a dollar now or a dollar in five years would choose the dollar now, for he or she is more certain of getting it now and can invest it so as to have more than one dollar in five years. Suppose that the dollar is invested at 10 percent and one can be just as sure of getting the dollar five years from now as now. Then, if it were invested, at the end of five years there would be $1.61. Under these conditions, the *future value* of a dollar five years from now is $1.61. Alternatively, the *present value* of $1.00 five years from now would be only 62 cents ($1.00/1.61). To compare costs that occur at different times, it is necessary to convert all costs to present values and then compare those values.

[8]Paul L. Reason and Alpheus L. White, *Financial Accounting for Local and State School Systems: Standard Receipt and Expenditure Accounts* (Washington, D.C.: Government Printing Office, 1957).

[9]Everett V. Samuelson and George G. Tankard, Jr., *Financial Accounting for School Activities* (Washington, D.C.: Government Printing Office, 1962); and Charles T. Roberts and Allan R. Lichtenberger, *Financial Accounting: Classifications and Standard Terminology for Local and State School Systems* (Washington, D.C.: Government Printing Office, 1973).

[10]For other descriptions see Henry M. Levin, "A Cost-Effectiveness Analysis of Teacher Selection," *Journal of Human Resources*, 5, no. 1 (Winter 1970), 37–52; and Barbara Wolfe, "A Cost-Effectiveness Analysis of Reduction in School Expenditures: An Application of an Educational Production Function," *Journal of Educational Finance*, 2, no. 4 (Spring 1977), 407–18.

Comparing two ways of providing beginning foreign language instruction illustrates an application of cost-effectiveness analysis. Both alternatives are assumed to result in 200 students per year educated to the same level in a foreign language. Thus, the benefits are identical.

Alternative 1 uses two teachers. Each teaches five classes of twenty students for a full year. Teacher salaries are $20,000 the first year, and increase $1000 a year thereafter. Each classroom costs $3000 per year for light, heat, and janitorial service. Books cost $20 per student per year. (All other costs are ignored for this example.)

Alternative 2 uses a language laboratory and only one teacher. Because the laboratory is a more efficient way of teaching, it is possible for a single teacher to bring 100 students (20 per period for a five-period day) to the same level of competency in one semester that the conventional method was able to do in a full year. Thus, one teacher is able to teach, with the aid of a laboratory, 200 students in a year. The teacher's salary is the same as in alternative 1, as are room and book costs. Of course, it is necessary to purchase and install the language laboratory. The laboratory costs $95,000, and $4000 per year is required for supplies and maintenance. At the end of five years it will be obsolete and have no salvage value.

The present value of the costs of the two alternatives can be compared (see Table 9.2) using a *discount rate* of 10 percent. (The discount rate is the interest rate used in making these present-value comparisons. There is no agreed-upon rate that should be used for cost-effectiveness analyses. A reasonable rate is the rate the district would pay if it borrowed the money.) Costs for each year are assumed for this illustration to be spent at the beginning of the year. Thus, the present value of the first year's costs is identical to their dollar value. However, the present value of costs in future years is less than their dollar value.

Note in Table 9.2 that the costs for one teacher are the same in both alternatives, and thus need not be included in the analysis. Similarly, the service cost for one room and book costs are the same in both alternatives. Thus, it is necessary to compare, for alternative 1, the cost of one teacher and one room with, for alternative 2, the cost of the laboratory and its maintenance.

If we are concerned only with undiscounted costs, it appears that purchase of a language laboratory will save $10,000 over five years. However, if one correctly assesses discounted costs (present values), the language laboratory actually costs $8226 more! The reason is that most of the costs for the second alternative must be assumed in the first year, whereas those for alternative 1 are spread over five years.

Budgeting, Decision Making, and Power

Individuals empowered to make decisions regarding resource allocation can determine an organization's direction. Frankly, budget control is organizational control; budget control is power. The appropriate conventional phrase is "the power of the purse." The budget process can be used to concentrate power in the hands of a relatively small number of individuals or to distribute it to an expanded number of actors. To illustrate this maxim we discuss the principles involved in *program bud-*

TABLE 9.2   An Example of Cost-Effectiveness Analysis

	COST	PRESENT VALUE
Alternative 1:		
Year 1:		
Teacher salaries	$20,000	$20,000
Room costs	3,000	3,000
Year 2:		
Teacher salaries	21,000	19,091
Room costs	3,000	2,727
Year 3:		
Teacher salaries	22,000	18,181
Room costs	3,000	2,479
Year 4:		
Teacher salaries	23,000	17,180
Room costs	3,000	2,254
Year 5:		
Teacher salaries	24,000	16,392
Room costs	3,000	2,049
Total Costs:	$125,000	$103,453
Alternative 2:		
Year 1:		
Purchase of laboratory	$95,000	$95,000
Maintenance	4,000	4,000
Year 2:		
Maintenance	4,000	3,636
Year 3:		
Maintenance	4,000	3,306
Year 4:		
Maintenance	4,000	3,005
Year 5:		
Maintenance	4,000	2,737
Total Costs:	$115,000	$111,679

geting and *zero-based budgeting*, budget development strategies that concentrate power, and *school-site budgeting*, a strategy that decentralizes decision-making discretion.

THE INCREMENTAL NATURE OF BUDGETING [11]

Budgeting in most organizations is said to be *incremental*. This is particularly the case in public sector institutions such as schools. *Incremental* in this context refers to the tendency to make resource allocation changes only at the *margin*. The vast bulk of expenditures continues year after year, budget cycle after budget cycle.

[11] See Joseph S. Wholey, *Zero Base Budgeting: Budgeting and Program Evaluation* (Lexington, Mass.: Heath, Lexington Books, 1979); I. Carl Candoli et al., *School Business Administration: A Planning Approach* (Boston: Allyn & Bacon, 1973); and Guilbert C. Hentschke, *School Business Administration* (Berkeley, Calif.: McCutchan, 1986).

The *base* changes little. The major reason for this is the political influence of individuals and groups advantaged by the status quo. For example, current employees, and the parent clients they serve are anxious to derive the benefits themselves should there be any added resources. Teachers, for example, might well lobby or bargain intensely for higher salaries and smaller classes should a school district have the prospect of increasing its revenues. For a variety of reasons, parents might side with teachers on these issues. Consequently, a school board and administration might be subjected to intense political pressure to accord added resources to those already employed, who believe themselves entitled to at least as much as they received the previous year and a "fair share" of any addition.

Under this scenario, the best that one can hope for is to gain control over a portion of any anticipated increase and direct such resources toward new goals. When resources are declining, entrenched interests, if anything, are more adamant in their protection of the base. To the extent that such organizational dynamics are present in schools, they render it difficult to make decisions about total revenues. Typically, it is only an increment to the base that can be redirected. Often this can occur only after successful negotiations.

PROGRAM BUDGETING AND ZERO-BASED BUDGETING

These mechanisms assist efforts to gain greater central control over an organization's resources. Each calls for resources to be aligned with organizational purposes, programs, or objectives, instead of with actual objects to be purchased, personnel, and materials. If a purpose is agreed to by decision makers, then expenditures necessary to accomplish the purpose are permitted. If a purpose or program is no longer thought to be fundamentally important or necessary by decision makers, then its expenditure base is reduced or eliminated. An old purpose or program may be replaced by a new one. Individuals employed to conduct an old program might be released or transferred and new or retrained personnel employed who possess the qualification necessary to perform new functions.

Although both planning–programming–budgeting systems (PPBS) and zero-based budgeting (ZBB) are centralized budgeting systems, PPBS establishes goals at the top, with budget development proceeding downward. ZBB builds from the bottom up, with budget requests at each level aggregated, ranked by the supervisor, and forwarded to the next level.

Program budgeting assumes that each program, or at least a significant number of an organization's programs, will be assessed periodically to determine their usefulness and effectiveness. Those judged wanting can be improved or eliminated. Similarly, zero-based budgeting assumes that annually, or at least regularly, an entire budget can be built from the ground up with few assumptions regarding existing obligations. A frequently used technique is for administrators to request that subordinates submit budgets assuming 5, 10, or 15 percent fewer funds for a forthcoming budget cycle and see what activities or programs are proposed for elimination or reduction.

Collective bargaining contracts, teachers' tenure, and the large capital cost already sunk into school building typically militate against a school district's undertaking a true form of zero-based budgeting. Even program budgeting is unusual. Districts periodically attempt such efforts, but they generally revert to incremental budgeting, attempting to spend added monies as wisely as possible and phasing out old programs if they show evidence of ineffectiveness or a lack of political constituency.[12]

SCHOOL-SITE BUDGETING [13]

In order to enfranchise a larger set of actors, some districts utilize a budgeting mechanism whereby a portion of a district's revenues are allocated by formula to school sites. School-level decision makers, usually the principal assisted by a site advisory council of teachers and parents, can then decide allocation patterns. Such systems must be carefully designed to work in tandem with central district collective bargaining contracts. However, well-developed technical mechanisms exist for budgeting and accounting for revenues school by school. School-site budgeting appears to be increasingly popular where state-level decision making is increasing.

PROGRAM EVALUATION

Program evaluation involves the systematic assessment of an endeavor in order to determine its effects. Once the effects on several selected dimensions are known, evaluation usually entails a judgment of the endeavor's relative success or failure. Such a judgment may involve measuring project results against a predetermined goal. Did reading achievement scores increase? Was student absenteeism and vandalism reduced? Was parent satisfaction enhanced? These are the kinds of questions evaluators pose. Their objective is to determine whether or not or to what degree a desired outcome occurred, to suggest how the undertaking might be rendered more effective, and to influence the allocation of organizational resources as a result.

[12]Difficulties involved in implementing PPBS are described by Jay Chambers and Thomas Parrish in *The Legacy of Rational Budgeting Models in Education and a Proposal for the Future* (Stanford, Calif.: Institute for Finance and Governance, Stanford University, 1984).

[13]See John Greenhalgh, *School Site Budgeting: Decentralized School Management* (Lanham, Md.: University Press of America, 1984); Lawrence C. Pierce, *School Based Management* (Eugene, Oreg.: School Study Council, 1980); James W. Guthrie, "School Based Management: The Next Needed Education Reform," *Kappan,* 68, no. 4 (December 1986), 305–9; Carl L. Marburger, *One School at a Time: School Based Management, a Process for Change* (Columbia, Md.: National Committee for Citizens in Education, 1985); Brian J. Caldwell, "Education Reform through School Site Management: An International Perspective on the Decentralization of Budgeting" (paper presented at the conference of The American Education Finance Association, Arlington, Va., 1987); and Daniel J. Brown, "A Preliminary Inquiry into School-Based Management" (report to the Social Sciences and Humanities Council of Canada), Grant #410-83-1086, University of British Columbia, March 1987.

Other than to illustrate cost-effectiveness analysis, this chapter does not explain program evaluation. This is a technical field in itself. Suffice it to say here that it is an important component of an organization's resource allocation cycle.[14]

SUMMARY

Resource allocation involves planning, evaluation, and budgeting. Planning is a future-oriented organizational activity, involving goal setting and determination of alternative procedures likely to result in achievement of goals. Technical planning methods—for example, PERT, linear programming, queuing theory, and computer simulation—can assist in this process by assigning probability to uncertain events or conditions and by more rapidly forecasting likely outcomes. Evaluation is a set of procedures undertaken to assess the effectiveness of a program. The intent can be either to improve the program or to make a judgment regarding its continuation.

Budgeting can be a practical bridge between planning and evaluation. A budget should serve as an organization's plan for allocation of resources. It should exhibit annualarity, comprehensiveness, and balance. In developing a budget, an organization should take into account its long- and short-range plans and evaluations of its current programs. Once the budget is developed, it is necessary to ensure that resources are allocated in a manner consistent with it. Known as budget administration, this involves responsible procedures for the disbursement and subsequent accounting of funds. The final budgeting stage coincides with an organization's evaluation cycle.

[14]For more information on program evaluation, see Lee J. Cronbach, *Designing Evaluations of Educational and Social Programs* (San Francisco: Jossey-Bass, 1982).

chapter ten

MANAGING FISCAL RESOURCES

The word *finance* has different meanings. In the term *school finance*, it connotes processes by which money for support of schools is raised and distributed. Once this money is in the hands of individual school districts, *business administration* describes more accurately the determination of how it shall be spent. This is a book about school finance, not about business administration. Nevertheless, there is a certain amount of overlap, and this chapter discusses facets of business management that impinge directly on the conservation and effective use of fiscal resources.

CAPITAL CONSTRUCTION

Capital construction can make enormous demands on the fiscal resources of a school district, yet much of it is outside the normal current-expenditures budget and tends to be ignored in discussions.

From World War II to the end of the 1960s an unprecedented number of new schools were built. Rapid increases in student population, combined with migration from farm to city and suburb, necessitated the construction of thousands of new schools. The decreasing birth rates of the 1970s produced dramatic changes. Although some areas, primarily in the sun belt, continued to expand in school-age population, most witnessed a decrease in number of students. This was particularly true in older cities and close-in suburbs. How to close unneeded schools became the primary problem for superintendents and boards. Invariably, parents agreed that for economic reasons schools should be closed, but "not in my neighborhood."

However, the 1980s have brought a slow reversal in pupil populations. Nationwide, enrollments are projected to grow by about 5 1/2 percent between 1985 and 1992.[1]

Where students are increasing in a district that has previously had decreasing enrollments, it may be possible in many cases to accommodate them by filling currently underused schools, or even by reactivating mothballed schools. In many other cases, however, new students are in places remote from where schools with available capacity are located. It is easy to predict that the remainder of the 1980s and the 1990s will see a rapid increase in the amount of school construction.

Dollars spent for school construction, land purchase, and major repair and renovation are *capital expenses,* and are normally budgeted and accounted for separately from current operating expenses. An important characteristic of capital expense is unevenness of expenditure. Construction of a school in one year may cost several million dollars, with expenditures in succeeding years being almost zero. Only the largest districts, such as New York and Chicago, can manage to smooth out these capital expenditures and spend about the same amount each year. This unevenness has important implications. Because construction of a new school is such a large investment, it is worth spending the time and effort necessary to be sure it is done properly. Because financing capital expenditures completely out of current revenues would mean large fluctuations in tax rate, borrowing is utilized.

Building a New School

Land purchase and new school construction are major undertakings. Large districts often do enough of this to have a special staff for the purpose; small districts must usually rely on the business manager to initiate the action. There are a number of books on the subject of construction, and an extended treatment is out of place here.[2] Nevertheless, a brief outline of the steps in a construction project is useful.

DETERMINING NEED

The first step is determining the extent of need. Projections of the number of students to be served by the district for at least the following five years are essential.[3] These projections, combined with careful analyses of present building capacity, provide a picture of future needs. There is a variety of ways in which these fu-

---

[1] Calculated from data in U.S. Bureau of the Census, *Statistical Abstract of the United States, 1985* (Washington, D.C.: Government Printing Office, 1984), p. 140, Table 224.

[2] Two examples are Basil Costaldi, *Creative Planning of Educational Facilities* (Chicago: Rand McNally, 1969); and *Guide for Planning Educational Facilities* (Columbus, Ohio: Council of Educational Facility Planners, 1969).

[3] For a brief discussion of projection techniques, see Walter I. Garms, James W. Guthrie, and Lawrence C. Pierce, *School Finance: The Economics and Politics of Public Education* (Englewood Cliffs, N.J.: Prentice-Hall, 1978), pp. 311–13.

ture needs may be met, and they should be carefully examined before the decision to build a new school is made. Some of the possibilities:

1. Space presently underutilized because of inconvenient arrangement of facilities could be remodeled.

2. It may be possible to utilize space in nonschool buildings nearby. This is particularly true for classroom uses that are not part of K–12 instruction, such as day care. Nearby church school classrooms have often been used for this purpose.

3. It may be possible to consolidate selected operations with a neighboring school district that has space. An example would be special education classes that are smaller than necessary in each district.

4. It may be possible to increase the number of periods in a normal day at the high school level, thus increasing classroom utilization.

5. Year-round schooling, using selected models, can increase the capacity of a building by 25 percent.

DETERMINING LOCATION

If, after a survey of the options, it is decided that construction is the most appropriate solution to actual or potential overcrowding, the next step is to determine location. Additions to present schools may be the least expensive alternative if space is available on the site and if shared facilities (multi-purpose room, playgrounds, etc.) are adequate for the additional student load. However, this lower cost may be balanced by higher busing costs if enough students live in a part of the district where there are no schools. Thus, it is vital that an enrollment projection include not only how many students are to be served but also where they live and will live in the future.[4] Necessary data may often be obtained from city or county planning departments, electric, telephone, and other utility companies, and major builders and developers.

LAND ACQUISITION

Assuming that it is desirable to build a school at a new site, a district must proceed to purchase land. The simplest solution is to find a parcel of land in the middle of an area about to become a subdivision and agree with the owner on a price. Where large subdivisions are being built, a district often does this well before it will be necessary to construct a school. The district may be able to negotiate a good price for the land by cooperating with the developer, who should realize the increased value that closeness to schools brings to houses. California is a case where state government and other local governments foster this cooperation. Each developer is required by state law to file an Environmental Impact Statement (EIS). This statement must be accepted by the city or county, which may require develop-

---

[4]James W. Guthrie and Terry R. Margerum, "Real Estate Assessment and Management Strategy," report submitted to the Board of Directors and Superintendent, Napa Valley Unified School District, Napa, California, 1987.

ers to deed a school site to the school district (or pay the district a specified number of dollars per house) before the EIS will be approved.

However, it is more likely that a suitable site must be assembled from parcels owned by a number of individual owners. A developer ordinarily does this by secretly obtaining options on each necessary parcel before making any purchases, to prevent owners from finding out what is occurring and holding out for a high price. It is difficult for school districts to deal in secrecy, particularly in states with *open meeting* laws. However, the district has an ultimate weapon not possessed by the private developer—the power of *condemnation*, also called *eminent domain*. Districts proceed in different ways on land purchases, some doing all purchasing through negotiation and others using condemnation exclusively. Condemnation has one advantage: the price is set by a court, which relieves the district of allegations of overpayment. Negotiation, however, is often more appropriate when establishing cooperative arrangements with developers of a large area, or where special concessions important to the owner and unimportant to the district (such as payments spread over a number of years) would result in a lower price. Each situation must be approached on its own merits. In any case, the district's legal counsel must be involved at every transaction step.

ARCHITECTURAL PLANNING

Having selected a site, the district must begin architectural planning. A good architect can plan imaginatively and save the district money; a poor one can be a catastrophe, the consequences lasting for the life of the building. Architects should not be selected on a bid basis. Most architects' fees are standard (indeed, state law may specify what they shall be), and any architect who promises to charge a lesser fee should be viewed skeptically. Rather, an architect should be selected on the basis of past performance in other situations. The firm (for it is seldom an individual architect) should certainly have built schools before. Stories abound of the famous architect who builds his first hospital, which is beautiful on the outside and absolutely unworkable on the inside. Firms should be invited to present sample photographs of their work, along with a description of the size of the firm and the kinds of expertise it offers. After a preliminary screening, district personnel should visit schools designed by firms under consideration and talk with administrators, teachers, and maintenance personnel. This will narrow the choice to a few architects, who should then be interviewed on preferred work method, current office workload, and particular employees to be assigned to the project. It is important that these individuals' personalities be compatible with those of the district personnel who are to be most closely involved in the project.

The school district should next develop *educational specifications*—the number of students to be housed and the kind of educational programs to be offered. The more careful and complete the specifications, the more likely the architect will be able to design the kind of school the district wants. Avoid an architect who says, "Tell me how many students you want to house, and I will design a school for you with no further worry on your part." Development of educational specifications is one of the most important parts of designing a school and should involve teachers, supervisors, and administrators. It should not be rushed, for time must be allowed for reconciling differing views.

With educational specifications in hand, an architect confers with district representatives to develop preliminary ideas. At this point it is desirable to keep the district delegation small so that it can reach tentative agreement on many facets of the plan in a reasonable time. However, a number of sessions may be necessary, and the district may need to gather additional data or refine its educational specifications. At some point the architect presents preliminary plans, usually consisting of plan view and elevations. When these have been sufficiently modified they will be ready for formal approval by the school board.

The architect can now develop detailed drawings and specifications. It is important that from this point forward the district's maintenance supervisor be involved, for the decisions made here can save or cost the district many thousands of dollars over the life of the building. Final detailed drawings should be carefully reviewed by district representatives. Errors found at this point are easy to correct. Found during construction, they result in costly change orders; if not found until after the building is completed, they are even more costly to correct.

BIDDING

The district now advertises for bids. Each bidder will obtain a set of plans from the architect, estimate the labor and materials necessary, and obtain commitments from subcontractors. Typically, the general contractor does all carpentry, performs some of the other work, and supervises and coordinates all construction. Subcontractors are usually obtained for electrical work, plumbing, site grading, mechanical work, and a number of other jobs.

At the date and time advertised, general contractors' bids are opened and read. The district is generally required by law to accept the bid of the lowest *qualified bidder,* but this need not necessarily be the lowest bid. The architect should be present, and should carefully review the two or three lowest bids. The financial status of the general contractor should be determined, if possible, and the contractor's performance on other contracts ascertained. The same is true of each subcontractor, who must be listed in the bid. Many other items must be assessed by an architect before recommendation of the bid award. (If recommending someone other than the lowest bidder, the architect should present good reasons, for there will probably be a challenge from the lowest bidder before the school board.) The board need not award the bid to anyone, although it usually will if the lowest acceptable bid is at or below the architect's estimate. Frequently an architect will specify alternatives, with a separate bid on each alternative, in order to be able to adjust total contract size to the funds available in case a bid exceeds the estimate. This complicates the selection of a bidder, for the lowest bidder on the base contract may be high on some alternative additions.

CONSTRUCTION

Construction now begins, under supervision of an architect, who visits the job site several times a week to ensure that plans are followed, to resolve problems in interpretation of drawings or specifications, and to develop change orders where necessary. However, it is difficult for an architect to be on the site at all times, and shoddy workmanship can be covered up by subsequent construction before the next visit. Thus, it is essential for the district to hire a full-time inspector. This should be a person thoroughly experienced in all facets of building. He or she should be on the job any time work is under way, and should insist on inspecting all work before it is covered. This is a crucial role, for opportunities for concealing poor workmanship or perpetrating outright fraud are great, and the potential cost to the district is much more than what will be paid to the inspector in salary.

Design-build construction. Private and nonprofit organizations rely increasingly upon *design-build* (or *managed*) *construction* for large buildings or projects such as industrial plants, commercial developments, or hospitals. This involves the services of a project architect and a prime contractor. However, the architect in this instance is not charged with both overall design and detailed drawing and specifications for the entire structure. Rather, once the functions to be performed within the proposed building are clearly known, the architect prepares requests for bids for various packages or components of the project: excavation, foundations, structural steel, heating and ventilation, interior finishes, and so on.

Bidders are provided with functional specifications, but not with detailed design drawings other than significant dimensions of the overall undertaking. Rather than simply expressing a dollar amount for which they will complete the component, a subcontractor also submits an overall plan with construction specifications for the component. In effect, the detailed work of an architect and structural engineer is completed by bidding subcontractors.

The design-build format has at least two advantages. It expedites construction of the overall project. Construction can begin early without being impeded just because the architect has not completed all drawings for every phase. More important, the managing contractor and architect have the advantage of subcontractor experience. By issuing overall performance specifications, but not detailed drawings, potential bidders can take advantage of their practical experience and offer better designs than otherwise might be the case, designs that often are less expensive to implement.

Design-build construction for public schools may not be possible in states that need to review detailed plans. Under such arrangements, whatever time was saved by the design-build mode would be lost by state review procedures. However, should managed construction become more widely adopted in the private sector, a means may be found to permit wider public sector use of similar techniques.

COMPLETION AND PREPARATION FOR USE

The final construction step is formal acceptance of a building after the architect has certified to the school board that construction is complete and satisfactory. Final payment may be made soon thereafter, although a percentage may be withheld for a legally specified period against the possibility of liens filed by employees or subcontractors for nonpayment by the general contractor.

This is not the final step in preparing a new school for students. The most important remaining activity (begun well before completion of construction) is purchase of equipment for the building. This involves careful planning to ensure that everything will be delivered in time. Lists of items must be compiled and cross-checked. Detailed specifications are drawn, based both on the educational needs expressed by principal and teachers and on the desires of the maintenance supervisor. These frequently conflict, for maintenance personnel prefer standardized equipment so as to minimize the problem of spare parts and of training mechanics, whereas teachers frequently want something unique, believing it will be more convenient or provide for better instruction. Equipment for a new building is a capital expense, usually paid for from proceeds of the bond funds used in building construction. Equipment other than that for a new building (such as additional desks for an existing school) is also a capital expense, but is usually purchased from current revenues instead of from bond funds. These capital expenditures from current revenues are usually minor compared with those from bond funds.

Surplus Facilities

Many districts, because of enrollment declines or population shifts, have underused or unused buildings and properties. This is a smaller problem currently than it was in the 1970s, for school enrollments nationwide are trending upward again. However, in older sections of the nation, and particularly in older cities of those sections, enrollments may still be declining. Surplus schools and property are a fiscal problem primarily because they are a political problem. Everyone is for more efficiency, but not for closing a school in the neighborhood. The result is often underutilized schools and small class sizes. The most difficult problem facing a school board and superintendent is often that of deciding to close a school.

Assuming a decision has been made to close a school, what is to be done with it? Sometimes the district itself can use the building and site for administrative offices or for special programs. However, unless the activities involved are being moved from rented facilities, this may simply mean shifting the surplus space to another spot in the district. (That may be good, if one part of the district is growing.)

In some cases, it is possible to convert surplus facilities to other community uses. A community hall, playground, library, or park are examples. The city, county, or state may need office space. In many states, law requires the district to offer the surplus property to other governmental agencies before it may market it publicly, and it may sell the property to another agency at lower than market value. This is often advantageous to the taxpayer, who supports both governmental entities, but that is scant comfort to the school district, which receives less cash than it might if it sold the property on the open market.

Unfortunately, nonschool uses for a surplus school may be limited, rendering sale difficult. Often the site is abandoned for school purposes because the clientele has moved away as the area becomes commercial or industrial. Even so, it is sometimes possible to find uses that make it possible to sell the property for a reasonable sum. Near Rochester, New York, Xerox Corporation bought a surplus school for warehousing purposes. In a number of cases, surplus schools in inner cities have been redeveloped into attractive apartments.

DEBT AND ITS MANAGEMENT

Categories of Debt

There are three categories of debt, and they apply equally to individuals, school districts, and corporations. The first category is the amount owed for items recently purchased and received but not yet paid for. For an individual, examples are the charge account at a department store or an amount owed for current purchases on a credit card. For school districts, this category of debt would be called *accounts payable* and is normally paid out of current revenues within a month of receipt of goods and invoice. Thus it need not be considered further as part of debt management. Of course, if a district should be unable to pay its accounts on time, it might try to stall creditors (dangerous if you want to deal with them again), or borrow from the bank. Borrowing converts this debt into the second type.

This second type of debt is the sort that individuals incur when they borrow on a short-term basis to pay for purchases, or pay less than the full balance on their monthly credit card statement. This is *short-term debt*. One can think of this kind of borrowing as meeting a *cash-flow* problem, whereby money comes in too slowly at one time of year and more rapidly at another time. This is particularly apt to happen with school districts, where tax money is received in large sums once or twice a year while expenses continue on a more even basis throughout the year. Districts faced with this problem usually borrow from a bank or other lending institution on a short-term basis, repaying the loan when tax receipts arrive. The district guarantees to pay interest at a stated rate. Such loans must typically be repaid within twelve months, and this period constitutes the dividing line between short-term and long-term debt.

Long-term debt is incurred almost exclusively for purchase or construction of capital assets. An individual incurs such debt when borrowing from a bank to buy a house, giving the bank a mortgage. School districts borrow also, but special circumstances dictate the use of a different evidence of indebtedness, called a *bond*. A bond is simply an acknowledgment that money has been borrowed. The district promises to pay a stated rate of interest on the debt, and to repay the principal amount at a stated time. However, there is not just one loan. Rather, bonds are issued in multiples of $1000 or $5000. Since the amount borrowed at one time may be several million dollars, there will be many bonds, and many individuals or corporations can own them. In addition, bonds can be sold by one person to another. The school district owes interest and principal to whoever owns the bonds at the time payment becomes due.

Another difference between a bond and a loan to an individual is that an individual typically pledges property as security. If payments are not made, the bank can seize the property and sell it, keeping what it is owed plus expenses and returning the remainder to the owner. School land and buildings are public property and cannot be seized for sale. Thus, the bond usually pledges the full *faith and credit* of the district. This means that the district is legally bound to tax its property owners a sufficient amount to pay principal and interest on the bonds, and it can be compelled to do so through court action. Because of this call on the taxes of property owners, school district bonds are relatively safe investments. However, it is possible that local conditions could cause a district to default on its bonds. In 1983, as a result of complications related to Proposition 13 and collective bargaining contracts, the San Jose, California, school district declared bankruptcy. The decision of the bankruptcy judge preserved bondholders' rights (employees forfeited negotiated pay increases), but until his decision there was serious concern among the district's creditors. The risk of default by a district is estimated by bond buyers and is reflected in the interest rate the district must pay when it borrows.

Reasons for Borrowing

Should a school district borrow? Some people believe any form of borrowing is wrong, or perhaps even sinful. However, there are several good reasons for borrowing under appropriate circumstances.

First, it is sometimes simply good business. Frequently, a vendor will give a cash discount for prompt payment. A typical bill might state, "Discount 1.5 percent 10 days, net 30 days." By paying 20 days sooner than required the district can save 1.5 percent of the purchase price. Figured on the basis of 360 days per year, this is equivalent to an interest rate of 27 percent per year charged by the vendor. If the school district can pay the bill promptly, it should do so. Even if it does not have the money to pay promptly, it can probably borrow funds for less than 27 percent and it will save money by so doing. Of course, this type of borrowing must be monitored carefully, for if more is borrowed than is necessary, the extra interest costs may negate the savings.

Districts could eliminate the need to engage in short-term borrowing to ease cash-flow problems by levying a higher tax than is currently needed and amassing a reserve fund to meet cash needs during the year. In most states, however, this is illegal. The law requires that property tax rates each year be sufficient only to make up the difference between budgeted expenditures and receipts, with receipts including all cash available at the beginning of the year. The reason for this is the basic principle of taxation that a government should not have tax revenues available until it is ready to spend money. In general, it is believed that individuals should have the right to use or invest cash themselves rather than giving it to government sooner than needed.

Of course, short-term borrowing can be abused. A prime example was provided by New York State during the 1970s. As a result of political pressure, the legislature voted a one-time large increase in school funding, hoping it would find the revenue to continue this in future years. However, there was insufficient money in the state's coffers to pay for the increase even in the year in which it was voted. The state solved the problem by a stratagem based on the difference between the fiscal years of the state and the school districts. This enabled the state to pay districts one year out of the following year's receipts. However, the strategy also necessitated borrowing by districts until they received the state money, and borrowing by the state to pay districts before it actually had tax receipts in hand. All this borrowing was a bonanza for banks and increased the cost of doing business for school districts and the state. Nevertheless, not much thought was given to it until normal state receipts fell short of meeting state obligations to local school districts. In the spring of 1976, at the last possible moment, the state was able to borrow the necessary $4 billion, part of it from state employee retirement funds. If the state had been unable to borrow this money, many school districts would have defaulted on their short-term loans, something that did not happen even during the Great Depression of the 1930s.

Management of Short-Term Debt

Short-term debt, usually incurred to solve cash-flow problems, may be a loan from a local bank, as is usual when needs are small or for a limited period. Where needs are more substantial, districts may sell *notes*. These are similar to bonds, for they are promises to pay, but they have a short life (typically no more than twelve months) and do not pledge the full faith and credit of the district. Because they do not commit the district to tax itself for repayment, electoral approval is not necessary and borrowing is not subject to bonding limits. As security, notes pledge the revenue to be obtained from some future assured source. If they are secured by a promise to repay from taxes to be received at a later time, they are known as *tax anticipation notes*. Those secured by future state aid payments are called *revenue anticipation notes*, and those secured by revenue to be obtained from the sale of bonds are called *bond anticipation notes*. Although notes are transferable, they are not usually bought by a dealer for resale, as are bonds. Rather, they are bought by the bidder who quotes interest cost, usually a bank.

In addition to notes, which solve cash shortages expected to last for several months, a district may borrow directly from a bank for periods of one day to several weeks.

The other side of the cash-flow coin is that at certain times of year a district may have substantial cash surpluses. Usually, keeping the money in bank savings is the least profitable way of investing it (with the exception of leaving it in a checking account, where it may draw no interest at all). Large districts typically have an employee whose duty is investment of idle funds (and usually also short-term borrowing as part of the cash-flow problem). This investment specialist estimates the cash position for each day several months in advance, taking into account anticipated revenues and expenditures. Then he or she makes investments in such a way that the necessary amount of money, and not too much more, will be available to meet the district's day-to-day needs. The specialist makes only short-term investments—those less than a year in maturity—typically in certificates of deposit, bankers' acceptances, treasury bills, and so forth.

To earn the most from funds, the specialist may even invest any cash left at the end of the business day overnight, and have it back again the next day. This is done through *repurchase agreements* with banks. Banks are required by law to have a certain percentage of assets available at all times in cash. However, they strive also to be as fully invested as possible. At the end of a business day they may find that their cash position is below requirement. Because government auditors always appear after business hours and without warning, the bank must borrow money overnight to cover its requirement, and it does so by means of repurchase agreements.

There are other types of repurchase agreements, all involving short-term borrowing. Unfortunately, as with many other transactions, one must be careful to deal with reputable companies and take reasonable precautions. The city of San Jose, California, lost $60 million in 1984 when two New York securities dealers went bankrupt and the securities San Jose presumably owned as a result of lending them money were never found.

Small districts usually cannot afford a specialist in short-term investment. However, even these districts can improve their cash flow management. School district revenues and expenditures are more predictable than those of a private business, both in timing and in amount. A business manager can therefore easily construct a calendar showing the predicted revenue and expenditure for each day of the school year, and from this estimate the excess or shortage of funds in the district's possession for each day. Using this information, the manager can plan to invest idle cash during periods of excess for appropriate periods in, for example, certificates of deposit that earn more than bank savings, and to borrow on a short-term basis only the amounts needed for the minimum period necessary to keep money in the district's accounts. Most small districts do not do this, or do it poorly, and as a result operate less efficiently than necessary.

Long-Term Debt

Because long-term debt commits a school district to repayments over many years, it usually must be approved by a vote of the people, frequently by a *supermajority* (votes of 60 percent or two-thirds are common). In addition, there are usually state restrictions on the total debt incurred. This limit is typically 5 or 10 percent of the assessed value of real property in the district. The intent is to prevent present district residents from saddling future residents with too large a debt, and to ensure that ability to repay present bonds is not overly diluted by future issues. Long-term debt may usually be incurred only for purchase of land and construction and initial equipping of buildings.

One reason for long-term borrowing is that school building construction is costly. To tax property owners sufficiently to pay for the entire construction cost during the year it is accomplished would usually mean prohibitively high tax rates, and in any case would result in extreme fluctuations of tax rates from year to year. By borrowing, the school district spreads costs over a period of years, giving more stability to tax rates. An alternative, possible in some states, is to pass a special tax levy that will be in effect a specified number of years. The trouble with this method for major construction programs is that construction will not be possible until some years after initiation of such a levy. School districts are seldom able to convince the public to pass such a levy sufficiently in advance of the need (and may in fact not be able themselves to project the need sufficiently). The idea is enticing to some because no money is borrowed and thus no interest need be paid. However, the presumed savings are illusory. Taking money away from taxpayers prematurely means they are prevented from using the money for their own ends, which might include earning interest on it.

Long-term borrowing is also defended as a reasonable way of spreading costs among generations. A school building will last many years, typically from thirty to well over sixty. It seems unfair to force the present generation to pay the entire cost of buildings that will be used by future generations too. If people always lived in the same place, this kind of generational inequity could be excused on the same basis whereby we defend parents paying for the education of their children. However, since individuals move while school buildings stay, it is more equitable to allow a school district's future residents to pay part of the building's costs. Thus, bonds are the most frequently used method of financing new school construction.

Bonding

AUTHORIZING THE BONDS

The steps involved in authorizing, approving, and issuing bonds are numerous and complex. Each step must be conducted with complete legality; otherwise the bonds will not be salable. For this purpose, a district should engage a *financial consultant* specializing in bonding. Such a consultant

1. surveys the issuer's debt structure and financial resources to determine borrowing capacity for future capital financing requirements;

2. gathers all pertinent financial statistics and economic data, such as debt-retirement schedule, tax rates, overlapping debt, and so forth, that would affect or reflect on the issuer's ability and willingness to repay its obligations;

3. advises on timing and method of marketing—the terms of bond issues, including maturity schedule, interest payment dates, call features, and bidding limitations;

4. prepares an overall financing plan specifying a recommended approach and probable timetable;

5. prepares, in cooperation with bond counsel, an official statement, notice of sale, and bid form and distributes same to all prospective underwriters and investors;

6. assists the issuer in obtaining local public assistance and support of proposed financing;

7. keeps in constant contact with rating services to ensure that they have all the information and data they require to evaluate credit properly;

8. is present when sealed bids are opened and stands ready to advise on acceptability of bids;

9. supervises bond printing, signing, and delivery; and

10. advises on investment of bond proceeds.[5]

---

[5] Arthur R. Guastella, "Municipal Finance Consultants," in Joint Economic Committee of the Congress, *State and Local Public Facility Needs and Financing* (Washington, D.C.: Government Printing Office, 1966), pp. 182-99.

In addition to a financial consultant it is necessary to engage *bond counsel*. This is a specialized law firm that reviews legal details of bonding procedures to ensure that bonds are indeed a legal obligation of the district. Each purchaser of a bond expects to find attached to it an opinion by bond counsel (often printed on the back of the bond) that there can be no reasonable legal challenge to the indebtedness represented by the bond. This function cannot be served by the board's attorney, for purchasers will want an opinion signed by an independent law firm. Indeed, sophisticated purchasers may insist that the opinion be written by one of a very small number of recognized bond counsels. The same firm may serve the functions of both financial adviser and bond counsel, if it has marketing as well as legal skills.

The *bond election* is the moment of truth when the district determines whether it will be possible to borrow money. District officials will, of course, have done all they can to ensure a successful outcome (school district elections are discussed in general in Chapter 8). From 1940 to 1960 over 80 percent of school district bond elections passed with the required majority, but since then passage has become increasingly difficult. In the 1970s and early 1980s fewer than half of these elections were passed by voters. Fortunately, the need also decreased; there were fewer children to be educated. However, the demographic pendulum is now swinging the other way, and with increases in school-age children one can expect schools to issue more bonds and to be better able to convince the electorate to pass them. In any case, the need must be justified and documented, and then presented to voters in a convincing manner.

SELLING THE BONDS

Assuming district voters approve a bond issue, the next step is to find a purchaser. School districts do not sell bonds directly to individuals. Rather, they sell an entire issue to a dealer, usually a bank, brokerage firm, or syndicate composed of several banks or brokers. Availability of bonds is advertised and bids are received. The bid resulting in the lowest net interest rate to the district is accepted. Frequently, bids will differ only in the second or third decimal place (7.244 percent versus 7.235 percent, for example), but this difference of 0.009 percent on a $10 million bond issue amounts to a difference of over $13,000 in interest paid over twenty years.

To obtain the best bid, the district needs at least two things—a *rating* of its credit by one of the bond rating agencies and a *bond brochure* describing an issue. Both have the goal of assuring prospective purchasers that interest and principal will be paid in full and on time. There are two important bond rating agencies: Moody's and Standard & Poor's. They use different codes to express the risk of a bond issue, but both rate issues on a scale from highest quality to extremely risky. If a district has sold more than $1 million in bonds fairly recently, it is probably already rated by one or both agencies. If it has not, or if the district's fiscal condition has changed markedly since it was last rated, the financial adviser will ask the agencies to review the rating. A small improvement in the rating can result in markedly lower interest costs over the life of the bonds, and is well worth pursuing. In making a rating, the bond analyst tends to look beyond the issue itself to the aggregated local economy and its burden of debt. He is interested in the "debt capacity" of the issuer (the maximum amount of debt that can legally be issued by the governmental unit) and in the untapped margin of debt capacity still available. . . . The analyst is also interested in a quantification of "indirect debt," composed of bond issues for which the issuer may be a guarantor, and "overlapping debt," the sum of all debt issued by all local governments in an area. Usually expressed in per capita terms, overlapping debt includes the individual citizen's proportionate share of city, county, school district, and other special district debts outstanding.[6]

Preparation of the bond brochure is the financial consultant's responsibility. The district should not attempt to do it unaided. Nonprofessional brochures are immediately apparent to purchasers, and tend to alienate sophisticated buyers. A professional knows what information is needed by prospective purchasers, and knows how to emphasize the most positive facets. A properly prepared brochure may also result in lower interest costs, which will repay many times the cost of preparing the brochure.

Economies of scale are immediately apparent in bonding. The cost of an election, of bond brochure preparation, and of printing bonds is almost the same regardless of issue size. The cost to bidders of the analysis necessary to make a bid (again reflected in the bid) is also almost independent of the size of the issue. The larger the issue, the lower the cost of all these fixed items per dollar of indebtedness. In addition, it is extremely rare for a small district to receive a high rating by agencies, and frequently they will not rate such a district's issue at all. A low rating will result in higher interest, and no rating may even mean no bidders. In this case the issue is usually privately placed with a local bank at a higher interest cost.

There is an alternative for small districts—the Municipal Bond Insurance Association. A school district can secure a commitment from the association to "guarantee unconditionally and irrevocably the full and prompt payment of the principal and interest to the paying agent of the bonds," with the result that rating agencies will give the issue a higher rating than otherwise. Districts pay a premium to the association for this guarantee, the amount based on the association's estimate of the issue's riskiness. It might seem that the premium would not be much less than the cost of higher interest rates if the issue went to market at the lower rating. The association, however, by specializing in small, fiscally sound districts, has been able to charge a premium sufficiently low to save money for these districts.

As with all other steps in the bonding process, care must be taken in the printing. The financial consultant assists in this. If the bonds are not correct in every detail, purchasing banks or brokers will discover the error and the bonds will have to be printed again. The bonds are then sold by the bank or broker to individuals or other institutions. The bonds may either be *coupon bonds*, whose coupons bondholders clip and return each six months to receive their interest payment, or *registered bonds*, the interest paid to the registered owner at the time each payment becomes due. Most bonds are now registered, and the Internal Revenue Service is taking steps to make coupon bonds illegal where the interest is taxable, so that it

[6]Alan Rabinowitz, *Municipal Bond Finance and Administration* (New York: John Wiley, Interscience, 1969), p. 35.

can receive the names of payees from the payer. (School district bonds are, of course, tax-exempt.)

INTEREST AND PRINCIPAL PAYMENTS

A school district could borrow, say, $5 million for twenty years through the sale of bonds, with interest payable semiannually and the entire principal falling due twenty years hence. Such a bond is called a *term bond*. This places a large repayment burden on the district at that future time, and to meet its commitment to redeem the bonds the district would have to establish a *sinking fund* into which it annually placed sufficient money (including interest on the fund) to add up to $5 million by the end of the twenty years. Bonds are not repaid, as are mortgages where each monthly payment is partly principal and partly interest. Instead, each individual bond is a term bond, with only interest paid on it until maturity. Typically, however, not all bonds of an issue will have the same maturity date. Instead, bonds are scheduled for sequential maturity dates: some may be only five-year bonds while others are twenty-year bonds. Maturities are scheduled so that the sum of principal and interest payments for the district is about the same each year. These are called *serial bonds*. An example is given in Table 10.1 for $5 million borrowed at 6 percent interest, with the first payment at the end of the present year, the last payment at the end of twenty years, and annual interest payments on the balance immediately prior to each principal repayment. Note that the sums of principal and interest are not precisely the same each year, for this would require paying a fraction of a thousand dollars in principal each year, but the schedule created here assumes that principal payments are in multiples of $5000. A given number of bonds mature each year, as shown by the schedule and as stated on the face of each bond. Owners of bonds that mature in a given year present them for redemption and are paid face amounts. Except in the last year, annual payments are between $433,000 and $439,000.

The entire issue of bonds schematized in Table 10.1 has a 6 percent *coupon rate*. This means that the school district will pay 6 percent annually on the principal amount of each bond. The bank or broker, however, will make an independent decision on the effective interest rate for each maturity date that will be necessary to attract buyers. The broker will establish this effective interest rate by selling at a higher or lower price than the *par value* of the bond. In the case of a discount, for instance, the buyer may buy a $1000 bond for $960. Nevertheless, interest of $60 per year is paid by the school district (6 percent of $1000), and this amounts to 6.25 percent interest on the purchase price. In addition, when the bond matures the owner will receive the full $1000, or $40 more than was paid. This further increases the effective interest rate. If the bond matures in ten years, the effective *yield to maturity* of the bond will be 6.55 percent; if it matures in twenty years, the yield to maturity will be 6.36 percent. The bank will make these calculations for each maturity date, setting a price on the bonds maturing in each year that will yield the effective interest rate it believes necessary to attract buyers. The sum of these will be the anticipated receipt from sale of the entire issue. The amount bid by the dealer

TABLE 10.1   Schedule of Principal and Interest Payments on a
$5 Million Twenty-Year Bond Issued at 6 Percent Interest

YEAR	INTEREST PAYMENT	PRINCIPAL PAYMENT	TOTAL PAYMENT	PRINCIPAL REMAINING, END OF PERIOD
1	$300,000	$135,000	$435,000	$4,865,000
2	291,900	145,000	436,900	4,720,000
3	283,200	155,000	438,200	4,565,000
4	273,900	165,000	438,900	4,400,000
5	264,000	175,000	439,000	4,225,000
6	253,500	185,000	438,500	4,040,000
7	242,400	195,000	437,400	3,845,000
8	230,700	205,000	435,700	3,640,000
9	218,400	215,000	433,400	3,425,000
10	205,500	230,000	435,500	3,195,000
11	191,700	245,000	436,700	2,950,000
12	177,000	260,000	437,000	2,690,000
13	161,400	275,000	436,400	2,415,000
14	144,900	290,000	434,900	2,125,000
15	127,500	310,000	437,500	1,815,000
16	108,900	330,000	438,900	1,485,000
17	89,100	345,000	434,100	1,140,000
18	68,400	365,000	433,400	775,000
19	46,500	390,000	436,500	385,000
20	23,100	385,000	408,100	0

may be more or less than the par value of the bonds, and the difference between anticipated receipts and amount bid is the dealer's gross profit. The award of the bid is based on net interest cost to the district.

It is also common for dealers to adjust bond coupon rates (within limits stipulated by the school district) as another way to establish a yield to maturity that will be attractive to investors. Table 10.2 displays a ten-year bond with different coupon rates.

Table 10.2 also displays calculations made to determine net interest cost to the district, bond offering price to individual investors, yield to maturity based on offering price, and calculations necessary to determine dealer profit. A brief explanation should clarify details of the table.

Principal and interest payments are assumed to be made at the end of each year (actually, interest payments are usually made semiannually, but for simplicity annual payments have been assumed). The principal amount due at the end of each year is shown in column 2, with the total amount of the issue being $5,000,000. Column 3 shows a separate coupon rate (the rate of interest paid by the district on the bond's par value) for bonds that mature in different years, ranging from 5.50 percent to 6.30 percent. In column 4 the principal amount is multiplied by the number of years to maturity. Column 5 multiplies the coupon rate by bond years to provide the total interest paid during the life of bonds of each maturity. The total of

TABLE 10.2 A Ten-Year Bond at Differing Coupon Rates

YEAR	PRINCIPAL AMOUNT	RATE	BOND YEARS (1)X(2)	INTEREST COST (3)X(4)	OFFERING PRICE	PRODUCTION (2)X(6)	YIELD TO MATURITY
(1)	(2)	(3)	(4)	(5)	(6)	(7)	(8)
1	$350,000	6.00 %	$350,000	$21,000	100.38	$351,330	5.60 %
2	400,000	6.00	800,000	48,000	100.65	402,600	5.65
3	450,000	5.90	1,350,000	79,650	100.54	452,430	5.70
4	450,000	5.85	1,800,000	105,300	100.35	451,575	5.75
5	500,000	5.90	2,500,000	147,500	100.64	503,200	5.75
6	550,000	6.00	3,300,000	198,000	101.00	555,500	5.80
7	600,000	6.10	4,200,000	256,200	101.13	606,780	5.90
8	650,000	6.20	5,200,000	322,400	101.57	660,205	5.95
9	700,000	6.30	6,300,000	396,900	102.06	714,420	6.00
10	350,000	5.50	3,500,000	192,500	95.92	335,720	6.05
	5,000,000		29,300,000	1,767,450		5,033,760	

Net Interest Cost $= \dfrac{\text{Total Interest Cost} - \text{Premium}}{\text{Bond Years}}$

$= \dfrac{1,767,450 - 1,000}{29,300,000}$

$= .060288$, or 6.0288 percent

Profit $=$ Production $-$ Amount paid for issue
$= 5,033,760 - 5,001,000$
$= \$32,760$

column 5 is the total interest paid during the life of the bond issue. This amount, less any premium paid by the dealer on the purchase, divided by total bond years, results in the net interest cost to the school district. In this case, the dealer offered to buy the bonds for $5,001,000, thus paying a premium of $1000. The calculations at the bottom of the table show that the net interest cost to the district is 6.0288 percent.

The dealer decides what yield to maturity must be offered to attract buyers. In general, the longer the maturity, the higher the yield to maturity must be. The dealer will decide what offering price will be attractive. Knowing offering price, desired yield to maturity, and years to maturity makes it possible, using a bond table or a special calculator, to calculate the coupon rate necessary for the bond. This rough calculation usually produces an uneven interest rate. For example, the dealer may decide to sell bonds maturing in three years at an offering price of 100.50. (The price of a bond is always expressed in terms of the percentage of par value at which the bond is priced. Thus, a $1000 bond priced at 100.50 will cost $1,005.00.) Using this calculation, we arrived at a coupon rate of 5.8837 percent. This rate is then rounded off to 5.90 percent and the offering price recalculated to 100.54.

Production, the money gained through sale of bonds at each maturity, is shown in column 7. It is a product of the principal amount and the offering price (divided by 100). The total of column 7 is the total anticipated by the dealer from the sale of the bonds, and this, less the amount paid for the bonds, is the dealer's gross profit.

Note that the dealer plans to sell most of the bonds at a premium. However, those with a ten-year maturity have been tailored for a particular customer, who for tax reasons prefers to buy a low-coupon bond at a discount rather than a higher-coupon bond at a premium. This customer still receives a higher yield to maturity than any other purchaser.

Money to pay principal and interest on bonds is usually set aside by the district in a special *bond interest and redemption fund.* Each year a tax is levied sufficient (along with any balance in the fund) to pay the interest on all outstanding bonds and to redeem all bonds that mature during the year. Bonds are a legal obligation of the district, and neither the school board nor voters can refuse to levy the tax necessary to pay them. The decision made at the time the bond issue was approved by voters binds the district as long as any bonds of the issue are outstanding.

Money from sale of bonds is received almost immediately (usually within three weeks of the bid date), but is spent over a period of perhaps two or more years as construction progresses. Meanwhile it is invested in whatever ways are allowed under state statute. Typically, it may be put into other government securities. It is interesting that it is frequently possible to invest idle funds at a higher interest rate than it is necessary to pay on them. Doing this is called *arbitrage.* Investment must be carefully planned, of course, so that portions can be liquidated as necessary to make payments on construction contracts.

Ways of Financing Capital Improvements

The way most school construction is financed presents several problems. One of them is the increased difficulty in passing bond elections. As mentioned, the rate of approval of bonds by the public plummeted in the 1970s and early 1980s. People may be reacting to the general taxation level by rejecting new taxes on which they have an opportunity to vote. That a number of states have passed laws or constitutional amendments restricting tax increases testifies to this.

Another problem is that the cost of borrowing has increased substantially. Shortly after World War II, interest rates on municipal bonds averaged only 1.3 percent; by 1967 the rate was 4 percent, in 1976 it was 6.8 percent, and by 1985 it was about 9.5 percent. Part of this upsurge reflects a general increase in the interest cost of all money, for reasons that have to do with the national and world economy. Part of the increase, however, has been the result of a narrowing of the gap between the interest rates of *municipal bonds* and those of taxable bonds. Interest on municipal bonds is not even reported as income to the IRS, and is thus completely untaxed. Such income is of great benefit to highly taxed individuals, who are thus willing to buy such bonds at an interest rate lower than they would pay for a taxable bond. However, some of the major money sources are now eligible for tax breaks on ordinary interest, among them life insurance companies, mutual savings banks, and pension funds. Nontaxability of municipal bonds thus becomes unimportant to them, and lower yields then make them unattractive. The clientele for municipal bonds is now limited chiefly to commercial banks and highly taxed individuals. But even to these buyers, the reduction of maximum tax rates accompanying the federal income tax reform of 1986 reduced the attractiveness of municipal bonds. Both of these occurrences have narrowed the difference in interest rates, and thus the subsidy conferred by the federal government on local governments.

Another problem with the usual way of financing school construction is the limit set by all states on the amounts a school district can borrow, usually expressed as a percentage of assessed valuation. The intent is to prevent present voters from saddling future residents with unmanageable debt. Rapidly growing school districts have found themselves reaching this borrowing limit with no way to satisfy the needs of unhoused students. Then too, many states do not aid districts with construction, but force them to do it on their own. The property-poor district, perhaps able to have a good instructional program because of aid provided by an equitable state system for current expenditures, may find it cannot afford to build schools to house the program. Although this may seem as inequitable as the current-expenditure inequities attacked in *Serrano* and its progeny, it has almost never been litigated, and inequities remain in most states.[7]

The most complete answer to the problem of equity is for the state to assume total responsibility for school construction, an experiment that has been tried with varying success in California, Florida, and Maryland. In California, the 1978 passage of Proposition 13 made it impossible for school districts (or any other level of government) to increase the property tax rate, which was frozen at 1 percent for all governmental purposes. Thus, bond elections could not be held, and districts could not borrow money through that mechanism. Prior to Proposition 13, the state had had an aid mechanism for helping school districts that were property-poor or fast-growing. It called for state loans to those districts, to be paid back over thirty years by a specified tax levy, with the unpaid balance at the end of that time forgiven. After passage of Proposition 13, the loan program became a grant program. The state provided all of the money for construction. The whole process became highly centralized. A district's need for school housing is determined by enrollment projections overseen by the state. The district must submit detailed plans of each school in the district, so the state may determine, through its square footage guidelines, how many students present schools will accommodate. The difference between capacity and need is what the district is entitled to from the state. However, the state also supervises every detail of planning and construction. The whole process generates an enormous amount of paperwork, which has overwhelmed the state agency. Construction authorizations and grants of construction funds have fallen far behind actual needs, particularly in fast-growing school districts. Part of the problem is clearly the result of the agency's being submerged in unexpected paperwork. But there are also problems that attend bureaucratic centralization—attempts to establish rules that fit all situations and thus become overly complicated; an insistence by state employees on adhering to the letter of the regulations, even when they clearly have an adverse effect on education in a particular district; delays

---

[7]Discrimination in capital outlay was declared unconstitutional by an Arizona court in *Hollins* v. *Shofstall*, Civil No. C-253652 (Arizona Superior Court, June 1, 1972) rev'd 110 Ariz 88, 515 P.2d 590 (1973), but the decision was overturned by the Arizona Supreme Court.

that result from many layers of required approval. All in all, the situation in California is a difficult one. It can, however, be said that all districts are being treated in a fashion that is procedurally equitable.

There are, of course, alternatives for financing school construction that lie between the extremes of full state assumption on the one hand and complete local effort on the other. New York provides state funds on a percentage equalizing basis. The district decides what it wants to build and how much it wishes to spend. The state shares the cost of construction, with the percentage share depending upon district wealth. This system allows much more local discretion in school construction, but is of little comfort to the district that is unable to pass a bond election or has reached its legal bonding limit.

At the other end of the scale is a system long in wide use in the South, although most southern states have now replaced it. A fixed number of dollars per student is provided to each district each year for construction, regardless of district need. Districts with declining enrollment find no need for this money and simply put it into interest-bearing accounts; districts with increasing enrollments usually find the amount grossly inadequate. Little can be said in favor of this plan except that it is simple and preserves local discretion.

Many states provide no assistance for capital outlay. Because construction cost accounts for a smaller proportion of the school budget than operating cost, there have been fewer efforts to equalize it. It is a fertile field for reform.

SUMMARY

This chapter has discussed two main topics—capital construction and debt. This is fitting, because major long-term debt is usually associated with construction of a school.

Building a school is a complex process. First the need must be determined. This involves making enrollment projections, as well as exploring alternatives to construction. Assuming that construction is necessary, land must be obtained. The problems a public body such as a school district has in purchasing land on the open market often make it necessary to use the government's right of eminent domain— its ability to take property (but for a fair price).

An architect must be engaged. This is a critical decision, for the wrong architect can make major errors that the district will have to tolerate for many years. The architect should be experienced in building schools, have an adequate and capable staff, and be able to work well with district representatives. Architectural planning is a cooperative enterprise between district and architect. The district must first develop its educational specifications. As the architect develops plans, they must be reviewed carefully by the district and finally approved by the school board.

Plans are made available to contractors, sealed bids are opened at a specific time, and the bid awarded to the lowest responsible bidder. During construction the architect frequently inspects progress. However, the district must have its own inspector on duty at the project at all times. Progress payments are made to the contractor during construction, but final payment is withheld for a specified period after acceptance of the building to allow for the possibility of mechanic's liens.

Long before the school is complete, furniture and equipment must be ordered and personnel selected for the school.

There are three kinds of debt. That which is owed to vendors and will be paid promptly is called accounts payable. It is debt in the sense that the district owes the money, but it is simply part of the ongoing business of the district. The second type of debt is short-term debt, usually money borrowed from a local bank because of cash-flow problems and repaid within the current school year. The third type of debt, long-term debt, is repaid over many years and is usually used as a source of money for capital construction. Districts issue bonds as evidence of long-term indebtedness.

Authorizing and issuing bonds is complicated and must be done carefully, for any legally questionable actions during the process will render the bonds unsalable. The process starts with official authorization of a bond election by the school board. All steps in this authorization and subsequent election must be carefully monitored for adherence to legal requirements.

If the bonds are approved in the election, the district may advertise them for sale. The whole issue is sold to a bank, brokerage, or consortium of financial houses. As with construction, sealed bids are received. The issue is awarded to the bidder whose bid represents the lowest net interest cost to the district. The bidder then resells the bonds to individuals.

chapter eleven

MANAGING HUMAN RESOURCES

Agriculture in the United States has evolved to the point where each farmer now produces food for forty other persons. Fifty years ago it took ten farmers to accomplish the same result.[1] Widespread use of machinery, development of high-yield seed stock and animal breeds, intense use of chemical fertilizers, and new planting and harvesting techniques have already resulted in extraordinary gains in farm productivity. Bioengineering based on gene splicing portends equally dramatic future gains in agricultural efficiency. Electronic automation has had a similar effect on the communications industry, and use of light amplification, superconductivity, and fiber optics may have an equal revolutionary influence. If the U.S. were still using outmoded manual telephone equipment, virtually half the population would now be engaged in servicing telephone calls for the remainder, assuming the current volume of traffic.

In contrast with agriculture, communication, manufacturing, and many other sectors of the economy, education has remained remarkably *labor-intensive*. There has been relatively little substitution of capital for labor. Indeed, education appears to have become even more labor-intensive over time. Fifty years ago there was one licensed teacher for every thirty public school pupils. Even as recently as 1960,

[1] U.S. Bureau of the Census, *Statistical Abstract of the United States, 1985* (Washington, D.C.: Government Printing Office, 1986), p. 631.

each professional educator was responsible for an average of more than twenty-five students.[2] By 1985, each public school teacher was serving only 17.9 students.[3] (See Figure 11.1.) This reduction in productivity took place at the same time as a substantial growth in the numbers of so-called nonclassroom professionals, such as school psychologists. If these additional personnel were taken into account, school labor productivity measures might sink even further.

The argument here is not for larger classes, nor are we contending that U.S. teachers have become lazy. Rather, the point is that few societal undertakings have depended so heavily upon labor and been so impervious to substitution of capital for labor as has education. As a consequence, more and more teachers have been hired and the cost of school services has steadily increased. Moreover, despite added per-pupil revenues, teacher salaries remain relatively low compared with those of other professional occupations and the purchasing power of teachers' salaries in other nations. Perhaps as a consequence the field attracts insufficient numbers of the most able individuals.[4]

Salaries for classroom teachers absorbed approximately $60 billion in 1987 dollars. To elevate average teacher salaries to $40,000 in that year would have cost approximately $35 billion additionally. Such huge increases are improbable. Society seems unlikely to continue allocating public resources to education in amounts that would permit ever more favorable educator-pupil ratios and substantially higher salaries for the entire teacher work force. Thus, unless an acceptable means is found to enhance education work force productivity, the delivery of school services is

FIGURE 11.1   Pupil–Teacher Ratios, 1938–90

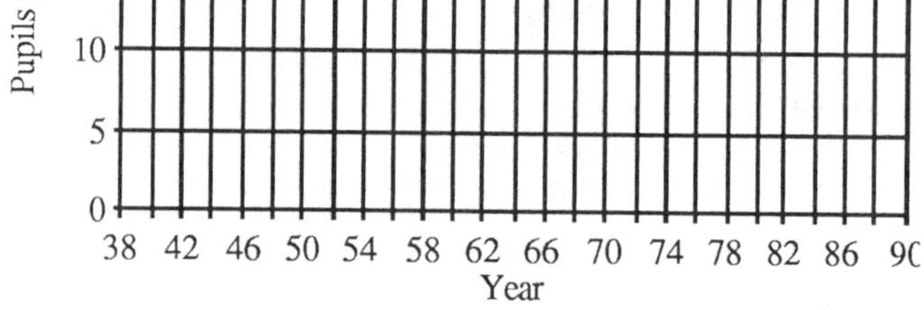

Source: *Digest of Educational Statistics,* Center for Education Statistics, U.S. Department of Education (Washington, D.C., May 1987), p. 57.

[2]W. Vance Grant and Thomas D. Snyder, *Digest of Educational Statistics, 1983–84* (Washington, D.C.: Government Printing Office, 1984), p. 197.

[3]U.S. Department of Education, National Center for Educational Statistics, *Conditions of Education* (Washington, D.C.: Government Printing Office, 1985).

[4]See Lee S. Schulman and Gary Sykes, eds., *Handbook of Teaching and Policy* (New York: Longman, 1983).

threatened by a sustained and self-reinforcing downward spiral in the quality of education personnel.

Chapter 12 describes selected technologies and the prospect they hold for improving instruction. Chapter 14 describes procedures by which schools generally can be rendered more productive. However, there is no technology or incentive system described in these chapters or appearing on the immediate horizon that promises to revolutionize delivery of instruction. Rather, improvements in education, at least in the short run, are more likely to result from improved performance by people. Such is the focus of this chapter, which describes the magnitude of the U.S. educator work force, its characteristics and costs, and the conditions that presently impede its effectiveness. The chapter concludes with an illustrative plan for professionalizing teaching in the United States.

THE U.S. EDUCATION WORK FORCE

Magnitude and Deployment

Public school systems in the United States presently employ approximately 4 million individuals.[5] Of this number, approximately 3 million are so-called *certificated* employees. (The comparable figure in 1950 was slightly less than 1 million.) These individuals hold professional licenses—certificates—from a state authorizing their eligibility for professional employment in public education agencies. There are also approximately 1 million persons who generally occupy civil service–like positions and work as school district cafeteria workers, bus drivers, maintenance personnel, secretaries, and so on. These are known as *classified* employees.[6]

The overwhelming proportion of certificated employees are teachers (approximately 2.3 million in 1987), responsible for regularly instructing students in day-long classes or in subject-matter areas, such as English, science, and history. Additionally, approximately 600,000 licensed employees serve outside of regular classrooms in positions such as counselors, supervising teachers, and school psychologists. Approximately 100,000 individuals are administrators—superintendents, central office staff, principals, and so on. The major change in this pattern has been the growth since 1965 in nonclassroom teaching personnel, many of whose salaries are paid from federal categorical aid program funds. The work force is divided almost evenly between elementary and secondary personnel.

Unionization and Political Dynamics

Between 1960 and 1985, the U.S. education work force underwent three major organizational changes. Its membership overwhelmingly became (1) unionized, (2)

---

[5]On the American education work force, see generally Arthur E. Wise, "Three Scenarios for the Future of Teaching," *Kappan*, 67, no. 9 (May 1986), 649–53.

[6]Figures in this and the following paragraph are taken from Grant and Snyder, *Digest of Educational Statistics, 1983–84*, p. 51.

fragmented into labor- and management-oriented groups, and (3) highly active politically. Both the American Federation of Teachers and the National Education Association have deep historical roots.[7] However, the NEA has long been the numerically larger organization. Moreover, until the advent of 1960s and 1970s union militancy, the NEA was also an umbrella organization encompassing educational administration associations as well as teachers. The NEA was an organizational base for both management and labor. Widespread adoption of collective bargaining altered this alignment.

In 1960 the United Federation of Teachers (an AFT affiliate) gained the right to represent New York City teachers at the bargaining table. This event signaled the beginning of unionization and collective bargaining throughout the United States and launched an intense, and often bitter, struggle between the AFT and NEA for membership dominance. To appear more attractive to prospective union members, each organization adopted an increasingly militant posture toward management. Unions attempted to define working conditions more specifically, challenged administrators' evaluation procedures, worked for agency shop provisions, and went on strike. By 1970 the NEA had emerged as a clear numerical winner with more than 1.6 million dues-paying members in its state and local affiliates. Though smaller (600,000 members), the AFT has remained dominant in many large city districts. The NEA majority is located generally in smaller cities and suburban and rural districts.

A consequence of the union organizing struggle was alienation of administrators and eventual formation of autonomous management associations, primarily the American Association of School Administrators (AASA) and the National School Boards Association (NSBA).

Union militancy also carried into the political arena. Beginning in the 1960s, educator organizations intensified their support of electoral candidates—local, state, and federal—and their advocacy activities in state capitals and Washington, D.C. (Local teacher advocacy takes place primarily, though not exclusively, in the bargaining process.) Frequently the highest-spending registered lobby in a state will be the NEA affiliate. Even if usually less well financed, the AFT can influence both state and local policy issues, both by conducting its own political activities and by lobbying as a member of the national AFL–CIO.

In 1976 the NEA altered its conventional stance of candidate neutrality and endorsed the presidential candidacy of Jimmy Carter. It is often reported that, in exchange, Carter promised to propose a federal Department of Education. He was loyal to what may have been a campaign promise, and early in his presidency he sent a bill to Congress to divide the Department of Health, Education and Welfare into a Department of Health and Human Services and a new Department of Education.

---

[7]Histories of the two unions can be found in William Edward Eaton, *The American Federation of Teachers 1916–61: A History of the Movement* (Carbondale: Southern Illinois University Press, 1975); Edgar B. Wesley, *NEA: The Building of a Teaching Profession* (New York: Harper & Brothers, 1957); and Lorraine McDonnell and Anthony Pascal, *Organized Teachers in American Schools* (Santa Monica, Calif.: Rand Corporation, 1979).

The proposal was controversial even among educators. The AFT, perhaps as part of its power struggle with the NEA, opposed formation of the new department. Nevertheless, the proposal was enacted. In 1980 the NEA again endorsed Carter and opposed Reagan. The latter specified in his campaign that if elected he would disband the new Education Department. However, at no time did the Reagan administration seriously attempt to dismantle the Education Department.[8]

Despite such conflict, at least at the rhetorical level, both the NEA and the AFT appear set on a sustained course of political activism. It is not so clear that their organizational rivalry will continue. Merger discussions between various state affiliates appear ever more serious. Should the two unions become one, it would be among the most powerful unions in the world.

Characteristics

Approximately 65 percent of all licensed elementary and secondary educators are women.[9] Elementary teachers are overwhelmingly women. At the secondary level the balance between men and women is slightly reversed, 53 percent male. (Most administrative positions are held by men, though the situation is becoming more balanced.) The average teacher is forty years old and has been employed as a teacher for more than fourteen years. Approximately 85 percent of the education work force is white, 12 percent is black, and the slender remaining proportion comprises Hispanics, Asians, Native Americans, and others. Seventy-five percent of all licensed educators belong to a union. (These and other data are summarized in Table 1.4, page 18.)

PREPARATION AND QUALIFICATIONS

If measured by level of education attained, the U.S. teacher work force appears highly qualified. The overwhelming majority (99.6 percent) of public school instructors and administrators possess a four-year college degree. An increasing proportion (49.3 percent) possess master's degrees as well. Virtually all of these advanced degrees are in education.

The modal U.S. teacher has seventeen years of schooling, five of which are at the college level. According to 1980 Census results, the median years of schooling in the adult U.S. population were 12.5. Only 9 percent of the adult population matches the average level of college education held by the teacher work force. However, the level-of-schooling gap between the general population and teachers has been closing rapidly. That most members of the total U.S. work force now have some college experience partly explains the diminished prestige of the education profession.

By measures other than level of education, teachers as an occupational classification do not appear highly qualified. Undergraduate students preparing to major in education possessed the second lowest Scholastic Aptitude Test (SAT) average

---

[8] A history of the dissolution effort is provided in Terrel H. Bell, *The Thirteenth Man: A Reagan Cabinet Memoir*, (New York: Free Press, 1987).

[9] Figures taken from Grant and Snyder, *Digest of Educational Statistics, 1983–84*, p. 51.

among thirteen undergraduate majors. Education majors are also among the lowest classification of those taking the Graduate Record Examination (GRE).[10] Moreover, the qualifications of those entering teaching appear to have declined between 1970 and 1985. This may be due in part to the added professional career opportunities now available to women and minorities. Teaching once represented a major, indeed virtually exclusive, avenue for professional advancement for women and many minority-group individuals. By the mid 1970s this condition had begun to change; for example, almost half of entering medical and law school classes are now women. Greater equity for women and others is doubtless in the long-run best interests of society. However, its short-run effect has been to dilute the talent pool of those individuals from whom the education work force is drawn.

The quality problem among new teachers is exacerbated by diminished public respect for teaching. Whereas teaching was once viewed as an effective avenue for professional advancement among low- and middle-income households, it now appears to have dwindled in attractiveness. For example, in a 1983 survey only 45 percent of parents responded that they would be pleased if their son or daughter selected teaching as a career. Only fourteen years previously, 75 percent responded that they would have been pleased. Not surprisingly, the proportion of entering college students expressing an interest in teaching declined concomitantly. In 1970, 19.3 percent asserted they were planning to become teachers. By 1982 the percentage had declined to 4.7. In part, dwindling interest reflects perceptions of decreased job availability during a period of enrollment decline. However, it probably also signaled a dip in the status of teaching as a career.[11] These conditions are not irreversible, and brighter job prospects and higher salaries in the latter 1980s may be altering the trend. A 1987 Bureau of Labor Statistics publication suggests that more people are being attracted to teaching by higher salaries.[12]

Professional Preparation and Licensing

States are legally empowered to establish minimum standards for teacher training and licensing. Local school districts are constrained by statute and may employ only those individuals possessing appropriate state-specified credentials. Local agencies are generally free to require personnel qualifications in excess of state minima. Their success in doing so, however, depends upon the market balance between teacher supply and demand.

[10]Gary Sykes, "Teacher Preparation and the Teacher Workforce: Problems and Prospects for the 80's," *American Education,* March 1983, pp. 23–29.

[11]Emily C. Feistritzer, *The Conditions of Teaching: A State by State Analysis* (Princeton, N.J.: Carnegie Foundation for the Advancement of Teaching, 1983); and Emily C. Feistritzer, *Teacher Crisis: Myth or Reality?* (Washington D.C.: National Center for Education Information, 1986).

[12]Daniel Hecker in Bureau of Labor Statistics, "Teachers Job Outlook: Is Chicken Little Wrong Again?" *Occupational Outlook Quarterly* (Washington, D.C.: Government Printing Office, 1987). Also, a 1986 poll of high school seniors revealed that 23 percent wanted to become teachers. David L. Clark, "High School Seniors React to Their Teachers and Their Schools," *Kappan,* 68, no. 7 (March 1987), 503–9.

States with the lowest teacher-training standards typically require only a bachelor's degree obtained in a four-year prescribed course of study at an accredited college or university. States vary in the extent to which they specify the balance in such undergraduate programs between subject-matter courses and professional training—*pedagogy*. States with minimum teacher-training criteria increasingly specify that once employed, a teacher must continue his or her professional preparation by adding more courses or even obtaining a master's degree. The most rigorous state requirements specify a fifth year of college or a graduate year of preparation as a minimum qualification for initial employment as a public school teacher.

Traditionally in the United States, little professional preparation has been required of prospective teachers. Daniel Lortie, a scholar specializing in the sociology of teaching, describes this condition as *eased entry*.[13] By contrast, requirements to be a licensed physician, attorney, engineer, accountant, or architect are more rigorous. This condition has also contributed to the diminished professional status of teaching in the United States. Indeed, teaching is sometimes referred to as a *semiprofession*.[14]

The mid 1980s were marked by a wave of proposals for injecting added rigor into teacher training. The National Commission for Accreditation in Teacher Education (NCATE) advocated higher standards, such as a higher grade-point average for admission, passage of subject-matter tests, and a longer internship. Another organization, the so-called Holmes Group (named after a former Harvard Education School dean) issued a far-reaching report in 1986 calling for vastly increased teacher-training standards, including a fifth year of training before certification.[15] The Carnegie Forum on Education and the Economy issued the most far-reaching report of all. This document, *A Nation Prepared: Teachers for the 21st Century,* advocated many pathbreaking ideas, including national teacher-controlled professional licensing boards.[16]

Unfortunately, efforts to intensify qualifications have often been diluted, particularly during teacher shortages. To contain salaries and still maintain a stream of entry-level teachers, state legislatures and other public officials, occasionally with the urging of professional administrators, reduce teacher certification requirements.

States rely primarily upon a *program approval* strategy for licensing teachers and other education professionals, such as school psychologists, administrators, and specialists. A state agency, perhaps a component of the state education department or an independent commission within the executive branch, specifies minimum

---

[13]Daniel C. Lortie, *School Teacher: A Sociological Study* (Chicago: University of Chicago Press, 1975).

[14]Nathan Glazer, "The Schools of the Minor Professions," *Minerva*, 12, no. 3 (July 1974), p. 350. The historical relationship between "professionalism" and public status of an occupation, teaching included, is described by Walter P. Metzger, "The Spector of 'Professionism,'" *Educational Researcher* 16, no. 6 (August-September, 1987), p. 10-18.

[15]*Tomorrow's Teachers: A Report of the Holmes Group* (East Lansing, Mich.: Holmes Group, 1986). The equivalent report for school administrators is *Leaders for America's Schools,* Report of the National Commission on Excellence in Educational Administration (New York: University Council on Educational Administration, 1987).

[16]Carnegie Forum on Education and the Economy, *A Nation Prepared: Teachers for the 21st Century* (New York: Carnegie Forum, 1986).

components of a professional course of study for a particular credential classification. Schools of education are then expected to ensure that credential candidates enroll in the required courses.[17] Completion of statutorily specified programs is then taken by the state as sufficient evidence of preparation, and a candidate is issued a credential qualifying him or her for initial public school employment. State agents may conduct periodic site visits to a school of education, much as an accreditation team would. Such visits are generally scheduled well in advance and preparation is undertaken by the school of education's faculty, staff, and student body so that the best image is presented. Withdrawal of state approval is rare.

In contrast with the eased entry condition of education, professions such as medicine, law, and architecture do not depend completely upon a program approval strategy for determining candidate eligibility. In these fields, candidates must sit for an examination, serve an apprenticeship under a mentor, and be interviewed by a board or panel of senior professionals in the field. In these instances, civil authority, the state, and the profession usually cooperate in assessing candidate qualifications. That a candidate for professional entry attended an "approved" institution is by itself insufficient.[18]

WORKING CONDITIONS AND ORGANIZATIONAL DYNAMICS

The physical and social surroundings in which teachers work also separate them from other full professions. Most instruction is conducted in a self-contained classroom. An elementary-level instructor typically will have responsibility for approximately thirty students during a five-to-six-hour school day. A secondary-level instructor typically will have responsibility for five classes of thirty students, each of which meets for fifty or fifty-five minutes five times a week. Secondary instructors may be assigned a "free" period each day for preparing for classes. Some school districts also accord preparation periods for elementary teachers, but this is not as common. It is unusual for a teacher to have a separate office. About the best that the typical teacher can expect is to be permanently assigned to a classroom that can be used as a home base for storing supplies and maintaining records.

Schools, as most everyone knows, are seldom architecturally imposing, nor are they sumptuous physically. They are generally constructed to be safe, but there is little about most of them that is commodious, either for teachers or for students. Seldom do teachers have surroundings as comfortable or pleasant as those available to the majority of physicians, attorneys, or business professionals.

[17]For more information on teacher training see Geraldine J. Clifford and James W. Guthrie, *Ed School: A Brief for Professional Education* (Chicago: University of Chicago Press, 1988).

[18]For additional information see Harold Orlans, *Private Accreditation and Public Eligibility* (Lexington, Mass.: Heath, 1975), chap. 1; Robert Kirkwood, "Accreditation," *Encyclopedia of Educational Research,* 5th ed., vol. 1, ed. H. E. Mitzel (New York: Free Press, 1982); and Kent W. Leach, "History of Purposes of Accreditation," *National Elementary Principal,* 43, no. 2 (May 1964), 36–41.

The social environment in schools is often on a par with their physical settings. Teachers generally engage in instruction isolated from other adults. Elementary teachers may be assisted by an instructional aide and occasionally by parent volunteers. It is otherwise unusual for another adult to be in the classroom with an instructor and students. Exceptions occur most notably when a student teacher may be present or an administrator is visiting for evaluation purposes. This degree of adult isolation is unusual for professionals and may contribute to the occupational burnout that afflicts many teachers.

In that virtually all teachers hold similar professional status, it is seldom that a school or school district has a formal organizational hierarchy for instructors. Higher status levels exist, but they are occupied by administrators. Teachers, in part because of the physical isolation accompanying their instructional duties, seldom share responsibility or have opportunities to engage in professional exchanges. It is unusual for teachers to observe and assess one another's teaching. In contrast, attorneys often cooperate in writing briefs or advising clients; physicians seek advice and cooperation from and are frequently subject to the scrutiny of professional peers; and the commercial success of architects often depends heavily upon team efforts and peer reviews.

Teachers are virtually unique in their professional isolation and the absence of a status hierarchy based on level of expertise or professional training. This insularity carries over into conventional areas of professional responsibility such as evaluation. Teachers, in the absence of clear professional performance standards and not possessing a professional identity, typically are reluctant to evaluate peers, leaving this task to administrators, if it is done at all.[19]

TEACHER OPINION

A national poll conducted by Louis Harris for the Metropolitan Life Insurance Company revealed that the overwhelming percentage of teachers (81 percent) are at least partially satisfied with their work, and 40 percent are very satisfied.[20] Comparable figures for the overall working public are 87 percent and 52 percent. The part of their job teachers like best is actually teaching. Ninety-six percent of teachers agreed with the statement "I love to teach." Seventy-eight percent agreed strongly. Teachers in city school districts felt less strongly about teaching, but otherwise there was no difference across ages, regions of the nation, or grade levels taught.

Seventy percent of teachers believe they are recognized for good performance. However, teachers also report a number of conditions that are distressing to them. For example, 72 percent believe they must spend too much time on administrative tasks. Half those surveyed think their training did not adequately prepare them for teaching. More than half report they do not feel respected by the public for their ef-

[19]In 1986 Albert Shanker, the AFT President, began to advocate greater peer responsibility for teaching standards. However, little practical change has yet occurred on this dimension.

[20]These opinion poll results are taken from a survey entitled *The American Teacher* (Hartford, Conn.: Metropolitan Life Insurance Co., 1984).

forts in teaching, and almost two-thirds do not think their jobs pay them a decent salary.

Most teachers rate their home schools highly. Nine out of ten report that the quality of education in their school is either excellent or good, and 42 percent say it is excellent. Only 7 percent report the quality to be fair, and 1 percent said it was poor. High school teachers, teachers with less experience, and male teachers are significantly less likely than elementary and junior high school teachers, teachers with more experience, and female teachers to say the quality of education in their schools is excellent.

Inadequate financial support for the school and students' lack of interest in their classes are seen by teachers as the two most serious problems. Each of these issues is seen as serious by almost two-thirds of the teachers surveyed, and one in five reports the problem to be very serious. Overcrowded classrooms, lack of discipline, drugs, difficulties in obtaining sufficient numbers of qualified teachers, and teachers' lack of interest in their work are, in that order, seen as the next most serious problems. One in four teachers also reports that drinking among students is at least a somewhat serious problem.

It is interesting to note that parents repeatedly report in national surveys that student discipline and use of drugs are the most serious problems. Teachers clearly hold different views.

Contrary to conventional wisdom, teachers report an acceptance of education reform proposals, including those directed at making teachers more accountable to the public. Rendering the school curriculum more rigorous, tightening high school graduation requirements, and elevating student discipline standards are all supported by large percentages of teachers. Similarly, teachers express support for testing new entrants to the profession, creating professional career ladders, being retested periodically on their subject-matter knowledge, and using student test scores as a means of measuring their productivity. Results such as these make it difficult to assert that teachers as individuals are major impediments to reforms intended to enhance educational productivity.

LABOR MARKETS AND TEACHER SALARIES

Education salaries are notably low, perhaps reflecting the eased entry, the relatively low qualifications of many entrants, the quasi-professional nature of the profession, and its low social status. Also, teacher salaries are sensitive to labor market conditions. For example, during a brief period in the 1960s, teacher salaries were slightly higher than the compensation awarded other occupations requiring comparable training. This condition may well have reflected the high labor market demand at that time; the post–World War II baby boom cohort of students was then swelling school enrollments, and there was a shortage of qualified teachers. Also, the entire U.S. economy was then in a state of high growth.

TABLE 11.1 Average Starting Salaries of Public School Teachers Compared With Starting Salaries in Private Industry: 1973–74, 1980–81, and 1981–82

POSITION/FIELD	1973–74	1980–81	1981–82	PERCENTAGE CHANGE 1981–82 OVER 1980–81	PERCENTAGE CHANGE 1981–82 OVER 1973–74
Average minimum salary for teachers with bachelor's degrees	$7,720	$11,758	$12,769	8.6	65.4
College graduates with bachelor's degrees:					
Engineering	11,220	20,136	22,368	11.1	99.3
Accounting	10,632	15,720	16,980	8.0	59.7
Sales–Marketing	9,660	15,936	17,200	8.1	78.3
Business Administration	8,796	14,100	16,200	14.9	84.2
Liberal Arts	8,808	13,286	15,444	16.2	75.3
Chemistry	10,308	17,124	19,546	14.1	89.5
Math–Statistics	10,020	17,604	18,600	5.7	85.6
Economics–Finance	9,624	14,472	16,884	16.7	75.4
Computer Science	N.A.	17,712	20,364	15.0	N.A.
Other Fields	9,696	17,544	20,028	14.2	106.6

Source: Emily C. Feistritzer, *The Condition of Teaching: A State by State Analysis* (Princeton, Carnegie Foundation for the Advancement of Teaching, 1983), citing *Prices, Budgets, Salaries, and Income: 1982a* (Washington, D.C.: National Education Association, 1981), p. 12; and *Prices, Budgets, Salaries, and Income: 1983* (Washington: National Education Association, 1983), p. 22.

Since that time, and particularly from 1978 to 1983, teacher salaries have lagged significantly behind occupations requiring comparable training (see Table 11.1). Rampant inflation in the late 1970s coupled with an intense economic recession in the early 1980s resulted in national average teacher salaries falling behind inflation by approximately 18 percent. Few other professional occupational categories were affected as deeply by economic instability during the period. There was a surplus of teacher candidates.

Public school enrollments in many states declined rapidly. Schools needed only a few new teachers; many districts undertook what came to be known as a *reduction in force* (RIF). The few districts hiring teachers had a large number of qualified candidates available and found it unnecessary to elevate entry-level salaries to attract new teachers. Teacher unionization expanded widely from mid 1970 through the early 1980s. Also, the average time of college education for teachers in training increased during this period. However, neither collective bargaining nor higher professional qualifications were sufficient to counter the apparent downward drag of a surplus labor pool upon educator salaries. Figure 11.2 displays average U.S. teacher salaries from 1950 to 1982. The value of the dollar is held constant in

FIGURE 11.2   Teacher Salaries 1950–82 (in 1981–82 Dollars)

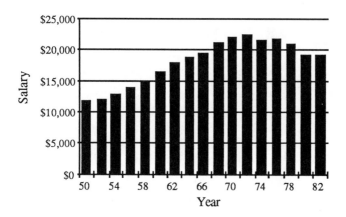

Source: *Digest of Educational Statistics*, Center for Education Statistics, U.S. Department of Education, selected years.

these analyses. What is evident is that salaries rise and fall consistent with the demand for teachers.

Potential teachers learn about employment market conditions and shape their behavior accordingly. However, there is sometimes an information lag; jobs may become available two or three years before the situation is widely publicized. Similarly, it took time before prospective teachers realized the growing surplus in the 1970s. Nevertheless, by 1980 enrollments in teacher training institutions had almost been halved in comparison with their 1970 level. By the mid 1980s, public school enrollments were again beginning to climb and the National Center for Educational Statistics (NCES) projected a teacher shortage. Enrollments in schools of education showed signs of expanding, and salaries increased in terms of purchasing power and relative to the overall work force.[21]

Market forces exert a strong influence, but labor supply and demand by no means offer a full explanation for teacher salaries. The potential effect of labor unions and collective bargaining has been already mentioned. Also, state governments can statutorily alter minimum qualifications for becoming a teacher, thus easily redefining the pool of those eligible for employment. Pressure is exerted by school administrators and school board members on state officials to ease teachers' entry conditions even further during periods of high demand—for example, permitting so-called *emergency credentials* and hiring teachers to instruct outside of their areas of subject-matter expertise. An expansion of the labor pool, by altering legal definitions of eligibility, can dilute salaries.

[21]Gary Putka, "Teachers Get More Pay and Power in the Wake of Reform Movements," *Wall Street Journal,* Monday, September 21, 1987, p. 27.

Projecting Supply and Demand

Few states undertake the systematic procedures necessary to project teacher supply and demand conditions.[22] This is regrettable from a policy planning standpoint because such projections are not difficult to construct, if an appropriate data base is available. The *demand* side of the equation is easier to specify. Major variable dimensions are (1) enrollments, (2) assumptions regarding class size, and (3) current work-force attrition.[23]

The *supply* side is more difficult to project. If an individual holds a bachelor's degree, time to employment eligibility in most states is a year at most. Also, the state has the ability to alter minimal eligibility requirements. These eased entry conditions render supply relatively fluid and able to respond quickly to employment incentives. Even with this indeterminacy, supply can be estimated from data about (1) teacher training institution enrollments, (2) past experience with out-of-state recruitment, and (3) size and employment elasticity of the reserve pool. This latter variable is particularly difficult to measure.

THE RESERVE POOL

The *teacher reserve pool* comprises those individuals (1) legally eligible to teach, possessing minimum qualifications and a state-issued license, and (2) who can be induced into teaching or into returning to teaching. At one time the U.S. teacher reserve pool was large. It consisted of housewives who, having raised their children, were willing to return to regular employment, or at least to serve as substitute teachers. Now that more than 70 percent of U.S. women between twenty-five and sixty-five are already employed outside the household, most mothers included, and now that women have many professional employment opportunities from which to select in addition to teaching, the reserve pool appears to have dwindled. Moreover, reserve pool members sometimes lack geographic mobility and may not be qualified for the fields of highest demand. A 1985 poll of California reserve pool members suggests that the incentives necessary to induce many such individuals to return to teaching, such as much higher salaries and vastly improved working conditions, may be costly.[24]

[22] A comprehensive economic model of teacher supply and demand is provided by Stephen Barro in "The State of the Art in Projecting Teacher Supply and Demand" (paper prepared under contract for the National Academy of Science, July 1986).

[23] Interesting ideas on teacher supply and demand are to be found in Judith E. Lanier and Judith W. Little, "Research on Teacher Education," in *Handbook of Research on Teaching*, ed. Merlin C. Wittrock (New York: Macmillan, 1986), chap. 19; Helen C. Cagampang, Walter I. Garms, Todd Greenspan, and James W. Guthrie, *Teacher Supply and Demand in California* (Berkeley, Calif.: Policy Analysis for California Education, 1985); and Linda Darling-Hammond, "Teacher Supply and Demand: A Structural Perspective" (paper presented at the 1986 American Education Research Association meetings, San Francisco).

[24] A 1986 Metropolitan Life Insurance Company–sponsored poll of former teachers suggests how difficult it may be to attract teachers back to schools. The majority polled enjoyed teaching, but were making much more in the private sector. Apparently, those who teach can also do.

REMUNERATION

Obviously, salaries, fringe benefits, and other forms of compensation also influence teacher supply.[25] Individuals make occupational choices for a complex and intertwined set of reasons. Some contend that teaching is a calling, which, like the ministry, should not be answered by those motivated by material rewards. Certainly many teachers are altruistic, greatly enjoy working with children and youth, and intensely believe in education's importance. However, individuals also seek employment as teachers in order to earn a living. Research by Ferris and Winkler demonstrates that remuneration is important in influencing the choice of teaching as an occupation. All other things being balanced, larger numbers of more able individuals are attracted to teaching when salaries are high than when they are low.[26] However crass it may appear to some, pay makes a difference in attracting highly qualified individuals to a field.[27]

Table 4.1 (page 80) displays three years of mean U.S. teacher salaries by state. Here we can see wide variation. Alaska has the highest salaries overall.

TABLE 11.2   Certificated Salary Schedule

STEP	CLASS I AB	CLASS II AB + 15	CLASS III AB + 30	CLASS IV AB + 45	CLASS V AB + 60	CLASS VI AB + 75
1	$14,929	$15,865	$16,801	$17,737		
2	15,865	16,801	17,737	18,673	$19,609	
3	16,801	17,737	18,673	19,609	20,545	$21,481
4	17,737	18,673	19,609	20,545	21,481	22,417
5	18,673	19,609	20,545	21,481	22,417	23,353
6	19,609	20,545	21,481	22,417	23,353	24,289
7	20,545	21,481	22,417	23,353	24,289	25,225
8	21,481	22,417	23,353	24,289	25,225	26,161
9	22,417	23,353	24,289	25,225	26,161	27,097
10	23,353	24,289	25,225	26,161	27,097	28,033
11			26,161	27,097	28,033	28,969
12			27,097	28,033	28,969	29,905
13			28,033	28,969	29,905	30,841

Master's: $350 in addition to a teacher's regular placement.
Doctorate: $500 in addition to a teacher's regular placement.

[25]See John Augenblick, *Teachers Salaries and the States* (Denver: Augenblick, Van de Water and Associates, 1984).

[26]James Ferris and Donald Winkler, "Compensation and the Supply of Teachers" (paper commissioned by the California Commission on the Teaching Profession, School of Public Administration, University of Southern California, April 1985).

[27]For detailed discussions of reasons teachers enter and leave teaching, see P. V. Bredeson, M. J. Fruth, and K. L. Kasten, "Organizational Incentives and Secondary School Teaching," *Journal of Research and Development in Education,* 16 (1983), 52–56; D. W. Chapman and S. M. Hutcheson, "Attrition from Teaching Careers: A Discriminant Analysis," *American Educational Research Journal,* 19 (1982), 93–105; and E. V. Frataccia and I. Hennington, "Satisfaction of Hygiene and Motivation Needs of Teachers Who Resigned from Teaching" (paper presented at the annual meeting of the Southwest Educational Research Association, Austin, Texas, 1982).

Among the contiguous forty-eight states, New York, Michigan, and California have the highest average teacher salaries, and Mississippi and South Dakota the lowest. (This is an interesting table because it displays the close connection between average class size and average teacher salary. California pays "high" salaries by sacrificing class size. Except for Utah, it has the largest number of pupils per teacher of any state in the U.S.) Variation in average salaries within states is at least as wide as variation among states.

States generally do not establish teacher salaries. School districts typically rely upon a *salary schedule* containing columns representing years of teaching service and rows representing number of academic units obtained beyond the bachelor's degree. (Table 11.2 illustrates one such schedule). A teacher's salary will be specified by the appropriate row and column intercept. Generally, minimum entry-level salaries (upper left-hand row and column) are set at approximately 50 percent of maximum salaries (lower right-hand row and column). Table 11.3 displays these minimum-to-maximum salary ratios for elementary and secondary teachers in the United States and six other nations. Districts frequently offer bonuses or permanent salary increments for earned M.A. and doctoral degrees. Such bonuses are seldom large.

A salary schedule is generally the outcome of collective bargaining in which the teachers union represents the district's certified employees. The scheduled salary will apply for a school year, be it nine or ten months long. Teachers are not paid for unauthorized absences, such as strikes. The salary for the teaching year, say 180 school days, is often spread over twelve equal pay periods. Teachers' pay usually reflects the assumption that they will not work during the summer. If a teacher is employed for any part of the summer, he or she will generally be paid an additional amount per day according to a ratio proportionate to the salary schedule for the academic year.

TABLE 11.3   Ratio of Minimum to Maximum Teachers' Salaries by Level of Instruction

COUNTRY	ELEMENTARY	SECONDARY	SECONDARY MAXIMUM/ ELEMENTARY MINIMUM
United States	1:2.0	1:2.0	1:2.0
Canada	1:2.1	1:1.8	1:2.1
Japan	1:3.3	1:3.1	1:3.4
Italy	1:1.6	1:1.6	1:1.9
Netherlands	1:2.0	1:2.2	1:3.0
Scotland	1:1.6	N/A	1:1.6
Switzerland	1:1.5	1:1.5	1:2.2
Average	1:2.0	1:2.0	1:2.3

Source: Stephen B. Lawton, "Teachers' Salaries: An International Perspective," unpublished paper, Ontario Institute for Studies in Education, Toronto, Ontario, Canada, 1987.

FRINGE BENEFITS

Fringe benefit costs have risen faster than salary costs. Benefits usually include retirement, health, dental, and disability insurance and may include an annuity or life insurance feature. Benefits typically amount to 20 to 25 percent of a teacher's total costs to a school district.

SALARY COMPARISONS

Table 11.4 compares U.S. teacher salaries with other nations. Here it is evident that teachers are generally lower paid than blue collar, technical, and professional workers, both in the U.S. and elsewhere. Table 11.5 utilizes other data but makes the same point.

Current data on the subject appear scarce, but it is frequently alleged that many teachers, particularly male and single teachers, *moonlight* (hold employment in addition to their teacher jobs). In a 1985 and a 1987 poll of California teachers, almost 50 percent of respondents reported holding second jobs outside of education.[28] This added employment was usually during the summer.

INCENTIVE EFFECTS

In addition to attracting individuals into education employment, or discouraging them from it, incentives influence their behavior once they are hired. It is here that education is particularly inefficient. Teacher salary schedules typically reward only two behaviors, growing older and gaining added academic units beyond the bachelor's degree. At the time these features were adopted, they were an improvement over the subjective and politicized dimensions which formerly influenced teacher pay. However, currently neither of these is particularly related to productivity.

Moreover, most salary schedules are *flat*: there are no categories of professionalism recognized for added remuneration. There is seldom a separate salary schedule for Master Teachers, as opposed to interns or apprentices. Bonuses are seldom awarded for being particularly productive with students. The only pay raise, other than for the two conditions just mentioned, is whatever is bargained for all teachers by the union. This raise is likely to be related to cost-of-living increases or teacher pay in surrounding districts. Such increases are also seldom related to any measure of productivity.

In American public education, if you want to "get ahead," get out of the classroom. More pay, more status, more interaction with adults, more discretion over one's time, and greater variety of assignment come by leaving classroom teaching. As a consequence, many able teachers are drawn away from instruction to become a specialist, a counselor, a vice-principal, a principal, or a central office administrator, and then may strive to be a superintendent, county office employee, state education department official, or professor. As important as these mostly non-

[28]Julia Koppich, William Gerritz, and James W. Guthrie, *California Teacher Opinion* (Berkeley, Calif.: Policy Analysis for California Education, 1985).

teaching positions may be, they do not constitute the major purpose of the institution—instructing students. The absence of a productively oriented career incentive system discourages many younger instructors from remaining in teaching. Figure 11.3 illustrates the financial facts regarding this incentive system.

TABLE 11.4 Teachers' Salaries Relative to Salaries in Other Occupations in OECD Countries, 1985

COUNTRY	SALES	INDUST. WAGE	CONST. WORKER	BUS DRIVER	TOOL-MAKER	ELECTRICAL ENGINEER	MANAGER
United States	52	73	95	97	120	146	204
Canada	46	60	83	78	85	124	159
Japan	59	69	69	104	94	130	248
Austria	63	82	89	119	125	225	226
Belgium	70	69	91	101	95	158	155
Denmark	79	70	92	93	108	142	195
Finland	64	62	97	98	98	154	224
France	61	78	57	119	113	309	305
Germany	45	68	66	98	95	137	180
Greece	55	55	71	112	104	136	180
Ireland	60	65	53	65	81	132	170
Italy	88	83	75	106	94	174	159
Luxembourg	37	58	41	80	79	141	158
Netherlands	70	73	80	98	97	152	231
Norway	68	81	124	105	101	138	132
Portugal	50	NA	50	78	73	155	175
Spain	46	51	48	64	83	174	127
United Kingdom	53	74	76	81	94	159	138
Average	59	69	75	94	97	160	160

Teacher's salary in each country = 100; salaries for other occupations are expressed as a percentage of a teacher's salary in that country. Position descriptions are as follows: *Sales,* salesclerk employed in ladies' wear department of a large department store received some training but not especially in selling, with several years of selling experience (about twenty to twenty-four years old, single); *Industrial Wage,* average annualized pay based on five-day week, forty-eight-week year, using data on hourly wages and hours worked per week or month; *Construction Worker,* unskilled or semiskilled laborer (about twenty-five years old, single); *Bus Driver,* employed by municipal system, about ten years' driving experience (about thirty-five years old, married, two children); *Toolmaker/Lathe Operator,* skilled mechanic with vocational training and about ten years' experience with a large company in the metalworking industry (about thirty-five years old, married, two children); *Electrical Engineer* employed by an industrial firm in the machinery department or completed university studies (college, technical institute, or institute of higher technical education) with at least five years of practical experience (about thirty-five years old, married, no children); *Manager,* technical department manager of a production department (more than 100 employees) in a sizable company in the metalworking industry, completed professional training with many years of experience in the field (about forty years old, married, no children).

Source: Stephen B. Lawton, "Teachers' Salaries: An International Perspective," unpublished paper, Ontario Institute for Studies in Education, Toronto, Ontario, Canada, 1987.

TABLE 11.5 Primary School Teachers' Salaries as a Percentage of Private Consumption per Head in U.S. Dollars, 1982 and 1985

Country	PRIVATE CONSUMPTION PER HEAD		SALARY AS PERCENTAGE OF PC/HEAD	
	1982	1985	1982	1985
United States	8,743	10,214	263	241
Canada	7,488	8,484	339	357
Japan	5,957	6,744	335	339
Austria	5,720	6,490	214	210
Belgium	7,099	7,637	245	236
Denmark	6,064	6,842	284	293
Finland	5,554	6,287	231	231
France	7,373	8,009	185	172
Germany	6,561	7,274	302	288
Greece	3,754	4,089	277	355
Ireland	4,180	4,338	398	464
Italy	5,724	6,251	205	258
Luxembourg	7,763	8,540	335	345
Netherlands	6,773	7,270	276	250
Norway	5,994	6,624	258	276
Portugal	3,002	3,076	N.A.	392
Spain	5,110	5,456	288	362
United Kingdom	5,733	6,535	268	279
Average	6,033	6,675	277	297

Sources: Salary data from Table 1. Personal consumption per head in U.S. dollars using current Purchasing Power Parities for 1982 and 1985 are from OECD (1986). Adapted from Stephen B. Lawton, "Teachers Salaries: An International Perspective," Unpublished paper, Ontario Institute for Educational Studies (Toronto, Ontario, Canada, 1987).

BUILDING AN EDUCATION PROFESSION

The picture painted to this point suggests that the U.S. education work force, while large in numbers, is in the case of many teachers insufficiently prepared academically or pedagogically, has low status in the eyes of the general public, is plagued by low and politically manipulable entry standards, is subject to substantial workplace indignity and professional isolation, is poorly compensated relative to comparable occupations, and has long been undermined by an incentive system that discourages sustained commitment to classroom teaching.

In sum, education is at best a weak profession that needs buttressing. By building a far more complete profession, educators could enhance school productiv-

FIGURE 11.3   **Salaries Paid Professional Personnel in Public Schools, 1986-87**

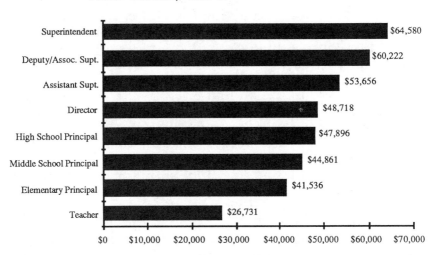

Note: These are the mean of mean salaries reported by districts throughout the United States.
Source: Data are from *Salaries Paid Professional Personnel in Public Schools, 1986-87* (Arlington, Va.: Educational Research Service, 1988), p. 9.

ity. The remainder of this chapter describes a set of proposals aimed at enhancing the professional capacities of those employed in education settings. These illustrative proposals include recommendations for preparation and licensing, the rearrangement of teaching into a professional hierarchy, and effective evaluation procedures.[29]

Preparation

Preservice professional preparation of teachers consists of three major components: (1) undergraduate concentration in a subject-matter field or the liberal arts, (2) graduate-level pedagogical training, and (3) supervised practical experience. Successful teaching assumes that an instructor possesses knowledge of the subject. A good teacher knows something, is confident about his or her expertise in at least one specific intellectual domain. Without this self-image teachers run the risk of appearing and acting in an unauthentic or illegitimate manner. The analog would be a physician skilled at interpersonal relations with patients, possessing a great bedside manner, but having no knowledge of pathologies or how to treat them mechanically or chemically. An able secondary-level teacher knows whatever field or fields he or she intends to teach, such as history, science, mathematics, or a foreign language. An able elementary-level teacher is sufficiently expert in several liberal arts fields to convey authenticity.

[29]The authors acknowledge the earlier efforts of Professor Charles S. Benson in developing many of the ideas contained in these illustrative proposals.

Because of the crucial need to have a field of expertise, it is necessary that individuals contemplating teaching as a career acquire a bachelor's degree in a specialized subject-matter field other than education. In order to constitute truly professional preparation, acquisition of pedagogy and supervised practice teaching should be graduate-level endeavors. Under this scenario, institutions of higher education would not offer undergraduate teacher preparation programs as majors for bachelor's degrees.

Entry into a professionalized graduate-level pedagogical preparation program should be difficult. Minimum qualification could consist of criteria such as a bachelor's degree in an appropriate subject field, satisfactory scores on a rigorous advanced examination such as the Graduate Record Examination (GRE), and a record of appropriate personal behavior and practical experience.

Professionalization advocates contend that graduate preparation programs for teachers should be at least one academic year in length. Some even assert that two years is necessary.[30] They believe that the amount of systematic knowledge regarding instruction may have at one time been insufficient to justify a year-long graduate-level preparation period. However, since 1970 education has been enriched with research discoveries regarding instruction in fields such as science and mathematics. Now the amount known scientifically about pedagogical matters such as sequential arrangement and presentation of subject content, evaluation and reinforcement of student performance, testing and measurement, and classroom management justifies at least a year of graduate-level professional preparation.[31]

Successful completion of an appropriate period of pedagogical preparation might qualify an individual as an *intern teacher* or *instructor*. Practice teaching for at least two years could then take place under the tutelage of a *master* or *mentor teacher*. The initial year of such practice teaching might well occur concurrently with enrollment in a pedagogical preparation program. Many contend that added pedagogy has the most meaning during this period of supervised practice, when the reality of teaching can impart meaning to theory and vice versa. However, if such a model is utilized, the pedagogical preparation period probably would need to be two years.

A Professional Hierarchy

Intern teachers could be granted a *preliminary credential* by the state licensing agency. This certificate could be accorded those who have successfully undergone entry-level pedagogical preparation. It would entitle an individual to be employed as an intern teacher, instructing under the supervision of a master. A preliminary credential would be valid for no longer than three or four years. An individual would thereupon be obligated to qualify for the next credential level in order to maintain employment eligibility as a teacher.

[30]Trish Stoddart, David J. Losk, and Charles S. Benson, *Some Reflections on the Honorable Profession of Teaching* (Berkeley, Calif.: Policy Analysis for California Education, 1984).
[31]See Jere E. Brophy and Thomas L. Good, "Teacher Behavior and Student Achievement," in *Handbook of Research on Teaching*, ed. Wittrock, chap. 12.

Successful completion of supervised practice teaching would render an individual eligible for the subsequent step on the professional ladder, e.g., *associate teacher*. Teachers holding this license could be qualified for regular employment as elementary instructors or secondary subject specialists, depending upon the kind of internship they had undergone. Such individuals would, presumably, constitute the bulk of the teacher work force. They ought to undergo systematic evaluations and sustained professional in-service training linked to their performance evaluation results.

Associate teachers could have gradations or levels within this rank to which they could aspire to rise professionally. The pay at each level would be greater. Such pay increases could be based upon an evaluation strategy, about which more is said subsequently. Such level advances would be in addition to cost-of-living adjustments or whatever total salary schedule advances were negotiated in collective bargaining.

Six years of successful service as an associate might qualify a teacher for a sabbatical leave, the purpose of which would be added professional preparation. Following a sabbatical and added training, an individual could request consideration for promotion to *master teacher*.

Another possible category in a restructured professional hierarchy for teachers is that of *special teacher*. These individuals, after receiving appropriate specialized pedagogical preparation and added supervised practice, could be eligible for employment in specialized roles such as instructors of handicapped students, or in administrative positions subordinate to principals. Their pay would be higher than that of associate teachers, reflecting their added preparation and specialization. Successful service as a special teacher, particularly in settings judged difficult, such as schools for juvenile offenders, might well contribute additional credits for those requesting promotion to master teacher.

Master teachers could be restricted to approximately 10 percent of the teacher work force in a state. They would be eligible for high pay, a topic about which more is said later. Their functions could vary. Some would serve as mentor teachers for interns. Others could serve as curriculum experts. Yet others might hold a range of quasi-administrative posts, such as department chair. Whatever their assigned duties, they would have to spend approximately 60 percent of their time in direct instructional contact with students. Not to do so would contribute to the existing set of disincentives that attracts able individuals away from classroom teaching.

Licensing

The previously described program approval licensing process suffices for granting intern teacher credentials. However, all advanced credentials, such as associate, special, master, and administrative, should be awarded differently—a process similar to that used for attorneys, architects, and physicians. Under such a revision the prospective licensee, and not the training program in which he or she had been enrolled, would be the subject of the examining process. Licensing could be legally undertaken by a state, but the state could rely upon the results of a national professional teacher licensing board, as recommended by the previously cited Carnegie

Forum Report. (Presumably, training programs could continue to be accredited by professional committees or boards, but these would be separate.)

How might a professional examination operate in teacher licensing? There might well be three sections. An initial component would be a pencil-and-paper test designed to assess subject-matter competence. A prospective associate teacher would sit for the test or tests in those fields for which he or she desired to be licensed to teach—for example, mathematics, biological science, U.S. history, or English literature. A second written examination would be given on pedagogical principles and the fundamentals of human development. A third component of a professional licensing examination for associate teachers (PLEAT) might well be a simulation (perhaps on a videotape) of an instructional problem. A candidate would be requested to respond in a written essay explaining the nature of the problem, possible diagnoses, and one or more solutions. Licensing examination procedures for special and master teachers might eliminate the initial test and concentrate on the remaining two components. Here they would be called upon to display their specialized and more comprehensive understanding of pedagogy, practice, and educational institutions.

Remuneration

Compensation should be tied to a teacher's position in the professional hierarchy. Figure 11.4 illustrates relative weightings for each level of professional status, as well as gradations within rank. It is assumed in this professional salary schedule that master teachers are paid on an eleven-month basis. Intern and associate teachers are paid for nine months, special teachers for ten months. If they are employed for a longer "year," they should be paid more on a prorated basis. The point of Figure 11.4 is to illustrate, using 1986 average teacher salary data for the U.S., that a career ladder can be constructed that offers teachers professional incentives and the prospect of higher salaries without raising mean teacher salary.

Master teachers could be paid almost as much as principals in the same district and even more than administrators such as vice-principal or central office administrators. Only district and perhaps county superintendents and chief state school officers should be paid significantly more than master teachers. The clear intent is to enable master teachers to be among the highest-paid education professionals. A power message should be made that those who receive the highest remuneration are those who are best prepared and the most able at performing the institution's central function—conveying knowledge to students through systematic instruction.

Evaluation

Assessing teachers' performance is difficult.[32] Professional isolation renders it awkward to observe a teacher's performance systematically. Also, there are few

---

[32]On this topic see generally, Linda Darling-Hammond, Arthur E. Wise, and Sara Pease, "Teacher Evaluation in the Organizational Context: A Review of the Literature," *Review of Educational Research,* 53, no. 3 (Fall 1983), 285–328; and Linda Darling-Hammond, "A Proposal for Evaluation in the Teaching Profession," *Elementary School Journal,* 86, no. 4 (March 1986), 1–21.

FIGURE 11.4 A Career Ladder

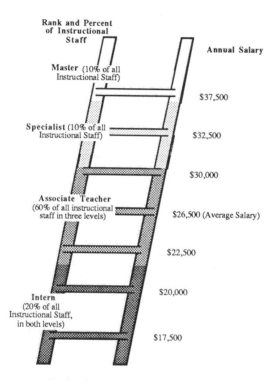

agreed-upon output measures that are fair when applied to teachers as individuals. (Chapter 14 describes Merit Schools, a strategy for using outcome measures to monitor and reward productivity of an entire faculty.[33]) Consequently, a procedure is needed whereby individuals can be considered for merit increases within a rank, say associate, special, or mentor teacher. A procedure adopted from institutions of higher education serves as an example.

A teacher seeking a merit promotion within a credential rank, such as associate teacher, would be responsible for assembling a *professional portfolio*. Items to be included in such a portfolio might, with one exception, be at the discretion of the candidate. Items might include exemplary lesson plans, funding proposals to outside organizations, curriculum units designed by the candidate, videotapes of outstanding instructional sessions, testimony from students and parents, awards, research papers, reports from supervisors and colleagues, transcripts specifying professional service, and journal articles or other professional publications.

[33]For more information on merit pay see David S. Stern "Compensation for Teachers," *Review of Education Research*, 13 (January 1986), 285–316. For a more complete list of agencies and individuals proposing merit pay see Richard Neal, "Merit Pay for Teachers, 1984," address to the Arizona School Boards Association seminar on merit pay, Phoenix, January 27 and 28, 1984; and R. J. Murnane, "The Rhetoric and Reality of Merit Pay: Why are They Different?" in *Merit, Money and Teachers' Careers*, ed. Henry C. Johnson, Jr. (Lanham, Md: University Press of America, 1985), pp. 57-76.

The portfolio item beyond a candidate's discretion would be a measure of student performance. This would be possible only if a district, and ideally the state, had a comprehensive testing program permitting an assessment of *value added*. This value would be the amount of understanding contributed by the teacher over the academic span involved. The value the teacher had added would be reflected by the gain in scores from pre- to post-testing intervals. Such a value-added arrangement, along with estimated or projected performance bands based on previous experience with similar students, would suggest whether or not a candidate was an effective teacher.

This illustrative scheme lends itself ideally to peer review, participation by professional teachers themselves. Procedures for guaranteeing appeals and due process considerations could also be part of such an evaluation plan

SUMMARY

Three million individuals constitute the certificated U.S. educator work force. This work force is highly unionized, and the unions are politically active. Without question there are many uncommonly able and altruistic teachers. However, teachers in the aggregate enjoy low public respect, which is reflected in their spartan work conditions and in their generally low pay. These unhappy circumstances limit the U.S. education system's productivity. Added efficiency—more student learning—is unlikely to occur in any significant amount until teaching can be restructured as a more complete profession that recruits, carefully trains, systematically evaluates, and appropriately rewards larger numbers of more able individuals. This chapter concludes with a set of proposals intended to accomplish such a purpose.

chapter twelve

Technology in Public Schools

INTRODUCTION

Why a chapter on technology in a book on school finance? Technology, primarily in the form of computers, is dramatically reshaping many sectors of American life. Even though the education sector has been remarkably resistant to many forms of technology, even it is now being affected by the revolution being wrought by computers. Thus, it is important to examine how this technology may affect education, in order to see whether its probable results will tend to favor more or less equity, efficiency, and choice.

Although the boundaries among them are inevitably blurred, general-purpose computers are usually classified by size, speed, and capacity as *microcomputers*, *minicomputers*, and large computers usually called *mainframes*. The microcomputer typically sits on the user's desk and is connected to an electrical outlet. It has capabilities that two decades ago were limited to mainframes (and in many cases its capabilities exceed those of earlier mainframes). The microcomputer is typified by the IBM personal computer (PC) and the Apple Macintosh.

A minicomputer can be housed in a single room that may be quite small, although *peripherals* (memory storage in the form of disk drives, printers, etc.) may occupy more space. The minicomputer has assumed many tasks of the mainframe of a decade ago. It is smaller, faster, more powerful, and more flexible than those machines. A typical minicomputer is Digital Equipment Corporation's VAX.

Today's mainframe is usually employed for tasks that necessitate millions of complex calculations in a short time. Researchers on college campuses need such machines. At the upper end of this scale is the *supercomputer*. Analyzing atmospheric mechanics to improve weather predictions is a typical job for such a computer. One such huge machine is the Cray I of Cray Research Corporation. However, most mainframe machines currently in use in school districts belong to an earlier generation. They are physically large, but often have less power than a modern minicomputer. They will be replaced with minicomputers as manufacturers stop supporting their repair and the software that operates them.

Most computers are general-purpose machines that may be converted into special-purpose machines through *applications* (programs that allow the computer to do word processing, spreadsheet operations, graphics, etc.). Increasingly, however, small computers are dedicated to a single purpose. An example is the automobile combustion analyzer, which continuously monitors engine performance and adjusts gas mixtures to facilitate efficient operation. This *dedicated computer* requires no knowledge on the part of the operator, who may be unaware even that the computer exists. In the future, there will be many of these, lessening even more the need for most people to learn the arcane ways of general-purpose computers.

Use of even general-purpose computers is growing easier. The older generation of micros, represented by the Apple II and the IBM PC, required knowledge of operating systems, the relationship of peripherals of different manufacture to the central machine, and a myriad of cryptic commands. The newer generation has eliminated many problems through the use of a *mouse* to point to places on the screen, *pull-down menus* instead of cryptic commands, and information in English instead of computerese. The earliest examples of this generation were the Apple Lisa and the Macintosh. Presumably, computers will continue to become even more user-friendly. However, the computer industry continues to be plagued by the absence of agreed-upon standards. As a result, programs that work on one computer often do not operate on another of a different brand, even though the two are supposed to have the same architecture. Peripherals that work with one machine do not necessarily work with another. Connecting computers of two different manufacturers so they can exchange data is often an exercise in frustration.

School districts will have little use for mainframes in the future. The capacity of these machines is far beyond the computational needs of administration or instruction in elementary and secondary schools. There are still many mainframes in school districts. They are obsolete, in the sense that it is not possible to do with them things that can now be done with minis and micros. Nevertheless, they can continue to perform the functions for which they were purchased. As it becomes more expensive to maintain them, they will be replaced by modern minis, supplemented by a great many micros.

There will be a great flowering of micros in school districts. They will be used on the desks of administrators for stand-alone purposes and to facilitate communication with other administrators. They will be used in classrooms for a variety of instructional purposes. Few people will actually write programs for them. Rather, most people will use applications written by experts. The application will enable an administrator or student to do things with a computer without having to learn a programming language.

Typically, a large number of micros will be connected to a minicomputer that will serve as a message center, for mass storage of data, and for processing what is beyond a micro's capability. Connections will be by means of telephone lines or through a small private set of lines (which may consist of optical fibers instead of wires) known as *local area network*. Whether communication between two or more computers spans only a few feet or an entire continent, the process is known as *telecommunications*. This promises to be one of the most important areas of future technological development.

All of these computers, of course, will be of no use without programs instructing them in what to do. Computers and peripheral devices are known as *hardware;* programs are called *software*. There are two main alternatives to acquiring the necessary software to accomplish the purpose with computers that a school district might desire: purchase it on the outside or develop it in-house. The former alternative is highly recommended. The advantages of outside purchase are as follows:

1. When a program, or application, is developed for a mass market rather than for an individual district, costs are distributed over many customers. Thus, the cost is apt to be much lower than that of in-house development. Also, an application is usually available immediately or within a short time, whereas in-house development usually takes much longer.

2. The time that a developer for the mass market is able to invest in a new program generally will result in a product that has more features and fewer bugs than an in-house product.

3. Programmers are notorious for disliking *documentation*. Documentation is of two kinds: that designed for the end-user and that designed to explain the internal workings of the program to the professional who may wish to fix a bug or make changes. It is possible to hire individuals to write end-user instructions, although the results will seldom be as good as those written by authors employed by a commercial developer of software. However, only the person who developed a program can adequately accomplish internal documentation. Turnover among these individuals is high, and the usual fate of in-house programs is that they are abandoned shortly after their developer departs, because they can no longer be repaired or adapted to new circumstances.

The only good reason for developing programs in-house is that nothing available commercially will meet requirements. However, software is now available for many of the things districts might like to accomplish. Most of this software can be customized to the specifications of an individual district.[1]

Purchase of software is an important undertaking. It is not just the cost of the software that is important. Software dictates data-base design and methods of storage. If an application is found to be inadequate and a new one must be purchased, it

---

[1]One book that discusses software for educational administration is Stanley Pogrow, *Evaluations of Educational Administration Software* (Tucson: Ed-Ad Systems, 1985). One should, of course, use only a recent edition of such a book as a guide, for software changes rapidly.

may be found that there is no easy way to convert all of a district's data files to the format required by the new application.

ADMINISTRATIVE USES OF COMPUTERS

Management Information Systems

Most current management applications of computer technology in schools concentrate on *data processing*. That is, computers perform the same tasks—accounting and purchasing—that used to be done with pencil and paper. Files are established to facilitate this. Typically, there are separate files for each department or function. This arrangement is effective as long as only routine operations are being conducted. However, when a superintendent or other administrator wants an answer to a nonroutine question, the existing programs usually cannot handle it. Either there must be extensive (and expensive) special-purpose programming to instruct the computer to find the answer, or those responsible must utilize hand calculation. Anyone who has been an administrator knows how frequently one is frustrated by the inability of a computer center to answer questions that are important to the management of the school or the district.

The result of this frustration in industry has been the development of *management information systems*. Such systems are usually constructed around *comprehensive data bases* that bring together much of an organization's data. Attached to such a data base is a powerful *query language* that enables individuals who are not programmers to ask questions management asks and obtain prompt answers. The combination of the comprehensive data base and the query language is usually called a *data-base management system (DBMS)*.[2]

RELATIONAL DATA BASES

The majority of new DBMSs are constructed around *relational data bases*. Such a data base uses a number of tables (or rather their equivalent in the memory of the computer), in which each row is a record and each column an item of data (called an *attribute*) about that record. The table is called a *relation*. Here are some examples of tables, or relations, for a portion of a DBMS related to instruction. Each relation contains information about one kind of relationship. The first attribute in each of the first three relations is the *key*. It is unique, in that there is only one record in that relation with that key. The fourth relation has a key consisting of a combination of the first *two* attributes, and that combination is unique, even though neither attribute by itself displays uniqueness. The remaining

---

[2]Useful, reasonably nontechnical texts on DBMS are Fred R. McFadden and Jeffrey A. Hoffer, *Data Base Management* (Menlo Park, Calif.: Benjamin/Cummings Publishing Co., 1985); and James Martin, *Principles of Data-Base Management* (Englewood Cliffs, N.J.: Prentice-Hall, 1976). The latter, while old, is still good on the fundamentals.

Student Relation:

STUD. NO.	NAME	ADDRESS	PHONE	PARENT NAME	ETC.
1001	Able, K.	415 Pine	445-6789	Able, Jane	
1005	Baker, T.	817 Oak	445-4432	Baker, Thomas	
Etc.					

Class Relation:

CLASS NO.	NAME	ROOM	TIME	TEACHER	ETC.
100	Algebra	C18	MWF 9–10	Jones	
103	Geometry	C18	TTh 10–11	Smith	
Etc.					

Teacher Relation:

TEACH. NO.	NAME	OFFICE	DEPT.	SALARY	ETC.
51723	Smith, J.	C23	Math	$18,000	
56789	Ames, K.	D32	English	$17,500	
Etc.					

Grade Relation:

STUD. NO.	CLASS NO.	GRADE
1001	100	A–
1001	205	B+
1005	100	A
1005	103	C
1005	205	B

attributes in a relation are closely related to the key. One would not, for example, put the salary of Smith in the class relation, for it is closely related not to class number but to teacher number, which is the key of the next relation. The advantage of this arrangement of tables, or relations, is that it prevents unnecessary duplication of data. If one put the salary of Smith (and other pertinent information about Smith) in the class relation, one would have to insert that same information for every class Smith teaches. If it became necessary to change an item of that information, one would have to change it everywhere it occurred. This leads to waste and error. Grade sheets for a particular class can be prepared through use of a query language. The teacher or administrator finds all occurrences of the class in the grade relation, then selects appropriate information from other relations to complete the grade sheet. For example, from the class relation the name of the class, room, and teacher's name would be selected; from the student relation the student's name would be selected. The information would be printed in any form desired. A similar query would print report cards. A different query would list teachers by department, with their salaries.

Use of the query language also allows administrators to ask for the average number of students in math classes, the names of students receiving a grade less than C– this grading period, or the number of students being taught by Ms. Smith. In other words, a large number of special tables can be constructed, each containing information about a special classification. Tables are then searched through use of a query language to generate answers to questions, whether they are routine data-processing questions or special management questions. Powerful query languages make it unnecessary for a user to understand how special tables are constructed. The language takes the question asked and devises the most efficient way of constructing tables to answer it. The power this provides can be appreciated only by an administrator of a large district who has asked an important question only to be told that the answer will take several weeks and extensive programming to prepare. Using a relational data base and its associated query language, the administrator or an assistant can often obtain an answer within a few minutes.

Although applications are being developed that incorporate a relational data base in a microcomputer, the amount of data to be stored in a typical district and the powerful query language make it necessary in most cases to operate such a DBMS on a minicomputer or a mainframe.

DESIGN

The design of data-base management systems is a specialized undertaking. It involves much time and great cost as existing files are remade into a relational data base. There are other less visible costs. Establishing an integrated data base for a district can threaten the semiautonomous empires of those who currently "own" data-processing files for a portion of the system (student files, purchasing files, accounts-payable files, etc.). It usually requires the interest of the person at the top to champion the change.

Another less-than-obvious problem is that there is usually a trade-off between a file design that facilitates queries frequently made by management and the design that facilitates updating files. The relational data-base system can do both kinds of operations, but one design will make updating more expensive whereas the other will make queries more expensive. The proper design is arrived at after comparing volume of queries with the amount and frequency of updating.

Electronic Spread Sheets

Perhaps the most important tool available to management for effective planning is simulation. Simulation allows management to ask "what if" questions: What if enrollment starts to increase after a period of decrease? What if proposed changes in state aid are made? What if there are large additional costs for a program for the handicapped? In the past, a superintendent and the board asked these questions. If the district was small, the staff donned their green eyeshades and sharpened their pencils, and in several days or weeks had the answer to one "what if" question.

If the district was large, they might have access to a mainframe computer and have a programmer who could develop a *simulation program* that would allow exploration of a variety of possibilities, rather than just one (suppose enrollment increases 2 percent in the early grades? suppose it increases 5 percent?). The situation of the larger district is better than that of the small district, but it leaves the superintendent and board relying on a program developed and operated by a programmer who may not completely understand the situation, and whose program may therefore be inaccurate or inappropriate.

Fortunately, the microcomputer and numerous business-oriented programs make it possible for senior staff, or even the superintendent, to develop and operate simulations. The most frequently used applications for this purpose are called *spread-sheet* programs. The earliest of the genre was VisiCalc. Many other spreadsheet programs are now available, and more are being developed. They are being used extensively by executives in business organizations. A microcomputer costs less then $2000, and the necessary software less than $500; thus any district can afford these useful tools. The spread-sheet program is like a sheet of paper with rows and columns. Here is an example of how it works. Calculations of revenue for a school district are shown below as they might be done by a business manager of a small district on a sheet of paper. The first column contains labels, the second data (both data that is input to the calculation and data that is calculated). The comments to the right explain how the calculation is performed.

Assessed valuation	$10,000,000	This is the business manager's estimate.
Pupils	1000	This is also an estimate.
Tax rate	20 mills	The district's current rate.
State guarantee per pupil	$1,800	The present state formula (a foundation program).
Required local millage	15 mills	The present state requirement.
Property tax raised	$200,000	Assessed valuation x millage rate
Foundation guarantee	$1,800,000	Guarantee per pupil x pupils
Less required taxes	$150,000	Required millage x assessed valuation
State aid	$1,650,000	Foundation guarantee – required taxes
Total revenue	$1,850,000	State aid + property tax raised

If the business manager now wishes to develop alternatives, such as estimating a different tax rate or a different assessed valuation, many of the entries must be changed or erased, or the whole thing written over again on another sheet of paper. In the simple case shown, this is easy to do. In the typical case, the number of calculations is large. The result is that each alternative takes a long time to calculate, and opportunities for error are legion.

The process is different and easier when computerized. A spread-sheet program might have a first column with exactly the same labels as in the example. The first five items of the second column would be filled with the input data just shown. (Typically, input data would be obtained by querying a data-base management system.) The remainder of the second column would consist of formulas. These formulas would automatically perform calculations. For example (note that the rows and columns are numbered or lettered):

ROW	COLUMN	
	A	B
1	Assessed valuation	10,000,000
2	Pupils	1,000
3	Tax rate	20
4	State guarantee per pupil	1,800
5	Required local millage	15
6	Property tax raised	B1 x B3 x .001
7	Foundation guarantee	B2 x B4
8	Less required taxes	B1 x B5 x .001
9	State aid	B7 − B8
10	Total revenue	B6 + B9

The formulas do not show on the printout, however. Instead, the results of the calculations would show. Thus, the electronic spread sheet would look like the information on the piece of paper. The power of the program becomes obvious, however, when we note that every time any change is made in the information, the sheet is instantly recalculated. For example, if the business manager decided to insert a different number of pupils, the sheet would be recalculated to show new values for the foundation guarantee, state aid, and total revenue.

Other features of the spread-sheet program improve on the paper calculation by making it easy to insert a row or column, or to move one to a different place. Of course, the sheet, or a portion of it, can be printed. Most important though, business people are finding the spread sheet something they can easily construct themselves, whereas writing a computer program in BASIC or Fortran is something most administrators will never do. The combination of not having to rely on a programmer and being able construct a spread sheet on your own personal computer means that administrators can assess ideas and proposals while preserving security until they are satisfied with the results.

The size of the spread sheet is limited primarily by the memory of the microcomputer. On a typical micro, a spread sheet might have available over 200 columns and several thousand rows, although the micro might not be able to use all of this unless it has a rather large memory. The spread sheet is particularly useful for situations that do not involve massive amounts of data. Typical applications might be a projection of cohort survival among students, and estimates of revenue or expenditure.

Larger Simulations

In some situations the typical spread sheet is inadequate because of the large amount of data to be handled. A simulation of school finance for a state might be an example. The simulation might involve fifty or more items of data for each of 500 or more school districts in the state, with more than fifty different data items to be calculated for each district, together with summary data. Such a simulation can usually be done only on a minicomputer (or, of course, a mainframe) and will typically require the services of a programmer to develop the simulation and in most cases to operate it.

Telecommunications

The mainframe computer has a large capacity. However, its complexity means that only certain specialists can control it, and this gives them the power to decide whose task will be done first, and how it will be done. The machine is often busy doing someone else's large job when one needs it, and the necessity to program it in some arcane language requires would-be users who do not understand computers to try to explain their problem to computer types who do not understand schools.

Microcomputers with applications (word processing, spread-sheet programs, etc.) that are understandable to busy administrators, teachers—and particularly students—are a great improvement, freeing people to do what they want without the problems of dealing with the mainframe. However, micros have suffered from inadequate memory and from their inability to transfer information rapidly to other computers. *Telecommunications* is often the answer to this problem.

Telecommunication is the process of communicating over a distance by electronic means. The telephone is one means of telecommunication, enabling two–way communications. Television usually is a one–way type of telecommunication. This chapter, however, deals mainly with telecommunication that enables computers to communicate with each other. If they are not too far apart, two computers can frequently be joined by a simple cable composed of a number of wires. This will enable information to be transferred between them.

However, this application is of limited use. Rather, one might want to obtain information from a minicomputer to use in a spread-sheet simulation on a micro. Of course, one does not want to receive a printout from the mini, then type the information back into the micro. This is time–consuming and prone to error. Rather, data should flow directly from the mini to the micro without being touched by human hands. A micro can communicate with a minicomputer (or with other micros) by sending information over telephone lines. *Modems* at each end of the line translate digital information from the computer into tones transmitted over the telephone line, then back to digital information at the other end. This is necessary because the normal telephone up to the present has been an *analog* device, dealing in continuously changing electrical currents, whereas a digital computer utilizes discrete bits of data. (This is changing, and some modern telephone systems are digital, enabling computer communication without modems.)

In some cases, the user only desires to obtain information from the minicomputer, and is not interested in passing information (except simple queries) back to it. This process is called *downloading* from the mini, and can end at a simple terminal that can only display information. Such a terminal is usually labeled a *dumb terminal.* A microcomputer with a modem connected to a mainframe becomes a *smart terminal,* for it can perform many kinds of operations on the information received from the mini. If it also sends information to the mini (for processing, say, in a simulation that is too large for the micro), it is said to be *uploading* data.

Many people use their computers to communicate with a mainframe, perhaps in another city, that contains a large data base. Commercial examples are *CompuServe* and *GEnie*. The micro can command the mainframe to send data, which are downloaded. The user of the micro can then store the information, print it, or incorporate it into an application.

There is much more to telecommunications than this.[3] An example is electronic mail. A number of micros are connected to a mainframe or minicomputer. The mainframe has storage space set aside on a disk for communication among micro users. One individual may send a message to another by typing it on his micro and sending it to the mainframe with the name of its addressee. The next time the addressee establishes communication with the mainframe, he or she will be told that there is mail waiting, and it can be read, printed, filed for future reference, or discarded. It is easy to send identical messages to a large number of individuals, while typing the message only once.

Another example of telecommunications is the *local area network (LAN)*. Typically, this consists of a number of microcomputers within a reasonably small area (a school, say), connected with one another and with devices that serve all of them. Such devices would usually include a large disk-based memory unit to augment the rather small memory of most micros, and a high-quality printer.

Perhaps the most important use of telecommunications is in *distributed processing,* a system in which a number of terminals or microcomputers operate on the same data base. An example is the airline reservation system. Not only is it possible for terminals in airports and travel agencies throughout the nation to obtain information on schedules, fares, and ticketing information for an individual, it is also possible to make reservations for individuals. Making the reservation updates the data base in the computer, which can then display that information to any terminal, retain a record of seats reserved for a flight, and, if desired, automatically issue an individual a ticket and bill it to a credit card. In other words, the system not only allows a microcomputer to convey information to terminals, but allows terminals to initiate information processing in a mainframe computer.

Distributed processing has important implications for school districts. Many districts consist of a central office and a number of geographically distributed schools. There is a constant flow of information between central office and schools. At present, where there is a central computer, data are gathered in the schools (on attendance, for example), committed to paper, sent to the central office daily or weekly by messenger, and entered into the computer. With distributed processing, data would be input to the computer through terminals in local schools, which would be connected with the computer in the central office through telephone lines.

[3]Useful texts that are not too technical are Charles T. Meadow and Albert S. Tedesco, *Telecommunications for Management* (New York: McGraw-Hill, 1985); Uyless D. Black, *Data Communications, Networks, and Distributed Processing* (Reston, Va.: Reston Publishing Co., 1983); and James Martin, *Computer Networks and Distributed Processing* (Englewood Cliffs, N.J.: Prentice-Hall, 1981).

The terminals would serve the same purpose as the present messenger system, with the advantages that updated information would be immediately available and that fewer errors would be made with information having to be entered only once.

The design of a telecommunications system is complicated and technical. In general, different models or brands of computers are not directly compatible, so it may be insufficient merely to link them to each other. The way in which machines package bits of data to send, the rate at which each can send, and the characteristics of telephone lines may all differ, and these are only the beginning. The incompatibility among computers has inhibited telecommunications, but in spite of such problems networks are becoming more extensive.

Distributed processing also has problems of its own, in addition to those associated with telecommunications. The data base must be safeguarded so that unauthorized persons cannot obtain or change data.[4] It is also necessary to ensure that accidentally simultaneous entries that change the data base do not leave it incorrect. These precautions can be observed, but they require skilled personnel operating the system.

In school districts, there will probably be several micros in the central office, connected through a LAN to a minicomputer that will contain all of the files of the district (including student files, accounting files, personnel files, and purchasing files). Administrative staff will be able to use a micro to access the data base for routine processing, or to pose queries that answer important management questions. Results will be directed to a laser printer connected to the LAN, which will do high-quality printing for all computers connected to the LAN. In schools, there will also be micros on the desks of administrators and staff, and they will be connected to the mini (and through it to the micros of the central-office LAN) by telephone lines. Those in schools will be able to obtain data from a central data base (while observing security procedures to prevent unauthorized access). In addition, they will feed information to a central data base through their micros. Not only will this improve efficiency, because data will have to be entered only once, but the data will also be available much more promptly. However, it will be necessary to develop procedures to ensure that input data are accurate, and that these geographically dispersed information sources do not accidentally render a data base internally incompatible.

Word Processing and Desktop Publishing

Word processing has become so commonplace that it scarcely warrants discussion. Word processing equipment is rapidly replacing typewriters (even electronic ones). Its advantages, of course, are ease and speed of correction. In addition, it is possible to send large numbers of nearly identical letters that are individually addressed (they may be individualized in other ways too), rapidly and automatically.

---

[4]Computer "hackers" have managed to infiltrate networked data bases to change grades or work other mischief. In most cases, this has occurred with systems not adequately modernized to safeguard against unauthorized access. It is more difficult to guard against access by an insider. After all, someone must have the authority to gain entry to a data base for maintenance and repair and to make desired changes in the system. The best safeguard against damage by insiders is trustworthy employees.

In the future, it will be important for school district administrators to choose word processing equipment that can be connected through telephone lines or a LAN to district micros and to its high-speed printing facility. Communicating with parents by means of individualized letters attractively printed can be an important public relations tool for a principal.

School districts also produce many small publications. These range from publicity brochures to curricular material. In the past, publications either consisted of typed copy and hand-drawn artwork or were sent to a local printing house. The former method is inelegant, the latter costly and time-consuming. The advent of computers that handle a variety of type fonts and pictures easily (the Macintosh was the first of these), laser printers that can produce pictures and also letter-quality printing in a variety of sizes and type fonts, and specialized software has made it possible to produce high-quality publications in-house. This use of computers, known as *desktop publishing*, is a rapidly expanding one, and most districts will probably wish to acquire this capability.[5]

INSTRUCTIONAL USES OF COMPUTERS

There is a variety of ways in which computers can be employed in teaching. They can be used to provide instruction, as a diagnostic aid, as a tool (as encyclopedias and calculators are tools), and for development of programming ability (which probably combines both use as instruction and use as a tool). These different uses have different potentials.

Computer Literacy

Computer literacy is the ability to understand computers sufficiently to utilize them for one's own purposes. Regrettably, computer literacy as usually taught in public schools involves learning to write computer programs in one of the higher-level languages such as BASIC or Pascal. This is probably a mistake. Most people will never be computer programmers, nor is there any need for them to be familiar (except in the most general way) with programming. Thus, the large number of students being given the rudiments of programming in BASIC are, to a great extent, wasting their time.

Programming is the process of developing a set of instructions that will direct a computer to perform certain operations. Originally, instructions were written in *machine language*, the sequences of zeroes and ones that are all a computer understands. However, *higher-level languages* were developed that could be translated by a special program in the computer into machine language. Programmers now write

---

[5]This textbook is an example of desktop publishing. The manuscript was created on the Macintosh computer, using Microsoft Word. Figures and graphs were created using Excel, MacDraw, MacPaint, and Cricket Draw. After copy-editing, the chapters were set in camera-ready form by one of the authors (Garms), using the Macintosh, Microsoft Word 3.01, and the Apple LaserWriter printer. Prentice-Hall produced the book by printing from offset masters made from the camera-ready pages.

instructions in a language similar to English. However, even in the most sophisticated of these languages, programming is a highly structured process. Since the computer does exactly what it is asked to do, it will consistently do the wrong thing if its instructions are wrong. In everyday life, humans give instructions that are often incomplete or ambiguous. A recipient of the instructions uses human intelligence to decide what was intended. Except in special situations, a computer is incapable of this. Learning to program, then, is an exercise in a special kind of logic, in which a sequential set of instructions is developed that will achieve a desired result. Learning to think in this linear, sequential sort of way is probably of value, particularly in fields such as engineering. It is, however, the antithesis of the kind of holistic thinking involved in the arts and much of the humanities.

That is not the principal reason for being opposed to the teaching of programming *per se*. The fact is that most programs written by amateurs are inefficient at best and work incorrectly at worst. In addition, they are usually simple. Development of a program that would cause the computer to function as a word processor, for example, would be beyond all but the most skilled of professionals. There are many general-purpose applications that can be used by amateurs to improve their skills in a variety of ways, and they could be encouraged to use these rather than spending time learning to program.

The Computer as a Tool

General-purpose microcomputers with judicious selections of software can be a more powerful tool in the hands of a student than the encyclopedia, dictionary, typewriter, and library—largely because computers can access or emulate all of these. Students should be taught to use software that includes a word processor, a filing system, a spread-sheet program, and a graphics package. In addition, they should have access through telecommunications to a variety of data bases. There are literally hundreds of these now, some general, some highly specialized. With these general tools, students can do research and writing typical of the best students of today many grades ahead of them.

WRITING

One of the most serious problems of the public schools is that they are so labor-intensive, and nowhere is this more true than in the teaching of writing. Writing teachers must spend many hours reading essays, and much of that time is spent in routine correction of spelling mistakes, repetitive phrases, and incorrect usage. Software already exists that finds misspelled words. Some is now being developed that will warn students about overuse of words or phrases, and even about incorrect usage. Electronic thesauruses are available. If students wrote essays on a microcomputer with a word processor, they could receive immediate feedback on these routine components of writing. This feedback would improve their writing because of its immediacy, and teachers would be free to concentrate on more creative facets of writing. Putting a system like this into effect might even attract excellent former English teachers back into the profession.

One of the reasons students dislike writing so much is that it is such a bother to correct mistakes. To be able to submit a presentable paper in any subject, the student often must go through several rough drafts and then laboriously copy a clean final draft. A computer used as a word processor can shortcut much of this, allowing easy changes and a clean final draft with almost no additional effort. Students who use word processors for their papers will probably turn in more and better work than they do at present.

A FILING SYSTEM FOR ORGANIZING WORK

One of the skills students have great difficulty learning is organizing information they have acquired in order to be able to use it. In doing a library research project, for example, they have been taught since time immemorial to copy information on three-by-five filing cards, which can then be sorted into an appropriate order for use in paper writing. Such sorting is not difficult if there are only a few cards. But when the number exceeds 100, sorting time gets onerous. Students find that one order is needed when doing a bibliography (alphabetical by author), and a different order when organizing references by content. There may be a variety of ways in which a student may want things organized, and a file-card system can put them in only one order at a time. A computerized filing system, on the other hand, will sort entries in any desired way, and will also search for that elusive comment on the Mediterranean fruit fly (or whatever). Of course, there are many other uses for a filing system, and when students realize the usefulness of such a system they will utilize it effectively. An example of a simple but powerful filing system application is Hypercard.

CALCULATION AND SIMULATION

The spread-sheet program was described earlier as a tool for managers. It is equally valuable for students. The program is useful for many routine purposes for which one would normally use a handwritten spread sheet. In addition, it is capable of sophisticated calculations. This author, for example, wanted to be able to calculate the great-circle distance and initial compass heading between any two points, the latitude and longitude of which were given. Assuming that the formulas are known, this can be done in several ways. The traditional way is to hand-calculate on a piece of paper, using tables of logarithms and trigonometric functions. When a second pair of endpoints is given, the process must be repeated. Mistakes are frequent.

A second way is to use a hand calculator with trigonometric functions. This takes much of the handwork out of the process. However, to calculate a second route requires the entire process to be done again, and the opportunity for error is still great.

The third way is to program a computer to do the work. The author has done this sort of thing frequently. Once the program has been written and debugged, it is easy to run it many times, whenever one wants to calculate the distance for a new route. However, the writing and debugging can take considerable time.

In this case, the calculation was done with an ordinary spread-sheet program. It took about half the time that writing a program would have taken, including testing to be sure it was correct, and required no knowledge of programming. With a tool this powerful, students will do much more sophisticated computational tasks because they will have to spend less time on computational mechanics.

GRAPHICS

Graphics capabilities of the first computers, even mainframes, were almost nil. The first microcomputers could usually draw pictures on a screen, but to do so one had to write a program that laboriously specified the position of every line and dot by giving its coordinates. The Macintosh opened a new graphics era, for the mouse could be used to direct the motion of a "pencil," "paintbrush," or "spray can" in making pictures on the screen, freeing would-be artists from past strictures. The ability to draw on the screen (and to print results) should not be thought of as a substitute for other kinds of art, but as a new kind that will appeal to many. Future improvements will leave would-be artists thinking even less of the mechanics and more of artistic creation.

Meanwhile, systems have been developed for minicomputers that allow designers to make a drawing on the screen consisting of several views of an object, and to combine those into a three-dimensional image. This image can then be rotated in any direction, allowing designers to see flaws before a model has been built. These are called *CAD* systems (for *computer-assisted design*). There are a few CAD applications available for microcomputers, although the memory and speed of these machines have thus far limited the complexity of the applications. The ability to make and manipulate three-dimensional drawings easily should be a boon to teachers of many subjects.

A RESEARCH LIBRARY AT HOME OR SCHOOL

To complete the arsenal of tools he or she should have utilizing a microcomputer, a student should be able to access through telecommunication the large number of data bases now established on the large mainframes known as *host computers*. CompuServe and The Source are examples of general-interest data bases, but there are also large numbers of special-purpose data bases. All of these are accessible by microcomputer through use of a modem (and usually payment of a fee). Students in a small rural school district need suffer no longer from lack of access to the world's accumulated information, for it is now available twenty-four hours a day on the micro. The kinds of information vary widely, from current weather reports to a complete encyclopedia to specialized information on programs for particular micros.

Of course, all of these applications should be integrated, so that, for example, data obtained from a remote data bank may automatically be entered into a spread-sheet program for performing calculations. Results could then automatically be entered into the graphics program. The resulting graph could be enhanced with the graphics program, and finally be transferred into a paper being written on the word processor. A set of tools like this would greatly improve students' creative abilities.

Computers for Delivering Instruction

Most people who think of computers in education think of *computer-assisted instruction (CAI)*. Such instruction has usually consisted of a program that conveys information to the student on the computer screen. If it is no more than that, the same thing can be done as effectively by, say, television. However, computers allow the student to interact with the program. If the student makes incorrect responses, the program can shift to a remedial section instead of proceeding forward. Several problems have inhibited computer-assisted instruction, however:

1. Until recently, computers have been so expensive that a school could not afford enough of them to deliver the CAI effectively. Prices continue to fall and computer capabilities continue to rise, however, so this is no longer a major obstacle.

2. Writing a program to deliver computerized instruction is costly in time and effort. It often takes five to ten times as long to write a CAI program as it does to write a textbook chapter dealing with the same information. *Authoring systems* (essentially, special-purpose languages for writing CAI programs) are helping to change this.

3. The current norms in many colleges and universities reward faculty for publishing, but not for writing computer programs. Some of the best talent is thus not enticed into producing CAI programs.

4. It is almost impossible to anticipate all the various difficulties a student will encounter in understanding material, and thus it is impossible to provide in advance material that will help to solve all of these difficulties. This is one of the most intractable problems of CAI, and has led some thoughtful people to abandon usual notions of CAI in favor of the use of the computer as a set of tools, as described above.

VIDEO DISKS

The marriage of the microcomputer and the *video disk* has the potential of being an important instructional tool. It is possible to put a very large number of visual images on a video disk. Of course, one possibility is to put a movie on the disk. However, the same number of individual images would record the entire Encyclopedia Britannica on a single disk. Any individual image can be accessed almost instantly with a microcomputer and appropriate software. In bulk, video disks are quite inexpensive to manufacture, and it might be possible to have a rather large reference library in every classroom through use of them. Of course, the reference need not be just textual material. A single disk could contain high-quality color images of much of the great art of the world.

For instructional purposes, a video disk could offer a variety of material about a single subject. For example, to teach a student to build something of wood, a disk could have textual material, still photos, motion picture sequences, and animated sequences. These could be accessed by students in a preset order, or in any order desired, and reviewed as often as a student wished. A video disk–computer combination can be thought of as being somewhere between CAI and a computerized tool.

One of the important problems of education is providing adequate education in rural areas, where population sparsity prevents establishment of schools large enough to have the variety of courses and programs that serve all students well. This problem will probably be substantially alleviated in the near future through telecommunications. This is already being done on an experimental basis, with high school students in several widely separated schools receiving calculus instruction on microcomputers connected by telephone lines with a remote instructor.[6] In Alaska, instruction is provided by television to remote villages through satellite transmission.

Computers as Diagnostic Aids

Computers can serve as *diagnostic tools* in a variety of ways. Among the simplest is the test given over a computer terminal and scored by computer, with a summary given to the teacher of the kinds of errors made, which may indicate areas of defective learning. Rather more sophisticated is a CAI package that provides not only instruction to students but also an analysis of each student's movement through the program, which indicates his or her progress in learning, types of errors made, and number of times a given type of instruction must be repeated before it is learned.

Recently, applications called *expert systems* have been developed for certain special cases. The name comes from the fact that one or more experts in a particular field is carefully questioned on how to make decisions regarding questions in that field. This expert knowledge is embodied in a decision–making program that asks questions and gives potential solutions depending upon the answers to those questions. The program tends to work best when art as well as science is involved in the decision making. A good example is in medicine, where expert systems are helping doctors to diagnose diseases. It would seem feasible to develop such systems to help in diagnosing learning problems of youngsters.

THE CONNECTION WITH SCHOOL FINANCE

Whether we wish it or not, computer technology seems destined to change drastically many of the ways we administer and teach in public schools. The result in the next ten years may be desirable changes in efficiency, equity, and choice in schools.

As we have seen, a major problem with promoting efficiency in education has been the labor-intensive nature of the enterprise. Whereas manufacturers have been able to increase productivity (units of output per unit of labor input) through introduction of additional capital in the form of labor-saving devices, schools have actually gone in the opposite direction. The number of students per professional de-

[6]Jane Perlez, "Computer Links Today to Tomorrow along Country Roads," *Democrat and Chronicle* (Rochester, N.Y.), December 29, 1985, p. 23.

clined from twenty-six in 1960 to eighteen in 1985. Such decline is often effected in the name of better instruction, through decreased class size (although average class size has not declined as rapidly as the number of pupils per professional; many positions added have been noninstructional), but it has also been a way of maintaining employment in the face of decreasing numbers of students. In any case, since labor costs are roughly 80 percent of the total cost of public education, the only feasible way to promote much efficiency is to reduce these costs. Technology such as that discussed in this chapter can probably help to do that.

In the classroom, computers can relieve teachers of much of the present routine activities of drill-and-practice, as well as helping to provide a higher quality of instruction. The result should be the possibility of larger class sizes without diminution of instructional quality. In the office, the ability of administrators to obtain information formerly unavailable, or not available on a timely basis, should result in better decisions. These gains will probably improve efficiency not by decreasing the office labor force but by improving the quality of education.

Equity may be improved primarily through individualizing instruction much more than at present. A major current problem is that students have many different kinds of learning styles and disabilities. It is possible generally to devise special programs for groups of students who suffer from the same class of disability, but within those groups (as within the "normal student" group) there are wide differences in student needs. The teacher can individualize among these students only to a limited extent because of time limitations. Computer-assisted instruction will probably become increasingly available and attuned to the many differences in learning styles of students, and should help each student to learn to the extent of his or her ability. Computers can also be used (as discussed earlier) to deliver specialized instruction to geographically dispersed students in rural areas.

There are those who believe that computers will result in a decrease in equity. They fear that only the schools that serve economically well-to-do areas will have computers, and they believe that administrative arrangements accompanying the introduction of computers will result in more racial or social segregation. The first of these concerns should have nothing to do with computers. If schools serving poor students cannot afford computers, it is because there is insufficient financial equity in the system at present. The problem should be attacked through the means discussed elsewhere in this book. The second concern apparently has to do with the notion that computers will result in much instruction being done in the home, rather than at schools, and that children will thus be spared the salubrious effects of contacts with children of other backgrounds. It seems unlikely that this will happen in the foreseeable future. The changes that will probably take place in the schools as a result of the introduction of computers will be extensive, but they will probably not result in most schooling being done at home.

Finally, it is clear that computers will increase the choices available to parents and students. A single classroom, through use of computer-assisted instruction, can offer instruction in a much greater variety of areas than is now feasible. Access to information in distant data banks through telecommunication will broaden students' horizons immensely. Of course, school instruction can be supplemented by programs available at home through a computer.

All of this will not be costless. Technology will increase capital inputs, but the extent to which it might decrease labor costs is not clear. Computers are not cheap. Although they are constantly decreasing in price,[7] demand for increased capability has resulted in a rapid increase in total expenditures for computers. However, the cost of computers that will accomplish many of the things discussed in this chapter has decreased to the point that most schools can afford to invest in them. Of course, school districts should not assume that they must buy computers and computerized instructional materials from the book budget. As discussed, the way computers eventually may make education more efficient is by reducing labor needs.

SUMMARY

Computer technology seems destined to change many of the ways in which schools operate both instruction and administration. The result in the next fifteen years may well be an increase in equity of education as schools become able to provide more individualized instruction; an increase in school district efficiency because administrators will have more timely and usable information and because computers can replace teachers for routine instructional tasks; and an increase in choices allowed students and their parents. However, these important changes are not without cost. Computers continue to decrease in price, but this seems merely to increase the demand for them. Schools will have to spend large amounts of money to equip themselves to use the new technology. In addition, everyone, from superintendents to teachers and students, will need to learn the basics of how to use computers for the specific purposes for which they need them. Finally, massive introduction of computers will change people's traditional relationships with one another, and involve potential infringement on turf that will create problems for the organization of schools.

---

[7]Hardware costs of equivalent capability have been cut roughly in half every two years for the last twenty years.

chapter thirteen

ENHANCING EDUCATIONAL EQUITY

This book emphasizes equity, efficiency, and choice as crucial qualities that may be used to judge an educational system. This final part of the book consists of three chapters, one for each of these values. This chapter discusses means for deciding how equitable school finance systems are and whether changes designed to improve equity actually do so. Chapter 14 describes a variety of means in which the allocative and technical efficiency of schools may be improved. Chapter 15 illustrates a system of school organization and finance that would greatly increase the choices available to students and their parents.

Chapter 6 described various features of school finance systems. Many of those features were concerned with improving equity. In addition, most of the school finance litigation described in Chapter 8 focuses primarily on issues of equity. Thus, it is important to define what is meant by equity and to develop ways of measuring the extent to which it has been achieved.

DECIDING WHAT TO MEASURE

An important question in enhancing equity is what to measure. Is the interest in outcomes, such as test scores, unemployment rates of graduates, or percentage of graduates who go to college? Is the interest in process measures, such as number of advanced placement classes, extent to which computers are used, or amount of emphasis on basic subjects? Or is the concern for input measures—dollars spent per student, average teacher salary, or pupil–teacher ratio? Ideally, we are interested in outputs, for these constitute the purpose of education. As a practical matter, however, outputs are difficult to measure. We would like to know how successful students are later in life, but it takes too long to determine this, and there are too many other variables affecting the result. Those who measure outputs usually utilize test scores, not because they are the optimal output measure but because they are available when the results are of more than historical interest, and because they are quantified and thus amenable to analysis.

Process variables are also difficult to utilize in many cases, primarily because they are not usually measured consistently among school districts in a state. For better or worse, most of the measurement of school finance equity has focused on input variables. By far the most frequent have been dollar inputs—revenues or expenditures per student. Even though there is little conclusive evidence of a close connection between dollar inputs and educational outputs, officials who must generate taxes believe that resources are important, and many of them want tax dollars spent equitably.

APPROACHES TO EQUALIZATION

Chapter 6 makes it clear that most school finance systems are concerned with disparities caused by three different categories of problems. The first is that local school districts differ in their ability to raise money through taxes. Accommodating this issue is the province of wealth equalization. Need equalization is necessary because some students require more expensive instructional techniques as a result of various handicaps, mental, physical, or emotional. Cost equalization is designed to compensate for the fact that it costs more in some school districts to deliver the same quality and quantity of education than it does in others. These environmental differences result in differing needs for bus transportation, differing amounts of snow removal, and differing pay scales to attract high-quality employees.

If all students in a state were completely normal, if all districts had identical tax-raising ability per student, and if there were no environmental differences, there would be no need to utilize state money for equalization. But it would still be necessary to define what is meant by equity, and to establish rules to see that it is attained. There are two general schools of thought here. The first is that it is the state's duty to ensure that all children are equally provided a basic education. *Basic education* is variously defined, but it is usually conceived as that level of education necessary for students to become productive members of society rather than public charges. Education above basic requirements is thought of as a locally preferred luxury. Localities may tax themselves to provide it, but they will receive no additional assistance from the state in providing it. The flat grant and the foundation program are based on this philosophy.

The second philosophy is that whatever services state schools provide should be provided equally, whether it is reading or driver training. This philosophy is divided into two subschools. One is that the education provided should be identical in all districts, resulting in complete state financing and provision of education. The other subschool maintains that it is sufficient to make it equally possible for districts to raise money for education while not specifying how much they shall raise. This is the philosophy of percentage equalizing, power equalizing, and guaranteed tax base plans.

All of these wealth-equalizing plans are concerned with equal treatment of equals. Similarly, plans that compensate districts for differences in the cost of providing equivalent education are also concerned with providing equal treatment to equals. On the other hand, special provision for handicapped children is unequal treatment of those who are not equal.

MEASURES OF EQUITY

One can think of equity as composed of *horizontal equity* and *vertical equity*. Horizontal equity applies to equal treatment of equals, whereas vertical equity involves unequal treatment of unequals to an end that is somehow equitable. Horizontal equity is by far the easier to measure, and devising measures of horizontal equity has attracted far more attention. The reason it is easier to measure, of course, is that it is relatively easy to determine whether two or more things are equal. It is much more difficult to determine whether an unequal distribution is equitable. We first consider measures of horizontal equity.[1]

Horizontal Equity

THE RANGE

The most frequently used measure is the *range*. This is simply the distance between the lowest number in a series and the highest. An item of data, typically expenditures per student, is examined for each school district in a state, and a comparison made between highest expenditure and lowest expenditure. For example, it might be noted that per-student expenditures in a particular state range from $1500 to $5000, a range of $3500. This clearly appears to be inequitable, and such comparisons have helped convince legislators and the public in several states to change their financial system. However, the range measure has severe drawbacks. To assess problems with this and other measures, we present two distributions of expenditures per student in Table 13.1. Each distribution displays data for ten districts, constituting a sample state. Each school district has 1000 students. Inspection of

---

[1] The best treatment of school finance equity measures is provided in Robert Berne and Leanna Stiefel, *The Measurement of Equity in School Finance* (Baltimore: The Johns Hopkins University Press, 1984).

TABLE 13.1 Expenditure Data for Two Sample States

STATE A		STATE B	
DISTRICT	EXPENDITURES	DISTRICT	EXPENDITURES
1	$1000	1	$1000
2	1100	2	2300
3	1200	3	2350
4	1300	4	2400
5	1400	5	2450
6	4600	6	2500
7	4700	7	2550
8	4800	8	2600
9	4900	9	2650
10	5000	10	5000

the data for the two states reveals that state A has five districts that are low-spending (between $1000 and $1400), and five that are high-spending (between $4600 and $5000). State B has one low-spending district, one high-spending district, and eight districts that spend similar amounts somewhere in the middle of the range of expenditures. To most observers, from the point of view of horizontal equity state B has the more equitable system. With the exception of two districts, all districts are spending about the same amount. However, the range is exactly the same for both states—$4000 (the difference between the highest-spending and lowest-spending district). A major problem with the range as a measure is that it employs data for only two districts, ignoring all of the other districts. Also, because the two districts are the highest- and lowest-spending, they are apt to be not at all representative of the state as a whole.

Why, then, has the range been used so frequently? Aside from ignorance on the part of those quoting the figure, the only good reasons are that it is easily understood by unsophisticated nonspecialists and is usually large and therefore alarming. Thus, the range has its political uses to those challenging the system, but it is perhaps the least accurate measure available.

THE RESTRICTED RANGE

In an attempt to retain ease of understanding while improving measurement, the *restricted range* was devised. The idea is that one should eliminate the highest- and lowest-spending districts and examine the range among districts that are more representative. For example, it could be agreed that the lowest-spending 10 percent and the highest-spending 10 percent of districts will be eliminated, restricting the range to the middle 80 percent . In the case of the two sample states in Table 13.1, if the highest - and lowest-spending districts in each are deleted, then the restricted range is $3800 ($4900 – $1100) for state A, and $350 ($2650 – $2300) for state B. The restricted range for B is less than one-tenth that for A. It would appear that the restricted range has accomplished its goal of distinguishing between these two distributions.

THE FEDERAL RANGE RATIO

There are other problems with the range as an equity measure that have not been discussed. For example, in either of our sample states the range (unrestricted) is $4000. Now suppose that the nation experiences serious inflation, and the dollar loses 50 percent of its value. In order to purchase the same amount of labor and supplies, each district must now spend twice as much as before. The lowest-spending district now spends $2000, the highest-spending $10,000. The range is now $8000, or twice as large. Does that mean that the distribution is only half as good as before? Clearly not. The only thing that has changed is the value of the dollar. Goods and services being purchased by districts are exactly the same as before. In other words, the range is sensitive to changes in scale. It is as though two persons measured the same distance, one with a foot ruler and one with a yardstick.

The *federal range ratio* was designed to address this problem. It is a restricted range in which the top and bottom 5 percent of the districts are dropped. (Actually, it is the top and bottom 5 percent of *students*.) This restricted range is then divided by per-pupil expenditure at the 5th percentile. Because there are only ten districts in our example, there is no way of deleting only 5 percent of the districts from each end. In order, then, to illustrate the federal range ratio, we drop instead the upper and lower 10 percent of the districts, take the ratio, and divide by the expenditure at the 10th percentile. For state A, the federal range ratio is ($4900 − $1100)/$1100 = 3.45. For state B, the federal range ratio is ($2650 − $2300)/$2300 = 0.15. Exactly equal expenditures would give a federal range ratio of zero. These results clearly reveal that state A is less equitable than state B.

Now, suppose that the same 100 percent inflation occurs. All of the numbers will double. But because both the restricted range and expenditures at the 10th percentile double, the ratio stays exactly the same. The federal range ratio thus accommodates the problem of sensitivity to changes in scale. This would also be true, of course, if one were comparing two states, one of which spends much more per student than the other.

The federal range ratio was devised for a specific purpose. Some federal funds, called impact aid, are provided to school districts affected by a federal presence, such as a large army base. The money is given in lieu of taxes, since federal property cannot be taxed (see Chapter 7). Kansas decided that this money was like revenue raised by local taxes, and counted the impact aid as part of the required local contribution to the school finance system. This, in effect, converted the impact aid into general aid to the state rather than aid to particular school districts. Since impact aid goes to districts in most congressmen's constituencies, the legislators were not pleased. Congress directed that only states with exceedingly equal finance systems could be allowed to do this. The federal range ratio was devised as a way to measure equality of state systems.

THE STANDARD DEVIATION

It should be clear that a measure that encompasses all data instead of only two items is preferable. One such measure is the *standard deviation*. This is a measure of the extent to which data are dispersed about the mean.[2] In a normal, bell-shaped distribution, two-thirds of the cases will fall within plus or minus one standard deviation from the mean, 95 percent of the cases within plus or minus two standard deviations, and more than 99 percent of the cases within plus or minus three standard deviations. State A has a standard deviation of $1903, state B a standard deviation of $974. On the basis of this, it would appear that B has a system in which dispersion from the mean is only half as great as that in A.

THE COEFFICIENT OF VARIATION

It should be clear that the standard deviation suffers from the range's problem of being overly sensitive to changes in scale. The solution is similar to that adopted for the federal range ratio. Here, we divide the standard deviation by the mean. The resulting ratio is known as the *coefficient of variation*. For our sample states, the coefficients of variation are as follows:

State A: 1903 ÷ 3000 = 0.63
State B: 974 ÷ 2580 = 0.38

The lower the coefficient of variation, the greater the equity. If all districts spent exactly the same amount per student, the coefficient of variation would be zero. This measure, like the standard deviation, is not so easily understood by laymen, but it is otherwise a good measure. It is a favorite of those who analyze school finance systems.

THE LORENZ CURVE AND THE GINI COEFFICIENT

For many years economists have used the *Lorenz curve* and its associated statistic, the *Gini coefficient*, to display inequalities of income. The horizontal axis measures percentage of the population (in, say, a state), and the vertical axis measures percentage of total personal income in the state. All individuals in the state are ranked in order of increasing income. Then, for each percentage of population, a dot is plotted displaying the percentage of total personal income possessed by all persons below that point (see Figure 13.1). If all persons had exactly the same income, the first 25 percent of the people would have 25 percent of the income, the first 50 percent would have 50 percent of the income, and so forth. Drawing this on the graph results in a straight diagonal line. However, since incomes are not equal, the lowest 10 percent of the population will have less than 10 percent of the in-

---

[2]As this is a nontechnical book, we make no effort to go into the derivation of the standard deviation. See any standard text on statistics. The formula is

$$s = \sqrt{\frac{\Sigma x^2 - \frac{(\Sigma x)^2}{n}}{n - 1}}$$

where s is the standard deviation, $(\Sigma x)^2$ is the square of the sum of the data items, Σx^2 is the sum of the squared data items, and n is the number of data items.

FIGURE 13.1   Lorenz Curve of Income

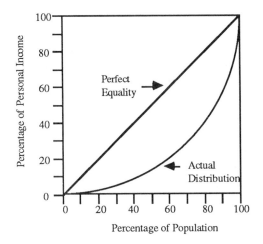

come, the lowest 50 percent will have less than 50 percent of the income, and so on. A line connecting the dots will sag below the diagonal line. The more unequal the incomes, the more the line will sag. The curve this line makes is known as a Lorenz curve.

It is also possible to construct Lorenz curves for a state's school districts using percentage of districts (or percentage of pupils, as discussed later) on the horizontal scale and percentage of total expenditure on the vertical scale. If Lorenz curves are constructed for the two sample states, they will look like Figure 13.2. It is clear that the line for state B sags less than the line for state A, substantiating the subjective assessment that state B has the more equitable distribution of expenditures.

FIGURE 13.2   Lorenz Curves for Sample Districts

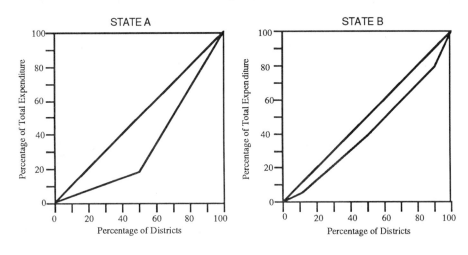

The Lorenz curve is one of the few graphic modes of measuring equity, and graphics are often helpful in visualizing information. However, graphs are time-consuming to construct and use a great deal of space. There is a natural desire to condense the information into a single number. This can be accomplished by considering the area between the diagonal line and the line of actual expenditures. This area can be expressed as a proportion of the total triangular area between the diagonal line and the bottom and right sides of the graph. If there were perfect equality, the area between diagonal and curve would not exist. If one district had all of the expenditures and none of the rest had any, the area would occupy all of the triangle. The ratio of area between diagonal and curve to the triangular area is called the Gini coefficient. It can range from 0.00 to 1.00, and the smaller the coefficient, the greater the equity. Calculating it is time-consuming, and best done with a computer. For the sample states, the Gini coefficient is .31 for A and .16 for B.

THE MCLOONE INDEX

At this point, it is important to make specific the criteria by which each measure judges a distribution. The range is concerned only with the total span of distribution; it is utterly unconcerned with what happens between extremes. The restricted range does the same thing within its boundaries, ignoring not only the distribution between its two end points but also any data outside its boundaries. The federal range ratio is the same.

The standard deviation is concerned with distribution of all data, as are the coefficient of variation, Lorenz curve, and Gini coefficient. All of these measures would be appropriate for those who say that whatever education is provided publicly must be provided equally to all. However, those who believe that the state is obligated only to provide a basic education equally would find these measures inappropriate, unless the only expenditures measured are those used to provide a basic education. In the absence of data on this dimension, some have decided that the important objective is to elevate districts that are in the lower half of the distribution. In their view, it is unnecessary to lower those in the upper half of the distribution, or to do anything with them. Implicitly, the average expenditure is sufficient to provide for a basic education, and expenditures above this point are local luxuries. The *McLoone index* is designed to measure the extent to which this goal is achieved. The measure is a ratio of the actual expenditure in all districts below or at the median expenditure to what the expenditures would be if all of those districts spent at exactly the median expenditure.[3] For state A, the median expenditure is $3000 (halfway between $1400 and $4600). The five districts that spend below the median have a total expenditure of $6 million (remember that each district has exactly 1000 students. District 5, then, with expenditures of $1400 per student, spends $1,400,000). If all of these districts spent exactly at the median expenditure,

[3]The median expenditure is the expenditure in the middle district when the districts are arrayed in order of expenditure. If there is an even number of districts, the median expenditure is halfway between the two districts closest to the middle. The median is chosen instead of the mean because if expenditures in the bottom half of the distribution were raised, the mean would change but the median would not.

the total expenditure would be 5000 students x $3000 = $15,000,000. The McLoone index, then, is $6,000,000 ÷ $15,000,000 = 0.4. For state B, the McLoone index would be 0.85.

The McLoone index has a maximum of 1.00, representing exact equality of expenditures for all districts below the median. This is unfortunate, because all of the other equity measures have a value of zero with perfect equity. The resulting difficulty of comparison has led us to develop a measure that we call the *inverse McLoone index*. It is the amount of money necessary to bring expenditure in all districts below the median to the median, divided by what the expenditures would be if all of those districts spent at the median expenditure. Mathematically, the inverse McLoone index equals 1 minus the McLoone index. For state A it is 0.6; for state B, 0.15.

THE CORRELATION

All of the measures thus far have been univariate measures. That is, they measure dispersion of only one distribution, that of expenditures. This is appropriate if the goal of the school finance system is to equalize expenditures. This is usually the goal of foundation programs and full state funding. On the other hand, percentage equalizing and power equalizing are not concerned with equalizing expenditures, but only with equalizing the access of districts to money. Two districts that levy the same tax rate should have the same amount of money to spend per pupil, but one that levies a higher tax rate than another should have more to spend per pupil. In assessing the extent to which this is accomplished, the appropriate comparison is tax rates with expenditures per student. If there is a perfect correspondence between them, the system is equitable by the criteria of those who believe in power equalizing. If there is no relationship between them, the opposite is true. The appropriate measure for such correspondence is the *correlation coefficient*. This coefficient is a measure with a maximum of 1.00, indicating perfect correspondence between two distributions, and a minimum of 0.00, indicating no relationship between them. It is usually more instructive to assess the square of the correlation coefficient (which also varies between 0 and 1), for it indicates the proportion of variation in one variable that is associated with variation in another variable. Thus, a correlation coefficient of 0.70 would have a square of 0.49, indicating that 49 percent of the variation in one variable is associated with variation in the other variable. The remaining 51 percent of the variation in one variable is unrelated to variation in the other.[4]

[4]See any statistics text on the derivation of the correlation coefficient and the line of regression. The formula for the correlation coefficient is

$$r = \frac{n\Sigma xy - \Sigma x \Sigma y}{\sqrt{[n\Sigma x^2 - (\Sigma x)^2][n\Sigma y^2 - (\Sigma y)^2]}}$$

where the x values are tax rates, the y values are expenditures, and n is the number of districts.

FIGURE 13.3   Regressions of Expenditures on Tax Rate

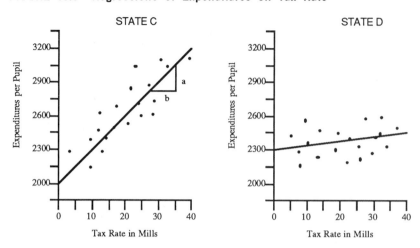

The correlation coefficient encompasses all data, it conveys a number that is easily understood subjectively by laymen (although, as said previously, the square of the correlation coefficient is more easily understood), and it is unaffected by changes in scale of the data. However, there may be a high correlation between tax rate and expenditures per pupil, but the amount of change in expenditure with tax rate may nevertheless be small. The idea is illustrated in Figure 13.3. Both graphs display data for districts plotted as points: a line is drawn through the points to provide the best fit to the dots. In both of the graphs, the points tend to be rather close to the line, and the squared correlation coefficient in both cases is about 0.90. However, in state C a ten-mill tax rate increase results in an increase of $300 per pupil in spending, whereas in state D a ten-mill increase results in an addition of only $50 per pupil in spending. Clearly, changes in tax rate are much more important in determining spending per pupil in state C than in state D.

THE REGRESSION COEFFICIENT

The extent to which changes in expenditure are affected by changes in tax rate can be measured with the *regression coefficient*. The regression coefficient measures the slope of the *line of regression,* which is the line of best fit through the data points (see Figure 13.3). The slope is defined as the ratio of the vertical component of the line to its horizontal component. For state C, the slope would be represented by the small triangle, the ratio being $a \div b$. There, a represents an increase of $600 in expenditure, and b an increase of twenty mills in the tax rate. The ratio is $30 per mill. For state D, of course, the slope, or regression coefficient, is $5 per mill.[5]

[5]The formula for the line of regression is $y = A + Bx$, where A is the point at which the line intercepts the y axis (where $x = 0$), and B is the slope of the line. For state C, A is $2000 and B is $30. The formulas for calculating A and B are as follows:

$$A = \frac{\Sigma y \Sigma x^2 - (\Sigma x)^2}{n\Sigma x^2 - (\Sigma x)^2} \quad \text{and} \quad B = \frac{n\Sigma xy - \Sigma x \Sigma y}{n\Sigma x^2 - (\Sigma x)^2}$$

Both the correlation coefficient and regression coefficient are helpful statistics in assessing a state school finance system that is based on the percentage equalizing or power equalizing concept. The correlation coefficient conveys the extent to which there is a relationship between tax rate and expenditures. The regression coefficient communicates the significance of that relationship. In Figure 13.3, there is a strong relationship between tax rate and expenditures for both states, but in state C the relationship is a much more important one in that a change in tax rate can make a much greater difference in expenditures. The correlation coefficient and regression coefficient are also frequently used to measure the relationship between expenditures and property value.

The Unit of Measurement

The discussion to this point has been about districts rather than pupils. In our examples we assumed for the sake of simplicity that all of the districts in states A and B had exactly 1000 students. Typically, however, a few districts in a state have many students and many districts have only a few students. To treat all districts alike may distort the picture. Consider, for example, the situation in state B in two cases. In the first case, district 5 has 100,000 students, and each of the remaining districts only 100 students. In the second case, districts 1 and 10 each have 50,000 students while each of the rest of the districts has 100 students. Subjectively, it would appear that the first case represents greater equity, for more than 99 percent of the pupils reside in one district, where the expenditure is a uniform $2450. In the second case, almost half of the students reside in a district where the expenditure is $1000, and almost half reside in a district where the expenditure is $5000. Yet, the district-based statistics just described would suggest the same results for both cases.

The solution to this problem is to base statistics on students rather than on districts. In this way, a weight is given to each district based on the number of students it has. Although an implicit assumption is made that within any district the expenditure on each child is exactly the same, this often is not the case. However, in most states there are no data that allow an analyst to go below the district level in examining expenditures.

Vertical Equity

All of the measures described thus far contain the implicit assumption that all students in a state are normal students, and that it is therefore equitable to spend exactly the same amount on each. This is horizontal equity. However, that is clearly not the case, for not only do school districts spend more on certain children (those who are handicapped or those who must be transported to school, for example), but often state school finance systems specifically take these needs into account and provide extra funds on their behalf. This confounds efforts to measure horizontal equity. Suppose that half of the districts in a state have large expenditures for transportation and the remainder have no expenditures for that purpose. Suppose further that except for this condition all districts spend exactly the same amount of money per pupil. All mathematical measures would show less-than-perfect horizontal equity for the state, since half of the districts would be spending substantially more than the other half. However, it could be argued that the system has perfect horizontal and vertical equity, for money is spent on transportation only to get children to school who live a long distance away, and once at school all students have the same amount spent on them.

We pose the illustration in this way to emphasize two points. The first is that the obvious way to examine horizontal and vertical equity is to separate expenditures on normal pupils from those on exceptional pupils. (Measures explained thus far assess expenditures on normal pupils for horizontal equity.) The main problem is making the separation. It is easy to do for transportation. Districts in almost all states maintain accounts for transportation separate from those for other purposes. But it is a completely different matter for handicapped pupils, particularly those who are mainstreamed. Typically, separate records are not kept, or are not kept in a way that would allow sufficient separation for purposes of an equity analysis.

The second point is that it is easy to establish criteria for judging horizontal equity (for example, that the range be zero, or that the correlation between tax rate and expenditures be one), but there are no agreed-upon criteria for vertical equity. How much more should be spent on an educable mentally retarded pupil than on a normal pupil? The answer often depends on unspoken or unverified notions of fairness, and on the technology available for education. It is clear that an educable mentally retarded child can never acquire the amount of learning that a normal youngster can. Those in the business of educating the handicapped speak of allowing each child to achieve to the limit of his or her ability. Though this is a laudable abstract goal, it is not subject to easy quantification. Even supposing that it were, if it cost twenty times as much to develop a mentally retarded child to the limit of his ability as it did for a normal child, would society be willing to spend that much? Would it be fair to the normal children if expenditures on them were reduced by half so that more money could be spent on handicapped children? Questions like these would be difficult to answer even if we knew how much additional ought to be spent. For this reason, often the best policy analysts can do is to indicate how much is being spent on certain groups or proportionately how much more is being spent on them than on normal children, and leave it to a political consensus to decide whether this is appropriate.

A different problem is posed by cost equalization. Does the fact that a mountain district spends more per pupil for snow removal mean that it has a better program? There is no answer unless the *extra* expenses that result from its location can be separated. To do this, given the kinds of records that are kept currently, is almost impossible. However, if a state attempts to equalize for such differences in costs, it is probably appropriate to deduct funding provided for special purposes from the revenues or expenditures being measured for equity.

Multivariate Methods

Almost all of those who have analyzed school finance systems quantitatively have used univariate or bivariate statistics such as those described previously. The result is that at best they can measure only horizontal equity. At worst, the statistics provide a misleading picture because of distortions introduced by attempts to introduce vertical equity into the system. In addition, there are two possible approaches to horizontal equity: equality of expenditures and equality of access to money. The measures to be used for the two are different. However, many states have elements of both in their school finance system.

A set of measures has been developed that attempts to capture the complexity of entire school finance systems.[6] The method relies on multiple regression techniques in which expenditure per pupil is the dependent variable; the independent variables measure dimensions such as assessed valuation, tax rate, number of handicapped pupils, number of pupils from poor families, number of bilingual pupils, and two district-size measures that attempt to capture diseconomies of scale in unusually small and unusually large school districts. The results display the extent to which variations in expenditures are associated with variations in each of the independent variables. These measures enable one to compare the profile of the system with the legislative intent in establishing it. For example, a system that is highly equalized, relying on power equalizing and special aids for the handicapped, would display a high multiple correlation, with a large percentage of variation accounted for by tax rate and percentage handicapped, and low percentages by variables such as assessed valuation and district size. A state system that is not well equalized but relies for what equalization it has exclusively on a foundation program would show a moderate multiple correlation, and the major proportion of variation would be associated with assessed valuation.

This is the only attempt made thus far to capture most of the value dimensions on which legislators attempt to achieve horizontal and vertical equity. It suffers from the problem that multiple regression is even more difficult for nonspecialists to understand than simple regression. The study utilized data from four states to illustrate the method, but thus far the method has not been used in analyzing a state's system for policy purposes.

RESULTS OF MEASURING EQUITY

Comparisons among States

Most of the studies undertaken on the equity of school finance systems are of a single state at a single point in time. Such analyses are of limited use. Individual studies usually cannot be compared with one another because of differing definitions of the dimensions to be measured. Usually there are measures of expenditures or revenue per student, but each analyst defines these differently. In 1978, however, the School Finance Cooperative was formed to develop measures of equity for a large

[6]Walter I. Garms, "Measuring the Equity of School Finance Systems," *Journal of Education Finance,* 4, no. 4 (Spring 1979), 415–35.

number of states based on consistent definitions of revenues and students.[7] Group members had access, among them, to data on twenty-eight states for selected years from 1970 to 1977. They computed all of the equity-appraisal measures described previously, and in addition some that are more exotic. However, the fact that the measures are for some years for some states and other years for other states renders the data of limited use for comparisons.

The 1978 amendments to the Federal Education Act mandated the Department of Health, Education and Welfare to publish biennial profiles of each state displaying the degree to which financial resource equalization has been attained among the state's school districts. Although these profiles have never been officially published, the National Center for Education Statistics did analyze data and issue a draft report in December 1979.[8] It contained measures for forty-eight states for the years 1969 and 1976.[9]

More recently, in 1987 the U.S. Department of Education commissioned a study of equity measures for thirty-one states for 1983 and 1984 using the same data definitions used in 1969 and 1977.[10] Results of these two studies, covering three selected years from a fourteen-year time span, are shown in Table 13.2. The mean for all three of the measures increased over the period, whether we look at forty-eight states between 1969 and 1976 or at thirty-one states from 1969 to 1983. In other words, on average the equity of the school finance systems in these states, as measured by these statistics, is worsening. However, depending upon the measure and the span of years selected, between one-fourth and one-half of the states improved in equity. Since in a steady state with random variation one would expect half of the states to improve over any period, the fact that fewer than half did reinforces the impression that school finance equality is being further diluted.

Comparisons of Measures for a State Over Time

Comparisons on a consistent basis of the equity in a single state over an extended period of time are also infrequent. Table 13.3 displays results for two states where such studies have been made. In both studies, the measure was of general-purpose revenues (exclusive of categorical revenues) per weighted student. The Illinois data shown in the table are for "unit" districts (those with grades K–12). Florida data are for all districts in the state.

---

[7]Published in Robert Berne and Leanna Stiefel, *A Methodological Assessment of Education Equality and Wealth Neutrality Measures* (New York: Graduate School of Public Administration, New York University, 1978).

[8]National Center for Educational Statistics, *School Finance Equity: A Profile of the States, 1976–77,* (Washington, D.C.: NCES, U.S. Department of HEW, 1979).

[9]The measures are not applicable in Hawaii, where there is only one statewide school district. Data were unavailable for Montana.

[10]The study was being done by DRC, Inc., of Washington, D.C., for the Department of Education. It was not complete at the time this book was set in type. Results for 1983 were furnished to the authors by Jay Moskowitz of DRC, and are printed with permission of the Department of Education.

TABLE 13.2   State Finance Disparity Measures, 1969-83

	COEFF. OF VARIATION			FED. RANGE RATIO			GINI INDEX	
	1969	1976	1983	1969	1976	1983	1969	1976
Alabama	.087	.122		.3	.5		.053	.068
Alaska	.141	.230	.469	.4	.8	1.17	.075	.111
Arizona	.088	.140		.2	.4		.044	.064
Arkansas	.174	.181		.7	.8		.091	.100
Calif. Unif. Dists.	.200	.140	.130	.6	.5	.42	.089	.071
Colorado	.163	.176		.5	.7		.087	.094
Connecticut	.237	.186	.210	1.2	.8	.81	.129	.103
Delaware	.162	.226	.166	.7	1.0	.54	.093	.117
Florida	.123	.121	.096	.5	.4	.32	.069	.067
Georgia	.165	.194		.7	.9		.088	.108
Idaho	.115	.147	.154	.5	.5	.58	.062	.077
Illinois Unit Dists.	.180	.174	.244	.6	.6	1.14	.092	.097
Indiana	.166	.157		.6	.6		.087	.088
Iowa	.192	.073	.069	.9	.3	.23	.083	.040
Kansas	.151	.144	.156	.5	.5	.55	.072	.074
Kentucky	.170	.210		.7	.8		.088	.111
Lousiana	.093	.120	.143	.4	.5	.52	.051	.068
Maine	.181	.150	.188	.6	.6	.64	.093	.082
Maryland	.133	.147	.175	.6	.6	.65	.068	.080
Massachusetts	.172	.249	.248	.6	1.2	.91	.094	.125
Michigan	.186	.205	.195	.8	.8	.80	.102	.106
Minnesota	.127	.186	.162	.5	.9	.66	.071	.099
Mississippi	.152	.146		.6	.7		.069	.080
Missouri Unif. Dists.	.264	.234	.441	.8	.9	.82	.114	.122
Nebraska	.166	.181	.224	.6	.7	.89	.082	.087
Nevada	.076	.075		.2	.1		.028	.020
New Hampshire	.116	.139	.343	.5	.6	1.01	.063	.077
New Jersey	.149	.151		.6	.7		.080	.084
New Mexico	.129	.132		.4	.5		.056	.059
New York	.149	.198	.236	.6	.8	.85	.075	.106
North Carolina	.101	.121	.095	.4	.4	.33	.057	.066
North Dakota	.142	.162	.277	.5	.6	1.08	.075	.083
Ohio	.217	.229	.292	1.0	.9	1.20	.121	.128
Oklahoma	.197	.172		.5	.5		.093	.079
Oregon	.089	.114	.126	.4	.4	.37	.048	.064
Pennsylvania	.216	.209	.195	.7	.8	.89	.112	.117
Rhode Island	.188	.136	.110	.8	.5	.35	.102	.077
South Carolina	.087	.136		.4	.6		.048	.074
South Dakota	.141	.180		.4	.9		.068	.091
Tennessee	.182	.227	.190	.7	.9	.74	.103	.128
Texas	.159	.181	.203	.7	.7	.79	.080	.093
Utah	.088	.097		.3	.3		.041	.047
Vermont	.226	.165		1.4	.8		.118	.092
Virginia	.246	.243	.228	.7	.8	.91	.128	.127
Washington	.160	.184	.148	.6	.8	.51	.090	.102
West Virginia	.105	.097		.3	.3		.059	.055
Wisconsin	.118	.144	.146	.5	.5	.52	.065	.081
Wyoming	.190	.150	.234	.6	.5	.93	.085	.081
Number of states	48	48	31	48	48	31	48	48
Maximum value	.264	.249	.469	1.4	1.2	1.20	.129	.128
Minimum value	.076	.073	.069	.2	.1	.23	.028	.020
Mean value	.155	.164	.203	.6	.6	.71	.080	.087

Sources: *School Finance Equity: A Profile of the States*, op. cit. (1969 and 1976) and Jay Moskowitz, DRC, Inc., personal communication (1983).

TABLE 13.3   Finance Disparity Measures for Illinois and Florida, 1972-87

	ILLINOIS		FLORIDA		
	COEFFICIENT OF VARIATION	MCLOONE INDEX	COEFFICIENT OF VARIATION	GINI INDEX	MCLOONE INDEX
1972-73	.147	.903	.076	.043	.968
1973-74	.134	.919	.045	.021	.953
1974-75	.134	.922	N.A.	N.A.	N.A.
1975-76	.133	.937	.064	.034	.948
1976-77	.129	.929	.028	.013	.978
1977-78	.137	.897	.039	.018	.974
1978-79	.157	.892	.029	.015	.976
1979-80	.139	.908	.027	.014	.980
1980-81	.163	.921	.029	.014	.976
1981-82	.145	.938	.047	.018	.971
1982-83	.167	.937	.025	.012	.975
1983-84	.165	.936	.028	.014	.977
1984-85	.158	.941	.030	.015	.977
1985-86	.139	.956	.034	.018	.971
1986-87	.141	.926	N.A.	N.A.	N.A.

Sources for Illinois: G. Alan Hickrod, Ramesh B. Chaudhari, and Benjamin C. Hubbard, *The Decline and Fall of School Finance Reform in Illinois, 1985 Revision* (Normal, Ill: Center for the Study of Educational Finance, College of Education, Illinois State University, 1986), with 1986-87 data provided by the first author. For Florida: Walter I. Garms and James W. Guthrie, *Assessing Educational Equity in Florida*, a report to the Florida State Department of Education, 1987, unpublished.

By both the coefficient of variation and the McLoone index measures, Illinois shows changes from year to year, but little general improvement over time. Florida had a major change in its school finance formula between 1972-73 and 1973-74, with little change in the finance system since. The data for the coefficient of variation and the Gini Index show improvement that resulted from that reform, and the McLoone Index shows the same thing to a lesser extent.

SUMMARY

Equity has been an important goal of school finance systems, and it has been the feature of those systems that has been most frequently litigated. Measuring the extent to which equity has been achieved, however, is a complicated task. It is necessary to agree upon what is to be measured, whether it is an output, a process variable, or an input. One must also decide whether the criterion of equity is equal provision of a basic education, or of all education provided, or whether one wishes only to equalize access to tax resources. Finally, there is the distinction between horizontal equity (equal treatment of equals) and vertical equity (equitable treatment of unequals). Only after these matters have been decided is it possible to choose an appropriate measure for assessing attainment of equity.

A number of measures of equity are available, some better than others. Among those often used in school finance studies are the range, restricted range, federal range ratio, standard deviation, coefficient of variation, Gini coefficient, McLoone index, correlation, and regression coefficient. All of them are useful for measuring horizontal equity. Measurement of vertical equity is much more difficult conceptually, and has seldom been attempted. The problem stems from a lack of agreement on a criterion for appropriately unequal treatment of unequals.

Data were provided for a majority of the states, measured at three different times over a fourteen-year period. Data were also provided for two states measured every year for fifteen years.

chapter fourteen

Enhancing Educational Efficiency

There are four major strategies by which educational institutions can be made more effective: (1) intensifying or improving the technology of instruction, (2) emphasizing "production" incentives, (3) increasing the professionalization of employees, and (4) privatization of services and enfranchising clients.[1] These strategies are not mutually exclusive; they can be employed in combination. All four can be used simultaneously, though it is not evident that this has ever occurred. The first two strategies rely heavily upon technocratic processes. The second two focus more upon human strategies, actions, and preferences. However, the latter two are themselves different in that the human beings involved are school employees ;in ;the ;first instance and clients in the second.

Each of the four strategies is explained in order. First, however, it should be understood that these are explanations for improving the efficiency or productivity of schools; these methods do not necessarily extend equality or choice. On occasion, the latter two values will be enhanced by one or more of the efficiency strategies. However, should this occur, it is a secondary outcome. The chapter begins with a discussion of the concept of efficiency when applied to schooling.

---

[1] A fifth means for enhancing student performance involves matters outside the immediate scope of school policy—improving students' lives through medical, mental health, social, and welfare means so that they can benefit more greatly from instruction.

EDUCATION AND EFFICIENCY

Almost everyone knows what *efficiency* means. If one wants something to be more efficient one generally wants it to cost less, perform more quickly, be less complicated, have more useful features, be of higher quality, and all for the same or a lower price. However, efficiency has other components for economists. One dimension is *allocative* efficiency. Another dimension is *technical* efficiency. Each has a quite different outcome, even though they have several common roots.

Allocative Efficiency

If a person went to the store to buy bread and the only available starch was spaghetti, he or she would probably be disappointed. At least in this instance, producers had not correctly anticipated individual preference. Even if the store had loaves of bread but did not have the whole-wheat bread the person sought specifically, he or she might be dissatisfied. This exemplifies a problem in *allocative efficiency*. Producers have not accurately anticipated consumers' preferences. Regardless of how efficiently manufacturers were making spaghetti or white bread, even though they might be offering them at exceedingly low prices, if it was not the product one wanted then the system was not efficient from the consumer's perspective.

How does allocative efficiency apply to education? At the extreme, imagine a school system that provides training only in fashion design. Potential clients wanting training in electronics, agriculture, foreign languages, journalism, or music would be disappointed. Decision makers for such a system would have misjudged the demand for other kinds of services, and potential clients or consumers would be unhappy. Similarly, an elementary school that stresses social skills and interpersonal relations might disappoint parents preferring greater emphasis on academic preparation and basic skills. In such a situation school decision makers—the "producers" of educational services—have misjudged the "market." They are allocatively inefficient.

This explanation suggests that providers are allocatively inefficient unless every consumer's product or service preferences are satisfied. Clearly there is no economic system that can completely meet such a stringent test. There seldom is a sufficiently available array to meet all demands. However, allocative efficiency is enhanced when providers are free to enter the marketplace with new ideas, products, or services, and when consumers are at liberty to select from what is available. In education, under present conditions the near monopoly of the public schools may restrict choice more than is necessary to protect the public welfare. If a greater range of choice could be accommodated by education providers, allocative efficiency would be enhanced. A few means for enhancing allocative efficiency are described in this chapter. However, a major illustration of strategies for encouraging greater choice is provided in the final chapter.

Technical Efficiency

This term refers to efforts to maximize *output* at any given level of resource *input*, or to minimize input for a desired level of output (the more frequent goal).

Technical efficiency encompasses attempts to reduce unit costs of producing any particular good or service, or producing a higher-quality "unit" for the same cost. In the private sector this kind of efficiency is motivated strongly by a desire for profit. The less expensively a good or service can be produced, *all other things being equal,* the greater the financial return to the owner or owners of the means of production. (Another means of maximizing profit is to eliminate all competition, create a monopoly, and charge as much as one can before exhausting elasticity of demand.) In the public sector, profit is typically not possible and a monopoly may exist. Under such conditions, incentives for seeking technical efficiency are weak.[2] (This explains why most gains in economic productivity are pioneered in the private sector.) The relative absence of public sector efficiency incentives is often used as a justification for imposing regulations, price ceilings, and revenue limits on public sector agencies and so-called natural monopolies, such as utilities.[3]

Technical efficiency can apply to educational services. Those desiring that schools be more efficient or productive are, at one level, asking that educational output be maximized relative to a given level of resource input. Definitional difficulties immediately become evident. What will be taken as measures of output? Is student achievement the measure? If so, then on what dimension—average SAT scores or Advanced Placement Test scores? If a school sought to enhance average SAT scores for all its secondary students, it might have substantially different resource allocation implications than if it chose simply to elevate the number of its most able students taking Advanced Placement exams and their scores on those exams. The *production function*—the technically most efficient means of maximizing a school's output—may well depend on the output measure selected. Relative lack of agreement regarding desired outputs, at least in public schools, renders technical efficiency in education difficult to achieve. Even when there is agreement on desired outputs, much of education continues to be more of an art and a craft than a science. Be that as it may, there exist four major strategies for enhancing school efficiency.

INTENSIFYING AND IMPROVING INSTRUCTIONAL TECHNOLOGY

Instructional technology refers to the nature and amount of the material a learner is expected to comprehend and the means by which that material is presented.[4] Excluded from consideration are whatever abilities, motives, and incentives may characterize individual learners and the educators with whom they interact. Electrical technologies are discussed in Chapter 12. This section illustrates strategic technologies.

[2] A classical explanation of this phenomenon is provided in W. J. Baumol, "On the Social Rate of Discount," *American Economic Review,* 58 (1968), 788–802.

[3] A comparison of production and efficiency behavior in private-sector and nonprofit agencies is provided by Burton Weisbrod, "Non-Profit and For-Profit Organizational Behavior: Is There a Difference?" (unpublished paper, 1986).

[4] For a discussion of the risk involved in mandating instructional technology reforms, see Arthur E. Wise, *Legislated Learning: The Bureaucratization of the American Classroom* (Berkeley: University of California Press, 1979).

The technologies included in this discussion are (1) school learning climate, (2) pupil assignment composition, (3) allocation of pupil time, (4) subject-matter requirements, curriculum alignment, and mastery learning, (5) cost-reduction strategies, and (6) evaluation. It should be understood at the outset that appropriate actions on these dimensions are likely to enhance only the technical efficiency of an educational agency. These strategic technologies have minimal bearing upon allocative efficiency.

School Learning Climate

Much research conducted in the 1970s and 1980s regarding school climate rediscovers and confirms conventional wisdom.[5] Nevertheless, the research is useful because the 1950s and 1960s witnessed much systematic violation of a number of time-honored principles about schools, such as the importance of setting high standards and maintaining an academically rigorous curriculum. What has emerged with increasing emphasis is that the "tone" of a school does matter for the learning of students, that reasoned discipline policies are important, that high expectations for pupil performance can influence student outcomes, and that schools are enhanced when a strong sense of academic purpose is shared by the faculty and communicated clearly to students.

It falls primarily to a school's chief executive and the faculty to agree upon and establish a positive sense of purpose for their institution. Research on school effectiveness suggests that schools can influence learning in subject-matter areas. Effective schools have been found to concentrate on academic outcomes. If too many additional objectives are established, schools' energies appear to become diluted.

Similarly, the disciplinary tone of a school, while not oppressive, must reinforce educational purposes. Students must feel physically safe and the learning environment must be free from frequent interruption from student misbehavior or administrators' overuse of classroom public address systems. A successful school is one characterized by a climate in which it is clear that the school exists for learning, that student misbehavior is unacceptable, that the faculty and administration cooperate in pursuing school goals, and that parent participation in reinforcing school purposes is encouraged.[6]

Publication in the late 1960s of *Pygmalion in the Classroom* and subsequent critiques of this research clouded understanding of the role that *expectations* play in

---

[5]The principles described in this section are synthesized from the following publications: Stewart C. Purkey and Marshall S. Smith, "School Reform: The District Policy Implications of the Effective Schools Literature," *Elementary School Journal,* 85, no. 5 (January 1985), 352–88; James Sweeney, "Research Synthesis on Effective School Leadership," *Education Leadership,* February 1982, pp. 346–352; and Dale Mann and Deborah Inman, "Improving Education with Existing Resources: The Instructionally Effective Schools' Approach," *Journal of Education Finance,* 10 (Fall 1984), 256–269.

[6]James S. Coleman, *Public and Private High Schools: The Impact of Communities* (Chicago: University of Chicago Press, 1987).

inducing student performance.[7] However, more recent evidence suggests that an effective school is one in which the general academic climate is suffused by the high standards instructors hold for student achievement and student conduct.[8] While it may be obvious, *the crucial role of leadership in organizing and sustaining these important characteristics should not be overlooked.* Educational research at times searches so diligently for procedural and structural variables associated with student achievement that time-honored understandings such as the significance of overall leadership can be overlooked.

Pupil Assignment Composition

Beginning in the 1960s, ever more sophisticated studies by sociologists and economists suggested the significance of peer socioeconomic (SES) characteristics in influencing students' achievement. The socioeconomic character of a student's household influences his or her own performance in school.[9] Also, student socioeconomic composition can influence the academic achievement of a classroom or school.

The precise dynamics of such situations are not fully known. Various hypotheses exist. For example, it may be that teachers expect higher learning of upper-SES students, thus pitch their instruction at a higher level.[10] If this hypothesis is accurate, such a dynamic creates a self-fulfilling academic prophecy. Another hypothesis involves more direct peer influence. Higher-SES students may contribute to higher teacher expectations, and may influence each other's learning, both by direct peer instruction and by contributing to a classroom and school environment conducive to learning.[11]

A third hypothesis, sometimes termed the *white hostage theory* by advocates of racial desegregation, is that school resources are unequally distributed in favor of upper-SES and white students. Designing attendance boundaries so as to gain a better school mix of students by income, and perhaps by race, is said to result in greater equality of resource distribution. Should this be the case it would, arguably, influence student achievement.[12]

Cost-effectiveness analyses conducted by Levin, Glass, and Meister suggest yet another important instructional component of student assignment composition.

---

[7]R. Rosenthal and L. Jacobson, *Pygmalion in the Classroom* (New York: Holt, Rinehart & Winston, 1968).

[8]J. E. Brophy and T. L. Good, "Teachers' Communication of Differential Expectations of Children's Classroom Performance: Some Behavioral Data," *Journal of Educational Psychology,* 61 (1970), 365–74.

[9]James S. Coleman et al., *Equal Educational Opportunity* (Washington, D.C.: Government Printing Office, 1966); and Russell W. Rumberger, "The Influence of Family Background on Education, Earnings, and Wealth," *Social Forces,* 61 (March 1983), 755–73.

[10]Herbert J. Walberg, "Social Environment as a Mediator of Classroom Learning," *Journal of Educational Psychology,* 60 (1969), 443–48.

[11]J. Ide, G. D. Haertel, J. A. Parkerson, and H. J. Walberg, "Peer Group Influences on Learning: A Quantitative Synthesis," *Journal of Educational Psychology,* 73 (1981), 472–84.

[12]James W. Guthrie et al., *Schools and Inequality* (Cambridge, Mass.: MIT Press, 1971).

Cross-age tutoring—older students assisting in the instruction of younger students—was found to be several times more cost-effective than three other instructional-improvement strategies, including reduced class size.[13]

School size, whether considered as a variable of school climate or of pupil assignment composition, may influence achievement. It may be possible for a school to become either too large or too small. At least to some point, a larger school and more pupils may be accompanied by scale economies. It may also be that beyond some point, large numbers of pupils under a single roof trigger alienation, anomie, lack of institutional identification, and an unfavorable discipline environment.[14]

Schools with fewer pupils may generally be more conducive to higher levels of student achievement, but the relationship is far from linear. An elementary school that is extremely small, having, for example, fewer than two classrooms per grade level, certainly restricts choice, or allocative efficiency, for parents. If a substantial personality conflict develops between student and teacher under such circumstances, there is often no recourse. A school containing at least two classrooms per grade level permits alternative placements. Similarly, extremely small secondary schools may have too few students to justify specialized academic courses. Students, especially advanced placement students, may suffer as a consequence.

ALLOCATION OF STUDENT TIME

Beginning in the 1970s, school-related research began to demonstrate the significance for student achievement of time allocation.[15] Several research studies appeared to be but quantified support for the conventional wisdom that the more a student studies a topic, the more he or she learns. What is evident is that time per se is not crucial. More important is how available time is used by both learner and instructor. However, greater research precision and better problem definition eventually resulted in concepts such as *academic learning time (ALT), time on task,* and *engaged time.*

Studies of instructional time reveal the importance of instructors' allocating sufficient time for learning, ensuring that learning environments are relatively free from interruption, and gaining the attention of students so that they are actually engaged with the task at hand. Teaching skills necessary to attract and retain student attention are complicated and beyond the scope of this text to explain. What is of particular note is that pedagogy has progressed to the point where it is now quite possible to train teachers to be effective in this undertaking.

[13] Henry M. Levin, Gene V. Glass, and Gail R. Meister, *Cost Effectiveness for Four Educational Interventions* (Stanford, Calif.: Institute for Finance and Government, School of Education, Stanford University, 1984).

[14] See James W. Guthrie, "Organizational Scale and School Success," *Educational Evaluation and Policy Analysis,* 1, no. 1 (1979), 17–27; Jonathan Sher, *Heavy Meddle* (Raleigh: North Carolina School Boards Association, 1986); and Richard Z. Gooding and John A. Wagner III, "A Meta-Analytic View of the Relationship between Size and Performance," *Administrative Science Quarterly,* 30 (1985), 462–81.

[15] See generally Henry M. Levin, "About Time for Education Reform," *Educational Evaluation and Policy Analysis,* 6, no. 2 (Summer 1984), 151–63.

Subject-Matter Requirements, Curriculum Alignment, and Mastery Learning

Students learn best those school subjects to which they are systematically exposed. This appears so obvious as to justify a reader's cynicism. However, throughout the 1960s and 1970s this truism appeared to have been neglected. The subject-matter curriculum in many secondary schools lost its cohesion. Students were permitted to select from among a wide range of electives, and analyses of student transcripts revealed wide gaps in sequential courses. Scores on standardized achievement tests dropped during this time and the decline, though complicated, almost certainly was related to the dilution of academic expectations and the laissez-faire nature of the high school curriculum.[16] The 1980s reforms focused added attention on the utility of having an integrated set of subjects building in intellectual complexity. Expectations of high performance are a *sine qua non* of effective schooling, and the expectations should center in learning important material. The curriculum cannot be forgotten in any effort to render schooling more effective.[17]

For a school or classroom to be an effective instructional setting, expectations for student achievement, *standards of achievement*, content of classroom instruction, textbooks and other instructional materials, and evaluation procedures or tests must all be consistently focused. This is known technically as *curriculum alignment* (see Figure 14.1). As common–sensical as such a procedure may appear, misalignment can substantially impede achievement. If at any point on this continuum there exists misalignment, achievement test results may be lower than they ought to be.

A second technical component of curricula to be kept in mind is *mastery learning*. Standards of achievement for any particular grade level or course should be sufficiently specified to facilitate careful assessment of student progress. A student generally should not be permitted to progress to the next grade level or next course in a subject-matter sequence until he or she has mastered the content in the present learning module.[18]

If policies such as these are followed, student failure will not be routinely conveyed from level to level. Also, if an accurate management information system exists in a school or school district, it becomes possible over time to identify those teachers in whose classes students frequently fail to master subject matter. Appropriate supervisory steps then can be taken to enable that instructor to overcome his or her weaknesses.

[16]Congress of the United States, *Educational Achievement: Explanations and Implications of Recent Trends* (Washington, D.C.: Congressional Budget Office, 1987).

[17]For more information on this topic, see Albert J. Oliver, *Curriculum Improvement: A Guide to Problems, Principles, and Process,* 2nd ed. (New York: Harper & Row Pub., 1977).

[18]Benjamin Bloom, *Human Characteristics and School Learning* (New York: McGraw-Hill, 1976). For an unanticipated consequence of mastery learning, see Michael Huberman, "How Well Does Educational Research Really Travel?" *Educational Researcher,* 16, no. 1 (January-February 1987), 5-13.

FIGURE 14.1   Curriculum Alignment

Before Curriculum Alignment

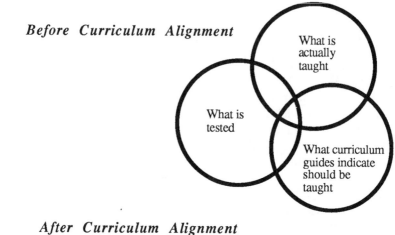

After Curriculum Alignment

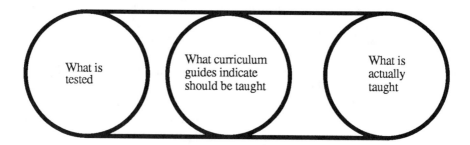

Mastery learning is particularly important when applied to basic skills at the elementary school level. It may also apply to fundamental understandings in science, mathematics, foreign language, and English at the secondary level. The important principle is that fundamental understandings be identified and that students be assisted in mastering them. To a reasonable degree, then, progress to the next level of schooling or the next course in the subject-matter sequence should depend on accomplishing these tasks.[19]

Cost-Reduction Strategies

A component of technical efficiency is holding outcomes equal while reducing production costs. The labor-intense nature of instruction has usually militated

---

[19]Mastery learning was attempted as a policy by the Chicago schools, but the district board of education formally abandoned it in 1985. However, there are strong suggestions that the strategy was not implemented correctly. See Kenneth S. Goodman, "Chicago Mastery Learning Reading: A Program with Three Left Feet," *Education Week,* 5, no. 6 (October 9, 1985), 20.

against reductions. For most local education agencies, 85 to 90 percent of expenditures are devoted to personnel, salaries, and wages. There certainly are ways to eliminate waste in the remaining 10 to 15 percent of an annual budget. For example, increases in petroleum costs from the mid 1970s until the mid 1980s motivated many school districts to implement dramatically effective energy conservation programs.

However, significant savings in the cost of schooling will have to come from more efficient deployment of personnel. History on this dimension is not encouraging. The mean number of pupils per teacher in 1930 was thirty. By 1983 this figure had declined to fewer than eighteen pupils per teacher (see Figure 11.1, page 258). Should the same rate of reduction be sustained over the next quarter century, average class size would be thirteen to one. In 1987 dollars, this translates to a national average per-pupil increase in school expenditures in excess of $800. (Such an analysis unrealistically assumes that sufficient numbers of qualified individuals would be available for employment as teachers and that enough space exists to house the additional classes.) If the pupil–teacher ratio had remained at the 1930 level, the United States would be spending approximately $30 billion less today for each year of schooling.

In order to counter past and prospective increases in labor costs, various proposals have been made to redeploy instructional personnel. A key ingredient in any of these cost-saving proposals is to alter the mix of expensive and inexpensive instructors by increasing class sizes, utilizing less expensive labor, or substituting capital for labor. It appears, however, that the United States has yet to undertake a serious effort to reduce personnel costs through widespread use of television or computers for instruction.

MASTER TEACHERS AND CROSS-AGE TUTORING

The professional career-ladder proposals described extensively in Chapter 11 possess cost-saving potential. Such proposals are generally justified on grounds of professionalizing teaching and thus rendering instruction more effective. However, at least in the abstract they could also be construed to reduce labor costs.

The presumption is that an unusually well trained and effective teacher is capable of supervising a cadre of less prepared, less experienced, and hence less costly junior instructors. Assuming an overly simplified situation in which a cohort of 200 elementary students was grouped in classes averaging 25, and mean teacher salaries were $30,000, instructional salaries under the conventional system would total $240,000.

Under a master teacher/apprentice configuration, a senior professional might well be paid $40,000 in 1988 dollars. However, eight junior professionals would each be paid only $20,000, for a total instructional salary of $200,000. Cost savings would be a substantial 20 percent under this scenario, class sizes would not have been increased, and the ability of the superior teacher is distributed over a larger number of students.[20] (Greater detail regarding such proposals is provided in Chapter 11.)

The so-called Lancastrian system of instruction, initially developed in Lancaster, England during the beginning of the industrial revolution, minimized labor costs. This system called upon a teacher to instruct students, presumably the most able or oldest, in the day's lesson and then depend upon them to act as "monitors" to instruct literally dozens of other pupils. Classrooms were constructed in ascending tiers to facilitate such tutorial arrangements and maintain the entire student body under direct line-of-sight supervision of a senior teacher. The contemporary version is known as *cross-age tutoring,* and the previously cited research by Levin, Glass, and Meister suggests that, appropriately used, it is a cost–effective means of enhancing student academic achievement.

SUBSTITUTING CAPITAL FOR LABOR

The history of education is filled with predictions and promises of an imminent revolution in instructional technology. In fact, despite the advent of motion pictures, television, and computers, American education has simply become ever more dependent on labor. The wide availability of microcomputers in homes, where parents can utilize them with children, might eventually alter this pattern. Perhaps enough students will eventually come to school already knowledgeable in computers to have a significant impact on classroom instruction. Meanwhile, it is clear that larger numbers of personal computers are to be found in schools. They may even be having a positive effect on instruction. However, there is little consistent evidence to suggest that they are substituting for labor, that they are replacing teachers.

Although it appears unlikely that massive substitution of capital for labor will reduce future education costs, it may be possible to contain future spending increases through such an avenue. The incentives are present. Enrollment increases in the 1980s and 1990s appear likely. Conversely, it is difficult to imagine that continued reductions in pupil–teacher ratios can occur, at least at the same pace as that of the last half century. Added use of technology is in order.

Pupil Evaluation

Frequent feedback regarding instruction can enhance learning. Two kinds of tests, *criterion–referenced* and *norm–referenced,* are needed.[21] The former are keyed to school or class standards of achievement. Often these are teacher-constructed tests. Regardless of their origin, criterion-referenced examinations assess student comprehension of the basic skills conveyed in classes. It is with these tests that decisions on mastery can be made.

---

[20]For added information on the economics of such plans, see James N. Fox, "Restructuring the Teacher-Workforce to Attract the Best and the Brightest," *Journal of Education Finance,* 10, no. 2 (Fall 1984), 214–37.

[21]See Purkey and Smith, "School Reform," p. 379.

Norm-referenced tests, allowing one to judge an individual student's performance relative to that of a group of students, are also an important part of instructional technology. Such tests enable judgments to be made on the effectiveness of one school relative to another or on the degree to which one SES ethnic or racial group is achieving relative to another. These latter measures are important in assessing equity outcomes, a topic discussed extensively in the prior chapter. States are increasingly enacting minimum competency statutes. By 1987, thirty-two states required such testing.[22]

ALTERING PRODUCTION INCENTIVES THROUGH OUTPUT DATA AND PAYMENT

A second means for educational institutions to increase productivity, or technical efficiency, is the use of effective extrinsic incentives. Incentives for whom? Should inducements be offered the learner? those who influence the learner, such as parents, siblings, or peers? or those who directly deliver educational services, such as teachers and administrators? Should rewards be directed at individuals or at groups? What should be the nature of the rewards—simple recognition? symbolic displays? money? Who should be decide rewards, and what criteria for rewards should be employed?

These are neither simple nor rhetorical questions. Education, being labor-intensive, is fraught with complex human interactions. This complexity, when coupled with the difficulty in agreeing on desired outcomes of schooling, suggests that any payment-by-results strategy should be approached with substantial caution. Otherwise, the risk of goal displacement is extraordinary. An example dramatizes the point.

Unanticipated Outcomes

If a school district decided to reward teachers for elevating student academic achievement and took as the performance criterion increases in class average scores on a standardized test, teachers might pursue multiple strategies in response. An ideal teacher-response strategy might be to focus on each student in an effort to elevate scores individually and thus achieve a higher aggregate class average. Under such a scenario, arguably, everyone would benefit.

However, imagine an instructor who calculates that for the time invested it was the intellectually most able students in the class who were capable of the greatest individual test-score gains. This hypothetical teacher then proceeds to ignore less-than-average students and concentrates only on those from whom the greatest achievement "payoff" is possible. Subsequent test administration reveals a higher class average, and the teacher receives a salary bonus. Below-average stu-

[22]Jon C. Marshall, *State Initiatives in Minimum Competency Testing for Students,* Consortium on Educational Policy Studies, Policy Issues Series No. 3 (Bloomington: Indiana University, 1987).

dents' test scores in the class actually decline, perhaps because of teacher neglect. It is unlikely that the school board desired such an outcome. Inappropriately structured incentives can displace legitimate organizational goals.[23]

Assumptions

Paying for results, regardless of the actual form of the incentive or reward, assumes the utility of extrinsic sanctions. Do humans beings respond to such incentives, and, if so, under what circumstances? McGregor has constructed an interesting set of principles based on assumptions about internal and external motivation.[24] Space prohibits full explanation of his theory here. Suffice it to assert that inappropriately applied organizational inducements can misfire. If individuals have been socialized to a strict professional standard—that is, if they have internalized the view that high performance and attention to client welfare is expected of one correctly performing his or her duties, regardless of external rewards—then application of payment for results can undermine professionalism, contribute to deteriorating performance, and simply be seen as insulting by employees. The point here is not that external rewards are bad or ineffective but that such a system must be carefully considered and implemented.

Another assumption embedded in education payment-for-results schemes is that a desired performance outcome has social utility: the outcome advantages not simply the individual learner but the larger society as well. It seems wasteful to allocate public resources to a result that benefits only the learner.

Incentives for Individual Pupils

Some learning apparently has its own rewards. Simply stated, acquiring new knowledge or a new skill can be pleasurable in and of itself. Additionally, behavioral psychology posits that learning can be enhanced through appropriate use of external rewards—positive reinforcement. Such reinforcement, to be effective, need be no more complicated than praise or commendation from the instructor. (Indeed, recognition need not necessarily even stem from a human being. Many CAI programs depend crucially on praise embedded in the program when a correct response is made by the learner.) Positive sanctions, such as rewards, are said to be substantially more effective in inducing learning than are negative sanctions, such as criticism.

What about paying pupils for learning—not simply giving praise or small candies when they display correct performance, but actually paying money for academic achievement? However crass or corrupting of the culture of education, this idea has actually been tried, albeit on an extraordinarily limited basis. In the 1960s, under President Lyndon Johnson's War on Poverty, a number of pay-for-results education "experiments" were sponsored by the now-defunct executive-branch Office of Economic Opportunity (OEO). Among these was an attempt to induce higher

[23]Guy Benveniste, *Managing Professionals* (San Francisco: Jossey-Bass 1987), contains an analysis of the problems of using quantitative measures.

[24]Douglas McGregor, *The Human Side of Enterprise* (New York: McGraw-Hill, 1960).

levels of achievement by paying individual students for higher test scores. The experiment was small, involved but a few classroom settings, was not enthusiastically endorsed by teachers, and had ambiguous results. Numerous individual psychology research studies have been built around this strategy. However, the limited OEO experiment was the only recorded public policy trial.

Enhancing Productivity through Peers

Pupil achievement is known to be influenced significantly by peers and peer-group composition. This influence occurs through the social mechanisms for which hypotheses are offered in our discussion of the technology of instruction. In addition, there is another potential dynamic operating in schools, a dynamic that appears too often overlooked by professional educators as a useful means for enhancing achievement.

Pioneering research on adolescent student culture conducted by sociologist James S. Coleman suggests the existence in most secondary schools of a set of peer-group-related learning disincentives. Coleman contends that the secondary school student culture esteems social popularity and athletic prowess more than academic achievement.[25] A student is more likely to gain peers' respect and friendship through competitive sports or social savoir-faire than through sustained scholarship. Schools reflect the larger society. Professional football players make more money than many doctors or lawyers. Schools cannot be expected to cure all society's ills, and it is unlikely that any pay-for-results scheme will eliminate this condition. However, proposals have been made to establish greater amounts of interscholastic academic competition in order to create scholar as well as athlete heroes. Aside from tactics, the principle involved is to reward a major purpose of schooling—academic achievement—with a level of recognition at least equal to that accorded by sports achievement.

"Paying" Producers

This is the external incentive dimension to which the greatest policy attention has been devoted. There exists such a wide variety of pay-for-results proposals regarding teachers and other "producers" that space permits no more than a selective description here. Among the more interesting policy suggestions have been performance contracting, merit pay for teachers, and merit schools.

PERFORMANCE CONTRACTING

Another much-publicized OEO pay-for-results experiment was conducted with performance contracting. In exchange for a specified educational service, such as operating an entire elementary school or a remedial reading program within a school, a qualified educational contractor would be paid an agreed-upon base amount plus bonuses tied to increases in student achievement. The more students learned,

[25]James S. Coleman, *The Adolescent Society: The Social Life of the Teenager and Its Impact on Education* (New York: Free Press, 1961).

the greater the payoff to the contractor. Contractors were free, within reason, to offer whatever incentives they wanted to students. Some offered trinkets such as transistor radios to students who increased their test scores.

However effective the results, or noble the concept, performance contracting in the 1960s came to an ignominious conclusion with press accusations of widespread contractor misfeasance. It was alleged that instructors employed by contracting companies were "leaking" test items to students before formal examinations. Students previously supplied with test questions increased their scores, but by a means judged fraudulent. A scandal involving a company under contract to the Texarkana schools was intensely publicized, and school officials lost what little enthusiasm they once had for added experimentation. Teacher-union officials nodded their heads in a "We told you so!" manner, and a number of private sector corporations dropped plans for expanding into the provision of public schools services under contract.[26]

Teacher unions, or any appropriately chartered group of teachers, could have become contractual providers under the OEO experiment. Such an idea presaged 1980s visions of teacher-managed schools.[27] However, no sustained effort at teacher-operated performance contracting resulted. Indeed, as with so many education reforms, performance contracting was a fad that endeared itself to virtually no one and left little legacy for contemporary educational policy or practice.

MERIT PAY

Unlike performance contracting, merit pay proposals for teachers are a continuing, or at least cyclically appearing, policy proposal. Chapter 11 details the personnel incentive system characterizing the overwhelming proportion of United States school districts. Simply put, to "get ahead" professionally in American public schools, one should get out of the classroom. Merit pay is an external reward scheme that attempts to dilute this condition by offering instructors added remuneration for added student performance.

A few school districts operate merit pay schemes; some have done so for a sustained period.[28] However, the idea is intensely controversial and traditionally opposed by the National Education Association. This organization frequently asserts that the idea is fine in the abstract but bogs down in the details of implementation. By what bases will student performance be assessed? Who will decide if a teacher is meritorious? Is the idea subject to collective bargaining as a term of employment? It is on questions such as these that the proposal usually founders.

[26]See generally Charles Murray, *Losing Ground: American Social Policy 1950–1980* (New York: Basic Books, 1984).

[27]See, for example, the previously mentioned Carnegie Forum–sponsored commission report *A Nation Prepared: Teachers for the 21st Century* (New York: Carnegie Forum on Education and the Economy, May 16, 1986).

[28]See Terry A. Astuto and David L. Clark, *Merit Pay for Teachers: An Analysis of State Policy Options,* Consortium on Educational Policy Studies (Bloomington: School of Education, Indiana University, 1987); and David K. Cohen and Richard J. Murnane, "The Merits of Merit Pay," *The Public Interest* 80 (1985), pp. 3–30.

Aside from difficulties in determining outcome measures, such as those illustrated by the pay-for-performance scheme hypothesized at the beginning of this section, teacher unions offer other criticisms of merit pay. An intense concern is expressed over the prospect of administrative favoritism. If criteria for merit pay are broader than test scores alone, then will they be fairly applied by principals? If not, teacher unions contend, then merit pay risks being divisive. Teachers not selected for a merit reward or bonus will resent those who were. In that a successful school depends upon a cooperative atmosphere, merit pay might erode, not enhance, productivity.

MERIT SCHOOLS

This is a pay-for-results proposal that appears to overcome many objections to other external reward schemes. Here, an entire school is assumed to be the unit of "production." Whatever the rewards, such as added money from the district or the state, they are accorded the whole school. Agreement upon output measures is still crucial to such a plan. However, assuming agreement on assessment procedures and reasonable cooperation on the part of the faculty, schools judged to merit rewards would have added resources. This money may be distributed evenly to faculty in the form of pay bonuses or divided between faculty bonuses and added resources for the school itself, such as more field trips, library books, or instructional materials. Florida has adopted such a policy, though it is too early to judge its advantages and disadvantages.[29] California utilized another version applicable only to secondary schools. The output measure was narrowly defined as increased test scores for graduating seniors. The program was enacted in 1983 and abandoned in 1986. Results suggest California's criterion was too narrow.[30]

PROFESSIONALIZATION

Chapter 11 describes current conditions that impede establishment of an education profession and proposes professionalizing reforms. There is no need here to repeat the message in detail. Suffice it to mention that investing in building a true teaching profession might well contribute significant gains to educational productivity. The major obstacle to be overcome is the current personnel incentive system, which rewards most those having the least contact with clients. Until able classroom teachers are readily identified and professionally rewarded, there is little prospect of recruiting and retaining enough talented individuals into teaching. Resistance to change by the education community has contributed to the downward spiral of the teaching profession. Until this political and economic logjam is broken, prospects

[29]Walter I. Garms, "Merit Schools," *Education and Urban Society,* 18, no. 3 (May 1986), 369–90.

[30]See Nancy Spaeth, "Cash for CAP: An Analysis of State Financial Incentives and School Improvement," unpublished paper (Berkeley, Calif.: Policy Analysis for California Education, University of California, 1987).

for enhancing school productivity through professionalization of the education work force are slender.

PRIVATIZATION AND ENFRANCHISING CLIENTS

There are critics of the current system who contend that public schooling suffers primarily from being oppressively bureaucratic and overly insulated from clients' preferences. Historic developments such as 1920s Progressive Era efforts to depoliticize public schooling, school district consolidation, growth of professional school managers, and educational administrators' efforts to ape the *scientific management* movement in the industrial sector, when coupled with the post–World War II development of collective bargaining, are said to have rendered schools' decision making the domain of educational professionals, a domain from which the public generally and school clients specifically are isolated.[31]

The logic underlying this set of criticisms suggests that schools would become more productive, more allocatively efficient, if client, parent, and pupil preferences could effectively be expressed in a manner that attracted the attention of professional educators. Proposals to facilitate expression of client preferences span a wide spectrum, from those that simply necessitate administrative reorganization of the current system to more radical recommendations that portend alterations of the basic decision-making unit in education. These proposals are described in three major classifications: (1) client opinion polling, (2) organizational restructuring, and (3) decision-unit reforms.

Client Opinion Polling

Popular mid-1980s studies of effective private companies stressed the tight linkage profitable firms often maintain between themselves and customers. Repeated sampling of customer opinion apparently aids both technical and allocative efficiency. Consumer views on new or contemplated products and services can prove useful to a firm trying to decide how to alter its product array. Also, customer views regarding recently purchased products offer "quality-control" feedback. Complaints, if acted upon quickly, can stanch the spread of negative rumors and help remedy whatever flaws are reported.[32]

Educators seldom engage in such monitoring. Administrator preparation programs lack a component on opinion sampling. A view frequently held by educators is that such marketing efforts are at once counterprofessional and technically beyond their comprehension.[33] Neither is correct.

[31]See James W. Guthrie, Diana K. Thomason, and Patricia A. Craig, "The Erosion of Lay Control," in National Committee for Citizens in Education, *Public Testimony on Public Schools* (Berkeley, Calif.: McCutchan, 1975), pp. 76–121.

[32]Thomas J. Peters and Robert H. Waterman, Jr., *In Search of Excellence: Lessons from America's Best Run Companies* (New York: Harper & Row, Pub., 1982).

[33]Kent D. Peterson and Chester E. Finn, Jr., "Principals, Superintendents, and the Administrator's Art," *Public Interest,* no. 74 (Spring 1985), 42–62.

Advocates of greater marketing in education assert that new techniques render survey research quite reliable with relatively small samples. District-level client surveys can be useful in matters such as bond and tax referenda, boundary alterations, location of a proposed new school, or districtwide curriculum alterations. The school site population—parents and, above some grade level, pupils—is the one from which feedback is particularly desirable. Schools, not districts, are the typical unit of "production" in education. Thus it is from the most immediate clients that opinions on course offerings, quality of instructional service, and preferred changes should be sought. When surveying school-level clients, one may not necessarily have to "sample." Even if by mail, a survey can be supplied to all parents. If cost is a factor, then survey questionnaires can be conveyed to and obtained from parents by students.

Although the school may be an appropriate unit of survey analysis, it need not be an individual school that is responsible for conducting the survey research. This is a function that can most appropriately be undertaken for all schools, unit by unit, by a district central office planning and evaluation division. Such a central management policy unit ought to report directly to the chief executive officer. Client survey results can be considered in much the same manner as internal audit reports in a large organization. Such reports, and client surveys, should not be the exclusive property of, or accessible to manipulation by, line administrators other than the chief executive and policy makers. Such results are necessary for evaluation and policy-planning purposes.

Organizational Restructuring

Seeking client views is easily accomplished and, if conducted appropriately, can contribute to allocative efficiency. However, critics sometimes assert that the insensitive bureaucratic nature of schools will not easily succumb simply to expressions of consumer preference. At a minimum, some contend, the system needs structural revision. Toward such an end four reform surges took place between 1955 and 1980: (1) the so-called community control movement, (2) efforts to establish "alternative schools," (3) administrative decentralization, and (4) school-site management and parent advisory councils.

COMMUNITY CONTROL

In the early 1970s the Ford Foundation sponsored a study of New York City schools.[34] The report recommended that steps be taken to disaggregate the huge New York City public school district into presumably more manageable units. Three experimental *community control* districts emerged and rapidly became a focus for intense political conflict. Eventually, the New York Legislature enacted a bill that divided the city's schools into thirty-one elementary districts with elected boards subject to the overall authority of the city's central school board. Each of these subdistricts contained more pupils than the overwhelming majority of school

[34]Authored principally by Mario Fantini, the report was entitled *Reconnection for Learning* (New York: Mayor's Advisory Group on School Organization, 1970).

districts throughout the United States. Community control proponents were dismayed that the new sub-bureaucracies would be touted as a way to return schools to the "people." Moreover, early political analyses asserted that newly elected local boards were heavily dominated by citizens supported by teacher unions.[35] Much discussion was devoted to similar disaggregating proposals in other city districts, but little came of it practically. A 1980s expression of this spirit was the return in several large cities to district- or ward-elected central city school boards. This early 1980s phenomenon, a return to the arrangements of the early 1900s, was also intended to render elected officials more responsive to their constituents. Almost predictably, by the late 1980s critics were asserting that decentralization had realized the worst predictions of corruption and inefficiency. They called for yet another cycle of reform.

ALTERNATIVE SCHOOLS

This concept, much like accountability, has continued to be a semantic umbrella of sufficient breadth to encompass numerous schooling ideas, some of them antithetical. In the 1960s, several notable authors wrote stinging critiques of public schools, asserting that they were debilitatingly uniform, repressive, stifling, and mindlessly administered.[36] "Alternative education" was proposed as a reform. British infant schools, frequently cited as a model for students' early years, easily assisted in the transition from home to scholarly activities. Many parents removed their children from public schools to place them in private "alternative schools." Public school systems themselves, unwilling to forego their market share easily, established public alternative school experiments. By the end of the 1970s, the movement had run its course and several of its major ideologues had revised their opinions,[37] confessed to a change of heart, and advocated more structured schools.

ADMINISTRATIVE DECENTRALIZATION

Large city school districts underwent a wave of decentralization during the 1960s and 1970s. The general justification was that organizational disaggregation would permit schools to be more responsive to clients and employees. The typical pattern was to divide a district into several administrative units, each with an executive officer nominally in charge of all subdistrict schools. Districts varied in degree of decision-making discretion permitted these units. In most instances, fiscal authority continued to be centralized. Personnel administration also typically remained a central office function. Curriculum planning and instructional emphasis were often permitted to vary in accord with the tastes of subdistrict administrators. Only in New York City was disaggregation accompanied by political reform—

[35] Marilyn Gittell, *Participants and Participation: A Study of School Policy in New York City* (New York: Center for Urban Education 1967).

[36] See, for example, Jonathan Kozol, *Death at an Early Age* (Boston: Houghton Mifflin, 1967).

[37] See, for example, Kozol's, *Children of the Revolution* (Boston: Houghton Mifflin, 1978).

namely, election of subdistrict school boards. In other cities, the central school board continued to be the policy-making body for the entire district. Consequently, critics contended that decentralization accomplished little more than added costs and insertion of yet another bureaucratic layer between local schools and "downtown" decision makers. It was difficult, outside of city school central offices and subdistrict administrators, to identify those favoring the reform.[38]

SCHOOL-SITE MANAGEMENT

The relative failure of community control, alternative schools, and administrative decentralization encouraged yet a fourth effort to infuse schools with greater citizen participation. This additional reform was described in detail initially by a New York State reform commission that utilized the label *school-site management*.[39]

The plan was intended both to gain a greater measure of lay control and to provide more accountability by using the school, rather than the district, as the basic decision-making unit for personnel and curriculum. School district central offices would continue to handle fiscal and business matters and serve as planning, coordinating, and record-keeping bodies. A parent advisory council (PAC) at each school would be responsible for principal selection and evaluation and for advising that officer on curriculum, instructional, and personnel matters. Principals were envisioned as being on multi-year contracts, renewal of which was subject to PAC approval. Within specified boundaries, the principal and parent advisory council would have discretion over funds budgeted for the school by the central office. Each school's budget allocation was to be determined by a set of uniform decision rules, including criteria such as number, grade level, and achievement records of pupils assigned to the school. The parent advisory council would issue an annual evaluation report including plans for the subsequent year.

Several states adopted PAC components for their state categorical aid programs.[40] Portions of the idea also were favorably received by federal authorities, which began in the 1970s to include PAC requirements for schools receiving categorical aid funds. The idea became so pervasive that school administrators were soon to ask that parent advisory councils undergo consolidation lest principals' nights consist of one council meeting after another and little else.

Aside from widespread adoption in form, there is slight evidence regarding the idea's effectiveness. In many instances, little budget discretion was ceded to parents, collective bargaining agreements with teachers continued to render most decisions a central office matter, parents claimed they were too easily co-opted by administrators, and few principals were attracted to the idea of having their job security tied to

[38] George R. LaNoue and Bruce L. R. Smith, *The Politics of School Decentralization* (Lexington, Mass.: Heath, Lexington Books, 1973).

[39] James W. Guthrie, "Social Science, Accountability, and the Political Economy of School Productivity," in *Indeterminacy in Education,* ed. John E. MacDermott (Berkeley, Calif.: McCutchan, 1976), pp. 253–308.

[40] *Improving Education in Florida: A Reassessment,* prepared for the Select Joint Committee on Public Schools for the Florida Legislature (Tallahassee, 1976).

parental approval. Also, the reform was proposed in the 1970s when enrollments were declining in many districts. Attempting to implement reforms on the back of reduced resources is difficult. These factors inspired the impression that the reform was widely adopted but was never of much consequence.[41]

Decision-Unit Reform

The relative lack of success of 1960s and 1970s structural revisions stimulated proposals for more radical reforms, alterations that would not simply change the bureaucratic layering of American education but would more dramatically shift fundamental decision-making processes. The two most prominent of these radical reform proposals are *vouchers* and *tuition tax credits*. Vouchers permit a greater amount of public regulation of education than do tuition tax credits, and to this degree are the less radical of the two reforms.

VOUCHERS [42]

Regardless of operational details, voucher plans possess a common fundamental principle. Their intent is to enfranchise households as the basic educational decision–making unit. Vouchers do not eliminate government interest in education. Rather, voucher plans retain the prospect of government responsibility for financing and otherwise maintaining a marketplace of education providers, which would require regulation.

This plan, should any state adopt it, not only would alter school financing but would also dramatically change the pattern of school governance. A voucher plan was enacted by Congress following World War II to help returning veterans pay for their higher education.[43] A complete lower education voucher plan has never been enacted by any state. Efforts were made by the now-defunct federal Office of Economic Opportunity in the 1970s to induce school districts to experiment with the idea. Only one, Alum Rock near San Jose, California, accepted the offer. Alum Rock dropped the plan within three years. The idea, usually espoused by fiscal conservatives and political libertarians, and sometimes by those who view it as a means of empowering school choice among the poor, has not yet proved attractive to a political majority either nationally or in a particular state. However, in the mid

---

[41] The 1981 enactment of the Education Consolidation and Improvement Act (ECIA) eliminated many federal requirements for parent advisory councils.

[42] In addition to the general references mentioned at the end of this footnote, see Laura Hersh Salganik, *The Fall and Rise of Education Vouchers*, Report No. 307, Center for Social Organization of Schools, Johns Hopkins University (Baltimore, 1981), p. 36; and John E. Coons, "Intellectual Liberty and the Schools," *Notre Dame Journal of Law, Ethics, and Public Policy*, 1, no. 4 (1985), 495–533. Generally, see Milton Friedman, *Capitalism and Freedom* (Chicago: University of Chicago Press, 1962); John E. Coons and Stephen D. Sugarman, *Education by Choice* (Berkeley: University of California Press, 1978); and Thomas James and Henry M. Levin eds., *Public Dollars for Private Schools* (Philadelphia: Temple University Press, 1983).

[43] Serviceman's Readjustment Act, P. L. 78, 346 (the G. I. Bill).

1980s there were renewed discussions at the state and federal levels about enacting voucher plans.[44]

Fundamentally, a voucher plan requires the state legislature to provide households with a financial warrant for each school-age child, redeemable only for the cost of schooling. What the characteristics of eligible schools would be is a crucial component of the voucher controversy. Most voucher proponents contend that both public and nonpublic schools should be eligible to accept vouchers. Others suggest that the idea is a good one in that it would inject a measure of market competition into schooling and might thus induce higher quality and more productive schools. However, they also fear that social cohesion might suffer if household preferences for styles of schooling paralleled racial, religious, or income stratification in society. These latter advocates would restrict voucher redemption to public schools.

Vouchers can be made more complex by weighting students such that, for example, handicapped pupils receive a voucher of higher dollar value than others. Similarly, other features can be imposed upon voucher plans to render them more socially sensitive. For example, requiring every school that redeems vouchers to accept any pupil who applies might be a mechanism for reducing racial or social discrimination.

Even though no state has seen fit to adopt a full voucher plan, the proposal continues to be made. In 1983, a presidentially appointed national school finance panel recommended that federal categorical aid programs for low-income students be transformed into a voucher scheme. The Reagan administration continued to make modified proposals of the scheme each year through 1987.

TUITION TAX CREDITS [45]

This mechanism, as with vouchers, enfranchises households as decision-making units regarding education services. However, tuition tax credits entail less government regulation of nonpublic schooling. Federal or state provisions would permit parents to deduct all or, as more commonly proposed, a portion of nonpublic school tuition payments as a credit against federal or state personal income tax obligations. Such tax credits can be graduated in terms of schooling level—for example, larger dollar tax credits for secondary school tuition than for elementary—or by taxpayer income bracket—for example, proportionally lower tuition payments allowed as a credit against the tax obligation of upper-income taxpayers. President Reagan espoused tuition tax credit plans early in his administration. The U.S. Senate has passed tuition credit bills six times, the House of Representatives once. This last case was in 1979, and the threat of President Carter's veto was then suffi-

[44]See, for example, the proposal by Governor Perpich of Minnesota described in the March 6, 1985, *Education Week*, p. 6.

[45]See James S. Catteral, *Tuition Tax Credits: Fact and Fiction* (Bloomington Ind.: Phi Delta Kappan Educational Foundation, 1983,, and, by the same author, "The Supply and Demand for Private Education: Rethinking the Impact of Tuition Tax Credits," *Journal of Education Finance* 12, no. 6 (Fall, 1987) pp. 702–16.

cient to discourage Senate approval. In 1985, Minnesota adopted a partial tuition tax credit plan. Early assessments suggest that the low tax-forgiveness amounts involved did not greatly influence parent choice of nonpublic schooling. Indeed, parents reported that state provision of transportation was a greater determinant of nonpublic school choice than the small net tax deduction for private school tuition. Regardless, the idea is likely to be the topic of debate for years to come.[46]

OTHER MARKET MECHANISMS

Proponents of added efficiency often suggest that schools would benefit from added use of market mechanisms. Sometimes these proposals are simple suggestions, such as permitting private providers to contract with schools for cafeteria services. Other proposals attempt to subject components of the school bureaucracy to greater accountability through the "invisible hand" of the market place. For example, a school district's central office budget for staff development and curriculum assistance might be decentralized and placed at school sites. Schools might then purchase central office services or they might buy such assistance elsewhere—local universities, other districts, or the private sector. Whatever the choices, their selections would reflect local school personnel judgment about the utility of central office services. Failure to "buy" staff help from "downtown" would display a market judgment and bring about greater accountability.

SUMMARY

This chapter explained the differences between so-called *technical* and *allocative* efficiency. The first involves minimizing production costs and maximizing output. The second pertains to producing goods and services consistent with consumer preferences. At least four strategic means exist for achieving technical efficiency in schools: intensifying instructional technology, utilizing output measures and extrinsic incentives for added productivity, relying upon greater professionalism in the education labor force, and privatizing services and enfranchising clients. This last strategy also contains the potential for aiding allocative efficiency.

[46]For a larger theoretical view and a novel empirical test of parent choice in education, see William Harold Gerritz, "Family Preferences for K–12 Education: An Explanatory Model" (Ph.D. dissertation, University of California, Berkeley, 1986).

chapter fifteen

Enhancing Educational Choice

The purpose of this chapter is to describe means for expanding choice in America's system of education. The focus here is not on an ideal system. Any education system for the United States will necessarily contain inconsistencies. The nation and American culture are too large and too complicated to be contained in a single uniform system. Thus, what follows is a set of proposals intended to exemplify important new ways in which the varied concerns for American education might be reconceptualized and reformulated into a system that enhances the nation's dynamic concerns for individual and societal equity and efficiency while simultaneously expanding liberty. The authors intend this as an illustration of one way to achieve a balanced system, rather than as the "the one best system."

FINANCING AND ORGANIZATIONAL VALUES

Alternatives can be packaged in a variety of ways. Each will have different effects on the basic principles of equity, efficiency, and choice. A useful plan must strike an appropriate balance among these. Here are the basic values and beliefs that have been considered in constructing this illustrative reform plan:

1. All children should have the right to a basic education without respect to wealth or place of residence.

2. The state does not have an interest in the provision of all schooling, but has a compelling interest in the provision of a high-quality basic education necessary to the fulfillment of individual ambitions and the proper functioning of government and the economy.

3. All taxpayers of the state should share in supporting the cost of a basic education.

4. An effective means of encouraging school efficiency is to leave as much choice as reasonably possible to consumers of education.

5. Education, even that which is not basic, is highly desirable, and the state should encourage citizens to pursue learning.

6. Low-income individuals should have as much opportunity as others to obtain the education they desire.

There is, in education, a *state interest* and a *private interest.* The state interest (it might better be labeled the *public interest*) is in ensuring that students are sufficiently well educated to serve as responsible and productive citizens. On the other hand, there is also a *private* interest in education. This has always been clear from the fact that there are educational activities not offered by the public schools for which people are willing to pay. Examples might be truck driving or square dancing lessons. Truck driving lessons could be thought of as vocational, and square dancing lessons as avocational. Vocational education provided by private industry is a major business; expenditures on it may equal expenditures on elementary and secondary public education. Expenditures on avocational education are also large. Clearly, these things are in the private interest, because private individuals are willing to pay their own money for them (or, in the case of industry, the company is willing to pay for them in order to increase employee productivity).

Most people would agree that the state should provide free education that is in the public interest, and that individuals should pay for education that is a private interest. The problem is in deciding just what constitutes the education that is in the public interest. That is addressed in the next section.

A main goal of this education system is to provide more choice than currently exists. That education is provided publicly has led in places to a bureaucratic organization of education that severely restricts choice. In many American communities, if a student does not attend a private school he or she must attend a specific public school. This is usually the closest one geographically. Once in the school, a student is assigned to a class taught by a teacher selected by a bureaucracy, with little or no counsel from student or parents. Even though there may be a severe clash of personalities, the student is often assigned to this teacher for the entire year. The curriculum is decided by professionals, with little influence from parents, and a student has little or no choice of courses in the elementary school, and only somewhat more in the secondary schools.

Students are required to attend school for a specific number of hours per day, and the schedule is usually quite uniform, without recognition of individual needs of parents. Students must attend a specific number of days per year, with vacations frequently having no necessary relation to parents' vacations. They must attend until age sixteen or eighteen, regardless of how much or little has been learned.

In short, a society that believes in individual freedom has created an educational system that in many respects is rigid and lacking in choice. A plan such as this would ameliorate that situation.

DESCRIPTION OF THE PLAN

The right to an equal basic education for all children is necessary for the proper functioning of a democracy, and is therefore a proper state responsibility. It is not easy, though, to decide the basic education that should be guaranteed to all. Ambivalence exists within and among the states. A state may have a foundation program that is supposed to provide a minimum basic education on an equal basis, but at the same time it may mandate a variety of curricula that appear not to be basic (because they are not required in all states), such as music, art, and physical education. A state's requirements for approval of a curriculum for a private school may come closer to what the people of the state believe are minimum requirements.

The Core of Schooling

Basic education consists of the things necessary for effective functioning in a democracy. This includes the ability to read, write, and do basic arithmetic and knowledge of the operation of democratic government. These goals are relatively clear-cut, and accomplishment is measured more easily than it is in other curricula. Most people would agree that they form the core of education, though there would be disagreement on other curricular objectives. Possible modifications of this position are discussed later.

Since this program involves the coercion of mandatory attendance, school operation should be kept flexible by allowing students to attend any public school selected by their parents, regardless of location. Transportation should be provided where the school is too far away for a student to walk but is within a fifteen-mile radius of his or her home; parents should be responsible for transportation to schools beyond this radius. The benefits of this arrangement are several. Parents can search for the school that provides an instructional method compatible with their child's learning method, or a teacher who can work well with the child. Different schools would probably schedule attendance hours at different times, and where both parents work they might choose a school whose hours coincided more closely with their own. Parents could also enroll children in a school close to their workplace, perhaps enabling more parental participation in school. Organizationally, the emphasis in this plan is on the individual school. There would be no more school districts, but only individual schools, with all financing provided by the state. With no need for local taxes, the need for school districts would disappear. Individual principals, probably with the counsel of parents and teachers, would make decisions about which hours to operate schools, which teachers to hire, what salaries to pay, and which teaching methods to use (the state interest would be safeguarded by required tests that would measure how well students were attaining state curricular objectives). This would not, of course, prevent principals from cooperating with each other to hire a reading specialist or to purchase supplies in bulk.

The number of hours a day, and days a year, that a school would operate would also be decided by the principal and teachers. Students would probably spend much more time on the basic subjects than they now spend, but even so they would not spend as much time in the classroom of the public school as is now the case.

Curriculum Options

Of course, parents want their children to learn more than just the basics, but not all would want their children to have the same mix of optional courses. Therefore, the plan provides much more freedom than currently exists. The system is based on *educational coupons*. These have some of the features of vouchers and food stamps. Coupons could be purchased by parents from the local school in any amounts desired. Cost of the coupons would depend upon family income and number of school-age children of the purchaser. A poor family with several children would be able to purchase coupons at as little as ten cents on the dollar; a wealthy family with one child would have to pay ninety cents or more on the dollar. The goal is to require roughly equal sacrifice, while requiring all families to make some sacrifice. Excess cost of the coupons, above that paid by the purchaser, would be paid by the state.

Coupons could be used to purchase additional educational services for children of the purchasers, either at a public school or through any private institution or individual certified by the state. Parents could spend these coupons on any kind of additional education they wished for their children: foreign language instruction, music, art, or swimming lessons, remedial reading, vocational instruction, flying lessons, study of medieval architecture, or baton twirling. Although the intent is to encourage the diversity provided by private entrepreneurs, public schools would not be excluded from providing these optional educational services. They would do so on the same basis as private schools: they would pay for their costs by charging parents, who would pay in educational coupons, and the coupons would be redeemed for cash from the state.

Compulsory education would end with the eighth grade. It should be possible for most children to obtain required competency in basic subjects by that time. The state would provide tests of this competency. Students who attained the necessary competency before the end of the eighth grade would be allowed to discontinue mandatory attendance at the public school when they could pass the tests. This would leave them free to spend more time in alternative education purchased with educational coupons, or to go on to additional public education, as described next.

Beyond the Eighth Grade

For the elementary grades, the system described is clearly divided into what is in the public interest and what is in the private interest. Most students would wish to continue on to secondary education immediately after elementary. Here, the division between public and private interest is more blurred. The plan recognizes that with a grant system that combines public and private interest. Each person would be provided with a *portable grant* that could be used at any time during the remainder of his or her life. It would entitle an individual to a maximum of six additional years of education at any school, public or private, that offered subjects covered by the entitlement. The amount of the entitlement in any one year would be equal to the average expenditure by the state on basic education in the elementary schools in the year the grant was exercised, possibly multiplied by a factor such as 1.3 to compensate for additional costs of secondary education. The state would provide money to both public and private schools for this education, at the specified rate. Courses would be those on a list approved by the state, and the individual using the entitlement could take six years of such courses. Through use of these grants, individuals could postpone education until they had learned more about the world and had decided what they genuinely wanted to study. In other words, it would be easier for students to drop out of high school, but also easier for them to drop back in again when they gained sufficient maturity and experience to realize that they needed more education.

In addition to this portable grant, individuals could continue to buy educational coupons throughout their lives, to be used for learning enrichment activities of various sorts. These coupons, for use by adults, would be issued by the state and purchased by individuals at a discount dependent upon family income. The excess cost of them, above the purchase price, would be paid for through state taxes.

FINANCING THE PLAN

Financing the plan is relatively simple. Public elementary schools would be fully state-supported, based on specified amounts of money per child enrolled. The amount of money provided each child would depend upon measures of need and cost differences, so that schools whose children have learning difficulties would receive more money per student, as would schools having to pay more to provide the same quality of education. Of course, full state funding implies no difference in revenues as a result of the wealth of a student's family or his or her neighbors, nor would there be any local tax contribution.

In addition, of course, principals could supplement the income of the school by offering optional programs paid for with educational coupons. Principals would tend to behave more like entrepreneurs. Rather than trying to maximize their budget allocation from a central office and to make things comfortable for teachers, they would be balancing revenues and expenditures. They would try to hire highly competent teachers and pay them accordingly, and to offer an instructional method popular with parents. They would try to adjust the hours of school operation to suit parents' needs, and to provide optional programs to be paid for with educational coupons that would be popular (and would cost no more than parents were charged for them). The competition among principals that would be engendered would result in better education, better tailored to student needs.

It will be noted that most of this proposal is fully state-funded. Only the enhancement of local public school efforts to furnish enrichment activities is supported with local taxation. This plan, then, achieves equity of state taxes while preserving local and individual options as to amount and kind of education to be obtained. The public cost of this program should be less than that in the present system because the state would be fully funding only basic and vocational education plus a portion of the cost of enrichment education. Nevertheless, the cost would be large, and it would probably be necessary for a state to finance it at least partially with a statewide property tax.

SCHOOL ORGANIZATION

Under this plan, elementary and secondary education would be divided into a public sector that operated elementary schools and some secondary schools, providing mainly a basic education, and private providers of educational services, both individuals and schools, providing mainly optional education. Public elementary schools would be supervised by the state, which would provide total financing for the basic education provided. The state would establish reasonable standards for health and safety, and would prescribe a curriculum. However, performance monitoring would be done primarily through student tests. Principals and teachers would be free to decide on texts and instructional methods, with the state intervening only if test performance did not meet expected standards.

Of course, some schools would be oversubscribed and parents would withdraw their children from others. This would create a housing problem at some sites, and the usual bureaucratic solution to this is to allow only as many students to attend as the school can hold, with admission on a first-come-first-served basis. Instead, crowded schools should be allowed to increase in size indefinitely through a variety of methods. The state could require that a school attempt to find room for students by using existing space more efficiently, identifying space in nearby buildings, or perhaps even taking over a nearby public school that was undersubscribed. Of course, a school taking over a nearby school would not be expected also to assume its teachers or administrative staff: presumably the reason it is undersubscribed is because the professional staff is inadequate. Principals would individually bargain with unions.

There would be no local school boards. Instead of an elected board making decisions that, ideally, reflected community beliefs, individuals would "vote with their feet." Those schools that were successful would grow, while ineffective schools would decline. Because the marginal cost of educating additional students is usually less than the average cost, but revenue from the state is based on average cost, the larger a school becomes, the more resources would be available for salary increases, teaching materials, and the like.

At the inauguration of this plan, existing secondary schools would continue to operate. However, their courses would be divided into those that constitute basic and vocational education and those that are more avocational. Students would pay for the latter courses with educational coupons. The basic and vocational courses would be paid for with the portable grant. The state would provide money for construction, and would perhaps subsidize operating expenses in somewhat the same way that public higher education is now operated. However, the amount of state subsidization would be limited to, say, 15 percent of cost. The idea is to encourage the continued existence of public high schools both to provide a standard by which to judge others and to provide education in rural areas where alternative education might not be readily available. As with elementary schools, public secondary schools would be operated by their principals as semi-independent entities, with no school district or local school board. The state would supervise schools mainly by testing students.

It is expected that many private secondary schools would open, offering both basic and vocational courses to be paid for with portable grants, and optional courses to be paid for with educational coupons. Diplomas of high school graduation would be offered only by the state. The state would test students graduating from these schools in basic and vocational subjects, and would not award diplomas where the student did not meet state standards. Parents (or students) would be free to choose any public or private secondary school, with transportation provided by the state to any school within fifteen miles of a student's home.

Secondary school would take up four of the six years of the portable grant. The remaining two years could be used to pay for part or all of the tuition at a community college, vocational-technical school, college, or university, public or private. Of course, a student could use educational coupons at any time to pay for courses provided publicly or privately.

A particularly difficult task in fleshing out this proposal is defining what constitutes approved subjects eligible for a portable grant. One suggestion is to limit four years of the portable grant to courses in an organized school that are designated as basic or vocational by the school and that are on a list of such courses approved by the state. Two years of the portable grant could be applied toward any kind of course. Probably the majority of students would use the first four years of the grant to take basic and vocational courses in a conventional high school, supplementing their program as desired with courses paid for with educational coupons. They might then use the final two years of the grant in a college or university, community college, or vocational-technical school, or for individual tutors. Some who found that eight grades of formal education were sufficient might opt to use only the two years of the grant not restricted to organized schools and designated courses. For elective courses designated by these two years of the grant, normal tuition might well be more than the state guarantee. The school (or tutor) could claim the guarantee from the state and then charge the student the difference, payable in educational coupons.

POSITIVE FEATURES OF THE PLAN

This proposal strikes a reasonable balance among equity, efficiency, and choice by providing an equal basic education for all and providing for additional education not limited by ability to pay, combined with the sort of client responsiveness that can accompany choice by parent or student.

There is no doubt that this plan would substantially transform public education. Most of the changes would be desirable. Public elementary schools, relieved of their present charge to be all things to all children, could concentrate on basic instruction in reading, writing, arithmetic, and citizenship. Of course, additional subjects would still be offered by schools that could do a better job teaching them than private institutions or individuals. This should certainly be possible in many cases, since the fixed costs of offering additional instruction are minimal: classrooms and administrators already exist for the basic program.

Parents would be accorded a wider opportunity to make choices about their children's education. They would be able to choose the public school attended for basic instruction, and although they would not be able to select the curriculum, they would be able to choose among instructional styles and teachers of different schools.

For enrichment courses, this plan offers freedom of choice of school or tutor, curriculum, subjects pursued, and time spent on them. Some students would choose to embark on a well-rounded course of study; others, particularly those talented in a particular field, would choose to spend many hours a week on that subject.

Parents would, of course, have to pay for a portion of this additional instruction, but the poorer they are, the larger the amount contributed from the public purse through the educational coupon system. This makes it much clearer that parents have a stake in the education of their children, for they must make a personal sacrifice that is directly connected to the education being obtained. Under the present system, taxes paid have no direct relationship to the education being obtained.

The program encourages diversity in provision. Public elementary schools would be encouraged to be diverse in the way they teach in order to attract students. Private schools would probably be even more diverse, just as they now are.

The plan ensures that public money is spent on programs on which there is a broad consensus. These programs should be offered in such a way as to equalize educational opportunity. Public elementary schools would concentrate on the basics, and the full state funding plus differential funding for those with special needs would assure greater equality of opportunity than now exists.

A particularly important part of the plan is the end of mandatory attendance after the eighth grade. High schools would no longer be forced to play a custodial role, and one result of this should be substantially fewer discipline problems. Provision of portable grants would encourage lifelong learning. Many students who now drop out of high school and then find it almost impossible to reenter would be encouraged by the portable grant to do so. A fair number of older students in the high schools would probably bring a more serious tone to studies there. Finally, the ability of all adults to buy educational coupons on a more or less equal basis (again because of state subsidies) would also encourage lifelong learning. It would probably be necessary to reduce the minimum working age in some states and freeze the minimum wage for teenagers in all states, so that those who drop out will be able to be employed productively. Unions have resisted such reductions in the past for fear that teenagers would compete for jobs, but this probably would not happen. The lower minimum wage for teenagers would encourage establishment of jobs that do not now exist because it is too costly to employ someone to do the job at the existing minimum wage. The result would be much more teenage employment. For every adult actually displaced from a job by a teenager, another probably would be employed in a more senior or supervisory position as a result of the increased employment. The benefits of reducing teenage unemployment should be great. On the other hand, most of these teenagers would soon realize that they are not apt to be able to continue to be employed after reaching the age of twenty-one, when the minimum wage would increase, unless they obtained further education. Many probably would return to high school.

Immigration into and out of the state should not be a problem. Residents of the state are entitled to the portable grant for six years of education after eighth grade and to buy educational coupons as adults as long as they are residents of the state. When they leave the state they forfeit the privileges so long as they are gone. Immigrants to the state (and former residents returning) would be entitled to the six years of additional education, less any already obtained elsewhere, and the right to purchase coupons.

In summary, this plan improves equity through full state assumption of the financing of basic education and through differential provision by the state for those with special needs. It improves allocative efficiency through the adoption of the free-market approach to most of education. The free market, both theoretically and practically, is the most efficient way to operate. The plan improves choice in a number of ways that can be categorized as resulting from use of educational coupons and from freedom to choose the public elementary school to be attended.

OBJECTIONS TO THE PLAN

Perhaps the strongest objections to such a plan would come from those who believe that it dismantles the public schools. It takes away the music, art, physical education, and other subjects that have been added to the mandatory list in most states during this century. The plan asserts that there is a certain amount of education that is the direct interest of the state. It is clear that reading is the *sine qua non* of educated, functioning, and productive citizens. The same thing can be said about the ability to communicate through writing, to do ordinary arithmetic, and to understand the way in which government functions.

Unless music, art, and other subjects are necessary for all students, to require them of all students not only detracts from the effort to provide all students with the ability to read, but also smacks of big-brotherism. The decision as to which of these subjects, and how much of each, are to be studied by each student should be left to students or their parents. Most public schools would continue to offer courses other than the basic ones, financed partly by local taxation and partly by educational coupons provided by parents. However, an artistically gifted student would not have to spend time being bored in music classes or physical education. If this student's parents desired, he or she could spend several hours a day in the art class of the public school, or could study art at a private school or with a tutor.

This plan, then, does not dismantle public education, but converts it to a system of high-quality basic education. Those whose teaching specialty is art, music, foreign language, or something similar say that it is necessary to introduce children to these subjects in order to allow them to decide whether they are interested in them. They have a point. It would be reasonable to allow the teaching of a limited number of survey courses that would introduce students to the many things that are not basic. Science as well as the humanities would be included in this category. It is no more necessary to teach all students science for a number of years than it is to teach all of them art for many years. Probably far too much time is currently spent on subjects that are not basic. A prime example of such a subject is driver education and driver training, currently offered in many high schools. However laudable the goal of reducing automobile accidents, the course is clearly not basic. And it is not necessary to teach it in the public schools. Even today, almost any teenager who can afford to drive a car can afford to pay for private lessons, and the state need only require the completion of such lessons before a license may be issued. That these lessons could be paid for with educational coupons would prevent discrimination against the poor.

Some insist that poor children and the children of poorly educated parents will not buy educational coupons and take elective courses, and that such a plan will thus result in unfair discrimination against these students. It is not at all clear that this would happen. Most parents are vitally concerned about the future of their children and want them to obtain a better education than they themselves acquired. They are often very upset with the quality of education available in the local public schools, but see no way to change the system. The fact that people could buy educational coupons at rates differentiated by income means that these people would have no greater difficulty buying education suited to their children's needs than would middle-class parents.

There are those who believe that the plan would result in massive racial segregation, but this is doubtful. Institutions and individuals who provided educational services in return for educational coupons would be required to abide by the same kinds of nondiscrimination statutes that apply to all other businesses. Most Americans, probably including most minority parents, do not believe in forced assignment of students to schools for racial balance. In general, minority parents may desire not so much attendance at racially integrated schools by their children as a better education for them. The fact that this plan allows free choice of a school and insists on nondiscrimination allows parents who want their children in a more integrated school to send them there.

It could also be argued that handicapped students would not be properly served. However, public school funding could be adjusted according to the number and type of handicapped students. Similarly, the portable grant could differ in amount according to a student's handicap. It might also be possible to adjust the price of the educational coupons downward for the handicapped.

Teacher unions might be expected to oppose such a plan because of a fear that it would damage the unions. Having to bargain with a large number of individual schools is much more difficult than bargaining with a smaller number of school districts. Unions would probably move to the state level, hoping to establish a statewide uniform salary schedule. Such a uniform schedule would be inimical to this plan.

Free choice of public schools for basic education would leave some schools with crowded classrooms and others with excess space. This is a natural result of the operation of the marketplace. It is inefficient from the viewpoint of those who favor a planned economy, but a market economist would state that allowing parents to choose promotes efficiency. The state could help solve crowding problems by making relocatable buildings available for rent to school districts. When no longer needed at a particular location, the state could move them elsewhere.

The fact that some parents could buy educational coupons cheaply while others would pay almost full price would encourage a black market in cheap coupons, with poor parents tempted to sell them to rich parents at a discount. Preventing this is a relatively simple bureaucratic exercise involving writing the pupil's name on the coupons and ensuring through occasional audits that coupons are redeemed for children actually enrolled in the school.

Many would assert that education is such a complicated endeavor that parents would be unable to make intelligent choices for their children. This has often been an excuse for asserting that educators should be allowed to make all of the important decisions about education. Parents may not know as much about education as teachers, but they frequently know a great deal more about their own children and their aspirations for them. Parents are frequently anxious to make decisions about their children's schooling, and are generally frustrated by their inability to do so under the present system.

It is true that it is always difficult to make good decisions in the absence of adequate information. Advertising is designed to emphasize strong points, ignore weak ones, and generally make comparisons difficult, and it is to be presumed that under this system schools would advertise. One cannot expect Consumer's Union to do a report on individual schools, for there are too many of them. Therefore, to be certified to redeem educational coupons for cash from the state, schools and individuals should be required to submit to the state standardized information about curriculum, teachers, instructional strategy, and other pertinent information. This information would be compiled and made available in libraries, schools, and other public places for parents to peruse. It would probably be wise to make it available in loose-leaf form so that parents could machine-copy information on those schools or tutors in which they are interested. Parents should also be permitted to redeem a specified number of education stamps to pay for the advice of licensed education counselors who could assist professionally in making school choices.

What other requirements should there be for certification to receive educational coupons? If these institutions and individuals were held to the same standards currently required of public schools, a large certifying bureaucracy would be formed, and established requirements would result in squelching the diversity this program is designed to encourage. Thus, certification should be limited to four areas:

1. Schools or individual tutors should be required to submit standardized information, as just described.

2. Schools or individuals receiving the coupons should not be operating fraudulently.

3. Facilities used should not endanger the health or safety of the students.

4. Students should not be denied admittance on any basis unrelated to the purpose of instruction. In most cases this would prohibit discrimination on the basis of race, religion, or sex. In the case of public schools it would also prohibit discrimination on the basis of residence.

Public schools would be subject to further certification requirements related to performance in teaching the basic subjects, as judged by their students' performance on standardized tests. Private schools wishing to receive educational coupons in payment for teaching the basic subjects would also be subject to these certification standards in the basic subjects.

Many people will feel that parochial schools, or other schools closely connected with an organized religion, should not be allowed to accept educational coupons on the basis that this would be a subsidy of religion. However, the fact that educational coupons are sold to parents at reduced cost is a subsidy of parents to aid their children's education. If they choose to spend the coupons at a religious school, they should be allowed to do so. It would fall to the courts to decide whether this would be legal. It is possible, based on decisions in other cases, that the system would be found constitutional.

Rural areas create a special problem because of their low population density. It is difficult under the present system to provide special programs of enrichment or remediation when schools are small. Private schools are less apt to be established and flourish in rural areas. Two things may tend to alleviate this situation. First, rural incomes are often low. This will make the price of coupons low for rural parents, who may then buy sufficient coupons to encourage establishment of small private schools or individual tutors. The other possibility has nothing to do with this plan and will probably improve rural education regardless of the system used. It is the use of telecommunications to bring special classes to students who are scattered geographically. This was mentioned in Chapter 12. Of course, this approach could be paid for with educational coupons.

POLITICS OF THE PROPOSAL

This proposal is not a radical proposal in the political sense. It has elements of both conservatism and liberalism. It caters strongly to the notion of equal educational opportunity, which has usually been thought of as a liberal attitude. On the other hand, it appeals for much more opportunity to allow the free market to work, and this is usually thought of as more of a conservative attitude. The plan strikes a balance sufficient to appeal to a broad spectrum of people in the United States. Some of those who would probably be in favor are the following:

- Private schools and their supporters could be expected to favor such a plan. Use of educational coupons reduces the cost of private education by the amount of state subsidy of the individual buying the coupons. The presumed result would be a greater demand for private schools, primarily by those with middle to low incomes (those with high incomes would receive little subsidy from coupons). There would be an increase in enrollment at existing private schools and establishment of additional private schools.
- Those who favor more choice in the education of their children would also be favorable.
- There are many parents and others who feel that public education has been saddled with too many expectations that are not of basic importance. These people complain about "frills" in schools. They could be expected to support a plan that separates basic education from all other education, and that insists on attainment in the basics.
- There are many who favor less government involvement in the lives of people generally. They could be expected to support a plan that reduces direct government involvement in much of education.

On the other hand, the plan proposes a radical change in the way education is financed and governed. As such, there is bound to be political opposition:

- Unions, particularly teacher unions, would be opposed. Not only does the plan make the school, rather than the district, the unit with which to bargain, but many of the teachers now in the public schools could be expected to become individual entrepreneurs, band together to form new private schools, or join the staff of a private school. Both of these developments could be expected to make it more difficult for the union to bargain, and to reduce the attractiveness of the unions to many teachers.
- Many teachers of special subjects, such as music and art, can be expected to be opposed. They feel discriminated against now, for many of the reductions in force that came about with the declining enrollments of the 1970s hit these special teachers the hardest. With the adoption of this plan, most of them would be forced into the private sector, although some public schools would continue to offer special subjects in return for payment by coupon. The best of these special-subject teachers, of course, will probably welcome the plan, for the number of students they could recruit privately through payment in coupons would probably enable them to earn more money than they now do in the public schools.
- Those who generally favor government intervention for social purposes would probably be opposed to the plan, for it reduces the amount of government intervention in education.

HOW TO PHASE IN THE PLAN

An attempt to solve a problem by means of a drastic change almost certainly creates another problem at least as intractable. As a result, a plan such as this should not be implemented at once in its entirety, even if that were politically feasible. There is a great deal to be said for incrementalism. It allows the process of consensus building to operate over a longer period, helping to smooth the way for change. In addition, inaugurating a plan step by step allows one to find the inevitable flaws that occur and to correct them before they become fatal.

Incrementalism, though, gives the opposition time to rally its forces, and also allows changes that could ultimately make the plan unrecognizable. Therefore, it is sometimes necessary to make a change at once and let the chips fall where they may.   Proposition 13 made a major change in the way government is financed in California. It almost certainly could not have been enacted in pieces, both for political and for practical reasons. It took a constitutional amendment enacted by the people through the initiative process. As might be predicted, Proposition 13 has created many serious problems in California, but it has had the effect desired by many of its supporters: rapid increases in property taxes have abated.

However, we assumed that it would be easier and safer to institute this education plan by increments, assessing progress toward goals and making adjustments to take care of problems as they arise. If this is desired, the following sequence of steps could be taken.

First, one could, within each school district, allow free choice of schools. Some school districts allow this now. There is really no reason, aside from administrative convenience, that this should not be the case in all districts, enforced as state policy. The price of this change would be almost nil, except for a minor increase in busing costs. Benefits should be immediately apparent. Those parents who believe they do not have sufficient voice in what is being imposed upon their children could exercise the exit choice, as could those whose children have a personality conflict with the teacher. The immediate result should be less conflict between parents and school personnel.

Of course, some schools would become oversubscribed. The usual bureaucratic response to this is to ration admission to the school. This should be only a temporary solution. As suggested previously, steps should be taken to provide more space at the crowded schools. Next, principals should be allowed to choose whether they wish to take into their schools particular teachers from schools that are undersubscribed. Gradually, principals should be given more control over their budgets, personnel, and instructional methods. The next step would be to allow free choice of schools, either within or outside the school district. Interdistrict transfer, however, brings financial problems if one district is spending more money per student than another. At this point, then, it is desirable to proceed to a fully state-funded financing scheme, with no local contribution. Such a scheme needs to be phased in because high-spending districts have personnel and other commitments that cannot be changed quickly.

Finally, after this system has been operating for some time, it should be possible to dissolve districts and move to a system of individual schools.

Meanwhile, concurrent with these steps it should be possible to phase in educational coupons. This should start as a modest experiment, in which the schools cease providing certain kinds of courses free. Prime candidates, of course, are driver training and driver education. Coupons could be sold through the local schools or some other agency, and individuals could spend them for the courses no longer taught free, either at a public school or a private provider. After the problems involved with selling and redeeming these coupons were resolved, more courses could be eliminated from the free local curriculum. This would involve some reductions in force or staff-reduction strategies for teachers of those subjects.

The goal, then, is to move slowly but steadily from the present system to the new one, adjusting the new system to unforeseen problems and opportunities.

WHAT ARE THE SHORT-RUN PROSPECTS FOR ENHANCING LIBERTY?

Public concern for any one of the three value streams—equality, efficiency, and liberty—are seldom steady or sustained. We have described the relative decline in concern for equality and the ascendance of efficiency during the 1980s. What is the likely prospect for liberty?

While proponents of efficiency, or productivity, have captured the education reform agenda during the 1980s, equality and liberty advocates have not disappeared altogether. Even as the Reagan administration advocated the rebirth of educational rigor and a return to more classroom discipline, it also proposed measures for obtaining greater choice. There are three related proposals: aid to private schools, tuition tax credits, and voucher plans for compensatory education.

The traditional wall between church and state has always been open to interpretation, and Reagan administration officials have consistently desired a relaxation of the rules that have been constructed over time by the United States Supreme Court. Some of the religious concerns are symbolic, such as permitting prayers to be said by public school children. Others, such as permitting an expanded amount of federal financial aid to be used in private schools, are quite practical. The 1985 Supreme Court decision in *Felton*, referred to in Chapters 1 and 6, angered Secretary of Education Bennett because it impedes use of federal funds for church-related schools.

Two policy avenues are viewed as possible solutions—tuition tax credits and vouchers. Both of these financial strategies are explained in Chapter 7 and reiterated in Chapter 14 so there is no need to describe them again in detail. Both share the fundamental manner in which decisions regarding choice of school are shifted to the household and away from the state. Despite periodic rhetoric by Reagan administration officials and the submission of bills in Congress, neither of these strategies has received much attention thus far.[1] Reagan administration proposals regarding choice are seldom viewed seriously. For example, two comprehensive reviews of

[1]For an example of the Reagan administration rhetoric regarding choice in education see A. Bridgman, "Reagan Pledges Administration Focus on Choice," *Education Week,* March 6, 1985, pp. 1, 29.

federal education policy proposals devote only one paragraph to the issue of choice.[2] Why is this?

Admonishing lower levels of government to restore rigor to schooling jeopardizes few interests. Seeking added productivity through the bully pulpit is a positive undertaking. It is aligned with widespread existing values and public views regarding schooling and efficiency. It necessitates no additional federal appropriations; does not call for redistribution of existing federal resources; and does not directly induce church–state conflict. Aid to private church-related schools is quite counter. Simply raising the issue incites remarkably intense conflict between proponents and adversaries. Moreover, tuition tax credits cost the federal government money, even if in the form of foregone tax revenues. In a time of awesome national deficits, proposed programs that diminish federal revenues face stiff opposition. Vouchers for compensatory education students call for a redistribution of funds. Current public school employees would have their federally funded jobs jeopardized by an ECIA Chapter One voucher conversion, and they certainly will resist, politically and legally.

Because of the intense political conflict involved, expanding liberty or choice in education calls for a greater level of political commitment than does efficiency, or at least the form of efficiency pursued in the 1980s. The Reagan administration was not willing to spend its political capital in support of such a cause. As long as the United States perceives economic pressures from its international competitors, or military threats from overseas, it is not likely to forego current concerns for efficiency. However, conditions can change.

SUMMARY

This chapter has outlined a plan for a very different way of organizing and financing schools. The plan is an attempt to suggest a set of ideas that does a better job than present schemes of acknowledging the values of equity and efficiency while optimizing choice. It is not presented as the one best plan, however, for this is not possible given the diversity of the states.

[2]See Richard Jung and Michael W. Kirst, *Beyond Mutual Adaptation, Into the Bully Pulpit: Recent Research on the Federal Role in Education,* Stanford Education Policy Institute, 86-ESPI-1 (Stanford, Calif., 1986). See also Elizabeth J. Whitt, David L. Clark, and Terry A. Astuto, *An Analysis of Public Support for the Educational Policy Preferences of the Reagan Administration* (Charlottesville: University Council for Educational Administration, University of Virginia, 1986).

INDEX

SUBJECT INDEX